Migration
without Borders

Migration
without Borders

Essays on the
Free Movement of People

Edited by

Antoine Pécoud and Paul de Guchteneire

UNESCO Publishing
PARIS

Berghahn Books
New York • Oxford

Published jointly in 2007 by
the **United Nations Educational, Scientific and Cultural Organization**
and by
Berghahn Books
www.berghahnbooks.com

The designations employed and the presentation of material throughout this
publication do not imply the expression of any opinion whatsoever on the part
of UNESCO concerning the legal status of any country, territory, city or area or
of its authorities, or the delimitation of its frontiers or boundaries.

The authors are responsible for the choice and the presentation of the facts
contained in this book and for the opinions expressed therein, which are not
necessarily those of UNESCO and do not commit the Organization.

Library of Congress Cataloging-in-Publication Data

A C.I.P. catalog record for this book is on record
at the Library of Congress

British Library Cataloguing in Publication Data

A catalogue record for this book is available from the British Library.

Printed in the United States on acid-free paper

ISBN UNESCO: 978-92-3-104024-5 (pbk)

ISBN Berghahn Books: 978-1-84545-346-6 (hbk) 978-1-84545-360-2 (pbk)

Contents

List of Tables

Foreword

Pierre Sané, Assistant Director-General for Social and Human Sciences, UNESCO

Imagine a world without borders, where people had the right to move freely from one country to another, to settle down, live and work wherever they wished. Today, with states strictly controlling their frontiers, this sounds like Utopia. But what if the idea of migration without borders was worth considering? Is it not natural to let people decide where they wish to live? Is it not natural to give people equal rights to move more freely throughout a globalizing world?

According to Article 13-2 of the Universal Declaration of Human Rights, 'Everyone has the right to leave any country, including his own, and to return to his country'. But the right to leave is not complemented by a right to enter; one may emigrate, but not immigrate. From a human rights point of view, we are faced with an incomplete situation that sees many people being deprived of their right to emigrate by an absence of possibilities to immigrate. It is therefore worth envisaging a right to mobility: in a world of flows, mobility is a resource to which everyone should have access.

It has become clear that migration is an essential element in the world economy. Sending countries benefit increasingly from remittance payments and the return of skilled migrants, receiving countries benefit from younger workforces, and migrants themselves find new opportunities through their move to a new country. Migration redistributes wealth at the world level and plays a central role in development and poverty reduction. Moreover, within the current globalization process, which favours an increasingly free circulation of goods, information and capital, it is worth considering including free movement of human beings as well.

International migration is one of the major moral and political challenges of our time. Throughout the world, people claim their right to migrate by attempting to cross borders clandestinely. This generates human costs that cannot be ignored; from the deaths of undocumented migrants to the rise in human smuggling and the social vulnerability of those living irregularly in receiving countries. It also leads to increasingly policed borders, higher walls and fences, and severe restrictive procedures affecting travelling, study abroad and even tourism.

Let us also recall that there have been long periods of world history in which those who wished to migrate could do so, and that this did not lead to chaos. People were often encouraged to migrate and migration was a decisive factor in the development of many countries. What would the world look like today if, historically, people had been limited in their movements, if there had not been any migration in the past? Let us also remember that the idea of lifting all restrictions to the movement of its citizens is one of the main policies behind the creation of one of the world's biggest regional cooperative structures – the European Union – and that other supranational organizations are currently considering free movement as part of their future cooperation agreements.

Of course, migration has profound implications for both sending and receiving societies that need to be dealt with very carefully. We must come up with innovative social transformations to make human movement compatible with welfare states, citizenship rights and democratic institutions. All too often, migrants are accused of threatening social cohesion; rather than fruitlessly trying to stop migration, however, policies should make people's right to mobility and societies' need for solidarity compatible. Free migration would then not jeopardize receiving societies, but would foster intercultural contacts, leading to societies based on openness and tolerance.

This book brings a breath of fresh air to contemporary debates. Is it not time to listen to the experts solicited by UNESCO and to rethink our approach to migration? Imagination, coupled with reason, can turn today's Utopia into tomorrow's options.

Chapter 1

Introduction: the migration without borders scenario

Antoine Pécoud and Paul de Guchteneire

What would happen if border controls were suppressed and people were granted the right to move freely throughout the world? This book explores the 'migration without borders' (MWB) scenario and investigates the ethical, human rights, economic and social implications of the free movement of people. In a globalized world in which migratory flows seem to elude the attempts of states to regulate such movements, the MWB scenario challenges conventional views on migration and fosters a critical rethinking of current policies and practices. This book is the product of a research project launched by UNESCO to better understand the theoretical issues surrounding 'open borders' and the regional dynamics governing the movement of people in the Americas, Europe, Africa and the Asia Pacific region. This introductory chapter reviews the main elements of the debate on free movement and summarizes the major findings of this project.

The MWB scenario is often dismissed as unrealistic. While it may indeed be an unlikely perspective for the near future, there are several arguments for going beyond a simplistic dismissal of free movement. The Universal Declaration of Human Rights states that 'Everyone has the right to leave any country, including his own, and to return to his country' (Article 13-2). Only *emigration* is recognized as a fundamental right, which raises the issue of the actual meaning of this right in the absence of *immigration* possibilities, and points to the necessity of envisaging a more comprehensive right to mobility. In today's world, most people are free to leave their country. But only a minority of them have the right to enter another country of their choice. The right to *emigration* remains problematic as long as major restrictions on *immigration* keep people from migrating, or even travelling, to other countries. The MWB scenario might therefore be morally desirable from a human rights perspective, in which case it would be worth promoting despite its apparent unfeasibility. Moreover, the unfeasibility of the MWB scenario is often taken for granted on the basis of fragile reasoning: one often hears, for example, that it would provoke huge migration flows, although few empirical investigations support this claim.

And of course, the future is difficult to predict. If one had told a French or a German citizen in, say, 1950, that free movement would be a reality in the European Union a few decades later, he or she may have been difficult to convince. Even in the 1980s it would have been difficult to predict that the free movement of people between Eastern and Western Europe would become normal some three decades later. Similarly, 'open borders' were a reality in the pre-1962 Commonwealth, within which citizens from the former British Empire had the right to move freely: people from South Asia or the Caribbean could for example move without restrictions to the United Kingdom. One also often forgets that until recently emigrating could be more difficult than immigrating: many states once prevented their citizens from leaving their country (Dowty, 1987), a practice that has decreased in the past few decades. In this regard, the world is actually progressing towards more, not less, freedom of movement.

Drawing on both a review of the literature and the contributions to this volume, the first section of this introductory chapter describes the context of the MWB debate and considers the contemporary evolutions in migration trends and border controls. The following sections investigate the MWB scenario from four different perspectives: ethics and human rights, economics, the social dimension, and practical aspects.

Migration and border controls today

Controlling immigration has become an important political issue. Most receiving states are strongly concerned with what they perceive as the porosity of their borders to flows of undocumented migration, and are developing new measures to police them. By envisaging a greater level of freedom in the movement of people across international borders, the MWB scenario directly challenges this trend and proposes a new vision, according to which nations should not fruitlessly – and often inefficiently – attempt to curb migration flows, but rather support them and recognize the opportunities they offer. This section examines recent developments in border controls and evaluates their efficiency, costs and advantages.

Contemporary trends in migration controls

Contemporary immigration controls are characterized by several trends. Governments are relying increasingly on new technologies to control their borders and are developing innovative measures to identify undocumented migrants once they have entered their territory, while receiving states are attempting to encourage sending and transit countries to cooperate in their fight against irregular migration. Security concerns play an important role in these developments, whose human and financial costs raise the issue whether it is possible to truly control people flows.

The borders between Western countries and less-rich countries have become increasingly fortified, and sophisticated tools are being used to control them. The most documented case is the U.S.–Mexico border, along which walls and high steel fencing have been constructed. A growing number of patrol agents rely on technologically advanced equipment that includes high-intensity lighting, body-heat- and motion-detecting sensors, and video surveillance (Nevins, 2002). A similar trend can be observed in Europe, notably around Gibraltar and the border between Spain and Morocco. New actors are involved in controlling migration – such as airline carriers, which are now required to check their passengers' right to travel to the country of destination (Guiraudon and Joppke, 2001).

If external controls fail, governments may be successful in establishing internal measures to trace undocumented migrants after their entry. Controls on the workplace are often envisaged and sometimes practised, but yield few results: they displease employers, have high economic and political costs, and require huge efforts to be significantly implemented. Another option is to control undocumented migrants' access to social services. Immigration status is increasingly used to restrict access to welfare provisions, but this policy meets resistance: it is questionable from a human rights perspective, as it generates even greater exclusion for migrants and contradicts the inclusive nature of the welfare system (Cohen et al., 2002). Once identified, undocumented migrants are sometimes subject to detention and expulsion. While these measures stem from the right of states to control the entry and residence of non-nationals, it is worth remembering that they have traditionally constituted responses to specific and exceptional circumstances such as armed conflicts and wars. Today, they are common practice (Schuster, 2004).

Another strategy to control migration relies on cooperation between countries. Sending states are pressured to stop outflows of undocumented migrants, while transit countries are encouraged to better control their borders. Countries such as Mexico or Morocco then become buffer zones to contain migration from Latin America or sub-Saharan Africa (Andreas and Biersteker, 2003). Development aid is sometimes conditional on sending states

.ı controlling migration or on their reaccepting expelled _ereby establishing migration as an issue in bilateral relationships. ∠nt years, security concerns have further reinforced the apparent need ιtrol borders, as porous borders are thought to facilitate terrorist .ıvities. In North America, even the long-neglected U.S.–Canada border has become a source of security concerns (Andreas and Biersteker, 2003). On both sides of the Atlantic, such concerns have prompted the introduction of new biometric technologies (Thomas, 2005). While security preoccupations exacerbate the pressure to control borders, it is worth remembering that immigration controls were already a hot issue before their emergence – they alone cannot explain recent trends in border controls.

The most disturbing consequence of these evolutions in migration controls is the number of people who die on their way to receiving countries. Undocumented migration has become a dangerous process: it is estimated that at least one migrant dies every day at the U.S.–Mexico border, mostly because of hypothermia, dehydration, sunstroke or drowning (Cornelius, 2001; Martin, 2003). Similar trends can be observed in Europe. Eschbach et al. (1999) estimate that at least 920 migrants died trying to reach Europe between 1993 and 1997, while NGOs have counted more than 4,000 deaths between 1992 and 2003 (Rekacewicz and Clochard, 2004). According to a 2002 statement to the UN Secretary General, over 3,000 migrants attempting to enter Europe died between 1997 and 2000, mostly when crossing the Straits of Gibraltar (Human Rights Advocates International, 2002). The tragic outcomes of undocumented migration are not confined to Western countries: the same document mentions casualties off the coasts of Australia, at the border of Mexico and Guatemala, and across the Sahara. We should keep in mind, too, that these figures are probably underestimated, as no one knows how many bodies have not been discovered.

The costs of border control measures are not only human but also financial: according to an IOM report, the twenty-five richest countries spend U.S.$25–$30 billion per year on the enforcement of immigration laws (Martin, 2003). These costs stem not only from controlling the borders, but also from the issuance of visas and residence permits; the prosecution, detention and removal of undocumented migrants; labour inspections and the implementation of sanctions on employers; the processing of asylum seekers' claims and the resettlement of refugees; and the search for undocumented migrants. To provide a better perspective, it is tempting to juxtapose this amount of money with the sums dedicated to development: according to the World Bank's 2004 *World Development Indicators* (World Bank, 2004), states spend some U.S.$60 billion on development, and it is estimated that some U.S.$30–$50 billion extra is needed to put poor countries on the path to achieve the Millennium Development Goals.

Is it possible to control migration?

The issue of migration controls has raised major debates in recent years, as states often seem unable to control their borders and, more generally, to successfully manage migration flows. The persistence of undocumented migration illustrates how even sophisticated forms of border controls do not manage to stop people from entering a country. Of course, some migrants are caught while crossing the border and some are expelled after having entered. But motivated migrants manage to escape controls: by taking more risks, by crossing at new border areas or by relying to a greater extent on professional people-smugglers. There seems to be a consensus among experts that tougher measures of migration control do not achieve their stated aims (Cornelius et al., 2004).

Several explanations have been proposed to explain the incapacity of states to control migration. Migration is now structurally embedded in the economies and societies of most countries: once both sending and receiving countries become dependent upon migration, migration is almost impossible to stop. In an era of globalization, states face the dilemma that borders must remain business-friendly and open to international trade or tourism (Andreas and Snyder, 2000). Moreover, migratory movements are self-sustaining processes (Castles, 2004): countries become connected via migrant networks that span the globe and facilitate further migration. This illustrates that migration is easy to start but difficult to stop. Finally, lobby groups can also impose domestic pressures on governments to allow migration for labour market reasons.

As the contrast between Western countries and oil-exporting states in the Middle East shows, controlling immigration is particularly difficult for liberal democracies. These are characterized by the preponderant role of the market and a respect for the fundamental rights of individuals (Hollifield, 1992). The market constantly strives for expansion, seeking new people to produce goods and services and new consumers, which quickly raises immigration as an option; as the state logic of control is challenged by market forces, this creates a tension 'between states and markets' (Entzinger et al., 2004; Harris, 2002). Respect for rights means that even undocumented migrants should enjoy a minimal degree of legal protection: according to the philosophy of human rights, individuals are protected on the basis of personhood, not of nationality or citizenship, and the enforcement of these rights sometimes takes place supranationally, thereby constraining governments' autonomy (Jacobson, 1996; Sassen, 1996; Soysal, 1994). This means that civil society, human rights groups and NGOs can contest government measures, and they have sometimes opposed them in the courts: in other words, control is controlled and states are limited in their initiatives.

While unquestionable, the difficulty states have in controlling their borders should be qualified. Historically, full control has never been the norm. It is sometimes argued that open borders were a reality in the nineteenth century. The picture of an era of laissez-faire migration policies is probably exaggerated, but it remains that states have only progressively acquired the ability and legitimacy to control individuals' movements, a prerogative that used to be shared with other social actors such as churches or private enterprises (Torpey, 2000). From this perspective, states are now better able to control migration than ever before, and their apparent loss of control relies on the myth of a once-perfect sovereignty that never was (Joppke, 1998). Moreover, officially declared policies may differ from actual intentions: a benign neglect towards undocumented migration may, for example, fit with the interests of states or employers wishing to have access to an unorganized and irregular workforce (Freeman, 1994). The strategies that states deploy may also not always be perfectly coherent, as economic concerns may conflict with security preoccupations.

Along the same lines, it is worth noting that border controls can be more a matter of symbols than of actual results. Frontiers have always played a psychological role in the formation of national identity and authority (Anderson, 1996), and governments need to communicate to their citizens that they control the gates. This may lead to a self-perpetuating process: border controls create problems (such as smuggling or trespassing), which then call for more control (Andreas, 2000). In this respect, border controls are policies that generate visibility but few results and enable governments to develop a pro-control (or even anti-immigration) rhetoric while maintaining access to a foreign labour force. In Europe, for example, countries strongly exposed to undocumented migration (such as Italy and Spain) feel the need to show both their citizens and other EU members that they are addressing the question.

While the social and political context exacerbates the issue of border controls in developed countries, the difficulty of controlling immigration is far from an exclusively Western concern. According to a 2001 UN survey, forty-four governments – including thirty in less-developed regions – indicated that levels of immigration in their country were too high, and seventy-eight governments – including fifty-seven in less-developed regions – had policies aimed at reducing immigration levels (United Nations, 2002, pp. 17–18). This represents a sharp contrast with the situation of the 1970s, when migration was hardly a topic of concern, and illustrates the globalization of migration preoccupations, not only in Europe and North America, but also in Africa, the Asia Pacific and Latin America.

Three issues for the future of migration controls

Whether or not it is possible to successfully control migration, it remains that contemporary practices raise a number of important issues. The first lies in the coherence of migration policies: should states stick to their claimed ambition of controlling migration perfectly, despite the factual evidence that they cannot achieve this goal? The risk is that the gap between what policy-makers claim and the actual situation may render policies incoherent, especially in the eyes of the public. It may foster a belief that governments are unable or unwilling to control people flows, thus feeding anti-immigration feelings. Coherent and successful policies are needed to address public concerns over migration issues.

The second issue relates to the sustainability of migration policies. As a decrease in the number of people on the move is unlikely, we must envisage long-term answers to the challenges of migration. Contemporary policies, rather than offering a clear perspective on managing migration, seem to be lagging behind and reacting restrictively or passively to changes in migration flows. But 'building walls is a peculiarly lonely job and an admission of the inadequacy of the system' (Nett, 1971, p. 224), and we need to envisage viable alternatives to face future challenges.

Finally, as Catherine Wihtol de Wenden argues in Chapter 3 of this volume, the human costs of border controls raise the issue of whether such controls are compatible with the core values of the international community. To what extent can tough border-control measures coexist with the harmonious functioning of democracies? The liberal values and human rights principles that guide our societies cannot stop at their borders; they must inspire countries to behave accordingly towards outsiders arriving at their gates (Cole, 2000). The way a society handles the fate of foreigners ultimately reflects the values upon which it is based and the price – in terms of dignity and human rights – developed countries are prepared to pay to control their borders (Brochmann and Hammar, 1999; Schuster, 2004). In other words, the evolution of migration controls towards greater harshness might eventually backfire and threaten the liberal principles and freedoms that lie at the core of democratic societies.

In this context, the MWB scenario offers a coherent and morally defendable way of envisaging migration policies in the long term. It is a challenging idea that may be possible to implement only in the distant future. But given the current difficulties surrounding migration control, free movement may be a stimulating source of new solutions to existing problems.

Human rights and the ethical dimension of the MWB scenario

The ethical perspective is the most fundamental approach to the MWB scenario (Barry and Goodin, 1992; Carens, 1987; Gibney, 1988). Recent years have also witnessed a growing concern with the moral and ethical issues surrounding migration at large. While political philosophers have long ignored migration in their reflections on freedom, equality or justice, the necessity to rethink migration from a critical and ethical standpoint and to bring values, agencies and policies together have inspired several ethical approaches to borders, migration and asylum (Cole, 2000; Dummett, 2001; Gibney, 2004; Isbister, 1996; Jordan and Düvell 2002, 2003; Miller and Hashmi, 2001; Schwartz, 1995). Bearing in mind the complexity of the arguments (analysed in greater detail by Mehmet Ugur in Chapter 4), this section reviews the major issues surrounding the human rights and ethical dimensions of the MWB scenario.

Human rights, emigration and immigration

As mentioned, emigration is recognized as a human right but immigration is not. There is thus a 'fundamental contradiction between the notion that emigration is widely regarded as a matter of human rights while immigration is regarded as a matter of national sovereignty' (Weiner, 1996, p. 171). This imbalance can be interpreted in two opposite ways. One can argue that 'immigration and emigration are morally asymmetrical' (Walzer, 1983, p. 40). The right to emigration is fundamental because it gives people an exit option in their relation to states and governments, thereby protecting them from authoritarian regimes. 'The restraint of entry serves to defend the liberty and welfare, the politics and culture of a group of people committed to one another and to their common life. But the restraint of exit replaces commitment with coercion' (p. 39). This reasoning does not imply that other states must welcome foreigners in an unlimited way: states must let their residents leave but do not have to let others in. As Dowty states:

> The right to leave does not imply the corresponding right to enter a particular country. Whatever the arguments over the authority of the state to block emigration, there is little dispute over its rights to limit *immigration*. The two issues are not symmetrical: departure ends an individual's claims against a society, while entry sets such claims in motion. Control of entry is essential to the idea of sovereignty, for without it a society has no control over its basic character. (Dowty, 1987, p. 14)

By contrast, one can argue that having the right to leave one's country is meaningless as long as one cannot enter another country. From a practical perspective, an individual wishing to leave his or her country who was authorized to do so but was not accepted by any other country would see his/her right to emigration violated:

> Logically, it is an absurdity to assert a right of emigration without a complimentary right of immigration unless there exist in fact. … a number of states which permit free entry. At present, no such state exists, and the right of emigration is not, and cannot be in these circumstances, a general human right exercisable in practice. (Dummett, 1992, p. 173)

Emigration and immigration then inextricably complement each other, and the Universal Declaration of Human Rights has somehow stopped half-way in its recognition of a right to move. This complex debate is unlikely to be resolved soon and illustrates how human rights, far from being defined once and for all, must constantly be rethought and, if necessary, complemented.

Migration and inequalities between people and countries

Another way of addressing the relationship between migration and human rights is to consider the inequalities migration creates between people and countries. Mobility is a privilege that is unevenly distributed among human beings: citizens from developed countries may travel and settle down almost anywhere in the world, while their fellow human beings from less-developed countries depend upon the uncertain issuance of visas and residence permits to migrate. In this respect, citizenship is a birthright privilege that is difficult to justify (Carens, 1987).

A different kind of inequality regards qualification. Today, trained workers are looked for by states and enjoy a much greater level of mobility than their unskilled compatriots. At other times, unskilled workers were privileged, illustrating skills-based differences of treatments towards migrants. Rafael Alarcón (Chapter 12) analyses how, in the context of the North American Free Trade Agreement (NAFTA), skilled workers have been granted the right to move and to accompany the free circulation of goods, services and information, whereas the numerous (and much-needed) unskilled Mexican workers in the United States are left out of these agreements. Australia, whose society is based on an openness to migrants that is still valid today, welcomes permanent settlers and students while developing a hard-line approach to asylum seekers and imposing visa requirements on virtually all non-nationals entering the country. These examples illustrate how states select desirable migrants to the detriment of 'undesirable' ones: their right to do so is hardly contested even if 'the line between preferences and discrimination ... is a morally thin one that is easily crossed' (Weiner, 1996, p. 178). In other words, restrictions on mobility violate the liberal egalitarian principle according to which people should have equal opportunities.

Border controls also play a role in inequalities between countries. Migration is grounded in the disparities between nations and partly functions as a redistribution mechanism: people from poor regions move where the money is and usually, through remittances, contribute to sending it where it is needed. It is morally difficult to prevent migrants from poor countries from having access to the wealth of richer countries. If receiving states close their borders, they remain compelled to find alternative ways of achieving greater equality between countries (Barry and Goodin, 1992). As Lucas (1999) clearly outlines, this may include trade, foreign investment and development aid. The problem is that these alternatives are far from successful: states have limited influence on foreign investments, while development aid has so far not proved efficient enough to reduce poverty. Development does not substitute for migration but tends to foster it: it leads to economic restructuring in sending countries and to rural–urban migration, creating a spirit of migration (Massey et al., 1998). Politically, developed states may be even more reluctant to freer trade in some sectors (notably agriculture), or to increased development expenses, than to migration. Migration may then not only be the most efficient way of reducing inequalities between countries but also, and contrary to widespread perceptions, the most acceptable solution.

Mehmet Ugur (Chapter 4) stresses that the key question is the level of analysis: closed borders may ensure the well-being of a nation, but what about the well-being of the world? How can one justify the priority given to a particular group to the detriment of the whole? While this can be interpreted as selfishness, it can also be understood, in a communitarian manner, as a moral imperative. In this view (best developed by Walzer, 1983), communities of people have the right to determine who is entitled to membership and to exert control over their nature and composition; this is necessary to achieve desirable goals (such as the development of a generous welfare system) and to develop the moral values that stem from involvement in a given community. States are legitimately responsible for the well-being of their citizens, and ensuring the well-being of the world implies having all states care for their own citizens, rather than letting people move wherever they want in a way that would ultimately destroy the values upon which communities are based. While this perspective rightly stresses the need to fully involve all residents in the community (which, as we will see, is not achieved in the case of many immigrant states), one can nevertheless object that the 'threat' represented by newcomers to community values is difficult to quantify and depends upon ideological and political factors. Moreover, while newcomers may initially threaten shared values, over time their eventual inclusion in the community is a process that may be beneficial for the community itself and for the evolution of its values: movement, rather than destroying the foundations of a community, creates a new form of community based on values of openness and justice (Carens, 1987).

Towards a right to mobility?

Nevins (2003) rightly argues that, while the human rights violations generated by border controls are usually condemned (especially by governments or NGOs), their very legitimacy is never questioned. At most, human smugglers are blamed for the deaths and poor living conditions of irregular migrants, and calls are made for only sketchily defined 'humane' border policies. This approach, which focuses on epiphenomena and neglects the roots of the problem, is unlikely to produce successful results. It is therefore time to push the human rights logic one step further and to question the moral basis of restrictions on people's mobility. In Chapter 3 of this volume, Catherine Wihtol de Wenden argues that, given the crisis of migration controls and their severe human rights consequences, it has become urgent to begin debate on a comprehensive right to mobility, which would encompass both emigration and immigration and complement the existing Declaration of Human Rights (see also Pécoud and de Guchteneire 2006*a*).

This right stems from the increasingly global and multicultural nature of today's world: in a world of flows, mobility becomes a central resource to which all human beings should have access. Graziano Battistella (Chapter 10) adds that undocumented migration can be interpreted not only as a consequence of inadequate migration policies, but also as the expression of people's claim to their right to migrate. Mobility might then be regarded in the same way as other fundamental human prerogatives:

> At some future point in world civilization, it may well be discovered that the right to free and open movement of people on the surface of the earth is fundamental to the structure of human opportunity and is therefore basic in the same sense as is free religion [and] speech. (Nett, 1971, p. 218)

A right to mobility would fit into other human rights principles. In a world of economic globalization and of gross socioeconomic inequalities, the human right to a free choice of employment (Article 23 of the Universal Declaration of Human Rights) and to an adequate standard of living (Article 25) seem hard to achieve in the absence of mobility opportunities. A right to mobility is therefore not a matter of adding a right to the existing list, it is about fostering respect for the human rights that are already acknowledged as fundamental.

The economic dimension

Along with the ethical perspective, another frequent approach to the MWB scenario is of an economic nature and reflects economists' interest in this issue. What would be the economic impact of free movement on the world economy? Conscious of the far-ranging developments of the economics of migration, this section outlines a few relevant points.

The national and international economic impact of migration

One can start to assess the economic impact of the MWB scenario by considering the current situation. Despite numerous studies on the topic, the picture remains complex. Regarding sending countries, the mainstream idea is that emigration generates remittances (which are positive but can be spent fruitlessly), reduces tax revenues, and results in a loss of skills, even if it is sometimes argued that brain-drain could be replaced by brain-gain, whereby sending countries rely on their emigrants' skills for their development. As for receiving societies, some studies highlight the costs of immigration and the large share of welfare benefits received by migrants (Borjas, 1999), while others – reviewed by Mehmet Ugur in Chapter 4 – show that migrants are net contributors and that receiving countries benefit from their presence. In any case, as Ugur also shows, the economic impact of migration on the well-being of a receiving country's native residents is limited; Faini et al. (1999, p. 6) confirm that 'immigration has played virtually no role in explaining the worsening labour market conditions of unskilled workers' in Europe and the United States. Having said that, one should note that it is obviously difficult to extrapolate from current migration conditions to the possible economic consequences of free movement.

One can then switch the analysis from the national to the international level and evaluate the economic impact of the MWB scenario on the wealth of the world at large. According to a classic article by Hamilton and Whalley (1984), the liberalization of the world's labour market would double the world's GDP. More recently, Rodrik (2005) argues that the biggest gains in terms of development and poverty-reduction do not lie in the much-discussed issues surrounding free trade, but in the international movement of workers, and that even a minor liberalization in this field would massively foster the development of poor countries (see also Iregui, 2005). For these reasons, neoclassical economists sometimes advocate free movement. The *Financial Times* is one of the few leading newspapers in favour of this; *FT*'s journalist Martin Wolf recently stated that 'controls on migration create the world's biggest economic distortion – the discrepancy in rewards to labour', but that 'nobody seems to be suggesting the obvious answer: free migration' (Wolf, 2004, p. 117). In this view, restrictions on the mobility of people, just like restrictions on the circulation of goods and capital, are economically counterproductive and should be banned in a globally integrated economy. Free migration would be the best way to achieve equality at the world level, which would then reduce the necessity to migrate:

> If labour is viewed as an export, and remittances as the foreign exchange earned from the export of labour, then the opening of the borders could allow labour-surplus countries to export labour and earn remittances. In so doing, the transfer of labour from poorer to rich countries would increase the world GDP (because workers earn more) and eventually reduce migration pressure as wages tend to converge as they rise in emigration areas and fall or rise more slowly in immigration areas. (Martin, 2003, p. 88)

Clearly, as Bimal Ghosh reminds us in Chapter 5, economic theory is based on assumptions that rarely correspond to reality, and one should be prudent in interpreting these results. But it remains that, from an economic standpoint, the MWB scenario would involve letting market forces handle the issue of inequalities between countries, with the belief that the non-intervention of states in human movement would achieve better results than their intervention. A counter-argument is that free migration would create opportunities for skilled workers in poor countries but not for their unskilled compatriots, who lack the minimal qualifications (literacy for example) to find jobs in developed countries: the MWB scenario would then hurt the interests of the poorest of the poor, which would be unfair and counterproductive from a development perspective. While this may be the case, the scale of this phenomenon remains uncertain and cannot justify closed borders (Piketty, 1997). More convincingly, one can object that the equalizing impact of free movement on wages and living standards may be achieved at an undesirably low level, and will in any case be hard to reach as 'it would seem that social and political objections to further immigration will arise long before it reaches such a scale that it has any major impact on the labour market' (Stalker, 2000, p. 91). The growth of inequalities between countries has historically gone hand in hand with the reduction of inequalities within countries (Giraud, 1996), and it might be difficult to win on both sides.

Globalization and the non-liberalization of migration flows

Whatever the impact of free movement on world inequalities, it remains that restrictions on migration contradict the spirit of globalization and liberalization. Indeed, 'whereas increased trade integration at the turn of the century and in the 1960s was accompanied by increased migration, this was not so during the increased trade integration of the 1980s' (Faini et al., 1999, p. 5); international migration is an exception in the globalization process. Borders used to stop everything – money, goods, people – but today they stop mostly people: 'there is a growing consensus in the community of states to lift border controls for the flow of capital, information, and services and, more broadly, to further globalization. But when it comes to immigrants and refugees ... the national state claims all its old splendour in asserting its sovereign right to control its borders' (Sassen, 1996, p. 59). As Nigel Harris (Chapter 2) argues, this is paradoxical given that the internationalization of the economy creates a world labour market in which some countries tend to specialize in providing particular types of workers to the rest of the world.

The Mexico–U.S. situation is the best example of this paradox: two countries united within a free trade agreement are separated by a militarized border. But it is not the only one. In Chapter 9, Sally Peberdy and Jonathan Crush describe how, within the Southern African Development Community (SADC) – comprising Angola, Botswana, Lesotho, Malawi, Mauritius, Mozambique, Namibia, South Africa, Swaziland, Tanzania, Zambia, and

Zimbabwe – agreements on free trade have been much more successful than those on free movement. In Chapter 13, Alicia Maguid reports that the initial ambitions of the Mercado Común del Sur/Mercado Comum do Sul ('Southern Common Market', or MERCOSUR) to facilitate the movement of people in the South American Cone have been progressively reduced and that the current focus is mostly on free trade. The European Union is the only region in the world in which free trade agreements have been coherently accompanied by a substantial degree of free movement of persons, as documented by Jan Kunz and Mari Leinonen in Chapter 7.

Comparing flows of people to flows of capital, information or commodities is, however, simplistic, as the circulation of people generates a high degree of social complexity and raises political challenges that cannot be ignored. Moreover, protectionism and state intervention are still very much present and free trade is strongly resisted, especially in vital sectors such as agriculture. In Europe, the Common Agricultural Policy imposes restrictions on the circulation of agricultural goods for the same reasons that are sometimes used to justify closed borders, namely social cohesion and national interests.

Yet, the contradiction between globalization and the non-liberalization of migration cannot be ignored. It is tellingly illustrated by the World Trade Organization (WTO) negotiations on the 'temporary movement of natural persons' ('Mode 4'). Recognizing that trade in services needs direct physical contact between suppliers and consumers, and wishing to foster the liberalization of international trade in services, WTO members have engaged in negotiations on cross-border movement of workers. In principle, these discussions concern temporary service providers exclusively and exclude the issues surrounding permanent migration, citizenship, residence or employment. But the boundary is not clear-cut, the issue remains largely unexplored and controversial, and discussions so far have dealt mainly with the mobility of skilled professionals within multinational companies (Bhatnagar, 2004). This however shows that trade and migration are interconnected in a globalized economy, and that pressures towards liberalization may one day promote a narrowly trade-oriented version of the MWB scenario.

Limits of the economic approach

While assessing the economic impact of the MWB scenario is an essential task, one should stress that migration policies have important implications in terms of ethics, human rights and global justice, and cannot be solely guided by economic concerns. For example, family reunification is sometimes criticized for bringing in immigrants' 'economically useless' relatives. Writing on U.S. immigration policy, Simon (1989, p. 337) argues that migrants should be chosen 'more for their economic characteristics and less on the basis of family connections'. But this would negate people's right to live with their family, and most states authorize family reunifications (Carens, 2003).

Moreover, migration policies cannot be a benefit to all: skilled migration is good for receiving countries, but less for sending ones; family reunification is important to migrants but not always useful to receiving countries; the individual interests of migrants can create an undesirable brain-drain, and so on. It is difficult to satisfy simultaneously the citizens of both countries of destination and origin and the migrants themselves; one needs to make social and political choices:

> Economic analysis raises questions regarding what welfare objectives we should assume. ...
> Should we seek to maximise the welfare of natives alone, or does the welfare of immigrants
> count as well? Should we seek to maximise national economic welfare or global economic
> welfare? Different welfare objectives will imply different optimal policies. Although
> economists can tell us what policies would maximise any given welfare objective, the choice
> of that objective is ultimately a moral decision. (Chang, 2000, pp. 225–26)

We are again confronted by the issue of the level of analysis. Usually, a nation's policies focus on its national interests, which, as argued above, raises moral questions. On the other hand, governments are responsible for their national interests and are expected to privilege their citizens' well-being. But even then, the picture is complicated, as determining the national interest may prove difficult. Different social actors – employers, unions, politicians – are likely to have different views and to try to influence policy choices (Humphries, 2002). Resultant migration policies might then be beneficial only to the most influential segment of the population, thus increasing internal inequalities. Moreover, focusing on the national well-being might be counterproductive if it creates tensions and social unrest in neighbouring countries: it is, for example, in the interest of Europe and North America to have friendly neighbours in northern Africa or Mexico, and hence to welcome at least some migrants from these regions (Borjas, 1999).

The social dimension

Whereas the ethical and economic dimensions of the MWB scenario have been substantially analysed, little attention has been given to its social dimension. This probably has to do with the near-impossibility of evaluating the numerous consequences of free movement on all dimensions of social life. As we will see, it is illusory to claim that we know what would actually happen if borders were to be opened; too many factors play a role and recent history reminds us that immigration policies often have unpredictable results (Castles, 2004). This should, however, not keep us from attempting to shed light on the social impact of the MWB scenario, as, whatever its moral or economic desirability, promoting free movement will be incomplete and unsuccessful without considering all its consequences.

How many people would migrate?

An often-heard argument against the MWB scenario is that it would lead to huge and unmanageable flows of migrants converging towards developed countries. The first obvious question is therefore: How many people would migrate under conditions of free movement? Contemporary policies focus on restricting people's mobility and it is fair to assume that putting an end to them would enable more people to move. But how many? A reasonable augmentation could be manageable, but what about a massive increase? One should first dismiss the idea that all inhabitants of sending countries are eager to migrate: after all, as the UN High Commissioner for Refugees (UNHCR) *Handbook* states, 'it may be assumed that, unless he seeks adventure or just wishes to see the world, a person would not normally abandon his home and country without some compelling reason' (UNHCR, 1979, Chapter 1, Article 39).

The history of the European Union – reviewed in this volume by Jan Kunz and Mari Leinonen (Chapter 7) – provides helpful indications here. Each step of its enlargement has been accompanied by ungrounded fears of massive migration flows. Today, many EU countries impose temporary restrictions on the mobility of people from most of the ten new EU members, but studies converge to show that substantial East–West migration flows are unlikely. In the future, the issue of Turkey's admission may raise the same issues, but, as Teitelbaum and Martin (2003) argue, it is impossible to make credible predictions on how many Turkish workers would leave their country, as this depends upon the evolutions of both the Turkish and the European economies.

One should further recall that migration flows and the legal conditions of migration are not always related. People reluctant to take the risk of migrating irregularly might be incited to do so legally under the MWB scenario, but, as mentioned above, restrictive policies do not keep people from trying to migrate clandestinely, and the MWB scenario would therefore have little impact on the numerous migrants who would leave their country no matter whether it were authorized or not: it would only reduce the dangers they are exposed to. Moreover, restrictions on mobility limit migrants' freedom to circulate, thus leading to a higher rate of permanent settlement. In this respect, the MWB scenario would enable more migrants to return, temporarily or not, which might to some extent counterbalance the increase in the number of people wishing to leave their country. Mexican migration to the United States illustrates these two points: migrants keep trying to cross the border until they succeed and, given the difficulty of doing so, tend to remain on a more permanent basis in the country (Cornelius, 2001).

The MWB scenario: welfare and social cohesion

Migration is often perceived as a threat to social cohesion, and it is therefore important to address the possible impact of the MWB scenario on the functioning of receiving societies. A major issue here regards the welfare state: as Milton Friedman once observed, 'it's just obvious that you can't have free immigration and a welfare state' (quoted by Raico, 1998, p. 135). As Han Entzinger (Chapter 6) argues, the core problem lies in the contradictory logic of welfare schemes and free migration; the MWB scenario is about openness and circulation whereas welfare systems are based on closure: people make a long-term commitment to a community and enjoy its protection. Putting aside the financial impact of increased migration on Western welfare systems, the risk is that free movement jeopardizes the sense of common national identity and solidarity that incites people to take part in welfare schemes. Jan Kunz and Mari Leinonen (Chapter 7) thus conclude that the MWB scenario is incompatible with collective welfare systems and would imply their privatization.

This is a real problem, not only because welfare states are hard-won and socially valuable achievements, but also because incorporating migrants would precisely require strong welfare systems. The MWB scenario challenges the viability of welfare states, but simultaneously demands efficient welfare mechanisms to make sure that the arrival of newcomers in receiving societies does not create situations of social vulnerability. This is also why, as mentioned earlier, welfare arguments are used – notably by communitarians – to advocate restrictions on migration. Another position is illustrated by Carens (1988), who acknowledges with regret the undesirable impact of free movement on welfare, but nevertheless believes that inequalities between countries are morally even more undesirable, and that welfare schemes must be sacrificed to people's freedom and to world justice.

This pessimism should be qualified. It is, for example, often claimed that migration would counterbalance the ageing of Western populations (United Nations, 2000). Welfare-based arguments may then also militate for *more* migration. In this respect, Iregui (2005) shows that the costs of skilled migration in terms of brain-drain may exceed welfare gains, but that this effect disappears if one allows both skilled and unskilled migration. As Han Entzinger notes (Chapter 6), states should then invest in migrants' linguistic and professional skills, thereby increasing their integration and the size of the workforce. Moreover, as Geddes (2003) argues, migration is far from being the main challenge to welfare states: other factors – labour-market situation, demographic trends or political decisions – play a much greater role. At a more immediate level, free movement would improve the well-being of undocumented migrants, whose status is a serious source of vulnerability; it would also reduce the size of shadow economies, thereby increasing employers' and workers' contributions to welfare schemes.

Another question regards the incorporation of migrants in receiving societies under conditions of free movement. Again, migrants are often blamed for their reluctance to 'integrate' and are accused of threatening the socio-cultural foundations of the countries in which they live. In particular, the MWB scenario is sometimes dismissed for its consequences in terms of racism and xenophobia. Free migration, it is argued, would increase the number of migrants and the tensions between them and the native population, notably concerning the labour market. This would lead to anti-immigration mobilization and foster populist and extreme-right political formations (Castles, 2004, p. 873). Walzer (1983) similarly argues that, if states do not control migration, people will reject foreigners by themselves through potentially violent methods.

But the correlation between xenophobia and the number of immigrants is not straightforward: very few migrants may sometimes cause disproportionate hostile reactions in regions not used to immigration. More fundamentally, border controls indirectly feed racism: they fuel the idea that foreigners and foreign-looking people are undesirable, thus casting doubts on the right of documented and naturalized migrants to live in receiving societies (Hayter, 2000). Ultimately, this reinforces internal boundaries along ethnic lines, jeopardizing migrants' access to decent living conditions and challenging social cohesion (Fassin et al., 1997; Wihtol de Wenden, 1999). As Dummett (2001) argues, Western public opinion has been subject to restrictive discourses on the need to close borders for decades, which can only support anti-immigrant feelings; any change in migration policies will imply stopping untruthful propaganda against immigrants and re-educating the electorates. The connection between the MWB scenario and racism is therefore equivocal.

The MWB scenario: democracy and citizenship

Closely related to the issues of welfare and integration are the issues of rights, citizenship and participation in the public sphere. In principle, access to citizenship rights depends upon nationality, thereby excluding migrants. In practice however, non-nationals enjoy certain rights. Human rights, for instance, are based on personhood rather than nationality, and protect both nationals and migrants. Migrants participate in unions, in the education system, in welfare schemes, have rights protecting their situation in the labour market, and sometimes even vote in local elections, thus illustrating how residency – and not only nationality – determines access to rights (Jacobson, 1996; Soysal, 1994). Hammar (1990) has coined the term 'denizen' to describe this intermediary status, in which migrants are not total foreigners, but not full citizens either. The MWB scenario would exacerbate this question, as it would enable people to move freely from one country to another, so raising the question of their status at the different steps of their peregrinations. Even under conditions of unrestricted mobility, people would probably choose to settle down in a given country and become citizens, but we nevertheless need to envisage situations in which nations are home to a large number of non-nationals on the move.

What seems obvious is that all people residing in a given country should have the same access to a minimal set of rights, including civil rights and social rights to education, health services and housing. This corresponds to a basic ethical principle and to the idea that all human beings should have access to fundamental rights, a notion that lies at the heart of the United Nations International Convention on Migrants' Rights (Pécoud and de Guchteneire, 2006b). This is also necessary to avoid the creation of an underprivileged sub-sector of the population subject to exploitation and misery, which is contrary to the national interest of states as such rightless migrant workers would create downward pressure on the well-being of the whole population. But what about access to unemployment benefits, political rights or cultural recognition? Unrestricted mobility would challenge the traditional distribution of these rights.

The same applies to migrants' participation in public affairs. It is easy to understand that two extreme situations should be avoided. In the first, non-nationals would have no access to political rights. Migrants would then live in a country without having any influence on its functioning, and would need to follow laws and obey governments over which they have no control. In immigration states with tight naturalization policies, this situation is already frequent; in Michael Walzer's terms, such states are 'like a family with live-in servants' (1983, p. 52), an unjust situation that excludes migrants and confines them to second-class status. At the other extreme would be the situation in which all migrants could have full citizenship rights. Even recent newcomers would then have the same influence over public affairs as nationals, a situation that may ultimately threaten the principles of democratic institutions: it seems illogical and unfair to grant people who have just arrived in a country the same rights enjoyed by nationals and long-term residents who share a strong commitment to the country in which they live. In other words, mobility is a challenge for democracy and we need to find ways to reconcile freedom of movement with the functioning of democratic institutions.

A first answer to these challenges is to decouple citizenship and nationality. As Castles and Davidson (2000) make clear, the classic form of citizenship, according to which membership and rights are based upon nationality, is inadequate in a world characterized by globalization and mobility. It creates situations in which people have no membership at all: they live in countries in which they have few rights, while being kept from participating in the life of the societies they come from. Citizenship should then be based upon residence on a state's territory. Following the same reasoning, Chemillier-Gendreau (2002) argues that, as long as rights are granted by states on the basis of nationality, situations of injustice will arise, because states can always be tempted to deny these rights to people under their authority, either by refusing naturalization or by (more rarely) depriving their citizens of their nationality. She then calls for a global citizenship in which people would enjoy rights irrespective of their nationality, solely on the basis of their being human beings.

The problem that remains is to decide when and to whom to grant rights. It would be absurd to expect states to grant citizenship rights to all foreigners entering their territory (such as tourists, students or business travellers). A creative solution to these issues is to unpack citizenship and consider that its different components (especially political, civil, social, family and cultural rights) can be distributed in a differentiated way. This approach avoids the binary logic of exclusion, in which people have either all possible rights or none at all. Migrants could then initially receive a first set of rights (civil rights and fundamental social rights). Only later would they receive, in a step-by-step fashion, full welfare rights or political rights. Such a system would ensure that migrants are not 'rightless' (as undocumented migrants tend to be), while enabling high mobility and addressing the fears of nationals and long-term residents who are reluctant to share their privileges with newcomers. According to Han Entzinger (Chapter 6), newcomers would not have to pay for the benefits to which they initially have no access, which would lower their labour costs and foster their integration in the labour market. The risk is that this system of 'differentiated inclusion' could transform into one of 'differentiated exclusion', but 'too much mobility is simply incompatible with a sustainable framework of rights [and] thresholds are needed to ensure durable rights' (Engelen, 2003, p. 510).

External borders and internal boundaries

Borders are only one kind of boundary. As discussed in this section, migrants are not only banned from entering a country; once they are in, they are often inhibited in their participation and incorporation in the receiving society, particularly in terms of welfare, rights and citizenship. One could therefore conceive a world of 'open' borders in which migrants would be free to cross borders between states, but banned from having access to the institutions of societies other than their own; the MWB scenario would then be about displacing (rather than suppressing) borders. This is particularly the case where international migration has contributed to the creation of social, ethnic or religious communities (Heisler, 2001), while at the same time restrictive migration policies have sought to reduce migrants' access to public resources (Cohen et al., 2002). As a result, 'bordering has become more multifaceted, taking on both geographic and non-geographic forms, of social, political, and economic characters' (Jacobson, 2001, p. 161).

It is therefore not enough to ensure that people have the right to cross borders and to settle down wherever they wish: we must also ensure that, once in a country, they are not stopped by internal borders but are able to fully participate in its society. This is a condition for social cohesion and for human emancipation, as people excluded from the society in which they live are likely to develop resentment and frustration. As Graziano Battistella (Chapter 10), Alejandro Canales and Israel Montiel Armas (Chapter 11) argue, this notably includes socioeconomic mobility within the class stratification of receiving societies. Labour markets are frequently segmented in a way that restricts social mobility and generates internal boundaries within the workforce, often along ethnic lines. Migrants are then left to do the dirty work, in conditions characterized by precariousness, low wages and non-existent future perspectives. This reinforces their exclusion and generates a 'ghettoization' of the society that jeopardizes the fair distribution of its resources and opportunities among all its members.

The practical dimension

Discussing the different dimensions of the MWB scenario highlights our ignorance of its practical consequences: 'nobody can claim to know in any detail what would be the consequences of a worldwide system of open borders sustained over a number of decades' (Barry, 1992, p. 280). While there are strong moral arguments in favour of the MWB scenario, its impact on wages, welfare, racism or citizenship is uncertain. It is probably exaggerated to argue that free movement would lead to chaos, but it would also be a mistake to underestimate the problems: as Castles (2004, p. 873) puts it, 'the elegant simplicity of the open borders slogan is deceptive, as it would create many new problems'. There is therefore a need to envisage the practical dimensions of the MWB scenario and what could be called its governance.

The need for a multilateral approach

A first principle of the governance of free movement lies in the cooperation among states it requires: no state can be expected to progress towards free movement if even some other states do not follow the same path. Unilateral openness is not only unlikely, it is also potentially damaging:

> Any country, rich or poor, that opened its borders might soon find other states taking advantage of its beneficent policies. A neighbouring country whose elite wanted a more homogeneous society could now readily expel its minorities. A government that wanted a more egalitarian society could dump its unemployed and its poor. An authoritarian regime could rid itself of its opponents; a country could empty its jails, mental institutions, and homes for the aged. (Weiner, 1996, p. 173)

To this we should add security issues: In Chapter 5, Bimal Ghosh notes that the MWB scenario would enable not only terrorists but also all kinds of criminals to escape surveillance more easily. These dangers point to the importance of international cooperation. After all, these dreadful consequences of free movement could take place within federal states, where regions are partly responsible for welfare provisions and security, and can be prevented by interregional cooperation. Of course, such agreements are more difficult to reach at the world level, but these obstacles are not inherently insurmountable.

A second principle should be the need for supervision mechanisms to study and monitor the social transformations induced by increased freedom of movement and to enable a less-chaotic opening of the borders. Both principles – cooperation and supervision – highlight the need for multilateral agreements (or organizations) to ensure the governance of free movement in a more comprehensive way than the trade-oriented WTO negotiations mentioned above. In recent years, many voices have called for a movement towards a multilateral approach to migration, with a series of similarly named propositions: 'New International Regime for Orderly Movements of People' (Ghosh, 2000), 'General Agreement on Movements of People' (Straubhaar, 2000), 'General Agreement on Migration and Refugee Policy' (Harris, 1995, p. 224), 'Global Agreement on the Movement of People' (Veenkamp et al. 2003, p. 98), or, modelled on the WTO, a 'World Migration Organization' (Bhagwati, 1998, pp. 316–17, 2003). Security concerns have also fostered the search for such agreements; Koslowski (2004) speaks of a 'General Agreement on Migration, Mobility and Security'.

Without describing in detail the nature, functioning and purposes of these approaches (they are reviewed by Bimal Ghosh in Chapter 5 and Mehmet Ugur in Chapter 4), their common point is that they all envisage a joint management of migration flows by sending and receiving states, which would avoid the pitfalls of unilateral policies while ensuring that the migration process does not harm the interests of sending and receiving states nor of migrants themselves. With respect to the MWB scenario, there are two ways to envisage the role of a multilateral approach. On the one hand, there are those who argue, as does Bimal Ghosh in Chapter 5 of this volume, that an orderly system of migration management would be fundamentally better than free movement as it would avoid the tensions and uneven benefits that characterize the MWB scenario while being much more acceptable to states. On the other hand, others see multilateral coordination as a temporary step towards free movement that would smooth the transition:

> In practical terms, even if states were to agree on a universal right to move in principle, it would probably cause chaos if all borders were instantly opened. But there are many matters on which states have agreed certain rights in principle and begun to implement these rights in a limited way, by agreement among themselves. … Could there not be

similar progress towards acknowledging a human right to freedom of movement across borders? Even if the aim could not be realized at once, would it not be worthwhile to begin the process by an international agreement whereby each state party to it would accept, in addition to those it admits under its laws of refugees and other migrants, a quota of people who merely apply? (Dummett, 1992, p. 179)

The MWB scenario and the internationalization and/or liberalization of migration policies finally raise the question of the asylum system. Today, asylum seekers are the only migrants whose situation is taken care of in a partly multilateral manner, notably through the United Nations High Commissioner for Refugees and the widely ratified 1951 Geneva Convention. In principle, the distinction between asylum seekers/refugees and other kinds of migrants is clear, and most states have distinct procedures to address their situations, even if empirical evidence illustrates that the boundaries between the two are often porous. Under the MWB scenario, this distinction would become meaningless, which, as Castles (2004, p. 873) argues, is regrettable because even the currently imperfect asylum system protects many vulnerable people. By contrast, one can argue that the fight against undocumented migration incites many receiving states to treat asylum seekers as disguised economic migrants, which leads not only to endless and unmanageable procedures to 'prove' the existence of persecution, but also to human rights abuses and sufferings for both 'genuine' and 'fake' refugees (Barsky, 2001; Hayter, 2000). In other words, sticking to the refugee/migrant distinction may not only be unrealistic: it may also counter-productively threaten the right to asylum.

Regional approaches to free movement

Establishing a multilateral approach to migration at the world level is clearly a difficult task, and it therefore makes sense to envisage regional approaches as a preliminary step. Significant cross-border flows take place within regions, and the countries involved tend to display a greater level of socioeconomic convergence. From an economic perspective, open borders should come first and equality should follow, but in practice, gaping inequalities between states may prevent any discussion. As a matter of fact, several regions in the world have concretely discussed regional migration management, an indication that they have indirectly acknowledged the shortcomings of national approaches. Some have even considered free movement as an option, and their experiences are useful in understanding the difficulty of concretely implementing the MWB scenario.

The clearest case is of course the European Union, which has achieved free movement for EU citizens at an unprecedented scale. In Chapter 7, Jan Kunz and Mari Leinonen relate how a core ambition of the European Union has been to create opportunities for its citizens to move freely from one Member

State to another. Yet migration flows have not increased substantially, which points to the importance of internal borders (including notably administrative, financial, cultural, linguistic and mental barriers). Mobility is mostly a feature of European elites while workers and employees tend to remain in their country of origin. In the meantime, European leaders have been engaged in the closing and monitoring of the EU's external borders, leading to what has been called 'Fortress Europe'. In principle, these two trends (the disappearance of internal borders and the consolidation of external ones) call for a common approach to migration, but European leaders have found it extremely difficult to move forward in this field. Regardless of these obstacles, it remains that the European experience is the most comprehensive attempt to establish free movement in a large supranational space.

But other less well-known cases exist, notably in Africa. As Aderanti Adepoju (Chapter 8) and Sally Peberdy and Jonathan Crush (Chapter 9) note, the African continent is characterized by recent and porous borders, as well as by a long history of human mobility in which free movement has often been the norm. While this should in principle provide a favourable context for the MWB scenario, post-independence nation-building has been a powerful process, sometimes inspiring exacerbated nationalism or xenophobia. Yet, since the early 1990s, the continent seems to have been engaged in some efforts to promote freer movement, which used to be grounded in a pan-African ideology but is increasingly apprehended in terms of economic benefits. Continental organizations such as the New Partnership for African Development (NEPAD) and the African Union (AU) have expressed their commitment to free movement, with the latter recently proposing the creation of an 'African passport' to facilitate the circulation of people throughout the continent. Efforts to go beyond national migration policies remain vague and uncertain however, as illustrated by the cases of West and southern Africa.

Aderanti Adepoju (Chapter 8) describes efforts to foster free movement and establish a 'borderless West Africa' within the Economic Community of West African States (ECOWAS). ECOWAS treaties aim at removing all obstacles to the circulation of goods, capital and people: an early step was to abolish visa requirements for ECOWAS citizens moving within the region, with governments agreeing to create an ECOWAS passport to facilitate internal migration. As Adepoju suggests, given the history of migration in the region, establishing open borders is more about re-creating free movement rather than shaping a new regional organization. Many obstacles remain however, and Adepoju shows that economic uncertainty and inter-state conflicts, along with the political strategies sometimes developed by ECOWAS governments, threaten the West African version of the MWB scenario by exacerbating tensions and fuelling nationalism and xenophobia, sometimes leading to the expulsion of foreigners. Sally Peberdy and Jonathan Crush (Chapter 8) document the efforts undertaken towards free movement in the southern African region, and the obstacles they face. The Southern African Development Community (SADC) drafted a protocol on the free movement of people in 1993–1994. This was strongly opposed by the South African government, who feared the consequences of open borders on unemployment, xenophobia and irregular migration; although these arguments were contested, they were sufficient to reduce the initiative to a much less ambitious version.

In the Asia Pacific region, regional organizations have focused on migration issues concerning business and skilled migration in accordance with the promotion of free trade. Other regional initiatives have focused on the fight against irregular migration, trafficking and refugees. As Graziano Battistella (Chapter 10) writes, the prospects for progress towards the MWB scenario seem more limited in Asia than in other parts of the world. In South America, Alicia Maguid (Chapter 13) reports that free circulation of labour was initially considered as part of MERCOSUR's ambitions to establish a common market and free trade in the South American Cone (Argentina, Brazil, Paraguay and Uruguay). While progress has been made in the harmonization of migrants' status in these countries, the free movement of goods and services has, as in the SADC, moved forward much faster than its counterpart in terms of human mobility. As in Europe, a felt need to fight against undocumented migration (particularly from the Andean region) has fostered a strengthening of border controls, while economic uncertainty has raised problems of racism and xenophobia. Finally, the North American Free Trade Agreement (NAFTA) is the most well-known example of a discontinuity between the circulation of goods and people: as Rafael Alarcón (Chapter 12) documents, it was clear from the beginning that migration would not be considered in the agreements.

These different experiences illustrate the extreme complexity of the establishment of free movement and the number of inevitable obstacles to such endeavours that exist. They also show, however, that free movement is not an absurdity that has only been considered by the Europeans: it is discussed, and even sometimes partly put into practice, in many regions of the world. The regional approach is not without critique, however. Mehmet Ugur (Chapter 4) argues that regional agreements only perpetuate world inequalities at another level; Bimal Ghosh (Chapter 5) stresses that migration always defies bounded geographical arrangements and that the different paths taken by regions in their migration management could lead to tensions: closing borders in one region may for example divert flows to other areas. This points to the necessity of envisaging a global approach to migration that would ensure that regional agreements are coherent with one another.

Conclusion

Throughout the world, states claim their will to control migration but are confronted with the extreme difficulty of developing policies that match this ambition. The number of people on the move is not going to decrease in the near future, and it will become increasingly apparent that even the most sophisticated and costly measures of control do not truly stop people. Migrants will probably remain the main victims of this unsatisfactory approach to migration, as they will be exposed to ever greater levels of risk in their cross-border movements. It is urgent to think of sustainable migration policies that will enable states to address the challenges of migration coherently.

It may seem naïve to suggest that the MWB scenario can provide answers to current problems. But it is equally naïve to assume that relatively minor arrangements of the contemporary migration system will provide long-term answers. The MWB scenario has the advantages of being ethically defendable and of usefully complementing the human right to emigration by a symmetric right to mobility. In a globalized world, movement of people is not an anomaly to be exceptionally tolerated; it is a normal process embedded in socioeconomic structures and in migrants' transnational lives and identities. There is ample evidence that the classic migration pattern of permanent settlement does not apply to all contemporary cases of human movement, and policies should therefore take new practices of circulation into account.

The social and economic consequences of the MWB scenario remain extremely complex, however, and this review has highlighted the numerous uncertainties surrounding it. It is therefore necessary to examine both the strengths and weaknesses of this scenario, and to keep in mind that, while free movement may be a desirable option, it is also a complex goal that requires careful thinking. The MWB scenario is not a straightforward and simple measure that would eliminate all injustices at once, nor an unrealistic Utopia. It is an inspiring vision for the future of migration and a precious source of ideas to imagine fairer migration policies.

Bibliography

Anderson, M. 1996. *Frontiers: Territory and State Formation in the Modern World*. Cambridge, U.K., Polity Press.

Andreas, P. 2000. *Border Games: Policing the U.S.–Mexico Divide*. Ithaca, NY, Cornell University Press.

Andreas, P. and Biersteker, T. J. (eds). 2003. *The Rebordering of North America: Integration and Exclusion in a New Security Context*. New York, Routledge.

Andreas, P. and Snyder, T. (eds). 2000. *The Wall Around the West: State Borders and Immigration Controls in North America and Europe*. Lanham, Md., Rowman & Littlefield.

Barry, B. 1992. The quest for consistency: a sceptical view. B. Barry and R. E. Goodin (eds), *Free Movement: Ethical Issues in the Transnational Migration of People and of Money*. New York and London, Harvester Wheatsheaf, pp. 279–87.

Barry, B. and Goodin, R. E. (eds). 1992. *Free Movement: Ethical Issues in the Transnational Migration of People and of Money*. New York and London, Harvester Wheatsheaf.

Barsky, R. F. 2001. An essay on the free movement of people. *Refuge*, Vol. 19, No. 4, pp. 84–93.

Bhagwati, J. 1998. *A Stream of Windows: Unsettling Reflections on Trade, Immigration and Democracy*. Cambridge, Mass., MIT Press.

———. 2003. Borders beyond control. *Foreign Affairs*, Vol. 82, No. 1., pp. 98–104.

Bhatnagar, P. 2004. Liberalising the movement of natural persons: a lost decade? *The World Economy*, Vol. 27, No. 3, pp. 459–72.

Borjas, G. J. 1999. *Heaven's door: immigration policy and the American economy*. Princeton, NJ, Princeton University Press.

Brochmann, G. and Hammar, T. (eds). 1999. *Mechanisms of Immigration Control: A Comparative Analysis of European Regulation Policies*. Oxford, U.K., Berg.

Carens, J. H. 1987. Aliens and citizens: the case for open borders. *The Review of Politics*, Vol. 49, No. 2, pp. 251–73.

———. 1988. Immigration and the welfare state. A. Gutmann (ed.), *Democracy and the Welfare State*. Princeton, NJ, Princeton University Press, pp. 207–30.

———. 2003. Who should get in? The ethics of immigration admissions. *Ethics & International Affairs*, Vol. 17, No. 1, pp. 95–110.

Castles, S. 2004. The factors that make and unmake migration policies. *International Migration Review*, Vol. 38, No. 3, pp. 852–84.

Castles, S. and Davidson, A. 2000. *Citizenship and Migration: Globalization and the Politics of Belonging*. Basingstoke, U.K., Macmillan.

Chang, H. F. 2000. The economic analysis of immigration law. C. B. Brettell and J. F. Hollifield (eds), *Migration Theory: Talking across Disciplines*. London, Routledge, pp. 205–30.

Chemillier-Gendreau, M. 2002. L'introuvable statut de réfugié, révélateur de la crise de l'Etat moderne. *Hommes & Migration*, Vol. 1240, pp. 94–106

Cohen, S., Humphries, B. and Mynott, E. (eds). 2002. *From Immigration Controls to Welfare Controls*. London, Routledge.

Cole, P. 2000. *Philosophies of Exclusion: Liberal Political Theory and Immigration*. Edinburgh, U.K., Edinburgh University Press.

Cornelius, W. A. 2001. Death at the border: efficacy and unintended consequences of U.S. immigration control policy. *Population and Development Review*, Vol. 27, No. 4, pp. 661–85.

Cornelius, W. A., Tsuda, T., Martin, P. L. and Hollifield, J. F. (eds). 2004. *Controlling Immigration: A Global Perspective*. Palo Alto, Calif., Stanford University Press, pp. 3–48. (2nd edition.)

Dowty, A. 1987. *Closed Borders: The Contemporary Assault on Freedom of Movement*. New Haven, Conn., Yale University Press.

Dummett, A. 1992. The transnational migration of people seen from within a natural law tradition. Barry and Goodin, op. cit., pp. 169–80.

Dummett, Sir M. 2001. *On Immigration and Refugees*. London, Routledge.

Engelen, E. 2003. How to combine openness and protection? Citizenship, migration, and welfare regimes. *Politics & Society*, Vol. 31, No. 4, pp. 503–36.

Entzinger, H., Martiniello, M. and Wihtol de Wenden, C. (eds). 2004. *Migration between States and Markets*. Aldershot, U.K., Ashgate.

Eschbach, K., Hagan, J., Rodriguez, N., Hernandez-Leon, R. and Bailey, S. 1999. Death at the border. *International Migration Review*, Vol. 33, No. 2, pp. 430–54.

Faini, R., De Melo, J. and Zimmermann, K. F. 1999. Trade and migration: an introduction. R. Faini, J. De Melo and K. F. Zimmermann (eds), *Migration: The Controversies and the Evidence*. Cambridge, U.K., Cambridge University Press, pp. 1–20.

Fassin, D., Morice, A. and Quiminal, C. (eds). 1997. *Les lois de l'inhospitalité: Les politiques de l'immigration à l'épreuve des sans-papiers*. Paris, La Découverte.

Freeman, G. P. 1994. Can liberal states control unwanted migration? *Annals of the American Academy of Political and Social Science*, Vol. 534, pp. 17–30.

Geddes, A. 2003. Migration and the welfare state in Europe. S. Spencer (ed.), *The Politics of Migration: Managing Opportunity, Conflict and Change*. Oxford, Blackwell/The Political Quarterly, pp. 150–62.

Ghosh, B. 2000. Towards a new international regime for orderly movements of people. B. Ghosh (ed.), *Managing Migration: Time for a New International Regime?* Oxford, Oxford University Press, pp. 6–26.

Gibney, M. (ed.). 1988. *Open Borders? Closed Societies? The Ethical and Political Issues*. Westport, Conn., Greenwood Press.

Gibney, M. J. 2004. *The Ethics and Politics of Asylum: Liberal Democracy and the Response to Refugees*. Cambridge, U.K., Cambridge University Press.

Giraud, P.-N. 1996. *L'inégalité du monde: économie du monde contemporain*. Paris, Gallimard.

Guiraudon, V. and Joppke, C. (eds). 2001. *Controlling a New Migration World*. London and New York, Routledge.

Hamilton, B. and Whalley, J. 1984. Efficiency and distributional implications of global restrictions on labour mobility. *Journal of Development Economics*, Vol. 14, No. 1, pp. 61–75.

Hammar, T. 1990. *Democracy and the Nation State: Aliens, Denizens and Citizens in a World of International Migration*. Aldershot, U.K., Avebury.

Harris, N. 1995. *The New Untouchables: Immigration and the New World Order*. New York and London, I. B. Tauris.

———. 2002. *Thinking the Unthinkable: The Immigration Myth Exposed*. London, I. B. Tauris.

Hayter, T. 2000. *Open Borders: The Case against Immigration Controls*. London, Pluto Press.

Heisler, M. O. 2001. Now and then, here and there: migration and the transformation of identities, borders, and orders. M. Albert, D. Jacobson and Y. Lapid (eds), *Identities, Borders, Orders: Rethinking International Relations Theory*. Minneapolis, Minn., University of Minnesota Press, pp. 225–47.

Hollifield, J. F. 1992. *Immigrants, Markets, and States: The Political Economy of Post-war Europe*. Cambridge, Mass., Harvard University Press.

Human Rights Advocates International. 2002. Violations of migrant workers rights. New York, United Nations Economic and Social Council (ECOSOC). (Document No. E/CN.4/2002/NGO/45.)

Humphries, B. 2002. Fair immigration controls – or none at all? S. Cohen, B. Humphries and E. Mynott (eds), *From Immigration Controls to Welfare Controls*. London, Routledge, pp. 203–19.

Iregui, A. M. 2005. Efficiency gains from the elimination of global restrictions on labour mobility: an analysis using a multiregional CGE model. G. J. Borjas and J. Crisp (eds), *Poverty, International Migration and Asylum*. Basingstoke, Palgrave Macmillan, pp. 211–39.

Isbister, J. 1996. Are immigration controls ethical? *Social Justice*, Vol. 23, No. 3, pp. 54–67.

Jacobson, D. 1996. *Rights across Borders: Immigration and the Decline of Citizenship*. Baltimore, Md., Johns Hopkins University Press.

———. 2001. The global political culture. M. Albert, D. Jacobson and Y. Lapid (eds), *Identities, Borders, Orders: Rethinking International Relations Theory*. Minneapolis, Minn., University of Minnesota Press, pp. 161–79.

Joppke, C. 1998. Why liberal states accept unwanted immigration. *World Politics*, Vol. 50, No. 2, pp. 266–93.

Jordan, B. and Düvell, F. 2002. *Irregular Migration: The Dilemmas of Transnational Mobility*. Cheltenham, U.K., Edward Elgar.

———. 2003. *Migration: The Boundaries of Equality and Justice*. Cambridge, U.K., Polity Press.

Koslowski, R. 2004. Possible steps towards an international regime for mobility and security. *Global Migration Perspectives, No. 8*. Geneva, Switzerland, Global Commission on International Migration.

Lucas, R. E. 1999. International trade, capital flows and migration: economic policies towards countries of origin as a means of stemming migration. A. Bernstein and M. Weiner (eds), *Migration and Refugee Policies: An Overview*. London, Pinter, pp. 119–42.

Martin, P. 2003. *Bordering on Control: Combating Irregular Migration in North America and Europe*. Geneva, Switzerland, IOM. (Migration Research 13.)

Massey, D. S., Arango, J., Hugo, G., Kouaouci, A., Pellegrino, A. and Taylor, J. E. 1998. *Worlds in Motion: Understanding International Migration at the End of the Millennium*. Oxford, Clarendon Press.

Miller, D. and Hashmi, S. H. (eds). 2001. *Boundaries and Justice: Diverse Ethical Perspectives*. Princeton, N.J., Princeton University Press.

Nett, R. 1971. The civil right we are not ready for: the right of free movement of people on the face of the earth. *Ethics*, Vol. 81, No. 3, pp. 212–27.

Nevins, J. 2002. *Operation Gatekeeper: The Rise of the 'Illegal Alien' and the Making of the U.S.–Mexico Boundary*. New York, Routledge.

———. 2003. Thinking out of bounds: a critical analysis of academic and human rights writings on migrant deaths in the U.S.–Mexico border region. *Migraciones Internacionales*, Vol. 2, No. 2, pp. 171–90.

Pécoud, A. and de Guchteneire, P. 2006a. International migration, border controls and human rights: assessing the relevance of a right to mobility. *Journal of Borderlands Studies*, Vol. 21, No. 1, pp. 69–86.

———. 2006b. Migration, human rights and the United Nations: an investigation into the obstacles to the UN Convention on Migrant Workers' Rights. *Windsor Yearbook of Access to Justice*, Vol. 24, Issue 2, pp. 241–66.

Piketty, T. 1997. Immigration et justice sociale. *Revue Economique*, Vol. 48, No. 5, pp. 1291–309.

Raico, R. 1998. Introduction. *Journal of Libertarian Studies*, Vol. 13, No. 2, pp. 135–36.

Rekacewicz, P. and Clochard, O. 2004. Des morts par milliers aux portes de l'Europe. *Le Monde Diplomatique*. www.monde-diplomatique.fr/cartes/mortsauxfrontieres (Accessed 2 January 2007.)

Rodrik, D. 2005. Feasible globalizations. M. Weinstein (ed.), *Globalisation: What's New?* New York, Council on Foreign Relations/ Columbia University Press, pp. 96–213.

Sassen, S. 1996. *Losing Control? Sovereignty in an Age of Globalization*. New York, Columbia University Press.

Schuster, L. 2004. The exclusion of asylum seekers in Europe. Oxford, Oxford University, Centre on Migration, Policy and Society. (Working Paper No. 1.)

Schwartz, W. F. (ed.). 1995. *Justice in Immigration*. Cambridge, U.K., Cambridge University Press.

Simon, J. L. 1989. *The Economic Consequences of Immigration*. Oxford, Basil Blackwell.

Soysal, Y. N. 1994. *Limits of Citizenship: Migrants and Postnational Membership in Europe*. Chicago, Ill., University of Chicago Press.

Stalker, P. 2000. *Workers without Frontiers: The Impact of Globalization on International Migration*. Boulder, Colo., Lynne Rienner /ILO.

Straubhaar, T. 2000. Why do we need a general agreement on movements of people (GAMP)? B. Ghosh (ed.), *Managing Migration: Time for a New International Regime?* Oxford, Oxford University Press, pp. 110–36.

Teitelbaum, M. S. and Martin, P. L. 2003. Is Turkey ready for Europe? *Foreign Affairs*, Vol. 82, No. 3, pp. 97–111.

Thomas, R. A. L. 2005. Biometrics, International Migrants and Human Rights. *Global Migration Perspectives, No. 17*. Geneva, Switzerland, Global Commission on International Migration.

Torpey, J. 2000. *The Invention of the Passport: Surveillance, Citizenship and the State*. Cambridge, U.K., Cambridge University Press.

United Nations. 2000. *Replacement Migration: Is it a Solution to Declining and Aging Populations?* New York, United Nations.

———. 2002. *International Migration 2002*, New York, United Nations.

United Nations High Commissioner for Refugees (UNHCR). 1979. *Handbook on Procedures and Criteria for Determining Refugee Status under the 1951 Convention and the 1967 Protocol relating to the Status of Refugees*. Geneva, Switzerland. (UNHCR, HCR/IP/4/Eng/REV.1.)

Veenkamp, T., Bentley, T. and Buonfino, A. 2003. *People Flow: Managing Migration in a New European Commonwealth*. London, Demos.

Walzer, M. 1983. *Spheres of Justice: A Defense of Pluralism and Equality*. Oxford, Robertson.

Weiner, M. 1996. Ethics, national sovereignty and the control of immigration. *International Migration Review*, Vol. 30, No. 1, pp. 171–97.

Wihtol de Wenden, C. 1999. *Faut-il ouvrir les frontières?* Paris, Presses de Sciences Po.

Wolf, M. 2004. *Why Globalization Works*. New Haven, Conn., Yale University Press.

World Bank. 2004. *World Development Indicators 2004*. Washington DC, World Bank Publications.

Part I

Theoretical issues

Chapter 2

The economics and politics of the free movement of people

Nigel Harris

Introduction

The development of modern industrial capitalism has always involved large-scale migration at various times. Where the population was historically settled – especially in the great river basins of Asia – was not where the modern economy, including its agricultural dependencies, developed. At least 10 million slave workers were moved from Africa to the Americas between the seventeenth and nineteenth centuries,[1] and when that transfer was ended, indentured labour systems moved Indians and Chinese to Africa, to Malaya, Ceylon, Australia, North America and the Caribbean. Much of this movement was developed to initiate and expand the supply of the raw materials, mining and plantation output (or to build the means to transport this output) required to feed the voracious appetites of the new industrial machines of the developed countries. In the same way, workers were moved within colonial territories for the same purpose – from central to southern Africa for the mines, from eastern India to the tea estates of the north-east and the coal and iron mines of Bihar and Orissa – as within North America they moved relentlessly westward to open the prairies to cattle and grain.

Meanwhile, masses of Europeans were freely moving to the Americas, to Australia and to South Africa, Rhodesia and Kenya. Late nineteenth-century European expansion could not be sustained without people moving from the periphery – Poland, Italy, Spain, Ireland – to Europe's heartlands of Germany, France, Belgium and Britain.

It was not a smooth process. The fluctuations in the demand for workers followed the surges of growth and contraction in the new world economy. But if anyone had suggested in, say, 1910, that migration was an unusual phenomenon, they would have been regarded by any knowledgeable person with astonishment.

What interrupted the process of long-term growth, which required insistently that a margin of the world's labour force move, was the Great Depression, the years of stagnation between the two World Wars, and the bitter wars fought between the Great Powers, disciplining each national population to a loyalty that could only embed an institutionalized and popular xenophobia. There were still movements in the rest of the world, local booms, but the overall picture in the heartlands of the system was stagnation. In North America, as unemployment rose in the U.S., the Mexican flow to the north dried up: failing labour demand accomplished far more effectively what xenophobic legislation by Congress to ban immigration had failed to achieve.

However, after the Second World War, economic growth resumed on an unprecedented scale and with an unprecedented geographical spread. Large-scale worker movements became inevitable. Part of this continued the former process of opening up sources of raw materials, as with the expansion of oil centres from the 1970s leading to migration to the Gulf and Iran, and to Libya, Nigeria and Venezuela, along with continued migration to South Africa and to Malaya/Malaysia (with its rubber and palm-oil estates). But there was also another movement, with a much wider recruitment area: to the old industrial centres of the world in Europe and North America. This migration enabled the native-born to upgrade out of, for example, agricultural labour, construction, transport and then manufacturing. Later, following the first major post-war recession (1973–1975), when governments in Europe endeavoured to close this supply, rapid industrialization in the 1980s and 1990s in a number of developing countries in Asia again stimulated new movements – of Javanese to Malaysia, of Burmese to Thailand and Thais to Singapore and Taiwan (and, for other reasons, to Israel), of Korean Chinese to the Republic of Korea, and of Filipinos to Taiwan and elsewhere. As its economy restructured towards services, Japan (which, during the days of its most rapid post-war growth, could rely on substantial reserves of native-born workers in agriculture) attracted increasing flows of low-skilled Chinese and highly skilled Taiwanese (among many others). At the same time, Japanese companies spread their manufacturing plants through South-East Asia. South Koreans were doing something similar – importing workers and exporting manufacturing plants. So ingenious are the labour brokers handling this business, like termites boring channels through migration control barriers, and so unpredictable are the patterns of growth, the observer is always a few steps behind.

However, demography's picture of migration – even if the data were reliable, which they cannot be – conceals the immense and all-important changes in the composition of flows in terms of skills, age, gender, etc. The Middle East is interesting here, because in a fairly short time span we can see a shift from the immigration of relatively low-skilled (but literate) men working in construction, agriculture and basic industry to those with a higher level of skills (and who bring their families) working in processing industries, management (including government) and maintenance, and to service workers, particularly maids (so the labour flow is feminized). It seems clear that the specific nature of labour demand, as managed by labour brokers and facilitated or obstructed by governments, determines who is selected to migrate; it is not at all a blind process. It follows that the scale and composition of migration will continue to change as the world economy continues to restructure (since innovation is now built into the very core of the system) and the location of its key points of activity changes.

As one would expect in a world economy characterized by local specialization, the emergence of a world labour market is encouraging some countries to specialize in providing particular types of worker (as well as particular types of goods and services). The Philippines is an advanced example, supplying the world with maids (facilitated by the competence of Filipinas in English), nurses and merchant navy personnel. India and a number of other countries are beginning to specialize in the supply of medical doctors, engineers and information technologists. Of course, this is not new – 150 years ago, a great number of the engineers working the steamships and ports round the world were Scotsmen (just as laundries in the U.S. were run by Chinese, ice-cream making and selling by Italians, etc.).

However, the present resumption of migration flows to the developed countries is not simply a recurrence of past surges in the redistribution of the world's workforce (and in any case, relative to the world's population, the margin redistributed is still very small – under 3 per cent or 150–200 million). Today, the surface of the world has been cut up into national territories, each part fenced to include some and exclude others, all in the name of the defence or affirmation of sovereignty and its psychic reflection, national identity. Thus, migration – of foreigners – becomes a major *political* issue: it affects the pretensions of sovereignty and national identity. Yet it does so when we are already well set on the process of globalization – the opening of national economies to flows of trade, capital and people, and the results of this in the restructuring of national economies to accord with new global patterns of economic specialization. In migration, we are in the midst of a process of transition from closed or semi-closed labour markets to a world labour market, with continual contradictions between the changing nature of domestic labour demand (itself reshaped by new specializations) and a world supply of workers, facilitated by the growth of a literate labour force in developing countries, a radical decline in transport costs and no less-radical reforms in developing countries releasing large numbers of workers for domestic migration (Martin et al., 2000, pp. 149–52). China offers a vivid illustration of this.

In the old order of national economies, the political boundary was assumed to coincide with the economic, and the economy was, as we have noted, relatively self-sufficient – neither imports, foreign capital nor immigrants were, supposedly, of decisive importance. However, in the newly emerging order, national output is the product of world interactions and no government can aspire to self-sufficiency in either the production of goods and services or capital; rather each government is concerned with managing flows that start and end beyond its authority and often its knowledge. Such a system requires growing mobility – of business people, students, tourists, consultants – within which it is almost impossible to identify those who wish – or might come to wish – to work without permission. In the field of labour, the instincts of the old national workforce planning and self-sufficiency in local supply collide with the imperative for economic growth.

Immigration policy has historically dealt with actual or potential settlers rather than transient workers. In important senses, it forced transients into exile from their home country if they wished to protect their access to work. Today, insofar as policy deals with migrant workers (and for many countries, family reunification still provides the bulk of immigration, although this is changing), it is a form of workforce planning – estimating future demand by skill level and setting quotas on the numbers of workers to be admitted in a given period for a set time. Such a policy approach has all the negative aspects of central planning. The unexpected fluctuations of a dynamic economy cannot be accommodated (as was shown so painfully in the mis-estimation of required information technology specialists just before the collapse of the 'dot.com' boom); the delays and costs of bureaucratic processing are notorious.

The demand that we rely on a self-sufficient national economy is constantly being revived, most recently in support of an educational and training policy that will make skilled immigration unnecessary. It is a significant aspect of this argument that it presents the options as alternatives – either educate the native-born or encourage immigration – rather than as being complementary. To make such an approach effective, it was proposed that Californian software companies should be required to pay a significant fee to employ an immigrant worker; the proceeds, it was said, would be used to finance U.S.-born students to train in the same fields. In fact, as the employers noted, there was no evidence that labour shortages in the U.S. were the result of a lack of funds to finance U.S.-born students; their preferences for particular disciplines was not determined by available finance. Thus, the fee was better regarded as an economically unjustified tax on employing foreigners. In fact, the preparation for large-scale immigration of highly skilled workers into the U.S. proved quite unnecessary – the collapse of the dot.com boom showed that, had American students been successfully induced to study software programming, there would now be a much higher rate of unemployment. Two lessons seem appropriate here. Employers should be allowed to recruit directly, bearing the costs and risks of their activity. Second, education and training policies cannot be governed by short-term fluctuations in the employment market without grave errors of policy. The reason for doing so is simply the desire not to use the world labour supply to ease the flexibility of the domestic labour market, which, in current circumstances, must lead to negative effects on domestic employment.

Workforce planning requires a closed or semi-closed economy. In an open economy, compensatory movements across borders are constantly nullifying domestic policy changes or leading to perverse outcomes. Thus, the attempt to make planning of the labour force effective requires the control of irregular movement. On the one hand, this would entail considerably greater internal police controls to check those who work while on a visa that does not allow this or has expired (in fact, it seems governments are unwilling to risk popular hostility to enforce this). On the other hand, borders would become militarized, brutalized and criminalized, and the asylum system would be effectively wrecked in pursuit of 'economic migrants'. In Europe and North America, we are within sight of restoring the border fortifications – backed by state terrorism – that divided East and West Germany in the Cold War: now between Poland and the Ukraine, Hungary and the Ukraine, Spain and Morocco (and, on occasions, between France and Britain), and between Mexico and the U.S. The fortified borders represent a permanent war against the compensatory imperatives of the labour market and its attempt to meet the demand for low-skilled workers – with the same discouraging results as the U.S. war on the narcotics that Americans so insistently demand to consume.

Temporary migration – already a major force in irregular movement – might seem to be some remedy here if there were not such a prejudice against it. The negative model is seen as the German guest-worker programme of the 1950s and 1960s, where large numbers of supposedly temporary workers were invited but proved impossible to remove at the end of their contracts – their human rights prevented expulsion. Yet this is far from what happened. The majority of workers, in fact, did leave Germany (emigration data do not allow us to say how many returned to their homes). Of those that did not, they stayed not simply because of their preferences or the moral constraints of the German authorities, but because of the wish of employers to retain workers (particularly experienced ones) when it was clear no more immigrants were to be available, and the agreement of the government to this. Thus, immigration controls were themselves crucial in forcing immobility – exile – on guest-workers. Of course, moral constraints exercised a role – and the negative political appearance of enforcing expulsion – but these were of lesser significance than the economic interests of the participants.

In the 1990s, there was a rapid growth in immigration through family reunification and asylum seeking. In policy terms, however, the crucial factor in the late 1990s was that the developed countries decided they could not compete in information technology without expanding their skilled workforce – they entered a competition to persuade IT workers to come to them. It was a startling reversal of the policy that had been entrenched in Europe for two and a half decades: a ban on new primary immigration, and a change in the emphasis on family reunification as the primary criterion for immigration (Canada and Australia, however, had long sought recruits by skill). However, the partial relaxation in the U.S. only underscored the inequality of the migration regime. As in South Africa's apartheid system, the skilled 'whites' have the right to migrate, while the low-skilled remain, supposedly, tied to the soil of their birth, denied the opportunity to escape poverty.

A little theory

The theory of international trade turns upon the proposition that where there are differences of factor endowment (raw materials, labour, capital, entrepreneurship, etc.) between countries or localities, disproportionate economic gains will result from exchanging factors. This is well known in trade and is the rationale for the liberalization of the world trading economy – it allows us to understand the high growth rates in activities in Special Economic Zones, border regions, off-shore, etc. But is the same proposition true of migration?

It would seem intuitively that it is and that, accordingly – to turn the proposition round – great losses are incurred by the world by sustaining barriers to labour mobility. A number of studies have endeavoured to put some figures on these losses, or – the other side of the coin – the gains from decontrol. Hamilton and Whalley (1984) in a pioneering study using 1977 data suggested, on set assumptions, that gains to the gross world product (then U.S.$7.8 trillion) from lifting migration controls could range from U.S.$4.7 trillion to U.S.$16 trillion. Recent reworking of more up-to-date figures confirms these outcomes (Iregui, 2005; Moses and Letnes, 2004). UNDP (1992, pp. 57–8) presents a different calculation of more limited changes. Walmsley and Winters (2005) offer a model in which worker migration to employment in services in developed countries equal to 3 per cent of the developed countries' labour force would yield benefits of U.S.$156 billion, shared between developed and developing countries, compared to the estimated U.S.$104 billion generated by a successful outcome to the Doha trade round (and the roughly U.S.$70 billion granted in aid to developing countries by the OECD group).

The direction of change – and its size – is important, even if the precise figures turn upon the assumptions that have been made. But workers are not commodities in a very important sense. They may be abstract 'labour' within an economy, but they are also part of society (citizens) and of a polity (electors, the embodiment of national sovereignty), apart from the detail of being human beings as well! Economics gives us a valuable perspective on some matters from one restricted angle, but it does not tell us how people will behave in general. The migration of foreigners can provoke astonishing fears. It may be demonstrable that the economic dislocation caused by immigration is far smaller than that caused by changes in trade patterns or capital movements, or by domestic changes in the supply of labour (for example, the entry of the post-war 'baby boom' generation to work, or the large numbers of women who entered employment in the post-war period), but the fact that migrants are foreigners, speak strangely, are of different physical appearance, etc., may prompt people to oppose them regardless of any real losses to their welfare.

The social issues are well known and are not the subject of this chapter. However, the problems of adjusting to higher levels of mobility need to be acknowledged – in particular, we must consider the rights attached to citizenship (voting rights, the right to participate in the exercise of sovereignty, etc.), the different degrees of 'temporariness' of temporary workers and the rights attached to their status, and the transition between these two. Issues of accommodation and services raise similar questions. In the past, migrant workers have often been housed by employers – and often in very bad conditions (for example, the hostels for single men in apartheid South Africa) that undermine the standards of housing of the poor in general. In principle, the problems are no different from those of maintaining minimum standards for the native-born (given, in some cases, different cultural practices), but the *foreignness* of workers can complicate any resolution. In an open housing market, poor immigrants tend to concentrate in areas of deprivation and then, quite unreasonably, become blamed for the deprivation. Again, in principle, the issues are no different for the native-born poor, but xenophobia – and the quality of political leadership – can turn such issues into intractable political issues, rather than questions of the quality of housing.

However, xenophobia or not, the emerging problems of labour supply are going to force some confrontation between the different dimensions of perception and discussion. Take Europe as an example.

Europe's labour market: the supply of workers

There are a number of self-reinforcing factors of relevance here:

1. The size of the European labour force over the next half century is set to decline – in 2005, over a third of Europe's regions face a declining size of workforce. The process of contraction will be exaggerated as the generation of the post-war 'baby boom' enters retirement.
2. However, within this projection there are other indications that show a more dramatic contraction in the available working time on offer:
   (i) An increasing proportion of working life (defined as the years between the ages of fifteen and sixty/sixty-five) is being devoted to education and training – thus simultaneously reducing the available work time and radically reducing the number of people available for jobs requiring less than a university education.
   (ii) An important part of the existing labour force is not engaged in paid or recorded work, but has retired early, lives on disability pensions, or in other ways has withdrawn from work. The size of this under-utilized workforce ranges from between 18 and 22 per cent of the labour force in Sweden to 40 per cent in Italy. This is not necessarily unemployment. The mark of an increasingly wealthy society is that people can afford to work less. On the other hand, such workers may be working in the black economy or other statistically unrecorded sectors, or may work unpaid in caring for the elderly, for the young, for the disabled, etc.
   (iii) A changing mismatch between the output of domestic training systems and the demands of a rapidly restructuring national economy is made worse by the aggravated lags in reshaping training systems.
   (iv) The working life, year, week or day are all tending to contract with growing wealth.

These trends coincide, in some cases, with high levels of unemployment (and especially of long-term unemployment), a sign of a mismatch between labour demand and supply (or also a lack of complementary low-skilled workers). Within the European Union, this allows areas of high labour-scarcity to coexist with those of high unemployment (or non-employment). Nor do Europeans seem willing, or not in sufficient numbers, at least, to move from one European country to another. Figures for the proportion of internal migrants to population in 1999 put it no higher than 0.2 per cent.

The result of this combination is peculiarly damaging – growing labour deficits with a significant under-utilization of the existing workforce. Assessing labour shortages is difficult, but we have some estimates for 2000–2003 in the OECD SOPEMI report of 2003 (pp. 124–5). It is interesting to note that, contrary to government assessments of what shortages they should respond to, it is the shortage of low-skilled workers that is most often mentioned. In many of the activities with high vacancy rates, the rising average age of the workforce, promising high rates of retirement in the short term, indicates a failure to recruit adequate numbers of new entrants despite rising relative wage levels.

In the short term, the deficits are already affecting the performance of the European economy and the capacity of governments to meet current objectives, thus affecting electoral prospects.

In the medium term, the picture is very much worse. Ageing, apart from the other factors cited, will increase the reduction in the size of the working population at the same time as the demand for age-related labour-intensive services increases.

Government responses

Despite the dangers of a negative political reaction, governments have made some attempts in terms of raising the discussion of increasing the retirement age, reducing the disincentives to work (encouraging housebound women to enter work, encourage those who have withdrawn to return) and raising the costs of leaving work, increasing training facilities to meet the requirement of mid-level occupations, and increasing productivity. In the Lisbon Agenda, the target is set of raising European participation rates to 70 per cent by the year 2010.

However, while the deficits are urgent and immediate, the remedies take much longer. Thus, alongside these measures there have been changes to ease the issue of temporary work permits, and not just for the highly skilled. There are schemes covering seasonal agricultural workers, working holidaymakers, work-experience schemes, contract workers and cross-border commuters. More importantly, the principle that migrant workers can be employed again has been established in practice even if political leaders have yet to set about convincing their electorates.[2]

The changes being introduced will, however, be insufficient to cope with future scarcities, particularly given the intensified competition for some types of workers – for example, nurses from the Philippines, Bangladesh and the Caribbean.

Nor is the search for labour necessarily consistent with other government priorities. The British 'working holidaymakers' scheme, originally directed at the old British Commonwealth dominions but now expanded, collides with British aid policy's promise not to recruit scarce middle-level skilled people from, for example, South Africa. In addition, occupationally specific quotas do not allow for the inclusion of non-specific, self-employed activities. Immigrants are over-represented in self-employment (OECD, 2002, p. 65) and have famously saved from extinction retail outlets, corner shops, news-agencies and cafes, in poor city neighbourhoods and in provincial towns, and seem now to be doing the same in rural localities (Greece is reported as a prime example of this last phenomenon). Such workers are not included in the current quotas.

Europe and North America are aspiring to be providers of highly skilled services and innovative technology to the rest of the world. However, as noted earlier, even if low-skill tradable sectors are relocated to developing countries, the high-skill economy will require a cluster of low-skill and non-tradable support services to be effective – from cleaners to retail trades, construction, transport, and domestic and caring services. The task, even in this extreme case, is to make such services affordable to the mass of the population without requiring high levels of taxation that, even if politically possible, stimulate the emigration of both the highly skilled and of business. In practice, the outcome is likely to be less sharp than this since irregular migration will meet the deficits with whatever incidental costs this incurs.

Migration and the poor

It is a persistent theme in much of the economic literature on migration that employers and the better off (who can afford maids, etc.) gain from the immigration of the lower-skilled, and that it is the lower-paid native workers who are disadvantaged. However, on reflection, this cannot be so. We can make two pertinent observations:

1. A large number of studies using data from the U.S. have found that increased immigration has no impact or an insignificant impact on native wage and employment levels (see, for example, Greenwood et al., 1997). Where there are small negative effects, they tend to affect earlier cohorts of immigrants rather than the historical poor of the U.S. This could be because migrants move to labour-scarce areas where wages are rising in any case, so that their effect is masked in the general movement. There is, however, much evidence that unskilled immigrants do the jobs that the natives, even if unemployed, are unwilling to do; rather than compete with the native population, new low-skilled immigrants compete with earlier low-skilled immigrants. Immigrants then fill places not because they are cheaper – in general, they seem not to be – but because they are the only workers available (as happens with seasonal migrant workers in some sections of European agriculture).

    On the other hand, few studies have tracked the impact of immigration on raising employment for complementary native workers – how the availability of foreign-born unskilled production workers increases the demand for native-born supervisors and managers, skilled workers and technical staff, truck drivers, etc. Fewer still estimate the multiplier effects of immigrant expenditure – on demand for accommodation, furnishings, foodstuffs, transport, and so on.

Borjas (1999), along with others, has changed the nature of this discussion by suggesting that native unskilled workers often take anticipatory action to avoid competition – by leaving sectors of the economy or geographical areas where such competition is likely to occur (great play is made of the changing balance between domestic and foreign migration of the low-skilled into California in this respect). Borjas argues that local studies of the impact of increased immigration greatly underestimate its effects, which can only be assessed at a national level. The argument is ingenious and well presented, and it may have some validity, but the deficiencies of the empirical evidence do not yet allow a decisive conclusion and, as a result, the case is as yet far from being a consensus among migration specialists (see Anderson, 2000; Bhagwati, 1999).

2. However, if we broaden the focus from work to consumption and prices, it seems intuitively that the case must be false. For example, immigrant workers in agriculture ensure fewer imports and the survival of small farmers and the rural economy, as well as lower food prices. The primary beneficiaries of this are the poor (who spend a larger share of their income on foodstuffs). Immigrant workers in manufacturing, construction, public transport and so on have similar effects. Women are able to undertake paid work outside the home if childcare and cleaning services are available, and often these are only available at affordable prices through immigrant carers. In certain regions, immigrants have saved the small corner shop in the poorer areas of big cities and provincial towns, as mentioned earlier, and they are beginning to do so also in rural areas. And the immigrant labour force is crucial in public healthcare services – particularly in the poorer districts of our larger cities. Indeed, the 'disadvantaged' may be the *primary* beneficiaries of the immigration of un- and semi-skilled workers, and would suffer most if the supply were curtailed. The better-off can afford to manage without the services provided by immigrant labour. Of course, it might be argued that wages should be paid that would induce native-born workers to do these jobs, and that this could be done without increasing taxation to an electorally suicidal level, or raising prices to a level that would make services prohibitive for the poor. That case, however, has to be demonstrated.

Migration and developing countries

It is well known – but worth repeating – that continued protectionism in world trade reduces the employment potential in developing countries, and that this may affect the propensity to migrate to work elsewhere. Nowhere does this appear to be more true than in agriculture, where, in the most notorious case, the Common Agricultural Policy not only deprives developing country exporters of markets in Europe, it also deprives them of other markets by subsidizing exports to Third World countries (and this is achieved through higher European food prices, affecting most severely the poorest consumers).

To the employment losses incurred through protectionism can be added those experienced through worker emigration. This is greatest with the highly skilled and magnified where such workers leave permanently or for the bulk of their working lives, depriving the developing country of skilled inputs (and the productivity of the average worker is strongly related to the average skill level of the labour force as a whole), of complementary employment of lesser skill, and of tax payments that the emigrant would otherwise have made. If the emigrant's skills were acquired with public subsidies, these also are lost (on the Indian case, see Desai et al., 2003).

Worker remittances returned to countries of origin are some compensation here. But a much greater benefit would accrue if migrant workers could return with enhanced skills. Low-skilled workers who travel without families have always tended to return; they work abroad primarily to strengthen their position at home. This tendency is much reduced the tighter the controls on migration: the higher the costs of accessing work, the greater the tendency to settle in order to secure continued access to work.[3] On the other hand, anecdotal evidence suggests some increase in the propensity of highly skilled workers to return to Asia if not to Africa. Domestic reform and stabilization are obviously crucial here. However, given relatively abundant labour supplies in developing countries, standards of living for the highly skilled at much lower levels of pay than are available in developed countries (even if much closer in Purchasing Power Parity terms) can be much higher. The development of high-level research facilities in developing countries supports tendencies to return (or indeed, not to set out in the first place). Numerous national and international schemes exist to support the process of return (International Migration, 2002), but more can be done to remove existing anomalies which force migrants to settle as a condition of work, and which weaken the 'social embeddedness' of migrants in their country of origin. Aid programmes can be of assistance here in financing training for migrants in preparation for their return and in employing returning migrants as agents of development, applying their funds to strengthen the creation of new businesses. Migration might then come to be seen by most migrants as an important part of their education, enriching their skills and work experience rather than being simply an opportunity to earn money.[4]

The issue of migration to the developed countries may prove temporary. Present demographic projections suggest that over the next half century, the bulk of the world's labour force will become concentrated in developing countries. It may be expected that the bulk of the world's tradable sectors will follow, led by those most sensitive to labour costs. It cannot be conceived that migration flows between developed and developing countries, even if completely free, would be on a scale sufficient to change this significantly. Furthermore, the developed countries' concentration on research and education, and on quality of life, may be expected to complement the concentration of the world's manufacturing and service production in developing countries. It could be that over the next half century, as a fully integrated world economy emerges, migration flows may come to decline or even shift to the reverse direction.

Remedies

The most obvious remedy to the problems of the present system is to accept the inevitable integration of the developed countries in a world labour market and move towards free migration and open borders. Employers would then recruit abroad as they do at home and bear the risks – the costs – of any errors made in assessing their future labour needs. The role of government would be restricted to extending its present responsibilities for the regulation of employment of native-born workers to the foreign-born. At the moment, private brokers and agents organize the regular and irregular recruitment and movement of workers, so the basic social infrastructure exists for such a change. Such a system would eliminate irregular migration and the bulk of asylum seekers who could take work immediately and not be obliged to call on public support (this would not be true of asylum seekers without the capacity to work, but that would be a much smaller problem than the current one).

Would direct recruitment by employers threaten the maintenance of acceptable levels of pay and standards of working conditions, as employers competed to lower costs? In principle, the problems are no more severe than those experienced with the native-born low-skilled workers. Indeed, they may be fewer insofar as migrant workers ought to be recruited on a standard – and government-approved – contract for a given period. Such standard contracts should be vetted and policed by both source and destination governments, by relevant trade unions and by NGOs. Of course, no system is foolproof – for native-born as much for foreign-born – but making such employment fully explicit offers some basis for regulation, whereas at present, with irregular migration, there is no such possibility.

However, the immediate needs of developing countries for the return of their migrant workers, combined with the fear that a significant sector of the European electorate has of being 'swamped' by foreigners, suggest that, while the aim should remain intact, we need a second-best transitional arrangement that allows governments to retreat if required. It is not the task here to design such transitional arrangements – and there are now increasing numbers of schemes on offer (for examples, see Veenkamp et al., 2003; Harris, 2003 [Appendix]; Ghosh, 2000). However, a number of points might be made concerning revisions to the present system:

1. The first issue of importance here is that, in principle, all migration should be temporary, even if some migrants apply to stay longer. The overwhelming bulk of evidence is that populations are relatively immobile, but that a small margin seek migration as, in the first instance, a means to broaden their experience and earn on a sufficient scale to improve their position at home. Of course, negative conditions at home can tilt the balance as a migrant becomes accustomed to life at the destination, but, even then, it is surprising how durable the loyalties remain and the hope of return. It has already been argued that immigration regulations (and the rising cost of getting past borders) and the pressure governments can place on migrant settlement can change this, forcing migrants into exile. The stress placed on assimilation, whether forced or voluntary, follows from a preoccupation with settlement; but if migrants were free to come and go, enforced assimilation would be a serious threat to the human rights of the migrant who does not wish to join in the host society at all, merely to work in order to return with enhanced skills and savings (from the migrant's point of view, assimilation could become an additional cost). Of course, access to social security can also tip the balance here, but arrangements can be made to reduce the impact of this (migrants could, for example, be exempt from all but the minimum social security contributions and benefits, or benefits could be accumulated and repaid in the home country at the end of the work period, etc.). There will always remain unresolved cases, but these should not be allowed to deflect the principle issue.

   Temporary worker status would be one element in restoring equality of treatment between high- and low-skilled workers. While it is assumed that most migrants will want to return home provided there is a reasonable possibility of future opportunities to work abroad, nothing should be done to weaken their commitment to return and to do so without any forms of compulsion. In some present schemes there are additional incentives – paying part of the wage in a cumulative sum in the home currency on their return (or possibly adding a bonus and/or refunded social security funds). I have mentioned the possibility of aid programmes financing training and offering business start-up funds on return. Given a well-managed pattern of circulatory migration, applications to stay longer for whatever reasons can be treated with generosity.

2. Irregular migration is first and foremost a response to a demand for workers (even if it may be precipitated by push factors), so that generally migrants move to previously identified jobs (or to agents controlling such work) and have very high rates of participation and low rates of unemployment. Accordingly, the expansion of the work-permit system should be designed to eliminate irregular migration. However, this cannot be done through government controls on recruitment on the basis of estimates of future labour demand. Not only must such estimates be erroneous in a dynamic economy, they cannot easily accommodate predictions for the type of demand that irregular migrants meet. Any system that is going to meet economic requirements has to end the idea of set annual quotas of workers and invest in the initiative of employers to recruit at their own expense in such numbers as they require, albeit within a framework of government supervision to ensure that the basic conditions of work and pay do not undercut alternative local supplies of workers and are clear to migrant workers before they leave home, and that robust provisions are made for the proper return of workers and for their social security during the period of their visit.

3. This chapter has not dealt with the family reunification category of immigrants, which raises a quite different agenda of policy issues. In general, with globalization, one would expect increasing mobility and growing crossovers between the citizens of a country – who live in that country or who live abroad (the present 'polity') – and those who work in that country or contribute to its output from locations abroad (the 'economy'). If this is so, then the family reunification category of movement will inevitably grow and, if the welfare of the country is to be assured, must be facilitated.

4. The ban on asylum seekers working – whether for six months or, as in some countries, until their claims are sanctioned or rejected – is one of the most obvious sources of social tension. The combined accusation of having entered a country irregularly (given there is, in many cases, no other way for them to obtain entry) and then 'living off social security' (as work is forbidden) seems almost deliberately designed to provoke the greatest xenophobia. With an expanded work-permit system to eliminate irregular migration, able-bodied asylum seekers can, if circumstances permit, apply for work before they arrive; if this cannot be done, then they can be granted temporary leave to remain while they seek work. Part of the funds at present devoted to supporting asylum seekers can then be directed to providing short-term support for those who cannot work.

Would increased temporary migration of low-skilled workers from the South to the North exaggerate the polarization between the two? In the larger picture, the capacity of developing countries to raise their incomes through the temporary emigration of workers will reduce this polarization, a change enhanced if workers return with upgraded skills and increased savings to expand their home economy. If this process is part of a reordering of the world economy, marked by the relocation of a major part of the world's tradable manufacturing and service sectors to developing countries, then present arrangements may be seen only as transitional, part of a process of moving to a much more equalized world order. On the other hand, the contrary policy – of preventing the poor from escaping from poverty through migration, even if it could be achieved (which is doubtful) – would vastly exaggerate the inequalities of the world.

Conclusion

The present system for all except the skilled is opaque and costly relative to its returns. A world labour market is in operation, but without any of the transparency required to put the right worker in the right job. Governments operate as large monopsonist buyers, while private agencies recruit and distribute irregular migrants without being subject to the open competition that reveals the marginal cost/value of the work proposed. Criminalization is inevitable in such circumstances. A global labour market requires a global exchange in which real scarcities in many different localities can be matched against the immense diversity of those offering work, and where wage levels reflect those scarcities.

If the developed countries are unable to establish an acceptable order in the field of migration, the danger is that their political leaders will continue to seek to exploit the issue for xenophobic purposes, that they will impede the development of developing countries (regardless of what aid programmes are employed), that they will lock out the poor, at whatever cost to the civil rights of their own citizens and the growing numbers of irregular migrants (growing because the labour shortages for low-skilled workers will worsen), and that they will damage the welfare of their poorest citizens. Protectionism here is, as elsewhere, directed to trying fruitlessly to capture benefits for a minority at the cost of the world at large – and particularly of the world's poor.

Notes

1. There have been debates surrounding the exact figures. The number of slave workers is often estimated to have been somewhere between 10 and 15 million, although other sources speak of 25 million.

2. As Papademetriou (2003, p. 9) writes: 'one of the issue's unfolding (and fascinating) paradoxes is watching how mainstream political leaders who have sought to accommodate the minority appeal of xenophobic impulses by adopting restrictionist rhetoric and policies will deal with the emerging realization that immigrants are fast becoming demographically and economically indispensable'.
3. This is shown in U.S. data following the tightening of southern border controls after 1986 (Massey et al., 2002; Cornelius, 2001). The return of Greek guest-workers from Germany once Greece joined the European Union and so secured the right of Greeks to return to work abroad suggests the same conclusion (Constant and Massey, 2002, p. 6).
4. German medieval craft apprentices were required to migrate between different localities or even countries to learn additional skills as the final qualification for craft accreditation.

Bibliography

Anderson, S. 2000. Muddled masses. *Reason Magazine*, February.

Bhagwati, J. 1999. A close look at the newest newcomers. *Wall Street Journal*, September 28. (Review of Borjas, op. cit.)

Borjas, G. J. 1999. *Heaven's Door: Immigration Policy and the American Economy*. Princeton, N.J., Princeton University Press.

Constant, A. and Massey, D. S. 2002. Return migration by German guest workers: neoclassical versus new economic theory. *International Migration*, Vol. 40, No. 4, pp. 5–39.

Cornelius, W. A. 2001. Death at the border: efficacy and unintended consequences of U.S. immigration control policy. *Population and Development Review*, Vol. 27, No. 4, pp. 661–85.

Desai, M. A., Kapur, D. and McHale, J. 2003. The fiscal impact of high-skilled emigration: flows of Indians to the U.S. Cambridge, MA, Harvard University, Weatherhead Centre for International Affairs Working Paper No. 03-01.

Ghosh, B. (ed.). 2000. *Managing Migration: Time for a New International Regime?* Oxford, Oxford University Press.

Greenwood, M. A., Hunt, G. L. and Kohli, U. 1997. The factor market consequences of unskilled immigration to the U.S. *Labor Economics*, Vol. 4, pp. 1–28.

Hamilton, B. and Whalley, J. 1984. Efficiency and distributional implications of global restrictions on labor mobility: calculations and political implications. *Journal of Development Economics*, Vol. 14, No. 1–2, pp. 61–75.

Harris, N. 2003. Economic migration and the European labour market. Brussels, The European Policy Centre. (EPC Issue Paper No. 2 – Part I.)

International Migration. 2002. Special issue: the migration-development Nexus. *International Migration*, Vol. 40, No. 5.

Iregui, A. M. 2005. Efficiency gains from the elimination of global restrictions on labour mobility: an analysis using a multiregional CGE model. G. J. Borjas and J. Crisp (eds), *Poverty, International Migration and Asylum*. Basingstoke, Palgrave Macmillan, pp. 211–39.

Martin, P., Lowell, B. L. and Taylor, E. J. 2000. Migration outcomes of guest worker and free trade regimes: the case of Mexico–U.S. migration. Ghosh, op. cit., pp. 137–59.

Massey, D., Durand, J. and Malone, N. J. 2002. *Beyond Smoke and Mirrors: Mexican Immigration in an Era of Economic Integration*. New York, Russell Sage Foundation.

Moses, J. W. and Letnes, B. 2004. The economic costs of international labor restrictions: revisiting the empirical discussion. *World Development*, Vol. 32, No. 10, pp. 1609–26.

OECD, Trends in International Migration (SOPEMI). 2003. *Continuous Reporting System on Migration 2002*. Paris, OECD.

Papademetriou, D. 2003. Reflections on managing rapid and deep change in the newest age of migration. Paper presented at Greek Presidency conference, Managing Migration for the Benefit of Europe. Athens, May.

United Nations Development Programme (UNDP). 1992. *The Human Development Report 1992*. New York, UNDP.

Veenkamp, T., Bentley, T. and Buonfino, A. 2003. *People Flow: Managing Migration in a New European Commonwealth*. London, Demos and Open Democracy.

Walmsley, T. L. and Winters, L. A. 2005. Relaxing the restrictions on the temporary movement of natural persons: a simulation analysis. *Journal of Economic Integration*, Vol. 20, No. 4, pp. 688–726

Chapter 3

The frontiers of mobility

Catherine Wihtol de Wenden

Introduction

A world without frontiers: is this an objective on the list of the major challenges facing humanity, or is it merely another pipe dream for the twenty-first century?

The final years of the twentieth century saw one upheaval after another have an impact on international migration, making it one of the burning issues of our times. Twenty five years ago it was widely believed that the era of mass migration was over: that immigrants would go back home; that unemployment would lead domestic labour forces to take immigrants' jobs; and that migration was to be restricted. But the only prediction to come true was the third one. Migratory pressure has remained high, despite the dissuasive policies applied around the world; asylum has rocketed; and regions previously closed behind walls have gradually opened since the collapse of the Communist bloc. Transnational networks have been created across state borders, leading not only to trade but also to irregular migration. Thanks to globalization, the poor have discovered the wealth of the North and realized that, if it does not come to them, they must go and seek it (though it is seldom the very poor who migrate).

Migration will unquestionably be a vital issue in negotiations concerning international relations in the coming century. The world is changing very quickly, and so are migration flows and borders themselves. Yet, both governments and populations remain impervious to the new situation, justifying strict border controls with the belief that rich countries would be undermined by an 'invasion' of poorer people from the South. Whereas the freedom to trade and do business has now been almost universally established, the freedom to travel, settle and work is still vehemently contested, both in principle and in practice. But closing borders is not a realistic option, and opening them remains idealistic. The question is: What restrictions can be placed on the principle of freedom of movement without restricting democracy? This is a dilemma few Western countries have so far successfully addressed.

After a description of how the globalization of migration has, over the past fifteen years, raised questions about the wisdom of closing frontiers and encouraged consideration of a right to mobility, this chapter will examine the transnational exchanges taking place, the changes that affect state sovereignty, and the new barriers that are being set up on either side of borders around the world. Finally, it will examine the idea of a right to mobility, which is increasingly understood as central to a modern conception of human rights and as an important instrument for democracy, citizenship and the fight against all forms of discrimination. The human rights violations that follow the closure of borders, such as the fact that migrants risk their lives to enter democratic countries, call for an urgent consideration of such a right to mobility.

The globalization of migratory flows and its effects on borders

The new factors of mobility

If we define globalization as a process of internationalization whereby barriers become less rigid and nations seem closer and more accessible to one another, leading to increased transborder communication, networking and interdependence, then it would seem that migratory flows have by now become part of that process. Migration is indeed a phenomenon with global political, economic, social and cultural dimensions, which could well undermine the very system of nation-states – leading to new or recomposed multipolar, transnational, transcontinental and regional networks, and turning the issue of the movement of people into a major international strategic challenge.

Until very recently, migration was confined to a limited number of host countries and regions of origin, often connected by a colonial past. The globalization of migratory flows is thus a relatively new phenomenon (Wihtol de Wenden, 2003). In the late 1980s, new patterns of migration emerged, characterized by new forms of mobility and by migrants from geographical areas where extensive population flows had seldom been experienced, particularly from central and eastern Asia, Eastern Europe and Central Africa. There are several reasons behind this phenomenon:

1. Pull factors are now stronger than those pushing migrants away from their homelands. Despite the growing inequalities between the North and the

South, it is currently not so much demographic pressure and poverty that generate migration, but a desire to live in Europe or in the West: this is fuelled by the spread of the consumer society and of democracy, brought closer by the media. Whereas in the 1960s, illiterate country dwellers used to migrate en masse, today's migrants tend to come from educated urban middle classes in search of greater economic – but also political, social and cultural – well-being.

2. Over the past two decades, passports have become easier to obtain, even in countries ruled by authoritarian regimes – with the exception of rare countries where they are still issued sparingly (notably China, Democratic People's Republic of Korea and Cuba). This has made it easier for people to leave their country, even though restrictions (applied through border controls and visas) to enter rich countries have become increasingly tight.

3. The massive increase in asylum seeking worldwide, no longer restricted to a few troubled regions, has raised the number of refugees to previously unknown levels (in the African Great Lakes region, South-East Asia, the Balkans, the Near and Middle East or the Caribbean region).

4. Fast-developing transnational networks have become responsible for large sections of migratory movements, notably in China, Romania, the Balkans or West Africa. Often clandestine by nature, this form of migration is hindered by state controls, but its actors turn borders to their advantage and even prosper on their reinforced existence.

5. Back-and-forth migration is increasingly frequent, whereby migrants no longer settle down permanently in a country, but stay on a temporary basis in order to improve their conditions at home. This can be observed between Eastern and Western Europe (following the fall of the Berlin Wall), but also between the North and the South or from one country in the South to another.

6. The creation of large regional free trade areas – NAFTA (the North American Free Trade Agreement between the United States, Canada and Mexico), MERCOSUR (Mercado Común del Sur, or the Southern Common Market), ECOWAS (the Economic Community of West African States), the Euro-Mediterranean Partnership, the European Union, and the European Nordic Labour Market – facilitates the circulation of goods, people and ideas. While some of these free trade agreements also provide for freedom of movement and settlement, the mobility of populations has so far been institutionally recognized only by the European Union.

These factors are symptomatic of a new world order, not only overturned by the end of the Cold War and by new regional and global conflicts, but also marked by widening economic, social, political and cultural rifts and new fissures. The emergence of highly symbolic crossing-points for people and goods illustrates these divides: the Rio Grande between Mexico and the United States; Gibraltar, the Canary Islands and the islands off Sicily between North Africa and Europe; Brindisi or Vlores between Italy, Greece and Albania; Sangatte and the Eurotunnel connecting France and the United Kingdom, or the former Oder-Neisse border between Germany and Poland. Geographical proximity is made easier by decreasing transport costs, especially by air. In the meantime, images of the West are broadcast by television and radio channels in migrants' countries of origin; manufactured products from the West are sold in local markets (often thanks to migrants' remittances), thereby opening up even the most remote regions of the world and creating a latent desire for the West among people who would not have previously thought of migrating.

Contrary to popular belief, the mobility of capital goes hand-in-hand with the mobility of persons. The circulation of Western goods, far from being an alternative to migration, encourages people to move. The more Western goods circulate, the more they create a desire to acquire these symbols of freedom and prosperity, and to travel to the countries that produce them.

Migratory pressure in the world today

According to the last report of the International Organization for Migration (2005), there are currently about 190 million migrants and displaced persons throughout the world (making up some 3 per cent of the world population). Albeit low, these figures are steadily increasing as part of the spiral of globalization. Although the overwhelming majority of the world's population remains sedentary, migratory trajectories are globalizing: the number of countries of destination and origin is constantly increasing, gradually blurring the importance of former colonial links and changing the bilateral nature of migratory flows. While most analyses concern host countries in the West (Western Europe, the United States, Canada, Australia and Japan), more than 60 per cent of all migrants do not leave the South, and three-quarters of all refugees settle in Third World countries, among their neighbours.

New flows appear, creating new connections between countries: Iranians in Sweden, Romanians in Germany, Vietnamese in Canada or in Australia, Bangladeshis in Japan, or North Africans and Egyptians in the Gulf countries and in the Libyan Arab Jamahiriya. This suggests that the globalization of migratory flows is likely to continue, due to a failure to reduce the development gap and to the growing capacity of the migration business to enable people to enter host countries. The scale of the phenomenon is such that policies designed to limit flows, however dissuasive and repressive, become largely ineffective.

Globalization also encourages the settlement of increasingly diverse populations, in search of socioeconomic, social, political, religious and cultural betterment. The possibility and legitimacy of closing borders are undermined by these many different forms of mobility, in relation to which national legislation often lags several years behind, leading to all kinds of mismanaged situations. Human rights are increasingly understood as a set of supranational references reaching beyond state sovereignty (the right to seek political asylum or to family reunification) or as guiding humanitarian concerns (such as the temporary protection of displaced persons). The idea that states cannot indefinitely prevent the mobility of people has begun to spread: the right to migrate has begun, albeit cautiously, to be thought of in the context of associated human rights, as very strict entry conditions are making the human right to leave one's own country difficult to implement.

In absolute terms, Germany and the United States have been the two major host countries in recent years, followed, in relative terms (regular entries vis-à-vis the foreign population) by Japan, Norway and the United Kingdom. Migration for family reunification and marriage dominates, especially in the United States and Canada, despite the number of asylum seekers and work-related migrants. Many immigrants are women, mainly from East and South-East Asia, and the contribution that migrants make in terms of demographic balance and addressing labour shortages is vital in Europe and Japan. All host countries endeavour to restrict clandestine immigration and the employment of undocumented migrants, but they lack the necessary will and means to do so because of a structural conflict between market pressures to open borders and state pressures to close them (Entzinger et al., 2004).

Some basic trends make it possible to evaluate this globalized mobility. First, the growth in the number of migrants over the past thirty years is striking: 77 million in 1965, 111 million in 1990, 140 million in 1997, 150 million in 2000 and 190 million at present. Also, migration is unevenly distributed around the world: 90 per cent of the world's migrants live in just fifty-five countries, mostly in the industrialized nations. Finally, there is an overall lack of coordination among national policies to address the rapid increase in transborder flows: despite its essentially international nature, migration has long been one of the least-discussed issues at the international level.

Globalization and migration

Globalization and migration go hand-in-hand, and they concern every continent. Europe, above all, has unwillingly and painfully become a land of immigration, whereas for a long time it regarded itself as a land of departures. It is struggling to include in its emergent identity its non-European – and especially its Muslim – residents. The effects of this changed situation are numerous and often undesirable: tense border controls and forced expulsions, irregular immigrants and arbitrary treatment of individual immigration applications (Wihtol de Wenden, 2004).

At the same time, the demographic prospects for the years 2020 to 2050 point to an ageing Europe, prey to labour shortages, to difficulties in replacing the generations reaching retirement, to demographic decline and to increasing numbers of very old people. A major United Nations study (UN, 2000), as well as reports by other institutions such as the International Labour Office or France's Economic and Social Council, more or less concur: immigration must increase again to maintain competitiveness, innovation, and economic, social, cultural and demographic dynamism (Gevrey, 2003; Grinblat, 2003). But public opinion lacks enthusiasm for immigration and is obsessed with its security aspects, as it is often linked in people's minds with terrorism and crime. Public opinion may, however, be a pretext, as it is manipulated by governments whose decisions – whether they are on the left or on the right of the political spectrum – are often based on an unspoken consensus about the need to control borders, based on a concern to protect sovereignty and a fear of losing control.

In the Americas, the Rio Grande between the United States and Mexico is one of the world's greatest dividing lines, but also a crossing-point, while, in the south, former destination countries have become countries of emigration (such as Argentina) and vice-versa (such as Venezuela). The continent is thus continuously criss-crossed by migration flows, mainly from the South to the North. Africa is a region that produces emigration, but also receives the flows generated by conflicts, economic disasters and drought; mobility patterns are perpetually changing, from south to north (as North Africa has become a region of immigration), and from north to south, since South Africa also attracts numerous migrants from neighbouring countries. Asia, the world's greatest demographic pool, is characterized by all kinds of mobility, of which some are recent while others have long characterized economies based on clandestine movement and displacement. Some countries, such as Thailand, are both receiving and sending countries, while others, such as the Philippines, massively export their workers and are above all countries of emigration; still others are exclusively countries of immigration, such as Japan. Australia, whose very identity is built on immigration, is the main destination country for the whole region, while openly implementing a highly restrictive policy towards asylum seekers and boat people.

As a result of the closure of borders by receiving states (which try to 'protect' themselves through visa regimes, readmission agreements and expulsions), grey zones are becoming ubiquitous. These are characterized by migrants' deaths, human trafficking, labour subcontracting, undocumented employment and prostitution. The journeys migrants undertake thus often become odysseys of horror towards which most of the world remains indifferent.

Yet mobility is neither invasion nor conquest: as mentioned, only 3 per cent of the world population takes part in migration, whether as family members, migrant workers, students, business people, experts, refugees or displaced persons. And the more open the borders, the more people circulate and the less they settle down, which leads to back-and-forth migration as mobility becomes a way of life. Following the fall of the Berlin Wall, this new phenomenon was observed in the countries of Central and Eastern Europe, when the need for short-term visas ('Schengen visas', or three-month tourist visas) was successively removed, between 1991 and 2001, for these new visitors to the European Union countries. The more borders are closed, the more migrants settle down and bring in their families, as they are afraid of being unable to re-enter the country if ever they return to their homeland.

It remains a little-recognized fact that migration can contribute to development, as money transfers are a vital resource for the countries of origin and help to reduce their isolation; even less recognized is the fact that development in turn generates migration as part of the modernization of sectors of traditional activity and the urbanization of the Third World (Sassen, 2003). The above-mentioned desire for the West is enhanced by peoples' awareness, in many areas of the world, that they have no prospect for personal improvement within their lifetime or generation, and that their situation is characterized by political, economic, social and cultural dead-ends, especially for the more adventurous or the more talented (Wihtol de Wenden, 2002).

Issues for political analysis

National borders in the face of mobility and transnational networks

Borders are zones of contact, barriers that regulate traffic and generate resources and are continuously shifting: the Mediterranean, far from being a place of exchange and dialogue for those who live on its shores (the 'Middle Sea' of Antiquity), has become a new Rio Grande, dividing its northern and southern banks. In the East, since the enlargement of the European Union on 1 May 2004, new borders have appeared between the eastern Member States and the former U.S.S.R. These are not only political borders, but also economic, social and demographic boundaries, dividing the East and West, the South and the North. Institutional borders distinguish between those who need no visas to cross borders and those who do, because they are nationals of 'high migration risk' countries. Cultural boundaries separate people from Others – the Muslims or asylum seekers – about which people often construct images and ideas based upon collective representations and identification processes.

The Mediterranean symbolizes one of the major North–South divides. Whereas the countries on the northern shores saw their populations grow by only around one-third between 1950 and 2000, rising from 158 to 212 million, on the southern shore, the population tripled, from 73 to 244 million – an increase of 32 to 53 per cent, varying from one state to another. In the 1990s, the natural growth rate (the difference between birth and mortality rates) averaged 1.5 per cent on its northern shores, compared with 20.2 per cent on its southern coast, despite the demographic stagnation observed in the countries of the southern and eastern Mediterranean during that period. As a result, 55 per cent of the population on the southern shores of the Mediterranean are under twenty-five years old. By 2025, the population of the countries of the Maghreb will have grown by another 48 per cent, compared with 3 per cent in the European Union, even though those countries have also begun their demographic decline. Another difference between the North and the South is the mobility of the population: the youth in southern Mediterranean countries are numerous and therefore able to bear the burden of older parents; at the same time, they have few children, which makes them particularly likely to migrate to escape high unemployment levels (Fargues, 2003). Employment is another dividing factor: the GDP per head in the European Union is fourteen times as high as in Morocco, Algeria and Tunisia. Migrant remittances account for 6.3 per cent of Morocco's GDP, 2.3 per cent of Algeria's and 4.1 per cent of Tunisia's (Brauch et al., 2003).

But whether closed or very slightly open, borders are a resource, as they fuel the business of the international networks that challenge states and facilitate new migrants' mobility. This travel (or migration) economy is built around borders and boosted by the transnational exchanges that prosper, whether legally or not, on their closure: trafficking in documents and visas, clandestine travel agencies, people smuggling, prostitution, cross-border trade (Peraldi, 2003). The harder it is to cross the borders, the higher the prices charged and the more sophisticated the proposed services.

Borders are areas of both crossing and closure. In an era of globalization, they generate all kinds of mobility: pendular migration, border zone migration, forced migration, migratory circulation, and migration of settlement. Borders also lead to transgressions: migrants do clandestine work for a day, for a few months, or for longer in order to fund their ongoing trip, sometimes becoming modern-day slaves. Borders further constitute important elements in the representation of national sovereignty, and are still perceived as symbolic checkpoints. Borders are finally about selection, about distant control – both before arrival (through visas) and after (expulsion, readmission agreements) – sometimes turning third countries into border guards that assume responsibility for the transit buffer zones.

Borders are also a matter of sovereignty-loaded sanctions: removal, repatriation or expulsion. But borders are evolving as the world itself is being recomposed: one witnesses new boundaries and new divisions within states, grounded in people's legal status (for example between EU and non-EU citizens), ethnicity, community, identity or religious beliefs, which lead to social exclusion and racism. These boundaries, both fuelled and challenged by migration, also question the cohesion of the state and its role as the main protagonist in international relations.

A challenge to the Westphalian sovereignty model

New global mobility patterns are characterized by the diversification of migrants' profiles: women, urban middle classes, isolated minors, skilled workers, merchants and business people, members of mafia networks, together with undocumented workers who come and try their luck despite the closure of borders. Areas of origin and destinations are similarly changing their profiles: we can no longer speak of countries of *emigration* or *immigration*, but of certain regions from which migrants flow towards urban areas throughout the world. Those who migrate are not the poorest, but those who belong to specific and often world-scale networks. Moreover, these new migrants develop patterns of mobility that do not necessarily aim at permanent settlement: in what is sometimes referred to as 'incomplete migration' (notably in the case of Eastern Europe), people live 'here' and 'there' and, being only settled in their constant mobility, circulate as a way of life.

As do established migrants, these new migrants challenge state practices in different ways. Many destination countries have, for example, changed their nationality laws, and now place more emphasis on residence rights, which has sometimes included the granting of voting rights in local elections for settled foreigners. The development of this residence-based citizenship frequently goes hand-in-hand with calls for multicultural integration policies, but also with questions regarding allegiances and loyalties of immigrants and their descendants – especially in the case of Muslim migrants, as the debates that surround headscarves or that have taken place on key occasions illustrate (the Gulf Wars; 11 September 2001).

Another consequence lies in the emergence of a migrant electorate and in issues surrounding the political behaviour of naturalized immigrants, as in California or France. The influence of migrants' specificity – linked to their countries of origin or to the cultural features of their community – have long been minor preoccupations, but now represent economically and politically strategic issues. Recent years have witnessed further concerns about the security aspects of immigration, now very much present in domestic and international political discourses (Heisler 1998/1999; Bigo, 1996; De Lobkowicz, 2001), along with the demonization of Islam – now widely perceived as one of the major threats to Western societies.

This global context calls for taking migration fully into account in the international political analysis of globalization and its consequences (Leveau,

1993) – the blurring of boundaries between internal and external orders, the declining role of the state, the impact of difficult border controls on their sovereignty, the role of international or supranational institutions such as the European Union (Zolberg, 1985). Migration is thus challenging the foundations of the international order, leading to recompositions in a way that not only announces new and improved patterns in terms of identities or fundamental rights, but also carries risks and disturbs existing equilibriums. Migrants are the anonymous actors of globalization (Sassen, 1996; Wiener, 1995): through their cross-border movements, money transfers, dual nationality and multiple allegiances, they contribute to decentralized co-development and construct transnational networks.

As James Rosenau (1997) shows, migration increases the number of non-state actors and points to the coexistence of two worlds (composed of state versus non-state actors); to the deterritorialization of identities; and to the role of infra-state, transnational and cross-border actors, while emphasizing the emergence of new borders – institutional, economic, social, cultural and religious – in the world arena. In many respects, the state is ceasing to be the leading player, whether in the external political order (dynamics of flows and transnational networks, clandestine immigration, refugees, etc.), or on the domestic front (the contribution of migrants to the definition of the national identity, dual nationality, the effect of any 'immigrant' vote on a state's diplomatic relations towards regions of emigration and, conversely, networks of influence in the countries of emigration exerted through non-state channels by transnational association movements).

Immigration further calls citizenship into question: not only does it question the relationship between nationality and citizenship, but it also introduces into the content of citizenship new cross-cutting values that go beyond the national framework (anti-racism, human rights, multiculturalism, multiple allegiances and a composite definition of a political community). Because of immigration, nations are no longer the basic community of the international system, and the notion of international actors needs to be re-examined, even if important disparities persist in terms of the influence of each actor.

The democratization of borders versus an elitist freedom of movement

The concerns of those who have not managed to have access to legal mobility (undocumented and deported migrants, victims of trafficking, or unsuccessful asylum seekers); aspirations to mobility in countries in which emigrating is a luxury and a privilege; the undermining of economic, demographic, political and cultural arguments in favour of closed borders – all are leading to a new reflection on a possible right to migrate, which is all the more relevant in a world where only the better off, the better informed and those with the best contacts manage to circulate freely and legally. This is also due to contextual changes over the last twenty years. There was once a need for unskilled labour in mines, factories or building sites, along with a rejection of skilled migrants, understood as potential rivals in jealously protected occupations: today, by contrast, rich countries are looking for qualified and highly skilled workers but are afraid of the poor – who are rejected, believed to be unable to integrate, and accused of engendering insecurity, violence or even terrorism.

Finally, the closing of borders following security concerns often leads to violations of human rights, in particular those of the least well off. This issue now pervades all approaches to migration and migrants, as if mobility was a new phenomenon for which nobody could have been prepared, despite the fact that it is as old as the hills.

Creating a right to mobility

The concept of a right to mobility draws its legitimacy from the 1948 Universal Declaration of Human Rights, whose Article 13-2 states that 'everyone has the right to leave any country, including his own'. This article remained incomplete, mainly because of its context: at that time, the issue was to send a warning to the Eastern bloc countries with regard to their dissidents (Chemillier-Gendreau et al., 1999). No text therefore recognizes the equivalent right to enter a country. But what value has the right to leave without the corresponding right to enter? What does a right to travel mean without a right to settle?

In recent years, various violations of human rights following the closure of borders (modern forms of slavery, trafficking, violent police interventions, forced deportations, detention of migrants in camps, and even deaths), along with the cost and undesirable effects of closed borders (which evokes a new prohibition and its correspondent mafias), and the diplomatic consequences in sending regions, have undermined the arguments in favour of dissuasion and repression. The frontiers of mobility are also the frontiers of democracy and human rights. A right to mobility is part of the universalist and individualist values of the citizen of the world, going back to Immanuel Kant's 'right to visit', which he contrasted with the 'hospitality right' in his 1795 essay *Perpetual Peace: A Philosophical Sketch*. A right to mobility would qualify the power of nation-states, which today tend to prevent people from entering, after having for centuries prevented them from leaving (Zolberg, 1993). A right to circulate fits into the modern conception of human rights, into the fight against all forms of discrimination, and into multiculturalism as a framework for democracy and citizenship in advanced countries.

As early as 1764, in an article entitled 'Equality' in his *Philosophical Dictionary*, Voltaire wrote: 'it has been maintained in many countries that no citizen has a right to quit that country in which he was born. The meaning of such a law must evidently be: "This country is so wretched and ill-governed we prohibit every man from quitting it, under an apprehension that otherwise all would leave it." Do better; excite in all your subjects a desire to stay with you, and in foreigners a desire to come and settle among you' (Morley, 1901). This comment, denouncing the decision by European countries in the eighteenth century to prevent their citizens from leaving (a policy that continued in many regions of the world at least until the fall of the Berlin Wall), challenges today's dominant conceptions. In Europe, even though the EU has had the courage to create an area without borders comprising twenty-seven countries, migration policies are still based on the desire to keep people out.

In Third World countries, migrants need visas to enter developed countries. The right to leave is the privilege of the richest sectors of the population or the best-informed, who succeed in migrating legally and leave clandestine entry and settlement to the less well off. This situation underlies the calls by philosophers, economists, sociologists and lawyers for a democratization of borders. Can countries that claim to be democratic, such as Europe and the United States, tolerate a situation where, in order for them to pretend that migration is controlled, people die on their doorstep every day, and criminal networks active in slavery and prostitution operate along their borders? Are there not other ways to manage migration, through dialogue and cooperation between sending and transit countries, whose interests lie in encouraging emigration and benefiting from it (contrary to popular beliefs about the plundering of the Third World)? Is it not because migration issues were long understood as minor aspects of state policy that they are now disdainfully and unprofessionally addressed, compared to other major policy matters?

It is worth repeating that migration is now a vital issue that will partly determine the future of states in most parts of the world.

Future prospects

What is to be done? Numerous proposals have been put forward and tried at different times and in different places, providing a range of options to choose among: abolish short-stay visas; diversify residence and work visas; introduce quotas or 'point permits' to reflect labour market needs (as Canada does and as Germany did in 2001); regularize undocumented immigrants to tackle labour shortages (as Italy did in 2004); sign bilateral seasonal immigration agreements in exchange for tighter controls at exit borders; foster co-development with sending regions and with the cooperation of migrants themselves; establish free trade agreements to replace the free circulation of people with that of goods (as in the NAFTA agreements or with the Barcelona

Process that developed from the 1995 Conference on Euro-Mediterranean Partnership); ban any form of statutory discrimination regarding the entry of foreigners into the labour market (such as European employment preferences); or reform asylum procedures.

In view of all the barriers reinforcing borders and encouraging people to find alternative ways to migrate, the right to mobility should become one of our key human rights. The fact that Western destination countries – rich, ageing and in need of both skilled and unskilled labour – will not be able to block human mobility forever is increasingly clear, not only among human rights organizations but also in the business world. In any case, migration will continue to contribute to redefining citizenship and the state's identity, thereby forcing states to rethink their understanding of what living together means.

Bibliography

Badie, B. and Wihtol de Wenden, C. 1994. *Le Défi migratoire: questions de relations internationales*. Paris, Presses de la FNSP.

Bigo, D. 1996. *Polices en réseaux*. Paris, Presses de Sciences Po.

Brauch, H. G., Liotta, P. H., Marquina, A., Rogers, P., Selim, M. (eds). 2003. *Security and Environment in the Mediterranean: Conceptualising Security and Environmental Conflicts*. Berlin, Springer.

Chemillier-Gendreau, M. 1999. Droit international ignoré, relations internationales de la France compromises. E. Balibar, M. Chemillier-Gendreau, J. Costa Lasoux and E. Terray (eds), *Sans papiers: l'archaïsme fatal*. Paris, La Découverte, pp. 63–87.

de Lobkowicz, W. 2001. *L'Europe et la sécurité intérieure: une élaboration par étapes*. Paris, La Documentation française.

Entzinger, H., Martiniello, M. and Wihtol De Wenden, C. (eds). 2004. *Migration between States and Markets*. Aldershot, Ashgate.

Fargues, P. 2003. L'émigration en Europe vue d'Afrique du Nord et du Moyen Orient. *Esprit*, December, pp. 125–43.

Gevrey, M. 2003. *Les défis de l'immigration future*. Paris, Conseil économique et social.

Grinblat, J.-A. 2003. Des scénarios d'immigration pour une Europe vieillissante. *Esprit*, December, pp. 92–101.

Heisler, M. 1998/1999. Contextualising global migration: sketching the socio-political landscape in Europe. *Journal of International Law and Foreign Affairs*, Vol. 3, No. 2.

International Organization for Migration. 2005. *World Migration 2005: Costs and Benefits of International Migration*. Geneva, IOM.

Kant, I. 1795. *Perpetual Peace: A Philosophical Sketch* 1795. www.mtholyoke.edu/acad/ intrel/kant/kant.htm (Accessed 21 December 2006.)

Leveau, R. 1993. Influences extérieures et identités au Maghreb: le jeu du transnational. *Cultures et Conflits*, No. 8, pp. 116–28.

Morley, J. 1901. *The Works of Voltaire, a Contemporary Version*. T. Smollett (ed.), W. F. Fleming (trans.). New York, E. R. DuMont.

Peraldi, M. 2003. La loi des réseaux. *Panoramiques*, No. 65, 4th quarter, pp. 100–12.

Rosenau, J. 1997. *Along the Domestic Foreign Frontier: Exploring Governance in a Turbulent World*. Cambridge, Cambridge University Press. (Cambridge Studies in International Relations.)

Sassen S. 1996. *Losing Control: Sovereignty in an Age of Globalization*. New York, Columbia University Press.

———. 2003. Géo-économie des flux migratoires. *Esprit*, December, pp. 102–13.

United Nations. 2000. *Replacement Migration: Is it a Solution to Declining and Aging Populations?* New York, United Nations.

Wiener, M. 1995. *The Global Migration Crisis: Challenges to States and to Human Rights*. New York, Harper Collins College Publishers.

Wihtol de Wenden, C. 2002. Motivations et attentes des migrants. *Projet*, No. 272, December, pp. 46–54.

———. 2003. La mondialisation des flux migratoires. Josepha Laroche (ed.), *Mondialisation et gouvernance mondiale*. Paris, PUF, IRIS, pp. 79–92.

———. 2004. L'Union européenne face aux migrations. IFRI, T. de Montbrial, P. Moreau Defarges (eds), *RAMSES Les grandes tendances du monde*. Paris, Dunod, pp. 109–23.

Zolberg, A. 1985. Immigration: l'influence des facteurs externes sur l'ordre politique interne. J. Leca, *Traité de Science Politique*, Paris, PUF. Vol. 2.

———. 1993. Un reflet du monde: les migrations internationales en perspective historique. Badie and Wihtol de Wenden, op. cit., pp. 41–58.

Chapter 4

The ethics, economics and governance of free movement

Mehmet Ugur

Introduction

After alarmist reactions to perceived threats of mass migration in the early 1990s,[1] the policy debate on international migration may now be going through a new phase. Although the official discourse is still coloured with a restrictive tone, implementation tends to reflect a degree of pragmatism in favour of 'managed' migration. There are also a number of regional and international initiatives geared towards the development of regional/international frameworks that would facilitate the management of international migration. This chapter contributes to this debate by exploring the ethical and economic case for free movement, which includes only the movement of people for employment purposes.[2]

A key argument developed in this chapter is that it is difficult to make an ethical or economic case against the free movement of workers. The analysis that leads to this conclusion also shows that free movement is not only feasible, but also more efficient than restrictive/protectionist policies. Another argument supported in this chapter is that a multilateral framework, similar to that of the World Trade Organization (WTO), would be an optimal arrangement that would enable member countries to tackle externalities and collective action problems associated with international migration, which can only be expected to increase given the extent of globalization and the persistence of international income inequalities.

The chapter is organized in three sections. The first part examines the ethical case for and against free movement as defined above. In this section I demonstrate that the level of analysis and the interdependence between actors at different levels are crucial issues that must be tackled by the ethical debate on free movement. Taking into account the consequences of strategic interaction between actors at the individual, national and global levels, I demonstrate that an ethical case against free movement cannot be made. Secondly, I examine the economic impacts of international migration – on national income, the labour market and fiscal balances of receiving countries. Theoretical and empirical findings suggest that international migration would have a positive but small impact on output, combined with some distributional effects that are in favour of capital but against the low-skilled section of the labour market. I conclude this section by arguing that the distributional effects can be tackled through compensation for the adversely affected sections of the host country labour force, which can withstand the erosion of their wages only by investment in skill enhancement. Finally, I propose a governance structure similar to that we observe in the area of trade. A World Migration Organization (WMO), just like the WTO, must be based on three principles: multilateralism, non-discrimination, and reciprocity. The conclusion to the chapter highlights its main findings and discusses the feasibility of free movement as a policy option in the current political climate.

Ethics and free movement

In examining the ethical case for and against free movement I will focus on the essential ingredients of the debate, even though this narrow focus may be an injustice to the richness of the existing literature. This chapter is limited to evaluating the existing ethical propositions with reference to a utilitarian criterion, which is defined as the social welfare of the receiving country. In that sense, my point of departure is the same as the 'communitarian' approach adopted by policy-makers and others who argue against free movement. The only difference between my understanding of social welfare and that of the 'communitarian' approach is that I take into account the strategic interaction between actors at different levels. Specifically, I consider interactions between individuals, groups and the government at the national level and between governments at the international level.

One implication of this strategic interaction is externalities, which draw a wedge between social welfare and the sum of individual/group welfares. In the case of negative externalities, certain individuals or groups are able to influence public policy in their own favour without compensating other individuals or groups for the negative effects the policy might have on their welfare. (In the case of positive externalities, the champions of the policy are not compensated by those who stand to gain from the policy.) Let me explain the negative externality and its implications with an example of policy choice – say immigration restriction.

Restricting immigration may benefit some groups – such as low-wage, low-skilled labour or those with a preference for a relatively homogenous community. The same policy choice, however, may affect adversely the interests of other groups – such as employers, highly skilled segments of the labour market, or those in favour of a more cosmopolitan community. Unless the winners from restrictive policy were made to compensate the losers, they would lobby for a level of restriction that is higher than the socially optimal level. This is mainly because they would not bear the full societal cost of the restrictive policy. Therefore, in the presence of negative externalities, immigration policy is highly likely to be over-restrictive – and inefficient.

The second implication of strategic interaction is what is referred to as collective action failures. According to Olson (1965), small groups are relatively better able to organize and lobby the policy-makers compared to large groups with diffused membership. There are two reasons for this type of collective action problem within large groups. First, the marginal contribution of a single member to the success of the lobbying process is small. Therefore, for the marginal member who chooses not to contribute, the perceived risk of group failure is small. This perception encourages lower participation rates. Secondly, the benefits derived from successful lobbying are distributed among a large number of claimants. Therefore, in large groups, the expected benefits of active participation are small. Given these dynamics, small groups formed around an anti-immigration objective may be more active and vociferous in their campaigns compared to large but diffused groups that may be in favour of immigration. To the extent that this is the case, immigration restriction will be not only inefficient, but also unfair.

The third implication of strategic interaction relates to the role of government. The realist/communitarian ethics tends to assume that the government is a social planner who maximizes social welfare (or national interest) and that the legitimacy of its action is derived from popular consent.[3] It is then ethical to restrict immigration if the latter is perceived to be posing a threat to the national interests. This proposition, however, is problematic because the government may be motivated by electoral considerations rather than social welfare. In addition, the government of a migrant-receiving country may adopt a restrictive policy without taking into account the effect of its action on other countries. In fact, this criticism constitutes the core argument of the natural law or egalitarian liberalist approach to immigration.[4] According to the latter, the unit of analysis should be the world itself rather than nation-states or communities.

In what follows, I will try to ascertain whether it is ethical to: (i) restrict immigration given the implications of strategic interaction summarized above; and (ii) to discriminate between movements of people and goods/capital. To do this, I will examine the propositions in favour of restriction as formulated by the libertarian and communitarian/realist ethics. I will also assess the coherence of the counter-propositions put forward by the students of natural law and egalitarian liberalism.

The ethics of restriction

The libertarian perspective

Libertarian ethics is based on individual sovereignty, the most explicit manifestation of which is the individual's ability to enjoy the benefits of private property and the associations formed with like-minded individuals. This premise has two conflicting implications for the free movement of people. On the one hand, it implies that sovereign individuals are entitled to free movement, subject to limitations that can be justified on the grounds of security and public order. On the other hand, however, it also implies that sovereign individuals are entitled to object to free movement if it is perceived to threaten their property rights and/or the 'club benefits' they derive from associations they voluntarily establish with like-minded individuals. In practice, the libertarian approach is in favour of immigration if it follows from an invitation from sovereign individuals or a contract between two parties. Otherwise, immigration amounts to trespassing.[5]

However, property rights are a poor basis for restricting the movement of people for three reasons. First, and as indicated by O'Neill (1992), the right to own and enjoy private property cannot be separated from the way in which the property was appropriated originally. If the original appropriation was based on closure or expropriation, people whose movements are restricted could well argue that the current income inequalities are a result of closure or expropriation. This is an argument likely to be voiced by developing country governments, who would argue that colonization by developed countries between the seventeenth and twentieth centuries constituted an exercise in expropriation. Then, restriction of immigration on the basis of property rights could be justified only if developed countries compensated developing countries through development aid.

Secondly, and from a natural law perspective, it can be argued that private property is a historical construct and was not a universal right before the emergence of capitalism. Therefore, the property rights argument can be criticized as an attempt at restricting a historically prior right (i.e., the right to free movement) by upholding a historically posterior right (i.e., the right to own property). Thirdly, the libertarian approach does not address the possibility of problems in relation to externalities and collective action indicated above. In other words, it does not allow for possible conflicts between the maximization of individual welfare and that of social welfare.

Finally, the libertarian ethics does not address adequately the issues that arise because of the existence of a 'public space' outside the realm of private property. For example, the delivery of essential public services, such as health, education or social care, may require the employment of foreign labour even if this is considered as a threat to the 'club benefits' associated with membership of the host community. The libertarian ethics suggests that a 'congestion criterion' can be applied to determine whether or not the entry of foreign labour is justified. However, congestion is not a robust criterion because its definition varies: congestion sometimes refers to the level of unemployment among the incumbent work force; sometimes it is the pressure that foreigners exert on local services; and sometimes it is the exceeding of an arbitrary threshold in the ethnic mixture of the local/national community. In addition, even if we agree on any of these congestion measures, the agreed measure would not be objective because it would inevitably be influenced by exogenous variables such as ideology, current policy, regime type, etc., which change over time and from one community to another.

In the light of the analysis above, we can detect two major shortcomings in the libertarian ethics of free movement. First, libertarian ethics may leave no scope for international migration when migration is perceived to encroach on individual property rights or to congest the public space. In practice, this may imply zero immigration – depending on societal perceptions and the organizational strength of the anti-immigration lobbies. The libertarian argument in favour of international migration (subject to preservation of existing property rights or 'club benefits') then becomes morally obnoxious, because it boils down to granting a right that may not be exercised. In fact, libertarian ethics could generate propositions that are more exclusionary than the realist/communitarian approach and might foster open hostility between defenders of existing property rights (i.e., incumbents) and trespassers (i.e., immigrants).

The second shortcoming is the high level of uncertainty and discretion that libertarian ethics would allow for in determining congestion thresholds. For example, what is an acceptable level of ethnic diversity in the host country? To what extent is the pressure on local services due to extra demand by foreigners and not to tax cuts induced by high levels of capital mobility? To what extent are unemployment and wage differentials due to other variables such as free trade, technological change or capital mobility rather than immigration? Finally, how should the policy-maker react to the diverse and sometimes conflicting perceptions about congestion?

The realist perspective

The realist arguments against free movement take two forms, both of which ignore the interaction between actors at different levels. One variant, described as communitarianism, is based on the premise that moral agents are rooted in particular contexts because people choose different ways of life and organize into different communities (Sandel, 1982; Walzer, 1983; and Kymlicka, 1988). Therefore, people are entitled to be protected against international migration that threatens their ways of life and association. In addition, popular sovereignty implies that states are under obligation to prioritize the interests of their political community vis-à-vis other individual or collective claims. Realists acknowledge that this stance inevitably implies exclusion, but they also argue that this exclusion would in fact be less severe than the exclusion that non-state actors, left to their own devices, are likely to impose (Walzer, 1983, p. 39).

The other realist variant is based on national interest as articulated by governments. For example, Weiner (1985 and 1996) argues that free movement of people and international regimes to regulate international migration are not feasible because sovereign states can always invoke the concept of national interest as a basis for unilateral action. In this case, he argues, we should be guided by the ethical requirement that 'ought implies can'. In other words, it is better not to have ethical norms if such norms are not likely to be observed. Weiner (1996, p. 193) also differentiates between individual morality and the application of morality to public policy. Based on this differentiation, he argues that 'personal ethics are a poor basis for public choices because they do not take into account the costs that such policies impose upon others.'

As a basis for restricting immigration, realist/communitarian ethics suffers from three shortcomings. The first is the ignorance of externalities that arise when governments adopt unilateral immigration policies. Just as the libertarian ethics criticized by Weiner above, the realist/communitarian ethics can be criticized for ignoring the costs that national policy choices might impose on other nations (see for example Keohane and Nye, 1977). True, realists are not against intergovernmental institutions that could mitigate or manage the spillover effects of unilateral actions. Yet, they leave such institution-building to the discretion of nation-states, which would prefer either unilateral action or rules/institutions that would be too loose to be effective. So the realist qualification concerning intergovernmental cooperation provides very little or no remedy to the externalities that may be associated with unilateral national action.

The second problem is that the negation of 'ought implies can' is not 'cannot implies ought not' (Goodin, 1992, p. 252). An action that would produce a superior outcome compared to the existing state of affairs may well be unfeasible. As Goodin indicates, however, 'the good remains good, even when it lies beyond our grasp.' Then, the realist approach cannot justify restrictions on international migration merely by pointing to the practical hurdles caused by the division of the world into sovereign state jurisdictions. It would still be ethically correct to argue in favour of free movement, not only because one has to be logically consistent but also because one has to call a spade a spade – i.e., one has to highlight the fact that the existing order is preventing the achievement of a superior outcome. Otherwise, the realist/communitarian proposition will boil down either to 'excuses' in defence of the existing order or to collusion with dominant actors in that order.

The third problem stems from the potential for 'veto groups' to form within national communities and the impact these groups have on national and global welfare. As suggested above, veto groups are likely to emerge when: (i) the group size is small; and (ii) the benefits to be derived from common group action are large (Olson, 1965). Therefore, the larger the number of veto groups in a country, the higher the probability of sub-optimal policy choices. In addition, the ability of veto groups to impose sub-optimal policy choices will increase to the extent that the group can equate its own interests with the national interest that the state is expected to defend against non-nationals (see Ugur, 1995). Unless it demonstrates that these complications do not exist, the realist approach cannot provide an ethical basis for rejecting free movement.

The natural law and egalitarian perspectives

The natural law or egalitarian approaches to the ethics of international migration try to overcome the shortcomings indicated above by focusing on global society or humanity. For example, the natural law approach argues that one's rights arise from one's being human – as opposed to being a citizen or a member of a community. The egalitarian approach, on the other hand, seeks a just distribution of wealth within a global society. Therefore, according to the natural law approach, 'any legal or political arrangement in which citizens have rights which aliens do not have' is unjust and in contradiction to natural law (Finnis, 1992, p. 205; see also Dummett, 1992). The liberal egalitarian approach, on the other hand, considers free movement as a human right comparable with other rights, and the exercise of this right to be necessary to reduce global inequality (Carens, 1992, p. 25; Woodward, 1992, p. 60).

The strength of these arguments stems from their non-contingent nature, which leaves little or no room for discretion or uncertainty. Yet, the natural law and liberal egalitarian approaches, too, ignore the implications of strategic interaction between actors (governments, individuals, groups) at different levels. For example, there is evidence suggesting that economic convergence between nations reduces (while economic inequality increases) the incentives to migrate. Then, the number of people exercising the right to free movement would fall as inter-country and inter-group equality increases. This is unlike the right to free speech, for example, the exercise of which not only contributes to achievement of equality but also becomes more feasible as equality increases. In other words, there is a symbiotic relationship between the right granted and the common good (equality) that it is expected to serve.

Therefore, the natural law and liberal egalitarian approaches must accept that free movement is not a basic right but only an instrument that could enable individuals to escape inequality. If this is the case, then the effectiveness of this instrument should be compared with that of others (e.g., fair trade, better access to capital and technology, etc.) that may also alleviate inequality through convergence of wages and other factor incomes. In short, free movement of people may not be considered as a basic human right, but only as a policy choice, which, preferably, should satisfy ethical and efficiency criteria.

Furthermore, free movement of people should be presented as a basic right only if it can be demonstrated that the exercise of this right does not harm others. All fundamental rights have a 'public good' character in that the exercise of these rights does not reduce the amount of rights available to others with legitimate claims. Neither free movement of people nor that of goods and capital satisfies this condition. All these so-called rights have redistributive effects that generate winners and losers, even though their exercise may lead to an increase in global welfare. Therefore, the ethicality of the free movement cannot be established on the basis of whether or not it constitutes a basic right.

The above analysis suggests that neither libertarianism nor political realism can provide an ethical basis for restrictive immigration policies. Both approaches ignore the possibility that restrictive policies may not serve the common good (i.e., they may not lead to the maximization of social welfare) within the countries that adopt them. Also, both approaches are conducive to a high level of discretion and uncertainty, either in the internalization of externalities or in the management of international migration. Therefore, I conclude that neither libertarian nor realist/communitarian ethics can be invoked against free movement.

However, my analysis also suggests that the ethical case in favour of free movement cannot be based on its conceptualization as a basic right. Yet, the impossibility of conceptualizing the free movement of people as a basic right does not imply that an ethical case for free movement cannot be made. Free movement can still be ethical, because the domain of what is ethical (i.e., right to do) is larger than the domain of basic rights (i.e., rights to enjoy).

The ethics of asymmetric treatment

The inadequacy of the ethical debate concerning free movement is also apparent in the debate on whether it is ethical to treat the free movement of people and that of goods/capital asymmetrically. On the one hand, the liberal egalitarian and natural law approaches argue that both types of movement should be treated symmetrically. Their argument derives from their assumption that free movement is a basic right. This is explicit in the case of free movement of people, but it is implicit in the case of free movement of goods and capital. In that sense, the natural law and liberal egalitarian approaches appear to be avoiding inconsistency at the expense of subscribing to a questionable characterization of free movement as a basic right.

The libertarian approach engages in a different trade-off. It refrains from discussing whether or not free movement of people is a basic right, but accepts explicitly that this is different from free movement of goods and capital. That is because the latter would result only from voluntary contracts concluded prior to the movement itself; whereas people can move between countries with or without prior contracts. The problem here is that this classification is based on questionable criteria. For example, the existence or lack of prior contracts may well be related to whether or not governments are permitting a market in which migrant workers can contract freely with potential employers. If such a market existed, migrants would prefer to secure an employment contract before they migrate to another country. For example, in the 1960s, almost all Turkish migrants secured such contracts before they left for Germany; the ratio of irregular to regular migrants tended to increase significantly afterwards, when securing such contracts was prevented by restrictive government policy. Therefore, the libertarian approach cannot justify the asymmetric treatment of the free movement of people on the basis of whether or not prior contracts exist.

Another problem with the libertarian asymmetric treatment is that it introduces *ad hoc* criteria in addition to the classification criterion mentioned above. For example, Lal (1992) appears to be suggesting *efficiency* and *feasibility* criteria. He argues that restricting the movement of capital may be unethical because restriction impairs economic efficiency or because it would be ineffective given the extent to which national boundaries have been eroded. This shifting basis for asymmetric treatment suggests that the 'objectivity' of the criteria for discrimination becomes even more questionable. In addition, it raises the question as to whether or not restrictions on the movement of people could also be inefficient and ineffective.

The lack of a coherent basis for asymmetric treatment is a problem in the realist approach too. Realism justifies asymmetric treatment by reference to national interest, which is characterized by two features. First, it is defended and maximized by the state. Second, the variable maximized differs from one state to the other because it depends on the position of the state in the international system (see Goodin, 1992, p. 257). One implication here is that asymmetric treatment is justified if states consider free movement of people as a threat to their national interest. The other implication is that one should not expect all states to treat free movement of people in the same way: some states may be more or less restrictive than others. Put differently, the realist logic can be invoked to justify *any* act of discrimination between people and money/capital – either over time or across countries. Then, realism cannot be relied upon to provide a yardstick with which one can distinguish between necessity and political convenience.

This problem is exacerbated by the non-quantifiable nature of the threats to the national interests. For example, realists draw attention to the impact of international migration on racial mix in the receiving country. Yet, they do not provide a consistent measure of how such change is going to harm the national interest. Communitarians refer to the threat posed by immigrants to existing values and norms; whereas conventional realists refer to security risks. However, the measures of such risks/threats are time- and ideology-dependent. In addition, there is no convincing evidence suggesting that countries of immigration have been subject to higher risks/threats because of immigration rather than other factors (e.g., past or current foreign policy preferences). All we have are tautologies such as the following: that 'admitting new people … will inevitably change the society' (Barry, 1992, p. 286); that any country that opens its borders 'may soon find other states taking advantage of its beneficent policy' (Weiner, 1996, p. 173); or that different people are entitled to lead their own different ways of life without undue influence from others. One can hardly rely on such speculations to justify asymmetric treatment.

The ethical case for free movement of people: a proposition

The analysis above suggests that the existing literature does not provide a coherent ethical basis for the argument against or in favour of free movement. We can avoid this shortcoming by defining what is ethical and proposing a measure to verify it. We define ethical as a quality, which implies 'right to do' rather than a 'right to exercise'. The measure that would be used to decide whether or not an action is 'right to do' is the impact of the action on social welfare, understood as the sum of individual/group welfare under strategic interaction between governments and individuals. If this specification is accepted, free movement of people can be considered as a *policy choice* rather than a *basic right*; and its ethicality can be derived from its positive impact on social welfare.

As a policy choice, free movement can be expected to increase social welfare in receiving countries for three reasons. First, free movement enables receiving countries to avoid *direct exclusion costs*. Direct exclusion costs are welfare-reducing because they result from non-productive activities such as increased border controls, increased costs of monitoring immigrants within the country, and increased costs of enforcement. These costs will tend to increase as the world economy becomes more integrated, globalization becomes a dominant trend, inter-country inequality increases, and governments tend to be more receptive to exclusion demands. In addition, some of the factors that increase the exclusion costs (e.g., globalization, market integration, etc.) would also reduce the effectiveness of exclusion. Therefore, exclusion costs are welfare-reducing not only because they result from non-productive activities, but also because exclusion becomes less effective as it absorbs more resources. Free movement will be ethical because it will enable receiving countries to avoid 'absolute waste'.

The second reason why free movement would be ethical relates to *indirect costs of exclusion*. A restrictive policy provides perverse incentives to citizens. For example, it perpetuates labour market rigidities as it strengthens the veto groups, who would deliberately confuse the *equality of employment opportunities* with *entitlement to employment*. In addition, restrictive policies prevent competition and reduce the incentives for skill enhancement and investment in human capital by the incumbent work force. Finally, restrictive policies increase the probability of illegal employment and, thereby, provide perverse incentives to employers to minimize productivity-increasing capital investment. Taken together, these perverse incentives will have a negative effect on social welfare – by discouraging investment, competition, and qualification. Free movement, coupled with the principle of equal treatment with nationals, can enable receiving countries to avoid such consequences by inducing employers and incumbent employees to engage in productivity-increasing investment.

The third reason why free movement would be an ethical policy choice can be deduced from its relative efficiency in stabilizing the flows of migration. The existing evidence suggests that restrictions are largely inefficient in curbing the flow of migrants from countries with low wages and employment opportunities to countries with high wages and employment opportunities. The cases of the U.S.–Mexican border and the continuing increase in the number of undocumented immigrants in the European Union are well known facts in this context.

Free movement is generally perceived as a recipe for unlimited flows of migrants from less-developed to developed countries. Yet, the EU experience concerning free movement demonstrates that this is not the case. The number of Italian, Greek, Spanish or Portuguese workers within other EU countries did not register a sudden increase after their entitlement to free movement. In fact, the number of the citizens of the new Member States registered a relative decline not only in comparison to historical trend but also in comparison to third-country citizens who were subject to strict restrictions (ILO, 1990; Ugur, 1999, p. 134).

One important reason for this trend was the fact that free movement removed the premium on pre-emptive entry (i.e., border jumping) and increased the probability of decisions based on the probability of employment in the destination country. In other words, free movement encouraged potential migrants to act in accordance with the signals about employment opportunities and wage levels in the destination countries. This is in contrast to taking high risks with the anticipation that entry into a closed market in itself would ensure sufficient compensation. In short, given reduced cost of entry and exit under free movement, migration will cease to be a one-way bet. In addition, the demand for labour in the destination countries will be a more significant determinant of migratory flows into and out of the developed countries.

On the basis of this analysis, we can argue that free movement of people would be an ethical policy choice because it can increase social welfare by: (i) questioning the legitimacy of individual or group privileges that cannot be justified on the basis of objective criteria such as skills, effort, productivity or investment in human capital; (ii) encouraging welfare-improving reforms in receiving countries; and (iii) inducing a self-regulatory dynamic that is conducive to manageable levels of migration. The task in the next section is to ascertain the extent to which: (i) international migration involves costs that outweigh its benefits; and (ii) free movement can be considered an ethical policy choice in the light of the findings of the economics literature.

The economics of free movement

In this section, we examine the economic literature on international migration. The aim here is to provide an empirical underpinning to the ethical conclusions derived above.

Theoretical findings on international migration

Attempts at formal modelling of migration date back to Harris and Todaro (1970). Focusing on rural–urban migration in a developing country, Harris and Todaro demonstrated that migration can lead to improvement in welfare, as it eliminates labour misallocation between regions, and that the larger the wage differential between receiving and sending regions, the larger this improvement in welfare will be. They also demonstrated that migration will increase as wages and employment opportunities in destination regions increase; but it will decline as wages in regions of origin and the cost of migration increase.

Borjas (1987b) introduced an important refinement to this model. Using Roy's (1951) model of income distribution, Borjas argued that migration models must take into account the extent of self-selection. Self-selection arises because migration is not a random process. A migrant makes two decisions before migrating: (i) the decision to leave his/her country; and (ii) the decision to go to country A rather than country B. Self-selection may be involved in both decisions, because not all potential migrants emigrate, and the distribution of income in the origin and destination countries can influence the type of migrants countries receive.

Borjas identifies two main types of self-selection. *Positive selection* occurs when only people with earnings higher than average income in the country of origin emigrate. These migrants are likely to be characterized by high skill levels and will move to countries where income distribution is widely dispersed – i.e., the variance of the income distribution is large. That is because a widely dispersed income distribution in the destination country signals to potential migrants that there is a good association between income and skill distributions and that the probability of rewarding high skills is high. A widely dispersed income distribution can also be interpreted as suggesting that it is a destination country where the probability of low earnings or of remaining unemployed is high unless the immigrant has high skills. *Negative selection*, on the other hand, occurs when potential migrants have lower skills and earn less than employees with comparable skills in both the home and destination countries. In this case, these migrants will move to a country where income distribution has a relatively lower variance. That is because the low variance (i.e., the more equitable income distribution) would signal to potential migrants that the risk of unemployment would be small and that the system would reward migrants even if their skill levels were low.

These findings do not suggest that international migration is conducive to lower social welfare. All they suggest is that self-selection may dampen the positive impact of international migration on social welfare and/or exacerbate its impact on earnings and on the employment prospects of low-skilled native workers. Yet, Borjas' findings provide significant insights as to why some policy makers would be inclined to restrict free movement. On the one hand, negative selection would lead to a flood of low-skill labour, which would cause the overall skill level to deteriorate. On the other hand, negative selection implies that income equality in the receiving country is a liability rather than an asset. That is because the more egalitarian a country is, the more likely it is to attract immigrants with low skills.

Although such theoretical possibilities strike a chord with anti-immigrant views held within the low-skill segments of the labour market, they can be questioned on a number of grounds. First, negative selection becomes less of a problem if labour shortages in the destination country are felt in the low-skill segments of the labour market. Secondly, an 'equal treatment' policy that treats migrants and incumbent workers equally will work in favour of the incumbent workers. This is because equal treatment in terms of wages and other employment-related benefits will limit employers' scope to exploit the immigrant labour and thereby will counter-balance any employer bias in favour of immigrants with similar skills to incumbents. Finally, Borjas' theoretical findings are not supported by empirical evidence. For example, Chiquiar and Hanson (2005) have tested Borjas' negative selection hypothesis, finding that: (i) Mexican immigrants into the United States may be less educated than U.S. natives, but they are on average more educated than residents of Mexico; and (ii) the wages of Mexican immigrants would have occupied the middle and upper segments of the Mexican wage distribution had they remained in Mexico and been paid in accordance with current skill prices there.

These findings suggest that negative selection may be a theoretical possibility, but it is not inevitable. True, one can argue that the absence of negative selection in the case of Mexican migrants in the U.S. could be due to dispersed income distribution in the latter. Such arguments, however, would fail to explain the absence of negative selection within European Union countries that are known to have extensive welfare regimes. There is no evidence suggesting that free movement within the EU has led mainly to movement of low-skill workers from relatively less-developed Member States such as Spain, Greece or Portugal into more developed Member States with well-established welfare regimes. If anything, free movement has generally led to increased mobility by high-skill workers across the EU.

Another refinement to the Harris-Todaro model concerns the assumption about the level of employment in the receiving country. The original model assumed employment in the receiving country to be variable. Ghatak et al. (1996, pp. 168–72), however, draw attention to the consequences of migration when employment in the receiving country remains at a constant level. Under this assumption, migration is sub-optimal from the perspectives of individual migrants and society in general. That is because every additional migrant is increasing the probability of unemployment in the destination country. As the probability of unemployment increases, the costs born by those employed in the destination country (whether migrants or natives) will be higher than the benefits accruing to the new, additional migrant at the margin.

However, the constant employment assumption can and should be questioned for two reasons. First, if migrants are *complementary* to incumbent labour, immigration will increase the workforce's productivity. In turn, increased productivity will lead to an increase in the demand for labour (hence employment) at current real wages. Secondly, even if migrants are *substitutes* for incumbent labour, immigration may lead not only to increased unemployment, but also to a fall in real wages. To the extent that real wages fall, the demand for labour (hence employment) will increase. So, irrespective of whether immigrant labour is complementary or substitutes for incumbent labour, there is scope for an increase in the demand for labour in the destination country.

The only qualification that can be made here concerns the distributional effects of migration. If the distribution of skills within the migrant population is similar to skill distribution in the destination country, there will be no distributional effects within the labour force but there will be redistribution from labour in general towards capital. If the distribution of migrant skills is biased towards low skills, there will be a redistribution effect within the labour force as well as between labour and capital (Borjas et al., 1997, p. 3).

This brief review suggests that international migration is conducive to improved global welfare under standard assumptions. In fact, welfare improvement would be possible (albeit dampened) even if full wage convergence does not occur or negative selection proves to be the case. Therefore, at the theoretical level, there is no economic case against free movement of people. But it also suggests that international migration is likely to have inter-group or intra-group distributional effects. Given the overall improvement in social welfare, however, these distributional effects cannot be used to support an argument against free movement of people.

Empirical findings on international migration

In this section, I will examine the findings of the empirical literature concerning migration's impact on gross domestic product (GDP), the earnings of incumbent workers, the risk of unemployment, and fiscal balances. I must indicate at the outset that not all of the findings reported below are based on a free-movement scenario. Even those based on a free-movement scenario relate only to Europe and the United States, and cannot be taken as definite indicators of the costs and benefits of free movement at a global level. Nevertheless, these findings are still pertinent, because they are in line with the predictions of the theoretical model discussed above – which assumes free movement and delineates the implications accordingly.

Migration and GDP

Brücker (2002, p. 7) provides simulation results for the European Union, using a one-good model of a closed economy along with different scenarios concerning labour-market characteristics and migrant composition. One of his findings is based on the assumptions that the labour market remains in equilibrium, manual workers account for 70 per cent of immigrants, and the share of immigrant labour in total workforce increases by 1 per cent. Under this scenario, total GDP in the host country increases by 0.7 per cent. Of this, only 0.006 per cent accrues to native workers, with the remaining increase in GDP accruing to capital. A similar distributional effect is also found by Borjas (1987a).

Brücker (2002) also considers the scenario in which the labour market does not clear. In this scenario, and assuming that the sensitivity of labour demand to wages is –0.4 for manual workers and –1.0 for non-manual workers,[6] the increase in the host country's GDP is nearly halved to 0.39 per cent. Although the change in GDP is still positive, rigid labour markets lead to a fall of –0.22 per cent in the total income of the native work force. The increase in GDP would be slightly higher if the sensitivity of the demand for labour to the change in wages increased – i.e., if the labour market became more flexible.

Borjas et al. (1997, pp. 19, 44) provide some simulation results for the United States. For example, change in total native earnings due to immigration in the 1980–95 period amounted to an increase of about 0.05 per cent of the 1995 GDP if the quantity of capital adjusts. The increase in native earnings would be higher, at 0.13 per cent of the 1995 GDP, if capital is assumed to be fixed. However, these findings are based on the assumption that all workers within a skill group are perfect substitutes. If complementarity exists, the gains will be higher. Another finding in Borjas et al. (1997) is that immigration would have a negative impact on a small group of the least-educated U.S. native workers, who in 1995 constituted 12.7 per cent of those 18–64 years of age.

These findings suggest that free movement is highly likely to have a positive effect on social welfare in receiving countries, even though the magnitude of the welfare gains is small – most probably less than 1 per cent of GDP. The policy implication is that a restrictive immigration policy cannot be justified on the grounds that immigration is welfare-reducing. In fact, one can make a case in favour of free movement under different assumptions about labour market flexibility, capital adjustment, and the extent of substitution or complementarity between immigrants and native workers. This case, however, requires attention to distributional consequences of migration, which are small and can be addressed more effectively through compensation and incentives for skill enhancement.

Migration and the labour market

As far as the impact of migration on the labour market is concerned, the following findings can be listed.

In his work on migration into West Germany, Smolny (1991) reports that migration had positive effects on employment and alleviated labour demand pressure on wage and price inflation. This is confirmed by Chiswick (1986) and Chiswick et al. (1992), who found that immigration had a positive long-term effect through capital deepening and rising native incomes. Similarly, Straubhaar and Webber (1994) found that this was the case for Switzerland. In their work on Australia, Withers and Pope (1985) and Pope and Withers (1993) report that immigration did not increase either the level or the risk of unemployment.

These findings are in line with that of Borjas et al. (1997), who report that a 10 per cent increase in the relative number of immigrants reduces the employment-to-population ratio of the natives only by 0.45 percentage point. In addition, any negative impact was diffused across the country. Borjas et al.

(1997, p. 18) also report on the combined effect that trade and immigration might have had on wage differentials between low- and highly skilled U.S. workers. The combined effect of trade and migration accounts for less than 10 per cent of the increase in the wage differential. Other factors, such as 'acceleration of skill-biased technological change, a slow down in the growth of the relative supply of college graduates, and institutional changes in the labour market', etc., account for more than 90 per cent of the widening wage differential since the late 1970s.

These findings enable us to put the distributional effects of international migration into context. Even though free movement is likely to have some distributional effects on the incumbent labour force, the effect will be small, and only a minority of the incumbent workers (specifically, the low-skilled workers) will be adversely affected. In addition, the adverse distributional effect of international migration accounts only for a small part of the relative decline in the earnings of less-skilled labour. The major causes of this relative decline have been either technological change or labour market flexibility, both of which had been embraced and encouraged by the governments of the destination countries.

A report by the European Integration Consortium (2000) provides similar insights into the likely consequences of free movement within an enlarged European Union. Focusing on Austria and Germany, the two countries that are expected to attract a disproportional share of the migrants from new Member States, the Consortium's Final Report (2000, p. 130) states the following: 'Against the background of empirical knowledge on the labour impact of migration, the projected flows and stocks of migrants will affect neither wages nor employment in the host countries strongly. ... One should recall that an increase of the foreigner share in one branch by one percentage point reduced wages by 0.25 per cent in Austria and 0.65 per cent in Germany. The risk of unemployment is increased by 0.8 per cent in Austria and 0.2 per cent in Germany.'

Brücker (2002) reports that manual wages would fall by 1.05 per cent and non-manual wages would increase by 0.18 per cent if the share of immigrants in the labour force increased by 1 per cent, and if we assume clearing labour markets. If the labour market did not clear (and assuming a semi-elasticity of wages of −0.4 for manual and −1.0 for non-manual workers), manual wages would fall by 0.48 per cent, non-manual wages would fall by 0.19 per cent, manual unemployment would increase by 0.85 per cent, and non-manual unemployment would increase by 0.05 per cent. Brücker also finds that the wages of the native work force fall slightly more as the replacement ratio (the ratio of unemployment benefits to post-tax wage) increases. Wages fall by 0.6 per cent when the replacement ratio is 20 per cent, by 0.67 when the replacement ratio is 40 per cent and by 0.73 per cent when it is 60 per cent.

Finally, ten empirical studies cited by Brücker (2002, p. 20) reflect similar results. Nine out of the ten studies show that 'a 1 per cent increase in the labour force through migration yields a change in native wages in a range ... between −0.3 per cent and +0.3 per cent.' These empirical studies also report that individual unemployment risks increase in a range between zero and 0.2 per cent.

The empirical findings cited above enable us to derive a number of conclusions about the impact of migration on the labour markets of receiving countries. First, the negative effects of immigration on wages and employment of the low-skill labour are small – i.e., less than 1 per cent. In addition, the impact of immigration may be significantly less than that of other factors such as technological change. Secondly, the negative effects of migration tend to increase as labour market rigidity increases. In other words, labour market institutions may be a more significant determinant of the negative effect compared to the characteristics (e.g., skill composition) of the immigrant labour. A study by Angrist and Kugler (2003) also confirms this conclusion and highlights product market imperfections as another source of adverse effects on wages and employment. Thirdly, the most severe distributional consequences of immigration would affect only a small minority of the native work force. Nevertheless, we should not ignore the fact that the earning capacity of this minority is already low. Therefore, the case in favour of free movement must be accompanied by an incentive-compatible compensation scheme that would compensate the low-skill labour and induce it to invest in skill enhancement at the same time.

Migration and fiscal balances

Another impact of immigration concerns fiscal balances. Drawing on analyses of the situation in Germany presented in Bonin (2001) and Bonin et al. (2000), Brücker (2002, p. 27) reports that the effect of migrants on public finance is positive. Net tax payments (i.e., the balance between tax payments and social security transfers plus government expenditures) are positive over the life-cycle of immigrants who arrive between the ages of eleven and forty-eight. At present, around 78 per cent of immigrants belong to cohorts that contribute to a budget surplus. Taken together, the net lifetime contribution of a representative immigrant is around 50,000 euros. These findings are parallel to those of Storesletten (2003), who finds that the net present value of the positive contribution of a young working immigrant to Swedish public finances is U.S.$23,500. This is larger than the loss incurred as a result of admitting a new immigrant, which is U.S.$20,500. The break-even participation rate (i.e., the employment rate at which the gain to public finances is zero) is 60 per cent, which is well below the empirical rate for this group. One should bear in mind the migrant's positive contribution to the Swedish public finances is realized despite the fact that Sweden has one of the world's most comprehensive welfare states. These findings demonstrate the lack of a credible basis for perceptions that portray immigrants as a drain on public finances.

As the above discussion demonstrates, when it comes to the welfare implications of migration, the findings of empirical studies are in line with predictions derived from theoretical models of free movement. These findings also suggest that policy-makers in receiving countries do not actually have an economically justifiable reason to take a stance against free movement. From the perspective of policy-making in destination countries, the only qualification is that there is a definite need for a compensation scheme to reduce the cost of immigration for a minority section of the labour force and induce this section to invest in skill-enhancement.

The governance of free movement

Free movement is often equated with a massive influx of 'foreigners' into developed countries. Even those who are less alarmist express concern about the long-term effects of continuing migration – especially its effect on the ethnic composition of the population in receiving countries. Yet, the European Union's experience of the free movement of people since 1968 suggests that such concerns may not be warranted. As indicated above, neither the number of Greeks nor of Portuguese have increased at alarming rates since the gradual introduction of free movement in the EU (Straubhaar, 1992). It can be argued that low rates of increase in intra-EU migration have been due to relatively small per-capita income differentials between the developed and less-developed members of the EU. Equipped with this argument, some policy-makers and the media in developed EU Member States have been drawing our attention to the flood of migrants from Central and Eastern Europe (CEE) that would occur after accession.

Yet these alarmist predictions are not supported by official estimates. For example, the European Integration Consortium (2000, pp. 121–26) reports that the rate of increase in the number of CEE migrants is likely to be (and remain) modest after the introduction of free movement. Focusing on Germany, the report estimates that the number of migrants arriving annually from CEE countries will grow by around 220,000 people initially, a figure falling to 96,000 by 2010. The total number of CEE migrants living in Germany is estimated to reach 1.9 million in 2010, 2.4 million in 2020 and 2.5 million in 2030. This implies that the proportion of CEE migrants in the German population will increase from 0.6 per cent in 1998 to 3.5 per cent in 2030. This baseline scenario is based on the assumption that the per-capita GDP in CEE will converge towards the EU average at a rate of 2 per cent per year.

When these results are extrapolated to EU-15, based on the present distribution of CEE migrants within these countries, the report estimates that the number of CEE migrants arriving annually will increase by 335,000 initially. The increase will slow down to less than 150,000 by 2010. The total number of CEE migrants will increase to 2.9 million in 2010 and 3.7 million in 2020. A peak of around 3.9 million will be reached by 2032. These figures imply that the proportion of CEE migrants living in the EU-15 countries will increase from 0.2 per cent in 1998 to 1.1 per cent in 2030.

These findings suggest that there might be an 'ideological' rather than a 'real' barrier to embracing free movement as a feasible and ethical policy choice. However, given the futility of the efforts to restrict migration since the collapse of the Soviet bloc, there is now an increasing awareness of the need to 'manage' rather than 'control' international migration. In fact, policy-makers in developed countries are now increasingly inclined to accept that international migration 'cannot be managed effectively … through national measures alone, and that collective efforts … are required to strengthen national capacities.' (Solomon and Bartsch, 2003; see also Salt, 2005). The following paragraphs will try to articulate some general principles that could enhance the chance of success in the quest for managing international migration.

Rethinking the role of the state

The first principle is that there should be a paradigmatic shift in our approach to the role of the state in the regulation of international migration. As is well known, the conventional approach is based on a strictly realist view of the world, in which the state is considered as the sole owner of the authority to determine who may enter and remain in its territory. Although it is not necessary to abandon the concept of the state as the ultimate regulatory authority within its jurisdiction, there are compelling reasons as to why this authority should be redefined.

First of all, positioning the state as the sole authority that determines who enters and remains in its territory may weaken rather than strengthen the state's policy autonomy. This is especially the case here because immigration policy decisions always involve trade-offs between some 'national' interests that the state must prioritize and interests of foreigners who are perceived as outsiders. As indicated in Ugur (1995), this type of 'insider'–'outsider' divide enables even a very small minority of nationals to emerge as veto groups. Such veto groups can easily block immigration policies that might be beneficial to the society at large. The irony is that the more the state is portrayed as a medieval gatekeeper, the more likely it is that such veto groups are able to impose their will both on the policy-maker and on the rest of the society.[7]

The other reason why a strictly realist view of the state reduces policy autonomy is that the failure of restrictive immigration policies generates an exponential increase in the demand for further restrictions. As restrictive policies fail to stem immigration, veto groups become more vocal and critical.

Their criticism will be based on the argument that the state has failed in the very area where it is accepted as the sole authority to act and where it is equipped with the necessary powers to defend the interests of its citizens.

Therefore, the paradigmatic shift in our understanding of the state must involve a move away from the concept of the state as a medieval gatekeeper towards a more modern concept. In this concept, the state is still the ultimate authority in the regulation of migration, but the legitimacy of its regulatory power should be based not on its ability to control immigration. Just as is the case in the area of free movement of goods and capital, the legitimacy of its regulatory policies should be determined by whether its actions are welfare-improving. In other words, and with the exception of security risks, the state's responsibility to its population should no longer be equated with erecting border barriers. The state's responsibility should involve regulation of the *free entry* of migrants with legitimate purposes (e.g., employment and service provision) with a view to increase welfare.

Multilateralism

The second principle should be to embrace multilateralism, just as is the case with respect to movement of goods and capital. This is because unilateral policies are not likely to be either effective or efficient in managing migration. That unilateralism is ineffective is proven by the failure of the restrictive policies to prevent immigration. For example, at the end of the 1990s, it was estimated that each year around 400,000 people entered the EU as a result of human trafficking and smuggling only (EU Commission, 2000, p. 13). This figure represents a four- to eight-fold increase compared to estimates at the beginning of the 1990s and does not include overstays or other types of irregular migrants. Strikingly, it is much higher than the peak number of migrants estimated to move from CEE to the current EU-15 as a result of free movement.

Unilateralism would not be efficient either, because in a world characterized by interdependence, it is conducive to sub-optimal outcomes such as migration deflection and the race towards excessive restriction. In addition, unilateralism involves a high degree of discretion, and thereby reduces the coherence and credibility of unilateral policies. The implication here is that either potential migrants or emigration country governments will always question the legitimacy of the unilateral action and, therefore, they will refrain from cooperation or compliance.

Bilateralism should also be rejected because, in addition to the coherence and credibility problems associated with unilateralism, it involves discrimination. As a result of discrimination, bilateral agreements are bound to remain non-transparent and will always be more costly to implement. Some policy analysts or practitioners (for example, Solomon and Bartsch, 2003; Lagenbacher, 2004;

or the International Organization for Migration) tend to think that regional cooperation may be conducive to an effective management of international migration. These expectations, however, are over-optimistic because regionalism may be conducive to effective global governance only if there is already a multilateral framework within which regional actors must act.[8]

In the absence of a multilateral framework that sets the parameters for collective action, regional arrangements may increase the risk of restrictive policies. This risk is likely to emerge for two reasons.

First, from the theory of international trade policy, we know that the larger the country, the higher its ability to improve its terms of trade by erecting trade barriers. Because a regional bloc is larger than any of its members, it enables a group of countries to improve their terms of trade at the expense of their trading partners. In the case of trade, the improvement in the terms of trade is due to the protectionist bloc's falling demand for imports that, in turn, depresses the export prices of trading partners. Therefore, in the absence of a multilateral framework, a regional bloc may well be motivated to be more restrictive than any of its members individually.[9]

In the case of international migration, welfare improvement is not necessarily the motive for excessive restrictions. The restrictive drive stems from the possibility of 'migration deflection' within a regional bloc. Migration deflection refers to a situation where migrants enter the most restrictive member of the bloc via other member(s) that may have less-restrictive policies. It is because of this deflection risk that the consolidation of intra-EU free movement after the single market has been accompanied by fortification of external borders. Put differently, regional arrangements for migration may become essentially hostage to the preferences of the most restrictive bloc members. The irony is that protectionist members will also be able to secure more effective exclusion, which may not be feasible when each country acts alone.[10]

The second reason as to why regional regimes may be conducive to restrictive migration policies relates to the limited leverage capacity of sending countries. In the absence of a multilateral framework, countries of emigration will be in a weak position to negotiate with destination countries that form a regional bloc. This will be the case irrespective of whether or not sending countries form a regional bloc of their own. The latter, faced with a common stance of the destination countries, can either comply with or reject the proposals on the table. If the first option is chosen, the agreements between the two blocs will reflect the lowest common denominator determined by the preferences of the most restrictive member of the destination-country bloc. If the second option is chosen, the destination-country bloc will react by erecting new restrictions in response to non-cooperation on the part of sending countries.

Overall, in the absence of a multilateral framework, a regional approach to the management of international migration is highly likely to perpetuate the existing levels of restrictions or to generate a drive towards further restrictions. A multilateral framework based on non-discrimination can enable both sending and receiving countries to avoid the prisoners' dilemma involved in non-cooperative interaction.

Non-discrimination

The third principle in the governance of free movement is that of non-discrimination. This should be similar to the non-discrimination principle of the World Trade Organization, which consists of two provisions: most-favoured nation (MFN) and national treatment. The MFN provision ensures that discrimination between trading partners is ruled out – i.e., countries or regional blocs are forced to extend liberalization to all trading partners. More significantly, however, the MFN provision will reduce the probability of resorting to restrictive measures as such measures will affect not only some targeted countries but other partners towards whom a more liberal policy is deemed appropriate.

The national treatment provision prevents another type of discrimination: between nationals and immigrants. This provision will ensure equality in the area of employment-related entitlements such as wages, working conditions, social insurance, health insurance, and hiring and firing conditions. National treatment will reduce any employer bias in favour of migrant labour and, thereby, moderate the wage dampening effect of immigration. Put differently, national treatment is necessary not only to prevent discrimination and possible 'social dumping', but also to limit the distributional effects of immigration.

Finally, national treatment will help eliminate employers' bias in favour of migrant workers employed at lower wages and with restricted entitlements. As a result, it will increase the probability that immigration will be determined by actual vacancies in the receiving country, rather than by the expectation that migrant workers would be able to underprice themselves into jobs through undeclared employment.

A multilateral organization

The fourth principle should involve agreement on the necessity of a new multilateral organization for the regulation of international migration. This can be labelled as the World Migration Organization (WMO) and should exist in parallel to but independently of the World Trade Organization (WTO) and the United Nations High Commission for Refugees (UNHCR). That is because neither the WTO nor UNHCR is appropriate for managing employment-seeking migration. The UNHCR is inappropriate because its main concern is the protection of the basic rights of refugees as a specific type of migrant. Of course, the UN still has an important role to play in terms of setting standards that the new multilateral organization for migration will have to internalize. An example of such contributions is the 1990 International Convention on the Protection of the Rights of all Migrant Workers and Members of their Families, which came into effect in 2003 after having been ratified by twenty (mostly sending) countries (Pécoud and de Guchteneire, 2006).

Recently, there have been suggestions that some principles of the General Agreement of Trade in Services (GATS) can be drawn upon in the global governance of migration. Although the MFN and national treatment principles of the GATS are relevant for the proposed WMO, the GATS regime is essentially a recipe for discretion rather than binding and transparent rules. According to the GATS, governments choose the sectors on which they will make commitments guaranteeing the right of foreign suppliers to provide services. Even for those services that are committed, governments may set limitations to market access and to the degree of national treatment they are prepared to guarantee. In addition, governments can also withdraw and renegotiate commitments. Given these high levels of discretion, the GATS is quite far away from being a model for free movement.

Return agreements

The fifth principle in the governance of free movement is that the proposed WMO should include a model return agreement that must be accepted by all members when joining the WMO. This is necessary in order to ensure that free movement is not a one-way flow and that migrants are aware of the risks involved in free movement. A free movement regime without return agreements would be compromised by an asymmetry that is a mirror image of the current asymmetry between emigration (which is free) and immigration (which is restricted). The current asymmetry is sometimes (and rightly) criticized as an indicator of inconsistency and even hypocrisy because, in a world of sovereign states, the freedom to emigrate cannot be exercised unless there is a state willing to accept the potential émigré.

To avoid the reverse asymmetry that might arise under free movement, governments of sending countries must accept the return of their citizens who fail to secure employment in the receiving country or who are expelled for reasons clearly laid out in the domestic law of the host country. Return agreements are also necessary to signal to potential migrants that they must balance the potential advantages of migration with the risks, including the risk of unemployment and return. In addition, return agreements will also put an end to the criminal stigma associated with deportation and make return a natural part of the migratory movements. As a result, return agreements will increase the probability that the migration decision is not a one-way bet. They will signal to potential immigrants that return to their country in periods of unemployment is not likely to prevent re-entry into the destination country in the future. Consequently, migrants will be less inclined to 'go underground' when their entitlement to remain in the destination country comes to an end because of their failure to find a job.

Conclusions

The analysis above enables us to arrive at a number of conclusions regarding the ethics, economics and governance of the free movement of people. The first general conclusion is that an ethical case *against* the free movement of people cannot be made for two reasons. First, the existing ethical arguments against free movement are based on non-objective and non-quantifiable criteria. Secondly, the analysis underpinning a particular argument against free movement tends to have a narrow focus that fails to capture the interactions between actors at different levels and with different interests, and the implications of such interactions for social welfare. If we define what is ethical as all actions that lead to an increase in social welfare (that is, if we minimize the linkage between ethics on the one hand and sectional interests on the other), then free movement can be defended as an ethical policy choice. Once this is established, it is no longer ethical to treat the movement of people and goods/capital asymmetrically either. Free movement of people, goods and capital are all driven by potential benefits for the parties to the transaction (exporters and importers in the case of goods and capital; migrant labour and employers in the receiving country in the case of migration).

True, all types of movement tend to generate distributional consequences. In the case of migration, the distributional effects emerge as an increased risk of unemployment for low-skilled labour in destination countries, or a relative decline in their wages.[11] However, such distributional effects cannot be presented as a basis for an ethical argument against free movement. This is especially the case when there is evidence suggesting that the distributional effects, in the form of unemployment or wage risks for the low-skilled labour force, tend to be higher as a result of free trade and capital mobility. The redistributive effects of free movement of labour (just as for the free movement of goods/capital) can only imply taxing the beneficiaries of the free movement to compensate those affected adversely. Such taxation will already be part of the tax paid by employed migrants, who pay taxes to finance not only current welfare services that migrants enjoy in the host country, but also infrastructure investments that the migrant may or may not benefit from to the degree that the natives of the host country do. In addition, it is possible to impose an access charge (or an entrance permit fee) that will supplement normal taxation. Such compensation payments will serve the long-term interests of the compensated better if they can be made compatible with incentives for them to invest in skill enhancement.

The second general conclusion is that free movement is likely to increase social welfare in the receiving country – even though the size of the increase is modest. Therefore, there is no sound economic case for rejecting free movement of people as a policy option for receiving countries. Economic analysis and empirical findings suggest that there is only a case for addressing the distributive effect of free movement, which, in any case, is found to be less significant than the distributive effects of technological change in particular and globalization in general. Obviously, one can argue that non-quantifiable impacts of migration may outweigh the quantifiable impacts, and that the economic case alone cannot imply a general case in favour of free movement. Such arguments may be relevant only to the extent that they call for appropriate governance structures that would reduce the risks associated with free movement. They cannot be presented as a basis for rejecting free movement in principle.

The analysis above also enables us to tackle the issue of governing free movement and to identify principles that would reduce the risks associated with free movement: including a welfare-based redefinition of the state's legitimacy, effective international cooperation, institutionalized governance, the principle of non-discrimination, and the principle of symmetry in the treatment of migration and return.

If an ethical or economic case cannot be made against free movement, to what extent is free movement a feasible policy option given the current political climate? The answer to this question is coloured with both optimism and pessimism. On the one hand, there are strong indications that developed countries are aware of the structural factors that would be conducive to higher levels of migration irrespective of the extent of restrictions in place. These factors include persistent and increasing per capita income inequality between countries, different demographic structures, ease of international transport and communications, and increases in the educational levels of people in less-developed countries (OECD, 2003, p. 1).

On the other hand, there are also indications of an emerging trend towards accepting the need for an international framework that would 'manage' rather than 'restrict' international migration. This trend is reflected in both OECD and Council of Europe reports and in the emergence of intergovernmental platforms such as the Berne Initiative (see, for example, Salt, 2005; Solomon and Bartsch, 2003). According to Salt, in the European context, the emerging trend reflects a degree of consensus on a number of principles that are compatible with the principles I identified earlier. These include: (i) management rather than control of migration – a necessity recognized by governments as well as intergovernmental organizations; (ii) recognition of the positive impact of immigration; (iii) a comprehensive approach that avoids unintended consequences of a piecemeal approach; and (iv) cooperation with third countries.

Yet, one should not be carried away with the optimism that these developments may justify. The debate on migration is still coloured with a 'realist' logic that tends to overlook objective criteria in favour of essentially subjective ones, such as nationality and national interests, as a basis for policy-formulation. That is why even in the EU (which offers the most developed regional free movement regime), movement of third country nationals is still considered a prerogative of Member States, which adopt common measures within a loose framework of cooperation and harmonization. In addition, the proposed framework reflects explicit preferences in favour of selectivity, monitoring, and limiting migration as a basis for the successful integration of existing migrants (EU Commission, 2000). These preferences are likely to clash with the principles I proposed earlier. Therefore, free movement and a truly global governance regime still seem beyond what is acceptable in the current political climate. Nevertheless, that something is not practically feasible in the current context does not imply either irrelevance or inferiority in terms of its outcomes. On the contrary, a policy proposal that seems practically unfeasible in the current political climate may be the only way to avoid the pitfalls of political convenience.

Notes

1. For example, Martin (1993, p. 13) warns that 'industrial countries are experiencing their highest ever levels of unwanted immigration, to which there is no end in sight'. On the 'securitization' of immigration, see Heisler and Layton-Henry (1993). For a reaction from the perspective of developing countries, see Matheson (1991).

2. Asylum seekers or the movement of people in the context of trade in services are outside the scope of this paper. This is because these movements are subject to already-existing rules and regulations, embodied in the work of the UNHCR and the 1951 UN Convention Relating to the Status of Refugees, as well as in the General Agreement on Trade in Services (GATS).

3. A classic example of the realist approach to international relations is Morgenthau (1960). Waltz (1979) provides a structural basis for political realism. For a state-centric critique of the realist/neo-realist approach on the basis of interdependence, see Keohane (1986). For a 'globalist' critique, see Linklater (1993). The realist approach to international migration is deeply rooted in international law. See, for example, Oppenheim (1905), Hendrickson (1992). For the application of political realism to international migration, see Weiner (1985, 1996). On the communitarian perspective, see Sandel (1982) and Walzer (1983).

4. For the liberal-egalitarian case in favour of taking international society as the unit of analysis, see Linklater (1993), Carens (1987) and Goodin (1988, 1992a, 1992b). For the case for open borders from a natural law perspective, see Dummet (1992) and Weithman (1992).
5. For a libertarian approach based on individual sovereignty, see Steiner (1992). On the case for capital mobility as opposed to free movement of labour, see Lal (1992). For a critique, see O'Neill (1992).
6. The assumption concerning wage semi-elasticity is based on a number of studies that found that this parameter ranges between 0.4 and 1.1. See, for example, Layard et al. (1991).
7. Examples of veto groups in the area of immigration policy may include trade unions in migrant-intensive segments of the labour market, regional authorities in migrant-intensive regions, xenophobic campaign groups in migrant-intensive neighbourhoods or schools, etc. Although opposing groups or voices can emerge against such veto groups, their influence is likely to be weaker than that of the veto groups when the state (the public policy-maker) is expected to act as a gatekeeper to keep 'trespassers' out.
8. Ugur (2000) discusses why this is the case in the area of trade policy. His main finding is that regionalism may undermine global governance of trade flows unless there is a superior authority to impose sanctions on regional blocs.
9. It must be noted, however, that trade restrictions are conducive to a decline in global welfare. This is because the gains for countries restricting imports are always smaller than the losses incurred by exporting countries.
10. The dynamic involved here is the same as that of veto groups within the national context of public-policy-making. A single bloc member (i.e., a definite minority) can block the relaxation of the bloc's migration policy.
11. Similar externalities are associated with international trade. In fact, as indicated above, international trade may be a more significant cause of income redistribution in importing countries. A different set of externalities is associated with capital movements, which lead to the destruction of traditional methods of production as well as the communities built around them.

Bibliography

Angrist, J. D. and Kugler, A. D. 2003. Protective or counter-productive? Labour-market institutions and the effect of immigration on EU natives. *Economic Journal*, Vol. 113, No. 488, pp. 302–31.

Barry, B. 1992. The quest for consistency: a sceptical view. B. Barry and R. E. Goodin (eds), *Free Movement: Ethical Issues in the Transnational Migration of People and of Money*. New York, Harvester Wheatsheaf, pp. 279–87.

Barry, B. and Goodin, R. E. (eds). 1992. *Free Movement: Ethical Issues in the Transnational Migration of People and of Money*. New York, Harvester Wheatsheaf.

Bonin, H. 2001. Fiskalische Effekte der Zuwanderung nach Deutschland: Eine Generationenbilanz. Bonn, IZA. (Discussion Paper No. 305.)

Bonin, H., Raffelhuschen, B. and Walliser, J. 2000. Can immigration alleviate the demographic burden? *FinanzArchiv*, Vol. 57, pp. 1–21.

Borjas, G. J. 1987a. Immigrants, minorities and labour market competition. *Industrial and Labor Relations Review*, Vol. 40, No. 3, pp. 382–92.

———. 1987b. Self-selection and the earnings of immigrants. *American Economic Review*, Vol. 77, No. 4, pp. 531–53.

Borjas, G. J., Freeman, R. B. and Katz, L. 1997. How much do immigration and trade affect labour market outcomes? *Brookings Papers on Economic Activity*. Vol. 1, p. 1–90.

Brücker, H. 2002. The impact of international migration on welfare and the welfare state in an enlarged Europe. Paper presented at the Oesterriche Nationalbank East–West Conference, 3–5 November.

Carens, J. H. 1987. Aliens and citizens: the case for open borders. *Review of Politics*, Vol. 49, No. 2, pp. 251–73.

———. 1992. Migration and morality: a liberal egalitarian perspective. Barry and Goodin (eds), op. cit. New York, Harvester Wheatsheaf, pp. 25–47.

Chiquiar, D. and Hanson, G. H. 2005. International migration, self selection, and the distribution of wages: evidence from Mexico and the United States. *Journal of Political Economy*, Vol. 113, No. 2, pp. 239–81.

Chiswick, B. R. 1986. Human capital and the labour market adjustment of immigrants: testing alternative hypotheses. *Research in Human Capital and Development*, No. 4, pp. 1–26.

Chiswick, C. U., Chiswick, B. R. and Karras, G. 1992. The impact of immigrants on the macro economy. *Carnegie-Rochester Conference Series on Public Policy*, No. 37, pp. 279–316.

Dummett, A. 1992. The transnational migration of people seen from within a natural law tradition. Barry and Goodin (eds), op. cit. New York, Harvester Wheatsheaf, pp. 169–80.

EU Commission. 2000. Communication from the Commission to the Council and the European Parliament on a Community immigration policy. Brussels, EU Commission. (COM. 757/ final.)

European Integration Consortium. 2000. *The Impact of Eastern Enlargement on Employment and Wages in the EU Member States – Analysis*. Milan and Berlin, EIC.

Finnis, J. 1992. Commentary on Dummett and Weithman. Barry and Goodin (eds), op. cit. New York, Harvester Wheatsheaf, pp. 203–10.

Ghatak, S., Levine, P. and Price, S. W. 1996. Migration theories and evidence: an assessment. *Journal of Economic Surveys*, Vol. 10, No. 2, pp. 159–98.

Goodin, R. E. 1988. What is so special about our fellow countrymen? *Ethics*, No. 98, pp. 663–86.

———. 1992. Commentary: the political realism of free movement. Barry and Goodin (eds), op. cit. New York, Harvester Wheatsheaf, pp. 248–64.

Harris, J. R. and Todaro, M. P. 1970. Migration, unemployment and development: a two-sector analysis. *American Economic Review*, No. 60, pp. 126–42.

Heisler, M. O. and Layton-Henry, Z. 1993. Migration and the link between social and societal security. O. Waever, B. Buzan, M. Keistrup and P. Lemaitre, *Identity, Migration and the New Security Agenda in Europe*. London, Pinter, pp. 148–66.

Hendrickson, D. C. 1992. Migration in law and ethics: a realist perspective. Barry and Goodin (eds), op. cit. New York, Harvester Wheatsheaf, pp. 213–31.

ILO. 1990. *Informal Consultation on Migrants from Non-EEC Countries in the Single Market after 1992*. Geneva, ILO Publications.

Keohane, R. O. 1986. *Neo-realism and its Critics*. New York, Columbia University Press.

Keohane, R. O. and Nye, J. 1977. *Power and Interdependence: World Politics in Transition.* Boston, Little Brown.

Kymlicka, W. 1988. *Liberalism, Community and Culture.* Oxford, Oxford University Press.

Lagenbacher, D. 2004. International migration management – Switzerland's approach. Paper presented at the European Population Forum, Geneva, 14 January.

Lal, D. 1992. The migration of money – from a libertarian viewpoint. Barry and Goodin, op. cit., pp. 95–114.

Layard, R., Nickell, S. and Jackman, R. 1991. *Unemployment.* Oxford, Oxford University Press.

Linklater, A. 1993. Men and citizens in international relations. H. Williams et al., *A Reader in International Relations and Political Theory*, Buckingham, U.K., Open University Press.

Martin, P. 1993. The migration issue. R. King (ed.), *The New Geography of European Migrations.* London, Belhaven Press, pp. 1–16.

Matheson, J. H. E. 1991. The immigration issue in the community: an ACP view. *ACP/EC Courrier*, No. 1298 (September–October).

Morgenthau, H. J. 1960. *Politics among Nations: The Struggle for Power and Peace.* New York, Knopf. (3rd ed.)

OECD. 2003. *Report of the Trade and Migration Seminar, 12–13 November, 2003.* Geneva, OECD.

Olson, M. 1965. *The Logic of Collective Action.* Cambridge, Mass., Harvard University Press.

O'Neill, O. 1992. Commentary: magic associations and imperfect people. Barry and Goodin, op. cit., pp. 115–24.

Oppenheim, L. 1905. *International Law: A Treatise.* 2 vols. London, Longmans, Green & Co.

Passel, J. S., Capps, R. and Fix, M. E. 2004. Undocumented immigrants: facts and figures. Urban Institute. www.urban.org/url.cfm?ID=1000587 (Accessed 21 December 2006.)

Pécoud, A. and de Guchteneire, P. 2006. Migration, human rights and the United Nations: an investigation into the obstacles to the UN convention on migrant workers' rights. *Windsor Yearbook of Access to Justice*, Vol. 24, No. 2, pp. 241–66.

Pope, D. and Withers, G. 1993. Do migrants rob jobs from locals? Lessons from Australian history, 1861–1991. *Journal of Economic History*, Vol. 53, No. 4, pp. 719–42.

Roy, A. D. 1951. Some thoughts on the distribution of earnings. *Oxford Economic Papers*, Vol. 3, No. 2. pp. 135–46.

Salt, J. 2005. *Current Trends in International Migration in Europe.* Strasbourg, France, Council of Europe.

Sandel, M. J. 1982. *Liberalism and the Limits of Justice.* Cambridge, Cambridge University Press. (Cambridge Studies in Philosophy.)

Smolny, W. 1991. Macroeconomic consequences of international labour migration: simulation experience from an economic disequilibrium model. H. J. Vosgerau (ed.), *European Integration in the World Economy.* Berlin, Springer, pp. 376–412.

Solomon, M. K. and Bartsch, K. 2003. The Berne initiative: toward the development of an international policy framework on migration. Washington DC, Migration Policy Institute.

Stark, O. 1991. *The Migration of Labour.* Oxford, Basil Blackwell.

Steiner, H. 1992. Libertarianism and the transnational migration of people. Barry and Goodin (eds), op. cit. New York, Harvester Wheatsheaf, pp. 87–94.

Storesletten, K. 2003. Fiscal implications of immigration – a net present value calculation. *Scandinavian Journal of Economics*, Vol. 105, No. 3, pp. 487–506.

Straubhaar, T. 1992. Allocational and distributional aspects of future migration to Western Europe. *International Migration Review*, Vol. 26, No. 2, pp. 462–83.

Straubhaar, T. and Webber, R. 1994. On the economics of immigration: some empirical evidence from Switzerland. *International Review of Applied Economics*, Vol. 8, No. 2, pp. 107–29.

Ugur, M. 1995. Freedom of movement vs. exclusion: a re-interpretation of the 'insider'–'outsider' divide in the European Union immigration policy. *International Migration Review*, Vol. 29, No. 4, pp. 964–99.

———. 1999. *The European Union and Turkey: An Anchor/Credibility Dilemma*. Aldershot, Ashgate.

———. 2000. Second-order reciprocity in the age of regionalism: the EU's market access strategy and EU-APEC relations. *Current Politics and Economics of Europe*, No. 10, pp. 73–92.

Waltz, K. N. 1979. *The Theory of International Politics*. Reading, Mass., Addison Wesley.

Walzer, M. 1983. *Spheres of Justice: A Defense of Pluralism and Equality*. New York, Basic Books.

Weiner, M. 1985. International migration and international relations. *Population and Development Review*, Vol. 11, pp. 441–55.

———. 1988. *The Company of Critics*. New York, Basic Books.

———. 1996. Ethics, national sovereignty and the control of immigration. *International Migration Review*, Vol. 30, No. 1, pp. 171–97.

Weithman, P. J. 1992. Natural law, solidarity and international justice. Barry and Goodin (eds), op. cit. New York, Harvester Wheatsheaf, pp. 181–202.

Withers, G. and Pope, D. 1985. Immigration and unemployment. *The Economic Record*, Vol. 61, No. 173, pp. 554–63.

Woodward, J. 1992. Commentary: liberalism and migration. Barry and Goodin (eds), op. cit. New York, Harvester Wheatsheaf, pp. 59–84.

Chapter 5

Managing migration: towards the missing regime?

Bimal Ghosh

Human mobility, in terms of the number of people moving across countries, has never been as high as it is today. More are still in the queue – willing and waiting to move. The number of countries in which migrants exceed 10 per cent of the total population has jumped from forty-three in 1960 to seventy in 2000 (United Nations, 2004). Paradoxically, we are also living in a time when governments, inadequately equipped to constructively manage these flows, are showing an increasing resistance to inflows of migrants, alongside a seemingly declining tolerance of foreigners in many receiving societies. Significantly, in 1976, only 7 per cent of the UN's 150 Member States viewed their immigration rates as too high; by 1993 the percentage had jumped to 35 per cent – a five-fold increase in less than three decades. Today, 40 per cent of the UN's 193 Member States have polices aimed at reducing immigration (United Nations, 2002).

The migration mismatch and the need for change

Germane to this paradoxical situation is a growing *mismatch* in the world migration system. On the one hand there are rising emigration pressures in sending countries, accentuated by the attraction, including powerful demand pull, of the destination countries. Opportunities for legal entry, on the other hand, are dwindling. Despite some feeble signs of a change, existing migration policies are proving inadequate to bring these conflicting trends into a sustainable and dynamic harmony. Mostly reactive and inward-looking in their orientation and thrust, and with a focus on unilateral immigration control rather than on migration management through cooperative or multilateral action, these policies are proving inadequate to meet the new challenges of international migration or exploit the opportunities it presents.

Worse still, these policies have been producing some perverse results. Indications abound. Many receiving countries have sharply increased personnel and expenditures to prevent irregular migration. And yet the number of irregular migrants has been rising faster than ever. Indeed, when there are high emigration pressures in sending countries, and powerful demand pull in the destination countries, and especially when the two converge, restrictions on admission do not, by themselves, stop migration; they only drive the movements into irregular channels – this is precisely what is happening today. Moreover, even if draconian measures might slow down irregular migration (as indicated by a temporary fall in irregular entries into the U.S. following the measures taken in the aftermath of 11 September 2001), liberal democracies cannot hold on to them for any length of time except at the risk of deep erosion of the fundamental rights and values on which they are based.

In the U.S., for example, the INS (Immigration and Naturalization Service) budget, at least half of which is devoted to enforcement, including preventing irregular immigration, rose twenty-fold from U.S.$250 million in 1980 to about U.S.$5 billion in 2000, alongside a sharp increase in its enforcement personnel. And yet the stock of irregular immigrants rose nearly three-fold from 3 million to 9.3 million (despite several legalization programmes), with a yearly increase of some 700,000 since the late 1900s (Passel et al., 2004; Chicago Council on Foreign Relations, 2004). Other industrial countries have had similar experiences. In Western Europe, for example, stringent measures and increased costs of controlling immigration have coincided with a rising level of irregular immigration, now estimated at 500,000 a year. To put it differently, at least one in every two people entering the U.S. or Western Europe is doing so in defiance of existing laws and regulations.

Human trafficking – increasingly interlocked with trafficking in drugs and arms, the prostitution of women and girls, and other forms of child abuse – is rising too, with anything between U.S.$10 billion and U.S.$12 billion being channelled annually into this business. Such large-scale movements in defiance of established laws, and often associated with a wide range of criminal activities, have generated a seemingly widespread fear that migration is getting out of control. Should new policy-making take place in a climate of crisis management and continue to be based on a reactive, fragmentary and lopsided approach, this would most likely create a vicious circle of further immigration restrictions and more irregular immigration.

Other human costs associated with the current situation are equally disquieting. Since 1993, thousands of people have died while trying to move, often with the help of traffickers, into Western Europe. For the same or similar reasons, one person is dying, on average, every day on the Mexico–U.S. border. Concurrently, anti-immigrant and xenophobic feeling is rising in many receiving societies, leading to race riots and civil strife and placing strains on inter-state relations. These are far from shining examples or signs of the efficacy of present policies; nor do they testify to the smooth working of the system.

If, as we have just seen, restrictive and unilateral migration policies have not been working well, should we opt for a policy shift to the other extreme of full freedom of movement? We had rather not. This chapter would argue that a regime of unfettered migration, however attractive at first sight, is not likely to do much better than the current policies, and that its political viability, at least from a short-to-medium-term perspective, is highly problematic. Instead, we should strive for a regime of managed migration that is based on the concept of regulated openness and sustained by close inter-state cooperation. But before rushing to any such conclusion we need to look a little more closely at the implications and viability of a regime of 'migration without borders'. This is done below from three different perspectives: economic, human rights and state security.

Migration without borders: the economics of open borders

There is a litany of theories that seek to explain economic migration. But none is more straightforward or assertive than the classical and neoclassical theories of economic migration in claiming its all-round beneficial effects. Given that these theoretical models also eschew any government intervention in migration, it seems appropriate to start discussing the economic merits of an open-door policy by using them as a frame of reference.[1]

According to these theories, when workers move from labour-surplus, low-wage countries to capital-rich, high-wage countries, it leads to a more efficient use of labour and narrows inter-country wage differences. The receiving country gains as immigration removes labour scarcity, facilitates occupational mobility, and often adds to the country's human capital stock. By doing so it reduces wage-push inflationary pressure, helps fuller utilization of productive capital and boosts economic growth, including exports. For the sending country, the movement implies less unemployment and a boost for economic growth through access to strategic inputs and returning skills. The migrants themselves gain from higher wages and improved productivity in the receiving country. These theories also suggest that with wages rising in the sending country and falling in the receiving country, factor costs, eventually equalized between the two countries, come to a stop.

Should these theories be right, how much can the world gain? In 1984, Hamilton and Whalley made an assessment of possible efficiency gains. They used a simple methodology to infer differences in the marginal productivity of labour between countries and across regions owing to barriers to inward mobility of labour and came to the conclusion that when these barriers were removed, the efficiency gains could double the world income. More recently, Dani Rodrik (2005) postulated that, because wages for similarly qualified workers in developed and developing countries differ sharply – by a factor of ten or more as against differences for commodities and financial assets that rarely exceed a ratio of 1:2 – the potential gains of openness could be enormous; roughly twenty-five times as great as the gains to be made from the liberalization of the movement of goods and capital. He thus estimates that even a modest relaxation of restrictions on the movement of workers – such as the temporary admission of workers from poorer countries equal to no more than 3 per cent of the richer countries' labour forces – could yield a benefit of U.S.$200 billion for the developing world. In a simplified world with no national borders and no limits to the internationally free movement of labour, migration overcomes country-specific scarcities or surpluses in factor endowments and enhances global welfare.[2]

These theoretical models bring out the positive outcome of free movement of people and suggest that it makes economic sense to strive for a policy of migration without borders. But there is an important snag: these models are based on a set of fixed assumptions, which are seldom valid. For example, it is assumed that labour is homogeneous; that perfect competition and mobility exist in labour markets; that there are no public goods and no public intervention; and that both economies of scale in production and the output mix in the economies remain unchanged. The reality is often different. Immigrant labour may be skilled or unskilled; even within the same skill category labour may not be fully homogeneous across countries; competition in the labour market may be hindered due to rigidities and segmentation of the labour market.

The more we relax these neoclassical assumptions, whether on theoretical or empirical grounds, the more we see that, despite its positive contribution to global economic efficiency and income, free movement does not lead to economic convergence between sending and receiving countries; nor does it imply that its benefits will be equally shared by different groups of population within the countries. For example, a regime of open borders is likely to lead to a massive outflow of skills from poorer to richer countries, fuelled by high unmet demand for skills in these countries. This will also be helped by the fact that skilled people in poorer countries have better access to market information, wider social contacts and more financial resources to migrate. As the endogenous growth theories indicate, the positive externalities of the deployment of such skills, and capital inflows, reinforced by their spillover effects, will help accelerated growth in the richer countries, while the large-scale depletion of their human capital will restrain growth in the poorer countries.

True, transnational networking can help countries of origin tap some of the skills and talents of the diaspora community, but there are limits to the extent that this can be done. Given the importance of human capital as a complement to capital and technology, skilled migration tends to depress the wages of unskilled workers and worsen the situation of those left behind. It can aggravate poverty in sending countries.[3] Free movement of persons can thus contribute to a process of further polarization of the world society and undermine domestic stability.

While the receiving country benefits from the positive externalities associated with skilled immigration, this can at the same time create distributional tension between immigrants and the local population within the host society. To the extent that there may be segmentation and rigidities in its labour market, part of its labour force may fail to benefit from the high growth, high wages sector. Wider wage and income disparities could then exacerbate the feelings of relative deprivation of those left behind. In such a situation, inflows of unskilled immigrants could make matters worse as they are likely to compete with those at the lower end of the local labour force. The average wage of these local workers will then fall and they may very well feel that their jobs are threatened.

Under a regime of free movement, receiving countries could also be exposed to negative externalities of a non-economic nature. Massive inflows of foreigners could place a heavy strain on the receiving country's physical infrastructure and public services, including housing facilities, transport system, schools and medical services. Costs of integration could be particularly high when foreigners have a sharply different ethnic, cultural and religious background from that of the resident population. If they overburdened the overall capacity of the receiving society to integrate them, exceeding the margin of tolerance of foreigners, tension and even conflict could follow, threatening economic growth and social stability.

To sum up, while a regime of open borders seemingly leads to substantial efficiency gains in the world economy, its distributional impact and its positive as well as its negative externalities are likely to widen wage and income disparities both within and between rich and poor nations, and generate both domestic and international tension. The overall economic case for open borders is further weakened by non-economic considerations. If, as is likely, a regime of free movement leads to massive inflows of foreigners, the institutions and social services of the host country – and its capacity to integrate these new arrivals – could come under heavy strain, undermining social stability.

International political economy and free movement

Looking at the issues involved from the perspective of international political economy, some analysts have expressed doubts about the existence of a valid basis for the emergence of a regime of free movement. They have further argued that, even if such a regime did emerge, it is not likely to survive, given the divergence of interests and bargaining power between the two parties. Their basic argument is that cooperation between the migrant-sending and migrant-receiving countries lacks some of the essential ingredients that could lead to the emergence of a true multilateral regime and subsequently sustain it. Most importantly, there is no common or collective good and no need for collective action binding the two groups (Meyers, 2002). This is because the (richer) destination countries can individually guarantee an adequate supply of labour to meet their needs. Given this situation, a regime of free labour mobility would be inherently unstable because a destination country could stop immigration at its will (e.g., in times of recession and due to domestic political pressure following large waves of immigration) and a (poorer) country of origin would not be able to reciprocate in kind. This is different from the case of trade, where reciprocity works because the flows as well as the benefits are assumed to be bi- or multi-directional.

Using some empirical evidence across regions, this line of argument also predicts that the more countries diverge in income and economic development, the less likely it is that an agreement for free movement will emerge; and even if it does, the more likely it is that it will suffer a setback. To put it differently, multilateral agreements on free mobility of labour between countries of similar levels of income and economic development, and involving relatively small number of migrants, are the ones that are most likely to emerge and survive. However, somewhat paradoxically, this goes directly against the allocational efficiency argument, which, as discussed above, shows that, other things being equal, the higher the inter-country wage disparity, the greater are the efficiency gains under the free movement model.

Although some of the assumptions underlying the view that a regime of freedom of movement is non-viable are open to question, it nonetheless cogently points to some of the inherent weaknesses of multilateral agreements based on full freedom of movement, as reflected in various setbacks suffered by a number of regional or subregional agreements providing for freedom of movement.

Ethics of human rights and freedom of movement

To what extent does a rights-based approach implicit in the concept of freedom of movement lend support to an open border policy for movement of people? Some analysts consider freedom of movement as an essential part of personal liberty, arguing that it is fundamental to the dignity and development of individual personality (Dowty, 1987). A rights-based argument also maintains that since freedom of movement for those lawfully present within a country is a widely recognized human right, there are no convincing grounds why this should not be extended across countries.

Free movement of persons, like free circulation of information and ideas, has also been a cherished ideal for Western democracies for a good part of their history. Western Europe takes pride in its liberal and humanistic tradition of freedom of movement, now enshrined in the EU treaties. Should this not be extended to the world at large?

But in dealing with the outside world, the EU Member States have so far applied the concept only selectively, in the light of contextual political circumstances and ideological considerations. For example, Western democracies, including the EU-15, had long pressed for freer emigration from the former Soviet Union and the communist countries of Central and Eastern Europe as a measure of their liberalization. In the wake of the fall of the Berlin Wall, many in the latter countries had imagined that this doctrine would give them open access to countries of their choice in the West. But when the ex-communist states stopped restricting exit, liberal democracies in the West imposed new restrictions on entry (which have not yet been fully suppressed even after the 2004 and 2007 enlargements of the European Union). In reality, the doctrine was never intended to recognize the individual's right to enter a state other than his/her own.

What about the juridical position? Numerous international and regional instruments, starting with the 1948 Universal Declaration of Human Rights, affirm the right to leave any country and return to one's own country. But none expressly grants non-nationals the right to enter a foreign state. In the absence of such a right to enter, freedom of movement remains an 'incomplete' right. The right to leave is conceded, but there is no corresponding obligation for states to receive non-nationals on their territory. A state can refuse a non-national's entry. Some limitations are, however, imposed on a state's prerogative to deny admission – when this could adversely affect family life, or the welfare of a child, or entails discrimination. In addition, the right to leave is completed in one specific context – 'the right to seek asylum' and the corresponding duty of states not to impede the exercise of the right by returning individuals to a country where they may face persecution, torture or other serious violations of their human rights. Although the receiving state may send the individual to a safe third state, in practice the right of non-refoulement amounts to a right to enter at least until an alternative safe state of refuge has been found.

However, these are very specific situations, and do not make a general case for open borders allowing free movement of persons.

Some of the internationally recognized principles governing fundamental human rights are of relevance to this discussion, nevertheless. For example, under the Universal Declaration of Human Rights, 'all human beings are born free and equal in dignity and rights.' The Preamble to the Charter of the United Nations reaffirms 'faith in fundamental human rights in the dignity and worth of the human person'. And the Annex to the ILO Constitution affirms that 'all human beings ... have the right to pursue both material well-being and their spiritual development in conditions of freedom and dignity, of economic security and equal opportunity'. Conceptually at least, such norms and principles can be used to justify free movement and open borders. And yet, as Goodwin-Gill (2000) puts it, 'the doctrine of inalienable rights, inherent in the individual, has frequently had to give way to sovereignty, considered in its high positivist sense, as an absolute assertion of right and power in a society of competing nation-states.' Not surprisingly, efforts made in the 1980s by the UN Human Rights Commission to extend the right to free movement by dealing with the correlative right to enter failed to make any headway (United Nations, 1989).[4]

In short, existing human rights norms do not provide an adequate basis to allow free movement of people. The primacy of state sovereignty prevails. *Freer* movement of persons is likely to be better achieved, as argued below, through mutually convenient agreement between states based on the principle of regulated openness, and within a multilateral framework.

Sovereignty, security and open borders

Can open borders and free movement be reconciled with state sovereignty and security? Basic to the concept of sovereignty is a state's prerogative to protect its borders and security. Control of immigration – the authority to decide who may or may not enter its territory – is a core attribute of such prerogative. Sovereignty and security are therefore frequently cited as an overriding factor that rules out free movement in a world without borders. How valid is this argument?

Although there is no comprehensive international law on state security and migration, exclusion and deportation of persons thought to pose a security threat is firmly established in state practices. In the wake of the terrorist attacks of 11 September 2001, the issue of state security has gathered an added significance and a new urgency.

The concept of state sovereignty, as it emerged in Westphalia in 1648, should not, however, be seen as a static one. Modern states have constantly adapted themselves in response to exigencies of transnational forces and changes in world society. The inter-penetration of markets and economies, the growth of transnational communities (including systems of dual nationalities) and the emerging concepts of post-national human rights and citizenship are no doubt having a discernible impact on the traditional authority and behaviour of the nation-state, with a shift of attention, especially since the end of the Cold War, towards inter-state cooperation and coalition. These changes in its behaviour or its modalities of operation are an expression of the evolution of the nation-state in an attempt to preserve its authority and influence in a changing world – and not of its diminished concerns for its territorial integrity or security.

However, even while admitting that a state's legitimate concern for security may circumscribe its willingness to admit non-nationals, thus leading to restrictions on freedom of movement, one needs to be clear about the concept of security *in relation to migration*. Broadly, a distinction can be made between (i) security defined in terms of the territorial integrity and military capability of the nation-state and (ii) security interpreted more widely to include human security, domestic political and economic stability, and social and cultural cohesion of its population.

The realist – or high politics – approach to international relations seeks to emphasize the narrow, geo-strategic and political dimension of security. Sovereign states shape international relations in which only war and peace really matter. Anything that threatens state sovereignty or circumscribes its self-seeking interest may be considered a security threat (Keohane, 1984), which arises principally from outside its borders and which primarily, if not exclusively, is of a military nature (Ayoob, 1995). The low politics approach, on the other hand, widens the concept of security by highlighting transnational relations as a factor that can significantly affect internal stability and subvert or undermine the authority and integrity of the nation state. State security is thus inclusive of the sustained ability to preserve dominant patterns of culture and behaviour within a society. Or, to put it differently, it includes the absence of threats – or a low risk of damage – to the acquired values and established culture in a national society (Wolfers, 1962; Baldwin, 1997).

Despite these differences, these two broad approaches – focusing on either external or internal security – are largely complementary, rather than contradictory or mutually exclusive (Keohane and Nye, 1977). Taking a broader view of security, some analysts, such as Myron Weiner (1995), have argued that population movements can destabilize societies and regimes, both in the industrial democracies and (especially) in the developing world, and that this destabilization could affect the receiving as well as the sending countries: migration, he argues, is thus a security issue.

There is little doubt that certain types of population movement and activities associated with them have a security dimension. These include irregular migration and human trafficking, intertwined with trafficking in drugs and arms. In the summer of 1993, when a series of smuggling ships with irregular Chinese migrants entered the U.S., President Bill Clinton declared that the tactic posed a threat to national security and authorized the National

Security Council to direct the response (*New York Times*, 16 September 1994). Experience in Africa shows that the presence of large numbers of irregular migrants can provide a ready reserve of recruits to create public disorder or support other subversive activities. The riots in Kano, Nigeria, in 1980 and 1982, in which undocumented immigrants from five West African countries were alleged to be involved, has been cited as an example of the security risk associated with irregular migration (Adepoju, 1983). Clearly, however, under a regime of free movement without borders, risks associated with irregular migration and human trafficking would cease to exist.

On the other hand, when groups involved in civil conflicts have ethnic, cultural, religious or ideological links across national borders, the conflicts – as the crises in Bosnia and Kosovo in Europe and in the Great Lakes region have shown – can suck the neighbouring states into a wider conflict, threatening national and regional stability. The situation worsens when the conflicts generate refugee flows that spill over into the neighbouring states. In such situations, a policy of open borders could easily aggravate the security risk, with refugees acting both as agents and victims of conflict. Significantly, during the Gulf crisis of 1991, it was the potential destabilizing effect of refugee flows on neighbouring states that was cited in the UN Security Council resolution (no. 68) as the immediate threat to international peace. The same argument – the threat to regional stability of large refugee flows – was frequently used to support NATO intervention in Kosovo. In the current conflict in Iraq, the porous borders of the country are viewed by many as helping insurgent activities, and thus undermining Iraqi security. Under a regime of free movement, international criminal gangs are likely to have an easy run across countries, threatening the stability especially of weak and vulnerable states.

The security dimension of migration can of course be overblown. For example, in April 2000, the governor of Tokyo suggested that foreigners and *sangokujin* (a highly charged term to describe Korean and Chinese immigrants) could stage an uprising during a natural disaster such as an earthquake (*Financial Times*, 12 April 2000). The Japanese government was of course quick to distance itself from the governor's remark. However the concern of a relatively homogeneous society over the entry and presence of a large, highly visible and culturally dissimilar foreign population cannot be lightly dismissed. Preservation of a national identity and social cohesion is often a cherished goal even for countries that are not closely wedded to a societal model of complete cultural homogeneity (see for example Schlesinger, 1992 and Huntington, 1996). Switzerland, with its structural labour shortages, has followed a liberal immigration policy since the nineteenth century. But in 1963, when the number of foreigners reached a million, constituting one-eighth of the total population, an increasing belief in a political danger that national traits would be debased gained ground. In the wake of the fall of the

Berlin Wall, sudden waves of East–West migration caused great concern in Western states: population movement came to be perceived as a security threat, although in the event massive flows did not materialize.

Should borders be thrown wide open it may be difficult for the potential receiving states to avoid concerns that massive immigration would undermine their culture and social harmony; just as sending states may feel threatened by the loss of their human resources. In the post 11 September climate, in the potential receiving states the threat could well be perceived to be to national security itself.

Managed migration and regulated openness

Before we go further to make a case for managed migration, we need to know more about what it really means. Central to managed migration is the establishment of a regime that is capable of ensuring that movement of people becomes more orderly, predictable and productive, and thus more manageable. Based on the principle of regulated openness and sustained by close cooperation between nations, the new arrangement will avoid knee-jerk reactions to the rising emigration pressure and will seek, instead, to bring emigration pressure and the opportunities for legal and orderly entry into a sustainable harmony. In doing so, it will balance and harmonize the needs and interests of the sending, receiving and transit countries and the migrants themselves. Basic to the whole approach are three main conditions:

1. In keeping with their joint commitment to the above objectives, labour-abundant sending countries should take all necessary measures to reduce the pressure for disorderly and unwanted migration. For their part, migrant-receiving rich countries should take measures to support the sending countries' efforts to reduce pressures for disorderly migration. In addition, they should provide new opportunities for legal entry to meet their own real labour market and demographic needs, both current and projected, and fulfil their human rights and humanitarian obligations.
2. Both groups of countries would agree to work jointly and adhere to a set of specific guidelines or norms to ensure coherence of policies and action to attain the above objectives. Nations would retain their right to determine the level of immigration levels in a flexible manner, but they would be guided by the agreed set of norms and principles. The normative framework would also help avoid policy contradictions, whether at home or abroad. In other words, migration policy objectives should be factored into the formulation of policies in other related areas such as trade, aid, investment, human rights and the environment.

3. The arrangement must be comprehensive to embrace all types of migratory flows – labour migration, family reunification, asylum seeking and refugee flows. While each type of these flows has its own characteristics, experience also shows that movement of people is being increasingly influenced by mixed motivations and composite factors. This accounts for the current trend of 'category jumping': when one entry channel is closed, a potential migrant seeks entry through some other channel that may seem more promising. To avoid undue pressure on one channel due to diversion of the flow from some other channel or channels, the arrangement must be based on a comprehensive strategy.

Specific objectives of the managed migration regime

Using the above as the broad policy parameters, the specific objectives of the managed migration regime can be summed up as follows:

1. Help capital-rich industrial countries meet their labour market and demographic needs through increased, planned and orderly intakes of migrants and through more effective integration policies, while enhancing the contribution of migration to the development of sending countries.
2. Increase the efficiency of the global economy through a more rational allocation of human resources, including through freer trade- and investment-related movements and other forms of temporary migration.
3. Encourage short-term inter-country exchanges conducive to scientific progress and the cultural enrichment of human society.
4. Enhance the credibility of the international migration system and the confidence that the public, including potential migrants, has in it by making national migration laws and practices more predictable and transparent.
5. Create conditions to make immigration control more cost-effective and minimize the negative externalities, including inter-state tensions, associated with irregular and disruptive movements.
6. Facilitate the return of migrants, including rejected asylum seekers and irregular migrants, in conditions of human dignity, and help in their effective re-integration in the country of origin.
7. Ensure, on grounds of both human rights and humanitarian considerations, effective protection and assistance, as required or genuinely needed under varying circumstances, to migrants, asylum seekers and refugees on a more predictable basis.

Comparative advantages of managed migration

A regime of managed migration, juxtaposed against one based on free movement of people, clearly has some distinctive merits and operational advantages.

From an economic point of view, the 'migration without borders' scenario has the merits of ensuring a more efficient allocation of available human and other resources, from which both the world economy and the migrants gain. However, it also creates losers and winners both between and within countries. As free movement unleashes a powerful but polarized process of development, its distributional effects could be explosive. A regime of regulated openness, based on a set of mutually agreed norms and principles among nations, can secure a good part of the efficiency-related benefits of openness while avoiding much of the distributional tension and negative externalities that free movement would generate. Unlike in the case of open borders, where asymmetries of interest could weaken the basis of cooperation between sending and receiving countries, a regime of regulated openness is likely to be more sustainable as it seeks to ensure orderliness and predictability in population movement in which all states have a common interest and also because of its built-in linkages to other issue areas such as trade and human rights in which they have shared stakes.

As for human rights, an adequate case cannot be made for an open borders policy on the basis of the provisions on freedom of movement in existing international human rights laws. Nor is such a regime likely to be directly concerned with the protection of human rights. A regime of managed migration, by contrast, has a direct stake in the protection of human rights. This is because orderliness and manageability of movement depend to a large extent on the protection of human rights. Gross violation of human rights in countries of origin is one of the principal causes of disorderly and disruptive movements of people. Experience has also shown that when the movements are disorderly – and especially when they are irregular and unwanted (as disorderly movements often are) – the risk is greater for further violation of human rights in countries of transit and destination. When this happens, management of migration becomes more difficult and costly; it also entails heavy social and human costs. By straining inter-state relations or provoking conflicts, the situation could even threaten regional and international stability.

Nation-states must be prepared to protect human rights, including those of migrants on their own territory, from another perspective as well. A state has a basic, internally driven, and widely recognized obligation to protect the rights and welfare of its own citizens, even when they are in another state as migrants. It cannot effectively meet this obligation except through inter-state cooperation based on reciprocity. Obviously, such reciprocity between states can best be guaranteed within a multilateral framework or regime. This requires a state to treat non-nationals in the same manner as it would like its nationals to be treated abroad (Ghosh, 2003).

Thus, those anxious to defend the human rights of migrants and those involved in managing migration clearly share a common interest. This two-way linkage between protection of human rights and orderliness in the movement of people finds due recognition in the proposed regime of managed migration.

Finally, viewed from the perspective of security, the case for an open-doors policy is particularly weak, especially if security is interpreted in a wide sense. As already noted, free movement across borders could be seen as a direct challenge to state sovereignty. Exercising their sovereign rights, nation-states can of course decide to accede to a regime of free movement, as EU Member States have been trying to do among themselves. But at a time when receiving countries are 'erecting an ever increasing number of barriers to all types of migratory movements' (UN, 1998) and, as noted earlier, as nations are becoming less and less enthusiastic about migration, it is difficult to imagine that they would be willing to give up control over their borders.

True, the nation-state cannot just be concerned with its own security. It needs to be sensitive to its other vocations and obligations as well, and must respond to the demands from the various groups of its citizens. For instance, if due to perceived threats to its security, a state systematically follows a policy of immigration restriction, it will fail to take advantage of the global labour market and address the needs and demands of powerful business groups; and the academic community and intellectuals will feel frustrated for lack of opportunities to interact with their peers who might otherwise have come from abroad. States, as discussed above, have an obligation to protect the human rights of their citizens abroad and those of the non-nationals on their territory.

A regime of managed migration should make it easier for the state to strike a balance between its genuine concern for security and its other obligations and vocations. It is also likely to be easier, or at least less difficult, for governments to accept, for a number of reasons. First, governments will not lose control over the national borders or the level or types of intakes (although they will be guided by a set of agreed principles). Second, given the active participation of governments in managing and monitoring the arrangement, they would also have the feeling of 'owning' it. Third, the transparency and predictability of the regime, coupled with the close inter-state cooperation on which it is based, should help build confidence among governments in protecting national security. Further, to the extent that the arrangement succeeds in enhancing orderliness in movements and lessening the current pressure and confusion affecting the immigration control systems, it will be more difficult for potential terrorists to take advantage of the situation.

Three pillars of the regime

The proposed regime would have three main pillars: a set of shared objectives, a normative framework, and coordinated institutional arrangements. The objectives of the regime and the normative principles, in the form of guidelines setting forth the obligations and commitments of the participating states, have already been briefly discussed above. What about the institutional arrangements?

Coordinated institutional arrangements

A normative framework, however sound, is not enough to achieve the policy objectives outlined above. Also needed is an adequate institutional arrangement at the global level to promote, and mobilize support for, the policy objectives: to provide timely assistance, when needed, to governments, migrant groups and others involved and to monitor progress in the implementation of the agreed principles and approaches. The present global institutional arrangement, marked by a multiplicity of agencies, a proliferation of programmes and a fragmentation of approach, is highly diffused, leading to at least three major negative consequences. It leaves a number of gaps in institutional mandates, and several situations affecting groups of migrants and refugees tend to be ignored or are given only marginal attention. At the same time, the multiplicity of agencies leads to wasteful overlapping and duplication of international effort. Finally, the fragmented institutional set-up inhibits a comprehensive and coherent policy approach to the multi-dimensional problem of migration management (Ghosh, 1995).

Under the proposed new regime, existing international arrangements would be streamlined and better coordinated, to (i) promote internationally harmonized migration policies and principles; (ii) ensure a coherent and concerted response to the various interrelated issues affecting international migration; and (iii) monitor the progress made and results achieved in these areas.

Would it be useful to have a single international body to bring the proposal to fruition? An increasing recognition of the present malaise in the world migration system has led some policy analysts and scholars to argue for the establishment of a World Migration Organization (WMO). Jagdish Bhagwati, for example, has been strongly pleading for a WMO (2003). His two interrelated arguments are that such a central organization would be in a position to (i) compile existing migration laws and regulations and codify 'enlightened' immigration policies and best practices; and (ii) establish a comparative 'immigration scoreboard' showing the degrees of openness of different countries towards immigration, in order to pressurize countries with restrictive immigration policies to open up. It is doubtful, however, whether these two arguments are strong enough to justify the establishment of a whole new international organization. Compilation of existing migration laws and regulations, while clearly useful, could well be done by existing legal and technical bodies of the United Nations system, in collaboration with other concerned intergovernmental agencies such as the OECD, with some limited funds made available for the purpose.

As regards the scoreboard, we need an internationally agreed set of criteria to serve as a yardstick to evaluate country performances. Migration is a sensitive and complex subject: different governments and individuals may have different ideas as to what constitute 'enlightened policies' and 'best practices'. The OECD's annual table of development aid performance, and the WTO's trade policy review, are credible and meaningful precisely because of the existence of a set of well-defined and previously agreed on norms and principles in each of these fields.

For sure, the existence of a WMO could be of enormous help in developing and negotiating the new international regime, including a set of agreed norms serving as a yardstick to evaluate country performances. But as matters stand now, governments seem hardly anxious to start a whole new organization to deal with international migration. On the other hand, the adoption of the proposed multilateral regime – or even a sufficiently broad global consensus towards it – would enhance the case for a strong WMO; just as the adoption of the UN Convention on the status of refugees in 1951 accompanied the establishment of the UNHCR in 1951. Clearly, if and when a new migration regime is adopted by the international community, a strong international body will be needed to facilitate and oversee its application, monitor progress made and ensure all necessary follow-up action.

What it is not or does not do

In order to avoid any possible confusion about the nature of the proposed regime, it is useful to explain further what it implies and what it does not.

A comprehensive arrangement to complement and reinforce existing international instruments, not to supplant them

The proposed regime reinforces and complements, but does not supplant, existing sub-regimes dealing with cross-border movements, namely, the 1951 UN Convention on the Status of Refugees and the 1967 Protocol and the GATS (General Agreement on Trade in Services) covering temporary trade-related movement of service providers; or the UN Convention Against Transnational

Organized Crime (2000) and its two Protocols concerning trafficking in persons and smuggling of migrants. Likewise, it reinforces, but does not otherwise impinge on, existing international instruments for the protection of rights of migrant workers such as the 1990 UN Convention on the Rights of All Migrant Workers and Members of their Families, and the series of Conventions and Recommendations adopted by the ILO on the subject.

An inter-state accord of convenience: not a supranational construct

The proposed regime is not to be seen as a supranational construct, imposed upon nations by an external authority, but as a freely negotiated arrangement of convenience between sovereign states to better control their borders and increase their capacity to manage migration. Globalization has enhanced the importance of transnational or extra-territorial issues. Nation-states forge alliances between them, as they have always done, to manage these important matters in the transnational space, to preserve territorial integrity and to meet obligations to their own citizens. Migration is one such issue. Participation in the new regime thus only strengthens and enriches the sovereignty of the nation-state. It implies evolution of the nation-state, not its erosion.

A hard or a soft instrument?

It is not a hard instrument with provision for sanctions in case of non-compliance with its principles or norms, but a framework agreement enjoining states to adhere to a set of agreed guidelines. In particular, as already noted, it does not impose any national quota for immigrant intakes. Although a binding agreement with provisions for sanctions has the advantage of discouraging free riders, two important considerations would seem to rule it out. On a technical level, it is doubtful if the comprehensive nature of the regime and especially the wide range of promotional measures included in it could lend themselves as subjects of a hard instrument. The framework agreement can however be complemented or reinforced by hard instruments in certain specific areas that are ripe for, and amenable to, such action – such as human trafficking as exemplified by the UN convention of 2000, or readmission and return of migrants.

A global or a regional approach? A false dichotomy

If close inter-state cooperation is a central feature of the new arrangement, how best to achieve this? Would it not be easier to develop such cooperation at least in the initial stage through a regional, rather than global, approach? Two arguments are usually advanced in favour of a regional approach. First, confidence-building is supposed to be easier and negotiation less difficult within a small group of contiguous countries, especially when they have a high degree of economic and social convergence, as in the case of the EU. Second, a significant proportion of cross-border movements is intra-regional. Countries within a specific region are therefore more likely to have a shared concern and a common interest to manage migration through joint action.

In reality, however, an exclusive reliance on a regional approach suffers from serious limitations. Confidence-building may prove to be more, rather than less, difficult within a specific region, especially when it is marked by glaring intra-regional disparities. As experience shows, fear and mistrust of the hegemonic influence of powerful neighbours often create tension and hold up progress towards genuine cooperation. Second, migration today is a truly global process. The main source and destination countries are not necessarily located in the same region. In fact, contrary to the popular impression, much of the migratory inflows to the U.S. and the EU, for example, stem from outside the respective regions (United Nations, 1998). As for Europe, figures for recent years showed that almost half of the foreign population resident in industrial (northern and western) Europe was from outside the European region.

Indeed, it is difficult to imagine how the pressure for emigration can be effectively absorbed within the confines of each specific region. Contemporary migration defies such a seemingly tidy geographical arrangement. Also, as exemplified by the constantly changing pattern of human trafficking, migration flows today can change directions at short notice in response to changing circumstances, suggesting the need for a global approach. In short, efforts at the regional and global levels can be mutually supportive as long as there is a common global framework to ensure policy coherence. If, however, different regional groupings move in different directions, tensions between them might be unavoidable. For example, tightening of immigration control by destination countries in one region (e.g., Western Europe) is likely to divert the flows to other regions (e.g., North America), and vice versa, creating interregional tension. As in the case of trade, they could then turn out to be stumbling blocks rather than building blocks constraining global cooperation. Efforts at the regional and global levels can also combine the advantages of both 'bottom up' and 'top down' approaches. But for this to happen, the global and the various regional processes must move in the same direction, interlocked by shared objectives and common principles.

The tasks ahead

The past few years have seen growing recognition of the rising financial, political and human costs of the malaise in the world migration system and of the need to reform it. One significant indication of this is the speed with which the international community in 2000 moved to adopt new international instruments to combat organized crime, including human trafficking and migrant smuggling. But mobilizing international efforts for punitive action against criminal and dehumanizing activities is one thing; launching comprehensive and pro-active policy measures to address the root causes of the migration malaise is quite another. The latter calls for more sustained and painstaking efforts at consensus-building, involving different stakeholders with conflicting as well as convergent interests and concerns.

Some tangible progress has, however, been made in this direction. Already in 1993, at the invitation of the Commission on Global Governance, I submitted a paper outlining a proposal for the establishment of a new, more coherent and comprehensive global regime to better manage the movement of people (see Commission on Global Governance, 1995). Following this proposal, an ambitious project, dubbed New International Regime for Orderly Movement of People (NIROMP), was launched in 1997 with the financial support of UNFPA and several European governments. An interregional meeting, held in Geneva in September 1997, generally endorsed the concept and objectives of a global migration regime and encouraged follow-up action. A second interregional meeting, also held in Geneva (December 1999) to help develop a common framework for the return and re-integration of migrants, generally agreed on a set of guidelines as a preliminary basis for an internationally harmonized approach to return and readmission. These guidelines subsequently found an echo in the Declaration and Programme of Action adopted at the West African ministerial conference on migration held in Dakar in 2000.

In 2001, the findings of the NIROMP project were widely debated in a series of meetings held in a number of capitals and university centres in Europe and the United States. The positive reactions from these meetings, as well as from a large section of the press, seemed to indicate a growing interest in a new multilateral regime to manage migration. With its consensus-building activities – through research, publications and networking – NIROMP seems to have been successful in setting into motion a process that is likely to gather further momentum in the years ahead, thus carrying forward the proposal presented in 1993 to the Commission on Global Governance.

This increasing interest in the matter is also reflected in the Bern Initiative, which was launched in 2001 by the Swiss government to mobilize support for closer inter-state cooperation and to develop a coherent policy approach to better manage international migration (Federal Office for Refugees, Switzerland, 2003). *The Hague Declaration on the Future of Asylum and Migration Policy*, launched in November 2002 in the presence of UN Secretary-General Kofi Annan and the heads of several international organizations, is still another example of the growing recognition of the need to develop a concerted global approach to migration management, and of the gathering support for it (Annan et al., 2002).

Finally, the Global Commission on International Migration (GCIM), established in 2003 by Switzerland, Sweden and several like-minded governments, further stressed the relevance of progressing towards migration management. Its 2005 report discussed possible reforms to the institutional framework. It addressed migration at the intergovernmental level and proposed the creation of a 'Global Migration Facility' to 'ensure a more coherent and effective institutional response to the opportunities and challenges presented by international migration' (Global Commission on International Migration, 2005, p. 82). While the outcome of this suggestion remains uncertain, the GCIM report spurred unprecedented activity concerning international migration at the international level, including the organization, in September 2006, of a High-Level Dialogue on International Migration and Development at the United Nations. These recent developments not only confirm the widely perceived need for changes in migration policies, but may also pave the way for innovative approaches to migration that would share the spirit of the propositions presented in this chapter.

Notes

1. For empirical evidence of the economic consequences for both sending and receiving countries of previous migration flows see Mehmet Ugur's contribution to this volume (Chapter 4). It should be noted, however, that under a policy of 'migration without borders' not only the level of international migration, but also its whole configuration, is likely to change profoundly – as are their economic consequences.
2. The potential economic gains from free movement to migrant-sending countries are thus used by some as an argument for open borders based on social justice, according to which immigration controls by rich countries perpetuate international economic inequality and so should be removed. 'Citizenship in Western democracies' is thus 'the modern equivalent of feudal privilege' (Carens, 1987).
3. This is a result of shifts in the distribution of wages and salaries in favour of highly skilled workers and against low-skilled workers and a possible decline in the average incomes of those left behind (Griffin and Khan, 1992).
4. The case for open borders is also sometimes challenged on the grounds that communities and, by extension, members of nations have the right to preserve their integrity and exercise at the collective level the equivalent of autonomy granted at the individual level (Miller, 1988).

Bibliography

Adepoju, A. 1983. Undocumented migration in Africa: trends and policies. *International Migration*, Vol. 21, No. 2.

Annan, K., Lubbers, R. and Rudge, P. 2002. *Declaration of the Hague on the Future of Refugee and Migration Policy*. The Hague, Society for International Development (SID), Netherlands Chapter.

Ayoob, M. 1992. The international security system and the Third World. W. C. Olsen (ed.), *Theory and Practice of International Relations*. New Jersey, Prentice Hall, pp. 224–41.

———. 1995. United Nations and civil wars. T. G. Weiss (ed.), *United Nations and Civil Wars*. Boulder, Col., Lynne Rienner.

Baldwin, D. 1997. The concept of security. *Review of International Studies*, No. 23, pp. 5–26.

Bhagwati, J. 2003. Borders beyond control. *Foreign Affairs*, Vol. 82, No. 1, pp. 98–104.

Carens, J. 1987. Aliens and citizens: the case for open borders. *The Review of Politics*, Vol. 49, No. 2, pp. 251–73.

Chicago Council on Foreign Relations. 2004. *Global Views 2004*.

Commission on Global Governance. 1995. *Our Neighbourhood: The Report of the Commission on Global Governance*. Oxford, Oxford University Press.

Dowty, A. 1987. *Closed Borders: The Contemporary Assault on Freedom of Movement*. New Haven, Conn., Yale University Press.

Federal Office for Refugees, Switzerland. 2003. The goal of the Berne Initiative. Berne, Switzerland, Federal Office for Refugees. (www.old.iom.int//DOCUMENTS/ OFFICIALTXT/EN/Goal_E.pdf Accessed 21 December 2006.)

Ghosh, B. 1995. Movement of people: the search for a new international regime. The Commission on Global Governance (ed.), *Issues in Global Governance*. London, Kluwer Law International, pp. 405–24.

———. 1998. *Huddled Masses and Uncertain Shores: Insights into Irregular Migration*. The Hague, Boston and London, Kluwer Law International/ Martinus Nijhoff.

———. (ed.). 2000. *Managing Migration: Time for a New International Regime?* Oxford, Oxford University Press.

———. 2003. *Elusive Protection, Uncertain Lands: Migrants' Access to Human Rights*. Geneva, International Organization for Migration.

———. 2005. Economic effects of international migration: a synoptic overview. IOM, *World Migration Report 2005*.

Global Commission on International Migration. 2005. *Migration in an Interconnected World: New Directions for Action*. Geneva, GCIM.

Goodwin-Gill, G. 2000. Migration – international law and human rights. Ghosh, op. cit., pp. 160–89.

Goodwin-Gill, G. and Newland, K. 2003. Forced Migration and International Law. T. A. Alienikoff, and V. Chetail (eds), *Migration and International Legal Norms*. The Hague, T. M. C. Asser Press, pp. 123–36.

Griffin, K and R. Khan, A. 1992. Globalization and the developing world: an essay on the international dimensions of development in the Post-Cold War era. Geneva, United Nations Research Institute for Social Development.

Hamilton, B. and Whalley, J. 1984. Efficiency and distributional implications of global restrictions on labour mobility: calculations and policy implications. *Journal of Development Economics*, No. 14, pp. 61–75.

Human Development Report Office (HDRO). 1992. *Occasional Papers*. New York, HDRO-UNDP, p.34.

Huntington, S. P. 1996. The West: unique, not universal. *Foreign Affairs*, Vol. 76, No. 6, November/December, pp. 28–46.

Independent Commission on International Development Issues. 1980. *North–South: A Program for Survival*. Boston, Mass, MIT Press.

IOM/UNFPA. 2001. The NIROMP process – an overview. Geneva, IOM.

Keohane, R. 1984. *After Hegemony: Cooperation and Discord in the World Political Economy*. Princeton, N. J., Princeton University Press.

Keohane, R. and Nye, J. 1977. *Power and Interdependence: World Politics in Transition*. Boston, Little Brown.

Meyers, E. 2002. Multilateral cooperation, integration and regimes: the case of international labour mobility. La Jolla, Calif., University of California. (Working Paper 61.)

Miller, D. 1988. The ethical significance of nationality. *Ethics*, Vol. 98, No. 4, pp. 647–63.

Passel, J. S., Capps, R. and Fix, M. E. 2004. *Undocumented Immigrants – Facts and Figures: Data at a Glance*. Washington DC, Urban Institute. www.urban.org/url.cfm?ID=1000587.

Rodrik, D. 2005. Feasible globalizations. M. Weinstein (ed.), *Globalization: What's New?*, New York, Columbia University Press, pp. 96–213.

Schlesinger Jr., A. 1992. *The Disuniting of America: Reflections on a Multicultural Society*. New York, Norton.

Society for International Development (SID). 2001. *Declaration of The Hague on the Future of Refugee and Migration Policy*. The Hague.

United Nations, Department of Economic and Social Affairs. 2004. *World Economic and Social Survey: International Migration*. New York.

United Nations Population Division. 1998. *World Population Monitoring, 1997*. New York, UN.

———. 2003. *International Migration 2002*. New York.

United Nations. 1989. *Report of the Working Group on Indigenous Populations*. New York, UN. (E/CN.4/Sub.2/1989.)

U.S. Congress, Senate Committee on Foreign Relations. 1911. *Treaty of 1832 with Russia*. Washington DC, Government Printing Office.

Weiner, M. 1995. *The Global Migration Crisis: Challenge to States and Human Rights*. New York, Harper Collins.

Wolfers, A. 1962. *Discord and Collaboration: Essays on International Politics*. Baltimore, Md., Johns Hopkins University Press.

Chapter 6

Open borders and the welfare state

Han Entzinger

The immigration/welfare paradox

In his book *Beyond the Welfare State*, the famous Swedish economist Gunnar
Myrdal stated – back in 1960 – that, in its essence, the welfare state is
protectionist and nationalist. Its functioning is based on feelings of solidarity
within a given community. The members of that community, usually a nation-
state, may be willing to accept income transfers, but preferably among those
with whom they share a sense of togetherness. In an era of globalization, and of
growing international migration as one of its expressions, this may become
increasingly difficult. Even though, according to many liberal economists, open
borders are, in the end, beneficial to the economic well-being of world society as
a whole, this does not mean that every single country would automatically
benefit from such openness. Welfare states in particular can only function
properly when the dividing line between insiders and outsiders is crystal clear,
because anyone who contributes to one is also a potential beneficiary, and vice
versa. In addition, the welfare state has been designed to redistribute scarce
resources between individuals, between generations and sometimes also between
regions. These transfers always take place from those who are better off to those
who are less well off *within* a given society and *within* one and the same system.

One may argue that immigration constitutes a challenge to that system.
Incorporating people who are not part of the welfare state from cradle to grave
threatens its logic, particularly its intergenerational nature. In certain phases of
their lives (e.g., working age) people are net contributors, in other phases (e.g.,
youth, old age) they are net beneficiaries. Most transfers in the welfare state
take place from the rich to the poor, from the higher to the lower social and

economic strata. In a situation in which immigrants are strongly represented in the latter, as in much of today's Europe, their reliance on social security provisions and on social policy instruments is likely to be relatively high. In several European welfare states, certain social policy schemes have now acquired a strong immigrant dimension (Ederveen et al., 2004; Ekberg, 2004). To insiders, this phenomenon is understandable: it can be explained easily as an outcome of low schooling, a lack of opportunities, and discrimination. However, if such a situation becomes permanent, it may become a basis for dissatisfaction with immigration in general and it may undermine solidarity, a quintessential condition for a proper functioning of the welfare state. This trend may be reinforced as a consequence of a lack of identification among certain immigrants with the nation of which they have become a *de facto* – or sometimes even a *de jure* – member. This too has a potential to undermine solidarity and may easily be exploited politically, as recent developments in several European countries illustrate. There is some research evidence that many migrants in Europe have stronger loyalties to their countries of origin than to the place where they actually reside (e.g., Phalet et al., 2000). This may become a liability, particularly in situations where immigrants are net beneficiaries of the welfare system.

The basic hypothesis of this chapter is that the openness that characterizes immigration societies and the closed nature of the welfare state are difficult to reconcile. Immigration asks for permeable borders, but the welfare state functions best within a closed system, which most often coincides with the nation-state. Will the two ever be reconciled? Even though some sociologists have pointed at what Grete Brochmann (1999) calls the *immigration/welfare paradox* (see also Bommes, 1999), this is not a very popular field of study – as it is full of pitfalls and political sensitivities that decent politicians do not always like to face. Yet, continuing immigration may force us to reconsider the foundations of the national welfare state, of which solidarity and equality are basic characteristics. Of course, globalization and immigration are not the only challenges to the welfare state. Ageing populations, growing individualization, changing perceptions of risk, bureaucratization, more flexibility in labour relations, an intrinsic trend of rising costs, and shifting ideas on the relationship between public and private responsibilities – all add to the need to reconsider the welfare state's foundations. The world did not stand still during the last hundred, or even fifty, years, nor did the welfare state. However, it is not always easy to convey this message to those with a vested interest in the present situation.

Forms of solidarity

In the previous paragraphs the hypothesis has been developed of a tension between the openness of an immigrant society and the closed nature of the welfare state. In what follows I will further explore the nature of this tension. How does it become manifest, what is its scope and how can its effects be handled? First, I will have a closer look at the concept of solidarity and what it means for the functioning of the welfare state. I will then analyse to what extent immigration actually has an impact on the welfare state. We will see that, in certain situations, immigrants indeed constitute a liability for its functioning, while in other cases they actually form an asset. I will try to find an explanation for such differences and will then embark on a discussion of some alternative routes towards a solution.

Solidarity is a crucial concept in understanding the functioning of the welfare state. More than a century ago, Émile Durkheim was the first modern sociologist to study this concept systematically. He saw solidarity as a major characteristic of a community that consists of individuals who have frequent contacts with each other and who share certain interests (Durkheim, 1967 [first published 1897]). Solidarity lies at the root of integrated communities, characterized by feelings of togetherness. On the basis of such feelings, individual members are prepared to share certain risks and to organize income transfers so as to make sure that everyone has a decent living and that peace and social order be maintained. Durkheim convincingly argued that, as society had modernized and as the division of functions – in a sociological sense – had become more differentiated, the basis of solidarity had shifted. More 'primitive' societies were characterized by a strong 'collective conscience', while the members of 'modern society' were not necessarily bound by a shared ideology, but rather through the division of labour and of other functions in society, which increases their interdependence. This shift from 'mechanic' to 'organic' solidarity has gone hand-in-hand with a growth in size, complexity and pluriformity of modern society. As a consequence, modern society requires more formal rules than did its predecessors. And rules require decisions on the scope of their application, as well as on inclusion and exclusion.

Solidarity in modern society is by definition exclusive. Anyone who claims to show solidarity with everyone else in the world shows in fact solidarity with nobody. Solidarity always implies including some people and excluding others. Whether or not an individual can be admitted into the community of solidarity depends on the type of solidarity under consideration. In this context, a distinction can be made between formal and informal solidarity (De Beer, 2004). Informal, or 'warm' solidarity as De Beer calls it, is generally shown towards people with whom one has a personal and concrete relationship, usually of an affective nature. In its strongest form it can be found between husband and wife, parents and children or, in more general terms, within families or among friends. Doing charity work for the underprivileged or giving money to a beggar also are forms of informal solidarity. Formal or 'cold' solidarity, by contrast, refers to those forms of solidarity between individuals who, in principle, are anonymous to one another. It is channelled through formalized intermediaries, such as the tax and social security system or insurance companies. Actually, the growth of the welfare state during the past century has formalized certain forms of solidarity that, in the past, were informal. Obviously, formal solidarity requires more precise criteria of entitlement than informal solidarity does.

Another relevant distinction is the one between unilateral and mutual solidarity. The former implies that the individual who displays solidarity with somebody else does not expect that person to reciprocate. This is the case, for example, in charity, but also in public assistance schemes. Those who contribute to that system as taxpayers are not usually the same people as those who benefit from it. Mutual solidarity is different: if you do the shopping for a neighbour who is ill, you expect that neighbour to do the same for you if you fall ill. At a macro level, this is the way insurance companies operate. The contributions you pay to that company in order to be protected in case of need are directly related to the likelihood that such a need may arise. Doing so enables people to run risks that they cannot cover individually. Therefore, a system of mutual solidarity is in principle beneficial to everyone who participates in it.

These four forms of solidarity are presented in Table 6.1.

Table 6.1: Forms of solidarity: mutual vs. unilateral and formal vs. informal

	Mutual solidarity	Unilateral solidarity
Formal ('cold') solidarity	Insurance	Public assistance; development aid
Informal ('warm') solidarity	Distribution of tasks between spouses; helping neighbours or friends	Care for one's children; giving to a beggar

Source: de Beer, 2004, p. 29.

A crucial characteristic of the welfare state, as we have seen, is the formalized nature of its solidarity. However, there is a substantial difference between unilateral and mutual forms of formalized solidarity. The latter requires its members to contribute in accordance with the risks they run or the benefits they may expect. This is not only the case for insurances, for example for healthcare or road accidents, but also for most private pension schemes or unemployment schemes. The level of individual contributions to such schemes is usually related to the level of the benefits one may expect upon retirement or after becoming unemployed. Therefore, the circle of those who are entitled to participate in these schemes is potentially unlimited. Anyone willing to contribute to the system in accordance with the perceived individual risks is free to become a member. Membership need not be limited to a specific category, such as citizens or residents of a particular country. In this light it is understandable that insurance companies have become very much internationalized. This enables them to spread their risks over a much larger population than before, but they can only do so successfully from a basis of mutual solidarity.

Schemes based on unilateral solidarity, by contrast, must set clear limits to membership, as major income transfers from rich to poor members take place within them. Here, issues of inclusion and exclusion are of particular relevance. Membership in the collectivity must be defined in clear terms, and it is here that the openness of an immigrant society and the closed character of the welfare state clash most visibly. Should newly arrived immigrants contribute to the system and – more importantly – be entitled to claim benefits in case of need? If so, what additional conditions should be fulfilled, for instance, regarding length of residence? There is a fairly common understanding that irregular migrants are not entitled to the benefits of schemes based on unilateral solidarity, even though they may contribute to such schemes, either directly or through their employers. However, under certain conditions, welfare provisions are made available to undocumented immigrants as well, for example in healthcare, particularly in emergency situations. Also, their children who are of schooling age have a basic right to education. In all European welfare states, legally residing immigrants are in a different situation. They are generally entitled to participate fully in formal schemes of unilateral solidarity, even if they do not hold citizenship of the country where they live. Certain restrictions, however, may apply, usually depending on the length of one's residence and employment records. In the United States, rules tend to be stricter than in much of the European Union: non-U.S. citizens are excluded from most national schemes of public assistance.

Public assistance schemes provide the most outspoken example of unilateral solidarity since there is almost no personal overlap between contributors and the beneficiaries. Other schemes, however, also have certain elements of unilaterality, though usually less outspoken. Examples here are public pension, family allowance and disability schemes. Most often employers or workers – or both – are the contributors to these systems, but anyone over a certain age, anyone with children or anyone with a disability is entitled to their benefits, irrespective of one's present or previous economic activities. In order to prevent abuse such as free-riding or other forms of evasive behaviour, contributing to these schemes has been made mandatory for workers and employers. Thus, even though public pension, family allowance and disability schemes are not usually funded with taxpayers' money, they can be considered unilateral welfare provisions, characterized by income transfers from the rich to the needy, though in a somewhat less outspoken manner than for public assistance schemes. The same applies to healthcare in countries with a nationalized health system.

Immigrants and welfare-state benefits

The next question that must be dealt with is to what extent immigrants actually make use of the social security system and, more precisely, how strongly they are represented among those who benefit from schemes that are partly or fully based on unilateral solidarity. As we have seen, this is a politically delicate question. Any overrepresentation of immigrants, no matter for what reasons, may easily foster anti-immigrant feelings and put a strain on solidarity between the established population and new arrivals, between 'insiders' and 'outsiders'. This may explain why relatively little research has been carried out on these matters so far. Existing data, however, present a rather mixed picture. Major variations do exist, not only for the different schemes, but also by country.

A most authoritative study on this subject resulted from a comparative project coordinated by Boeri, Hanson and McCormick for the Fondazione Rodolfo Debenedetti (Boeri et al., 2002, p. 66). They compared levels of social security dependency among people of immigrant origin for ten of the EU-15 Member States. The authors of this econometric study allowed for some relevant differences between native populations and immigrants, for example in their educational levels and in age. In many countries, but not in all, immigrants tend to be younger and less well-educated than non-immigrants. This may enhance their dependency on certain welfare benefits, such as those that cover the risk of unemployment. Immigrant status indeed has a positive and significant impact on unemployment benefit dependency in some European countries, particularly in Denmark, the Netherlands, France, Austria and Finland. However, this is not the case in other countries, particularly in Germany, the United Kingdom, Greece and Spain. Immigrant populations also benefit more strongly from family allowance schemes than non-immigrants do. This is the case in all European countries included in the study. However, these differences disappear if one accounts for the fact that immigrants tend to have more children than natives, and at a younger age. Only in France and Spain does reliance on family allowances among immigrants remain above the national average even after this correction, while it is below that average in the United Kingdom. The authors explain these differences by pointing at what they call 'residual effects' such as self-selection (migrants may be attracted by high levels of social security), migration network effects, discrimination or differences in portability of entitlements. Finally, in the sphere of old-age pensions, there is a strong under-consumption in absolute terms in all countries concerned, simply because immigrant populations are younger than the national averages. Among those who are entitled to old-age benefits, no differences could be found between the two categories in any of the countries studied.

In absolute terms, important differences in the levels of social security entitlements for immigrants and non-immigrants exist in all European countries included in the study. Immigrants draw more than non-immigrants on unemployment allowances and on family benefits, but substantially less on old-age pensions. However, if one allows for relevant factors such as level of education, age structure and length of residence, most differences become much smaller or even disappear altogether. Inter-country differences are more persistent for unemployment benefits than for the other schemes studied. The authors note that countries with relatively ungenerous unemployment schemes (Spain, Greece, United Kingdom) tend to have significantly lower proportions of beneficiaries with an immigrant background than countries with more generous systems. Germany constitutes the exception to this general pattern: in that country, fewer immigrants are unemployed than in other EU countries with more generous employment schemes; this may be because in the past Germany actively encouraged its migrant workers to return to their countries of origin after they had become unemployed.[1]

The most direct and outspoken form of formal and unilateral income transfer is public financial assistance to those who have no or too little income of their own, but this was not included in the above-mentioned study. I am not aware of any systematic inter-country comparative research on this matter, but some data are available for individual countries. In the Netherlands, for example, it has been found that 40 per cent of the funds for public assistance are allocated to the 10 per cent of the population that has a non-Western immigrant origin. This gap is smaller for second generation immigrants than for first. Immigrant reliance on disability schemes, which in the Netherlands sometimes serve as a more generous substitute for public assistance, is also quite high. This is particularly so among the first generation of 'guest workers' who were recruited from Turkey and Morocco around 1970, but who lost their low-skilled jobs as a result of a restructuring of the Dutch economy during the 1980s (Roodenburg et al., 2003).

Similar findings have been reported for Sweden, where in 1999 the total budget on a per capita basis for social welfare allowances, housing allowances and unemployment benefits in the age group of sixteen to sixty-four for immigrants was more than double that of native-born Swedes. The differences were particularly striking for social welfare allowances (public assistance), where, also measured per capita, entitlements among immigrants were almost ten times higher than among non-immigrants (Ekberg, 2004). Unlike the results reported by Boeri et al., these data have not been controlled for age and skill levels. They do reflect a labour-force participation rate that is considerably lower among immigrants than among non-immigrants. For some immigrant communities in countries such as Sweden and the Netherlands, that rate is no less than fifteen percentage points lower than the national average (Ederveen et al., 2004). In a report on this phenomenon for Sweden, Ekberg concludes that the cost of poor labour market integration of immigrants in Sweden adds up to 3 billion euros per year (Ekberg, 2004, p. 209). Von Loeffelholz and Thränhardt (1996) drew a similar conclusion in an older study on Germany, while Wadensjö (2000) did the same for Denmark. On Denmark, Ekberg concludes that because of their poor employment situation immigrants make more use of the public sector than they contribute to the system in taxes. This implies a negative effect on the native Danish population's disposable income. He then suggests an immediate link between this phenomenon and the enormous impact that issues around immigration and the integration of immigrants into Danish society have had for the political system in Denmark in recent years (Ekberg, 2004, p. 209). A study carried out jointly by three Dutch government agencies also suggests a link between the migrants' poor economic performance and the 'commotion surrounding immigration' (Ederveen et al., 2004, p. 104).

These studies may well be right in their analyses. A relatively heavy reliance by immigrants on certain welfare provisions has the potential of provoking inter-community tensions in our increasingly diverse societies, thus putting solidarity at a strain. However, this is not the situation in all European countries. In their comparative analysis, Boeri et al. found large differences across these countries with respect to welfare dependency among immigrants (Boeri et al., 2002). Much of the existing literature attributes these differences to the specific characteristics of the respective migrant populations.[2] From their analyses, however, they conclude that there are also residual factors that cannot be attributed to migrant characteristics. These residual factors are strongest in countries with generous welfare systems. Discrimination is one of these factors, but Boeri et al. also find a high correlation with welfare generosity, expressed as the overall level of social benefits. This high correlation, particularly evident in the use of unemployment benefits, leads them to suggest that the most generous countries, such as Denmark and the Netherlands, may act as 'welfare magnets' (p. 89). Through self-selection and network migration, they may have attracted more migrants than other countries have. If they are right in their conclusions, we now have some empirical evidence for the immigration/welfare paradox, which states that the openness of an immigration society is hard to reconcile with the protectionist nature of the welfare state.

Immigration as an asset

We should not be tempted to conclude from the preceding section that immigration automatically and under all circumstances constitutes a liability to the welfare state. A situation where migrants are not net beneficiaries, but net contributors, is equally conceivable. The first large-scale recruitment of low-skilled workers from the Mediterranean by the welfare states of northern and western Europe was very successful in fostering economic growth in these countries, thus enabling them to maintain and even expand their welfare arrangements. Only after a dramatic and rather sudden economic restructuring that wiped out many of the low-skilled jobs did these (then former) migrant workers begin to rely on welfare arrangements themselves. This trend was reinforced by large-scale family reunification, which tied the migrants even more strongly to their country of residence and its welfare arrangements. Returning home would mean losing one's income, but staying on meant being trapped into the welfare system, and thus into marginality, in a country to which one hardly identified. This explains many of the integration problems that several European countries experience today, and which are the outcome of a rather unique historical combination of economic developments and social policies.

Today's situation at the lower end of the labour market is different, but equally paradoxical. The majority of migrants who enter Europe legally are family members of earlier migrants or refugees. Neither of these two categories is being selected on the basis of their potential contribution to the economy, and these new arrivals therefore constitute a potential challenge to the welfare state. Their qualifications are not necessarily in demand. Consequently, many have to fall back on social security and to follow costly integration programmes (although these can just as well be seen as an investment in their future). Meanwhile, gaps at the lower end of the European labour markets are being filled with undocumented migrants, who have no entitlements. It is truly paradoxical that many of those newly arriving migrants who contribute to the economy – and therefore indirectly and sometimes even directly support the welfare system – are excluded from its benefits, while those new arrivals whose presence (except for refugees) is only a consequence of earlier immigration are included into it. The paradox lies exactly in such differential treatment, which runs counter to the egalitarian principles that are at the basis of the welfare state.

There are more reasons to believe that the immigration/welfare paradox is a product of specific developments of the past decades and, therefore, that it is not unavoidable in future. As we have just seen, the paradox arose from a situation where low-skilled migrants came in shortly before their jobs began to disappear. Today's needs for migrants lie primarily at the intermediate and higher skill levels. As a result of demographic developments, these needs are likely to grow, rather than to decrease, particularly in Europe. As a general rule we may argue that the higher their skill levels, the more likely migrants are to become net contributors to the system rather than net beneficiaries. Besides, it must be kept in mind that letting in highly skilled migrants may save welfare states from spending considerable sums on educating and training them. Moreover, many of these people may return to their home countries when the work is done, or upon retirement. This again saves considerable sums on healthcare and on other forms of support at old age. The higher the migrants' skill levels, the more potential they have and the less likely they are to be forced to life-long dependency on welfare provisions in a host country where they do not feel at home. This phenomenon may also explain the growing reluctance in Europe to grant formal residence to migrants with low skills. If, however, the demand for low-skilled migrants in certain sectors of the labour market persists, they will continue to come. Social tensions stemming from the denial of social security entitlements to these people may then be replaced by social tensions that result from large-scale irregular residence.

Even though the immigrant situation as it presents itself today in parts of Europe puts a strain on solidarity, we may conclude that this is not unavoidable. It is rather the outcome of a specific conjuncture of developments.[3] Can these developments be avoided in future by making welfare states more 'immigration proof'? I can see two types of possible solutions; one is in the field of immigration policy, and the other requires changes in the welfare system. The two types are not mutually exclusive.

Immigration policy

Changes in immigration policy in order to protect the welfare system almost automatically imply limiting immigration to those whose skills are needed in the labour market now and in the foreseeable future. In the present situation in Europe, this means giving priority to highly skilled migrants in certain sectors of the economy. There is, of course, a problem of timing here. It would be unwise not to attempt to mobilize the potential that may be present in the local labour market, even though that usually requires more time and effort than recruiting abroad. In the current context, limiting immigration to the highly skilled will not be easy to achieve. The need to observe international treaties concerning refugees, the right to a family life, etc., all set clear limits to a state's freedom to select immigrants. Besides, the number of highly skilled people in the world is limited, and many of the best prefer to go to North America, rather than Europe, where opportunities for skilled immigrants are perceived as being fewer. Last but not least is the well-known fact that Europe cannot fence itself off from the rest of the world. Irrespective of the immigration policy pursued, considerable numbers of migrants will manage to enter Europe without authorization. Given the continuing demand for cheap labour, it is most likely that irregular immigration will go up as formal immigration policies become stricter. This will only add to a dichotomization of European societies, a trend that is exactly the opposite of what the welfare state aims to achieve.

On the other hand, certain people claim that Europe now has rapidly growing concerns over its ageing population. Some even advocate a less-restrictive admission policy in order to preserve the welfare system. Of course, this will only be effective if the migrants admitted are economically active and become net contributors. However, the numbers of migrants needed to keep the active vs. non-active ratio more or less at its present level is inconceivably huge: net immigration should be about eight times higher than it actually was in the 1990s (United Nations, 2000). Therefore, immigration can at most be a very partial solution to Europe's ageing problems. Besides, immigrants also get older, and more immigrants will be needed again as long as the structural nature of this demographic change is not sufficiently recognized. Stepping up efforts to mobilize members of underrepresented categories in the labour market – such as second generation migrants, women and older workers – is a much better alternative than immigration if one wishes to preserve the welfare system.

From this discussion we may conclude that a welfare state and immigration need not be incompatible, but only in situations of selective admissions policies, attuned to the long-term labour market needs, that must also be effectively implemented. The less selective and the less effective immigration policies are (in other words, the more borders are open), the more it will be difficult to maintain the welfare state as it currently is. Under such conditions several types of modifications in its functioning may be considered. I will consider four such types of adaptations, two that maintain the principle of equality, so characteristic of the traditional welfare state, and two that imply abandoning, or at least stretching, that principle.[4]

Four routes towards accommodation

While maintaining the principle of equality, it should be possible in a welfare state to *step up integration efforts for new arrivals*. This should aim at improving their language and other skills and qualifications, and at enhancing their opportunities in the labour market, for example through jobs programmes or affirmative action. Increased efforts to combat discrimination are also part of this approach. In fact, this is the road that many Western European welfare states have been following for a long time, but it requires time and some patience, as well as substantial sums of money. It is doubtful, given the current political climate, whether Europe is ready to continue on this road. On the contrary, recent developments in several countries point in a different direction: while immigrants are indeed encouraged – if not obliged – to step up their integration efforts, fulfilling that obligation is increasingly seen as the migrants' own responsibility. It is uncertain whether all those concerned will be able to comply with these demands. The (un)intended consequence of this may be that those who are unable to do so may have to fall back on welfare state provisions, unless their entitlements are discontinued or severely reduced, which would seriously challenge the principle of equality.

A second approach may be found in *limiting welfare state entitlements and benefits for everyone*, migrants and non-migrants alike. In much of Europe this has been a general trend anyway, and for a variety of reasons mentioned earlier. In the light of all those reasons, growing immigration would only be a minor excuse for such cuts, but one of high political significance. In fact, if the welfare state were to be reduced to a much more basic system, the immigrant situation in Europe might become similar to that in the United States. This will not necessarily harm immigrants' opportunities. On the contrary, if certain benefits were to disappear, migrants might be lured more easily into the labour market, particularly at the lower skill levels. Many analysts have argued that it is precisely the virtual absence of social security entitlements for newly arriving immigrants that forces these people to take up a job that is often far below their level of education. This explains why in the United States the labour market is a much more powerful channel for integration and upward mobility of immigrants than it is in Europe (e.g., Ederveen et al., 2004, p. 53).

Stepping up integration and reducing benefits for everyone have the advantage that two of the basic principles of the welfare state – equality and solidarity – can be maintained, even under conditions of a continuing and only partly controllable immigration. But how realistic are these options? As an overall rule, social rights and entitlements to welfare provisions are not linked to citizenship, but to residence. Certain exceptions, however, have always been generally accepted, such as linking unemployment benefits to the period of active employment. As immigration has continued, and as the numbers of undocumented migrants has grown, many states have felt the need to determine more clearly than in the past who is entitled to certain benefits and who is not. As the geographical borders have been losing their significance, the 'borders' of the welfare state system have been increasingly strengthened: more computerization, more identity checks and more exclusion, particularly of undocumented migrants. In much of Europe, border controls have been partly replaced by controls at the desks of social, healthcare and housing services, in what may be referred to as the 'dual border of the welfare state' (Entzinger, 1994). It has created a situation of greater difference between residents in their rights and entitlements. This runs counter to one of the basic principles of the welfare state.

This trend seems hard to reverse. As geographical borders open up even to those who are not legally entitled to cross them, alternative means of protecting the welfare state and its arrangements will have to be developed. A further *differentiation of entitlements* may be one answer to this. This could be done, for example, by introducing longer waiting periods for certain benefits for all newly arriving migrants, whether workers or family members. Workers would have to make their own arrangements or have to fall back on arrangements in their country of origin. Family members would only be allowed in if relatives can support them. In order to keep the balance right, these newcomers should not be asked to contribute to those elements of the welfare state from which they do not benefit. This will lower their labour costs and give them a fairer chance to become integrated in the labour market. Of course, the domestic labour force may experience this as unfair competition, but today such unfair competition is already experienced from undocumented migrants, who have no protection whatsoever. It is an illusion to expect that this approach will wipe out irregular migration, but it can at least provide a perspective for some undocumented migrants and encourage newcomers to find a job, which will facilitate the integration process.

Another form of differentiating entitlements may be found in *deterritorialization*. Many welfare state entitlements are actually linked to residence in a given territory. This is precisely the reason why so many migrant workers did not return home after losing their jobs in the 1980s. They were caught in the web of the welfare state. The findings of Boeri et al., according to which the more generous welfare states tend to act as magnets for new migrants, may announce additional claims in future. In order to avoid such developments it would be interesting to reflect on ways of disentangling entitlements and residence. Instead, entitlements may be acquired on the basis of other criteria, such as one's employment record, and it should also be made easier to export them. Such an approach may not only facilitate return migration, but it may also be a more adequate response to the growing phenomenon of transnationalism: migrants commuting back and forth between two (or more) countries with which they have links and to which they may feel attached. This approach may even pave the road towards finding an answer to the problematic issue of dual citizenship, with which many governments are struggling. One idea might be to distinguish a full or active citizenship, linked to actual residence, from a more restrictive or passive form of citizenship. The latter may not automatically entitle the holder to permanent residence with all benefits linked to it, but it may be (re)activated under certain conditions. In recent years, several countries (e.g., Turkey, India, China) have introduced legislation that enables such differential forms of citizenship, but they have done so primarily with regard to their emigrants abroad, rather than to their immigrants (Groenendijk and Ahmad Ali, 2004). This is a field worth exploring further.

Conclusion

The welfare state and open borders are not incompatible per se. However, under its present conditions a welfare state is more likely to cope successfully with immigration if migrants are economically advantageous and if the established population develops a sufficient degree of solidarity with the newcomers. In much of Europe, neither of these two conditions seem to be fulfilled at present. As a consequence, immigration puts the welfare state under pressure. In this chapter I have attempted to analyse the nature of this process and have developed four possible routes for coping with the challenges that lie ahead of us. Two of these routes would enable us to maintain the major principles of equality and solidarity, which have been so characteristic of the welfare state throughout the twentieth century. Two others would have us venture into new territories, of which we can see only the contours now. They have in common an attempt to disentangle entitlements, residence and membership of a nation-state without, however, creating unacceptable forms of poverty and marginalization, which would disrupt social order.

Notes

1. Another explanation for this phenomenon may be related to the fact that, until a few years ago, German naturalization policies were stricter than those of other European countries. As a consequence, Germany hosts relatively large numbers of foreign citizens with long residence records and second-generation immigrants who hold foreign passports. Many of these people may be well integrated into the local labour market. Therefore, the risk of becoming unemployed is smaller for them than for newly arrived migrants.
2. Certain EU Member States, particularly those in the south, exclude large segments of their immigrant populations from social security entitlements because of their undocumented status. This affects low-skilled migrant workers in particular. As the unemployment risks are higher for low-skilled workers than for the highly skilled, it is not unlikely that, as a consequence of their immigration policies, fewer immigrants benefit from social security systems in southern European countries than in countries in the north of Europe.
3. I am leaving aside here a serious methodological problem, which is to what extent second-order effects of immigration should be included in an analysis of the impact of immigration on economies in general, and on the welfare state in particular. This is a problem that several economists who have attempted to calculate costs and benefits of immigration have tended to overlook. Should we look at all migrants, for example, or only at certain categories – usually the more problematic ones? Should we include the costs of educating a second generation, which, after all, is an investment in the future of the local economy? Should we also include the costs and benefits of emigration of a country's own citizens? For a discussion see, for example, Von Loeffelholz and Thränhardt (1996).

4. What follows is a brief summary of the main conclusions of a project on social policy, migration and world development, partly financed by the Dutch government (Entzinger and Van der Meer 2004).

Bibliography

Boeri, T., Hanson, G. H. and McCormick, B. (eds). 2002. *Immigration Policy and the Welfare System: A Report for the Fondazione Rodolfo Debenedetti.* Oxford, Oxford University Press.

Bommes, M. 1999. *Migration und nationaler Wohlfahrtsstaat. Ein differenzierungs-theoretischer Entwurf.* Opladen, Germany, Westdeutscher Verlag.

Brochmann, G. 1999. The mechanisms of control. G. Brochmann and T. Hammar (eds), *Mechanisms of Immigration Control: A Comparative Analysis of European Regulation Policies.* Oxford, Berg, pp. 1–27.

De Beer, P. 2004. Insluiting en uitsluiting: de keerzijden van de verzorgingsstaat. H. Entzinger and J. van der Meer (eds), *Grenzeloze solidariteit: Naar een migratiebestendige verzorgingsstaat,* Amsterdam, De Balie, pp. 26–42.

Durkheim, E. 1967. *De la division du travail social.* Paris, Presses Universitaires de France, 8th edition. (First published 1897.)

Ederveen, S., Dekker, P., van der Horst, A., Joosten, W., van der Meer, T., Tang, P., Coenders, M., Lubbers, M., Nicolaas, H., Scheepers, P., Sprangers, A. and van der Valk, J. 2004. *Destination Europe. Immigration and Integration in the European Union.* The Hague, CPB/SCP.

Ekberg, J. 2004. Immigrants in the welfare state. B. Södersten (ed.), *Globalization and the Welfare State.* New York, Palgrave MacMillan, pp. 195–212.

Entzinger, H. 1994. De andere grenzen van de verzorgingsstaat; Migratiestromen en migratiebeleid. G. Engbersen, A. C. Hemerijck and W. E. Bakker (eds), *Zorgen in het Europese huis; Verkenningen over de grenzen van nationale verzorgingsstaten,* Amsterdam, Boom, pp. 142–72.

Entzinger, H. and van der Meer, J. (eds). 2004. *Grenzeloze solidariteit; Naar een migratiebestendige verzorgingsstaat.* Amsterdam, De Balie.

Groenendijk, C. A. and Ahmad Ali, H. A. 2004. *De juridische vormgeving van de band van Surinaamse immigranten met Suriname.* Zoetermeer, Netherlands, Centrum Surinaamse Ontwikkelingsvraagstukken.

Myrdal, G. 1960. *Beyond the Welfare State: Economic Planning and its International Implications.* New Haven, Conn., Yale University Press.

Phalet, K., van Lotringen, C. and Entzinger, H. 2000. *Islam in de multiculturele samenleving: Opvattingen van jongeren in Rotterdam.* Utrecht, Netherlands, ERCOMER.

Roodenburg, H. J., Euwals, R. W. and ter Rele, H. J. M. 2003. *Immigration and the Dutch Economy.* The Hague, CPB Netherlands Bureau for Economic Policy Analysis. (CPB Special Publications series No. 47.)

United Nations. 2000. *Replacement Migration: Is it a Solution to Declining and Ageing Populations?* New York, UN Population Division. www.un.org/esa/population/publications/migration/migration.htm (Accessed 16 December 2006.)

Von Loeffelholz, H. D., Dietrich and Thränhardt, D. (eds). 1996. *Kosten der Nichtintegration ausländischer Zuwanderer.* Düsseldorf, Germany, Rhine-Westphalia Institute for

Economic Research (RWI), Institute for Political Sciences of the University of Munster, and the Ministry of Labour, Health and Social Affairs of North Rhine Westphalia.

Wadensjö, E. 2000. Immigration, the labour market and public finances in Denmark. *Swedish Economic Policy Review*, No. 7, pp. 59–84.

Part II

Regional perspectives

Chapter 7

Europe without borders: rhetoric, reality or Utopia?

Jan Kunz and Mari Leinonen

Introduction

Migration is a hotly debated issue in Europe.[1] On the one hand, the population in the European Union (EU) is ageing rapidly, unemployment is high in many EU Member States, and there is a lack of both professional experts and people willing to take low-wage and low-status jobs. Migration is said to be a tool to overcome at least some of these problems in the short term. On the other hand, there are all kinds of fears that open borders would lead to labour market distortions, to a collapse of social security systems, to uncontrollable security risks, and to the loss of national identities. Hence policy-making in this field is slow and painstaking, as the debates concerning a common European migration and asylum policy indicate. The most prominent metaphors of the political discourse in this context are 'Europe without borders' and 'Fortress Europe'. They are not contradictory, although at first sight they may appear to be; rather, they refer to two different dimensions: the internal and the external.

With regard to the former, 'Europe without borders', the EU has created opportunities for its citizens to move without restrictions from one Member State to another and to enjoy the multicultural complexity of Europe. However, the abolition of national frontiers has not increased migration within Europe excessively. This fact underlines the need to examine obstacles to migration that lie beyond border controls; such as administrative, financial, cultural, linguistic, social and mental barriers. These can be referred to as 'invisible boundaries'. It is important to note that these obstacles are not identical for all EU citizens. While the European elites, among them academics, business people and professional experts, are highly mobile, ordinary workers and employees usually remain in their country of origin.

Concerning control and security issues, the EU is commonly described as 'Fortress Europe', in reference to the closing and monitoring of its external borders. But if we take the term in a wider sense, it could also be applied to various areas of everyday life. In contemporary Europe, 'guarding duties' are not limited to external frontiers, but also concern access to public institutions, to the labour market, to social security systems and to welfare services, as well as to key positions within the political system. Much control is thus executed by street-level bureaucrats from labour-inspection agencies, public-housing agencies, or welfare and social security departments, instead of by border guards (Engbersen, 2001, p. 242). Sophisticated identification and control systems such as Eurodac, which enable the sharing of information about asylum seekers and irregular immigrants in the EU (see European Union, 2006a), play an increasingly important role in this context.

Against this background it is a challenge to imagine a Europe without any internal, external or invisible boundaries. On the other hand, borders are not given facts, but result from social and political definitions and agreements. Eiki Berg and Henk van Houtum (2003, pp. 1–2) put it as follows: 'border as a concept is not so much an object or phenomenon, something to erase or install but rather an ongoing, repetitive process that we encounter and produce ourselves in our daily lives'. Hence borders can be changed. The processes of de-bordering and re-bordering are therefore dynamic discourses and practices.

To assess whether talk of a 'Europe without borders' is simple rhetoric, actual reality, or merely a utopian dream, this chapter addresses five key issues: the experiences of the European Union in opening its internal frontiers; the phenomenon of labour mobility and its active promotion by the EU; the factors that prevent or foster mobility in Europe; the eastward enlargement of the EU and its anticipated effects on the mobility patterns of Europeans; and last but not least, the interdependence of migration policies and migration in the European Union, which we analyse through three possible future scenarios.

Migration in Europe

The removal of frontiers

By signing the Single European Act in 1986, the then twelve Member States of the European Community agreed to establish a single European market from 1993 onwards. This was defined as 'an area without internal frontiers in which the free movement of goods, persons, services and capital is ensured'

Table 7.1: Foreigners in the European Union

- *Foreigners:* There are about 23 million foreigners living in the EU-25 (precise figures are difficult to obtain due to the phenomenon of irregular immigration and the reluctance of temporary migrants from EU Member States to register). Approximately 7 million (primarily Italians, Greeks, Irish and Spaniards) are nationals of other EU Member States; the remaining 16 million are non-EU nationals. The total number of foreigners corresponds to 5.1 per cent of the population of the European Union (European Commission, 2006a)

- *Geographical mobility and net migration:* While the geographical mobility of EU nationals is lower than the levels reached during the 1950s and 1960s, the number of non-EU immigrants continues to rise. Since 1984, net migration in Europe has been positive, which means there have been more people moving to the EU than leaving it. This positive net migration is the main cause of population growth in the European Union (Eurostat, 2002, pp. 18–23).

- *Asylum seekers:* With regard to asylum seekers the picture is inconsistent, as the trends depend on global geo-political developments and legal regulations. The number of asylum applications increased from 397,000 in 1990 to 672,000 in 1992, before going down again to 242,000 in 1997. Five years later the figure stood at 352,000 (European Commission, 2006c; Eurostat, 2003, pp. 120, 179).

- *Place of residence:* In 2003 about 29 per cent of the 23 million foreigners living in the EU-25 countries lived in Germany, 14 per cent in France and 12 per cent in the United Kingdom.

- *Share of foreigners:* With the exception of Luxembourg (about 37 per cent) and Estonia (about 20 per cent), the share of foreigners in relation to the total population was highest in Cyprus (9.4 per cent), Austria (8.8 per cent), Germany (8.3 per cent) and Belgium (8.2 per cent). The EU average stood at 5.1 per cent (European Commission, 2006c).

(Consolidated Version of the Treaty establishing the European Community, 2002, Article 14-2). The agreement, which went far beyond the existing freedom of movement of labour (see below), meant that all EU citizens had the right 'to move and reside freely within the territory of the Member States' (Article 18-1).

In practice, the creation of a single market in Europe made internal frontiers and border controls between Member States superfluous. This was an experiment that had never been undertaken on such a large scale before. As a result, everybody (Europeans and non-Europeans) residing in any one of the EU Member States could move without restrictions within Europe. This had consequences for the national security and immigration policies of the

Member States: these were no longer domestic matters, but needed to be dealt with at the European level. While internal control mechanisms (e.g., police activities at railway stations, airports, highways and city centres) increased across the national territories of the individual Member States (see Best, 2003, p. 198), the control and securing of the EU's external borders gained greater priority (see Rodrigues, 2004, p. 1).

The first steps concerning the removal of internal frontiers in the European Union had already been taken one year prior to the Single European Act. In 1985, Belgium, France, Luxembourg, the Netherlands and Germany signed the Schengen Agreement. By doing so, the five states agreed on an intergovernmental basis to 'gradually remove their common frontier controls and introduce freedom of movement for all individuals who were nationals of the signatory Member States, other Member States or third countries' (European Union, 2004a). The Schengen Convention, which was signed by the same states in 1990 (but did not come into force until 1995), laid down, among other things, common rules concerning immigration issues, visas, border controls and police cooperation. The 1997 Treaty of Amsterdam incorporated the content of the Schengen Agreement and the Schengen Convention into the Treaty on the Establishment of the European Union. All EU Member States, with the exception of Ireland and Great Britain, which cooperate only in certain areas, signed the agreement. In addition, non-EU nations Norway and Iceland joined the Schengen Convention in December 1996 (see European Union, 2004a; Rodrigues, 2004), and Switzerland joined in June 2005. It is expected that the new EU Member States will do the same as soon as their administration, police, and border guards are able to fulfil the required criteria.

Immigration and asylum policy

The Dublin Convention, which was signed by the EU Member States in 1990 and finally ratified in 1997, was an important step towards a common EU immigration policy. It stipulates that refugees have the right to have their application for asylum reviewed in one EU Member State, usually the one in which they first arrive. The convention was established primarily to prevent refugees from moving about in Europe seeking asylum once their case has already been dismissed in other Member States. It was further agreed in 1992 – in the London Resolution on Host Third Countries – that refugees who arrived in the EU from a safe third country could be sent back to it without having their cases reviewed in the EU, which meant that applications without any sound basis could be dealt with more quickly than normal asylum applications. But due to their restrictive and superficial character, the Dublin Convention and the London Resolution came under strong criticism from human rights organizations (Rasmussen, 1997, pp. 157–9).

During the 1999 European Council in Tampere, Finland, the heads of state and governments resolved to create an area of freedom, security and justice for all citizens of the European Union by 2004 (Rodrigues, 2004, p. 1). One of the key elements in this context was the development of a common policy on asylum and immigration, with a special focus on four areas:

1. Partnership with the countries of origin (in order to prevent migration).
2. A common European asylum system (in order to develop common proceedings and a common status of asylum seekers in the long term).
3. The fair treatment of third country nationals (in order to promote integration and prevent discrimination).
4. A more efficient management of migration flows (in order to prevent irregular immigration).

Another important topic of the Tampere Council was the need for a united approach to fight crime, through police and judicial cooperation (Council of the European Union, 1999).

Despite some progress – for example, in the shape of general rules on asylum (Dublin II) and plans to introduce a common visa-information system and an agency to control the EU's external borders (Rodrigues, 2004, p. 5) – establishing a common policy on asylum and migration has turned out to be a difficult undertaking. It was not until April 2004 that ministers of the Justice and Home Affairs Council finally reached agreement on this politically sensitive topic. The new Asylum Qualification Directive of the European Union 'sets out the eligibility criteria for both refugee status and for subsidiary protection in the EU and entitlements of those persons who qualify for that protection' (McDowell, 2004). It, too, stipulates that refugees who enter the EU via 'safe third countries' can be rejected; and that the same applies for asylum seekers who originate from countries considered to be safe (McDowell, 2004; 'EU einigt sich auf Asylrecht', 2004; 'Ministers Reach Breakthrough on EU Asylum Policy', 2004).

These directives have been much criticized: human rights experts, for example, consider the EU asylum policy too restrictive, and argue that it presents numerous shortfalls with regard to non-discrimination against third country nationals, and their integration in the EU ('Ministers Reach Breakthrough on EU Asylum Policy' 2004; Amnesty International U.K., 2003; Scagliotti, 2003). The European Parliament has criticized the slow progress made in this area, and has pointed out an inherent imbalance in European migration and security policy: while the Council of Ministers is quick in deciding on measures to fight terrorism or to prevent irregular immigration, few steps have been taken towards a more pro-active migration policy (European Parliament, 2004).

In November 2004, EU heads of state and government established the Hague Programme, which aims at creating a common European asylum system: with common procedures and a uniform status for those granted asylum or subsidiary protection in the EU (objectives for the period 2005–2010). Importantly, the Hague Programme also demands improvements in the exchange of information on migration and asylum issues among EU Member States. In addition, it takes into consideration the external dimension of asylum and migration, by acknowledging that the European Union cannot ignore global migration pressure or the situation in third countries.

In certain respects the Hague Programme has managed to reach beyond political rhetoric. A good example is the Regional Protection Programme (RPP), which was realized by the European Commission in close cooperation with the United Nations High Commissioner for Refugees. The RPP aims to deliver direct benefits to refugees and to contribute to improving the human rights situation in host third countries. A number of new funding programmes have subsequently been developed. The AENEAS Programme, for example, contributes approximately 250 million euros between 2004 and 2008 for migration- and asylum-related actions in third countries (European Commission, 2006a).

Labour migration in Europe

The freedom of movement of labour

The freedom of movement of labour in the EU has its origins in the Treaty of Rome, which was signed in 1957 and led to the founding of the European Economic Community one year later. However, it was not until 1968 that the free movement of labour was fully achieved, and even then safeguard clauses remained in force until the end of 1991 (European Commission, 2001b). The initial idea behind the establishment of the freedom of movement of labour in the 1960s was to create a legal framework for migrants from southern Europe (particularly Italy), who were desperately needed in the labour markets in central Europe (particularly Germany).

Due to a changed labour market situation and the fear of 'migration waves' from southern to northern Europe, the freedom of movement of labour was restricted when Greece (1981), Portugal (1986) and Spain (1986) joined the European Union. It took Greek workers six years before they were allowed to choose their place of work freely within the EU. Their Spanish and Portuguese counterparts had been expected to wait for seven years, but as no strong flow of migration occurred, they were granted the freedom of movement of labour one year earlier. Over the years, the right of EU nationals to choose their place of work and live wherever they wish has become one of the main principles of the European Union, and has now the status of a basic right. It is confirmed in many international contracts and agreements (see European Commission, 2001b; Vandamme, 2000; Graham, 1992).

However, despite the high ideological value attributed to this principle, few citizens make use of it in practice. A labour market analysis by the European Commission (2001a) indicates that geographic mobility is strong only among young and highly skilled employees and workers. This is a reversal of the trend in the 1960s and 1970s when primarily low-skilled people with only basic education moved from southern to central Europe in order to find work. The number of students studying abroad in the framework of the Erasmus exchange programme, for example, rose steadily by about 10 per cent throughout the 1990s and amounted to 181,000 in 2000. This shows that mobility can be promoted with the help of appropriate initiatives. On the other hand, it should also be mentioned that participants in the Erasmus programme represent less than 2 per cent of the 12 million students in Europe.

With regard to EU citizens as a whole, only 225,000 people – or 0.1 per cent of the EU-15 population – changed their EU country of residence in 2000. The number of people working in a country different from their country of residence was also relatively low (600,000). According to a study by the MKW GmbH (2001), the total number of permanent migrant workers in the EU is approximately 2.5 million, which represents about 1 per cent of the total EU-15 labour force. The situation has not considerably changed with EU enlargement. According to the European Commission (2006d), nationals of the new EU Member States represent less than 1 per cent of the labour force in the EU-15 countries, with Ireland (3.8 per cent) and Austria (1.4 per cent) as exceptions.

An assessment of the European migration legislation

The EU has introduced numerous measures to increase the mobility of its citizens, especially with regard to labour force mobility. The transferability of social security rights and the planned introduction of an EU health insurance card are just two examples (European Commission, 2002). Nevertheless geographical mobility remains low. According to Vandamme (2000, p. 441), 'the labour mobility of EU nationals may be perceived as enjoyment of rights and facilities guaranteed by community law and encouraged by business developments'. This means that there is generally no need for EU nationals to move to other Member States in order to overcome economic misery or even to ensure their own survival. The authors of the MKW GmbH study (2001) argue that, from a strictly legal point of view, the actual level of geographical mobility does not really matter, as long as obstacles to mobility are reduced and EU nationals looking for additional opportunities in other Member States are able to exercise this basic right.

Efforts made to strengthen mobility within the EU are partly based on the 'integration theory', according to which high wages will guide migrant workers to the places where they are needed most, if all legal obstacles are removed (Tassinopoulos and Werner, 1998). This again ensures economic prosperity and balanced labour markets in the Member States. However, the reality in the EU casts doubt on this theory. Despite the fact that EU labour markets are far from being balanced, there is growing reluctance on the part of EU nationals to work in other Member States. One reason for this may be that the theory underestimates the 'value of immobility' and the risks of, and obstacles to, migration. Another reason is the increasing convergence of incomes and wages within the EU, reducing people's desire to move to other Member States. In addition, the choice to migrate does not exclusively follow an economic logic, but is also affected by personal interests.

The so-called 'classical foreign trade theory' analyses decreasing migration from a different point of view and argues that the intensification of economic activities among the Member States is responsible for the decline. As goods and capital are more mobile than people, they are brought to places where experts and companies exist already. Hence trade and foreign direct investment (FDI) can be considered as 'substitutes for labour mobility' (Langewiesche, 2001, p. 326). The classical foreign trade theory also gives an explanation for regional specialization and regional differences within the EU. Labour mobility is, however, still necessary in fields where products cannot be transferred, such as special services in the construction or tourism sector.

Migration in context

A person's decision to move to a foreign country is influenced by different factors, including economic reasons (e.g., higher wages), social and cultural reasons (e.g., friends or family members living in the country of destination, an existing culture of migration), work-related reasons (e.g., career possibilities), political reasons (e.g., repression in the country of origin), or humanitarian reasons (e.g., ethnic discrimination or deadly peril due to conflicts in the country of origin). From an individual point of view, the decision to migrate depends on an assessment of the transaction costs involved, which range from the probability of finding a job and the costs of moving and housing to taxes and contributions and access to information. Migration will occur only if personal gains from a change of residence are considered to be higher in the long run than these transaction costs (Tassinopoulos and Werner, 1998).

Individual factors such as age, family status, education and knowledge of languages, as well as economic situation, play an important role in this context (see Kunz, 2002; European Commission, 2001*b*). According to the European Foundation for the Improvement of Living and Working Conditions (2004), migration in Europe is dominated by financial and employment considerations and the prospect of enhanced living conditions.

There are also a number of obstacles that prevent migration (see MKW GmbH, 2001): first of all, the EU is no homogenous cultural zone. In addition to different traditions and religions, one of the most important cultural barriers is the great variety of languages spoken in the twenty-seven EU Member States. Secondly, there are sizeable information deficits that can be traced back to geographical distance; limited communication networks; a lack of personal contacts; or limited cultural, political and economic knowledge. Thirdly, migrants can face problems in having their qualifications recognized. These must be viewed alongside the different school and education systems (whose harmonization is the key goal of the Bologna Process), and the diversity governing job regulations. Fourth, economic and financial problems can result from different income, taxation and social security systems (e.g., the transfer of entitlements). Fifth, migration can entail legal and administrative problems, such as a lack of common rules in residence-permit applications, problems concerning family reunifications, or difficulties in accessing social security.

Besides migration obstacles, there are also factors that encourage people to stay in a given region, which Tassinopoulos and Werner (1998, p. 35) refer to as the 'value of immobility'. Among the factors that discourage migration are, for example, good jobs, work that is strongly connected to a specific region or employer, strong social relations, involvement in political and social activities, a high level of integration, or good cultural and economic information about a region. These are reinforced by difficulties in assessing the risk factors and transaction costs associated with migration.

Samorodov (1992) argues that, from the point of view of sending countries, migration is a two-sided conundrum. On the one hand, its development has advantages: such as fulfilling the desires of certain people to work abroad; reducing political, economic or ethnic tensions; providing training for workers abroad; or enabling the remittance of money from migrant workers to their families. On the other hand, if too many young, skilled and well-educated people leave a country, migration can endanger regional development and jeopardize regional social security systems. These phenomena, which are known as 'brain drain' and 'youth drain', were witnessed in the Baltic states (Estonia, Latvia, and Lithuania) at the end of the 1990s and the beginning of the twenty-first century (Wiegand, 2002).

Fear factor – the perception of migration as a threat

The general attitudes towards human mobility in Europe are contradictory. While migration from poorer parts of the world to Europe (described in terms of unpredictability and abnormality) is seen to represent a threat to host societies' territorial-based identities and to personal and societal security, as far as internal labour migration is concerned, at the beginning of the European integration process the mobility of EU citizens was perceived as a sensible and organized process. The different waves of EU enlargement, however, have altered this perception. According to EU Commissioner for Justice and Home Affairs, Antonio Vittorino, interviewed for TV5 France's *Rideau Rouge* ('Immigration: les rêves et les peurs', broadcast on 24 February 2004), as much as two-thirds of Europeans think there are already too many immigrants in Europe. And attitudes towards migrants are geo-politically biased: migration from developing countries in the East and South is especially perceived as a threat. As statistician Mehdi Lahlou point out during the same 2004 television programme, Spain has 3.3 million immigrants, the biggest segment of which comprises immigrants from Europe and Latin America. Yet, it is the presence of 300,000 Africans in the country that the public describes as problematic.

Immigrants from developing countries are often associated with smuggling, illicit work, drugs, social problems, organized crime, fundamentalism and terrorism. In addition, the citizens of the rich European welfare states are worried about the future of their social rights and benefits. Further worries are connected to demographic development; such as fears of gradual invasions resulting from differences in birth rates between an ageing local population and various ethnic communities. These narratives are often spiced up with metaphors such as 'world of chaos' or 'the clash of civilizations'.

In the view of nationalists, multiculturalism boosted by migration symbolizes a disregard for and a violation of traditional state borders. In many European countries, populist parties have claimed the right to protect their native soil from 'contamination' by restricting the number of migrants. The need to protect cultural particularities is expressed most explicitly among communitarians, according to which the right to immigration is justifiably limited by the right of a political community to preserve the integrity of its way of life (Habermas, 1996, p. 513). In this view, places are 'thick' – i.e. rich in cultural traditions, feelings of local belonging, civic resources, and human fulfilment – and may be legitimately preserved by erecting political, social and cultural boundaries to restrict entry and access. The demand for open borders is clearly at odds with this communitarian philosophy (Entrikin, 2003, p. 54; Walzer, 1994, pp. 85–104).

Nationalists and communitarians are not the only groups that perceive migration as a threat. Discourses in which migration is represented as a threat to societal or personal security have become a natural part of Western politics and media coverage. Even influential international institutions such as NATO and the EU have placed migration on their security agendas (Bigo, 2000, p. 123). Discourses linking migration and security issues have consequently received a status of commonplace truth that is hardly challenged (Foucault, 1994). In this process the notion of security is placed over liberty of movement.

Western media often present migration in terms of 'flows'. In 1999, for example, the Finnish media reported on a 'stream of refugees' when three hundred Romany from Slovakia arrived in the country to seek asylum. This created the impression that there was an endless stream of refugees from Eastern European countries coming to Finland to abuse its social security systems at the expense of native Finns. Three years later, the fuss was still in everybody's memory; the arrival of just fifty Romany from Slovakia was enough for the media to speak again about a 'refugee flow'. As a result of public and political pressure, Finnish immigration laws were finally tightened (Horsti, 2003, pp. 14–15). Using the term 'security' is thus never an innocent act: in this case it transformed migration into a security problem and fed images to the public that created a climate of anxiety or moral panic, leading to the stigmatization, marginalization or even criminalization of immigrants (Huysmans, 1998). Western democracies usually fall back upon similar discourses to justify their exclusionary immigration policies and increasing control of human mobility, which are otherwise at odds with liberal political philosophy and universal ideas of equality.

At the moment, there is a trend in Europe towards ever more restrictive migration policies – a trend reinforced by these often ungrounded threatening images. To steer migration policies towards more open borders, a serious unpacking of such eclectic discourses, in which migrants are represented as a threat, is needed. This means first of all disentangling migration and security issues, which is a big challenge as far as political agendas and the public debate are concerned. One should also take a more critical view of discourses in which the emphasis is on 'immigration' instead of 'migration' and all migrants are lumped together.

Migration and EU enlargement

When a new country joins the European Union, its citizens enjoy the same rights as citizens of the other Member States, including the freedom of movement of labour. This principle itself has never been a problem, but economic crises and increasing mass unemployment have led to a perception of labour mobility as a threat to labour-market stability. As a result, transitional agreements were, as mentioned, put in place when Greece (1981), Portugal (1986) and Spain (1986) joined the EU. A precautionary measure, these agreements restricted the mobility of Greek, Portuguese and Spanish workers for a limited period of time.

Twenty years later, the topic of labour mobility was high on the political agenda once again when the EU discussed its eastward enlargement. Unlike in the case of former accessions, highly developed welfare states in the EU would share internal borders with considerably less-developed countries for the first time (e.g., Finland/Estonia, Germany/Poland or Austria/Slovakia). Thus the influx of migrants appeared to be more likely than in the past (see Kunz, 2002). Corresponding public fears were fuelled by the media and policy-makers alike. The EU's political reaction to these fears was to put into place transitional agreements for most new Member States (the Czech Republic, Estonia, Hungary, Latvia, Lithuania, Poland, Slovakia and Slovenia), with the exception of Malta and Cyprus, which were neglected because of their small size. Based on the so-called '2+3+2 formula', the agreements allowed the restriction of labour-market access for a limited period of time, in case of actual or anticipated labour-market distortions.

From 1 May 2004, all EU Member States could prevent workers from the new Member States from joining their national labour force for two years. It is possible to prolong this period by three years in 2006 and, if considered necessary, by another two years in 2009. All restrictions are to be abandoned by 2011 at the latest. As these interim provisions are optional, however, Great Britain and Ireland chose to open their labour markets immediately. In 2006 Finland, Greece, Portugal, Italy, Sweden and Spain followed their example. Denmark, Belgium, France, Luxembourg and the Netherlands are planning to lift their restrictions gradually until 2009, whereas Austria and Germany are likely to prevent migration for as long as possible (see European Commission, 2006d). It is important to note that these restrictions concern only labour migrants (and thereby often their general access to social-security systems), but not students, tourists, or seasonal workers (see 'The Coming Hordes', 2004, and Wiegand, 2002).

From a political point of view, transitional agreements are considered to be a good compromise, as they respond to the above mentioned 'threat debate' and thereby help to ensure public support for the enlargement (see Kunz, 2002). Concurrently the maximum restriction period of seven years buys time for the new Member States to improve their socioeconomic situation. This may to a certain extent prevent 'brain drain' or 'youth drain' processes. On the other hand, the transitional agreements make it difficult for companies to hire needed specialists from the new Member States. In this context, companies located in Great Britain or Ireland (where no transitional agreements are in place) have an advantage over those in countries such as Austria or Germany (where a restriction of seven years appears to be likely). And for citizens of the new Member States wishing to work in other EU countries, the restrictions are a limitation of their personal freedom.

With regard to the field of academic research, it is difficult to predict future migration trends as they are usually based on current developments. However, there seems to be general agreement that, after an initial increase when freedom of movement of labour is first granted, there will be no further major influx of migrants from the new Member States (see Kunz, 2002). The European Foundation for the Improvement of Living and Working Conditions (2004), for example, expects East–West migration would be as low as 1 per cent if full freedom of movement were granted immediately. Similar levels of migration were experienced after the southern enlargement of the EU during the 1980s. So far these estimations have proved to be correct, as citizens of the new Member States have been less mobile than expected in most EU-15 countries. Immigration figures have only increased to a greater extent in the case of Ireland and the United Kingdom, but this was due to a higher demand for labour (European Commission, 2006d).

Three future scenarios of borders and migration in Europe

Societal reality can develop in many, often contrary, directions. Futurologists speak about different 'future paths' in this context, which refer to possible courses of events. After each event a new 'world stage' is reached. Although human development is an ongoing process and there is no ultimate outcome, scientists, for reasons of simplicity, usually describe some ideal or final point. This means that 'future paths' and 'world stages' together form some kind of 'possible world' or future scenario. The values and risks connected to future scenarios vary greatly in many cases, hence they appear more or less desirable for different social groups or individuals (Kamppinen et al., 2003).

With regard to borders and migration in Europe, we have developed three scenarios for the purposes of this discussion (see Table 7.2). One envisages an EU with rigid internal and external borders (Scenario 1); one an EU with no internal, but with rigid external borders (Scenario 2); and one an EU with no internal and no impermeable external borders (Scenario 3). These three scenarios are partly opposing and partly complementary. They are based on observations of current trends, which will ultimately lead to different directions depending on the decisions taken by Europe's politicians and policy-makers. When looking at these scenarios, it should be kept in mind that societal reality is far more complex than can be presented here. These are just some examples that highlight the complexity of numerous 'possible worlds' in order to draw attention to current trends and future prospects.

Table 7.2: Three future scenarios for borders and migration in Europe

	Scenario 1 (rigid internal and external borders)	Scenario 2 (no internal but rigid external borders)	Scenario 3 (neither internal nor external borders)
Key features	Only selective labour migration within the EU; effective monitoring of external borders as well as economic and social gateways (Europe of multiple petty fortresses).	A high level of equality, mobility and integration within the EU; effective monitoring of external borders as well as economic and social gateways (Fortress Europe).	A high level of equality, mobility, and integration within the EU; openness towards and integration of migrants from non-EU countries.
Position of migrants	Scepticism toward migrants from other EU Member States (first- and second-class citizens); non-EU migrants are marginalized and criminalized.	Migrants from other EU Member States integrated into economic and social spheres; non-EU migrants are marginalized and criminalized.	Equal opportunities for migrants regardless of their origin; migrants are approved on the basis of economic and other rational considerations alone.
Ideology and key actors	Nationalism and Euro-scepticism promoted by the centre right; calls for protection of cultural particularity.	Neo-liberalism promoted by European elites and controlling agencies.	Universal justice claimed by global civil society and promoted by grass-root movements.
Long-term tendencies	Politics of difference; aspiration to keep things the way they are (stability and preservation).	Progress towards equality, justice and sustainable development at the EU level.	Politics of unity; progress towards global equality, justice and sustainable development.
Openness and control	Effective control and monitoring in the Member State; strong national identities; emphasis on border control.	Openness at the Member State level; omnipresent monitoring of non-Europeans inside Europe; Eurocentric racism in the course of building a European identity.	High degree of openness towards difference; the EU as a cosmopolitan state that respects transnational and momentary identities and cultures.

Table 7.2: *continued*

	Scenario 1 (rigid internal and external borders)	Scenario 2 (no internal but rigid external borders)	Scenario 3 (neither internal nor external borders)
Security and policy aspects	Restrictive and assimilative immigration policies; monitoring, control and isolation in the name of security; state-centric approach and traditional security view.	Inclusive migration and citizenship policy for EU nationals; exclusive policies towards others; transition towards a common security policy; traditional view of security concerning external relations.	Inclusive migration and citizenship policy; multicultural integration; security thinking and policy based on a cosmopolitan world view; global responsibility of local actions.
Relation to the welfare state	Migrants are perceived as a burden to the welfare state; fears of 'social tourism'; passive role ascribed to migrants.	Transition towards a European welfare state model; minimum social security for EU citizens; non-EU migrants are seen as a burden.	The end of traditional welfare states; everybody is responsible for him- or herself (individual social security).
Points to ponder	Strong national identities pose a problem to migrants; rich European states isolate themselves from the less-developed world.	The Euro-centric focus may lead to politics of indifference concerning global problems that trigger migration flows.	The challenges posed to the welfare state systems and national identities could lead to public resistance.

Scenario 1 (rigid internal and external borders)

Scenario 1 describes the European Union as an entity with rigid internal and external borders: a Europe of multiple petty fortresses, of Member States, regions and localities trying to resist the mounting migration pressure. From a feeling that territorial-based communities will otherwise be invaded by migrants, national and European policies in this scenario accentuate the importance of identities and particular cultures. At the same time, Member States intensify their control over human mobility from outside Europe to affirm a sovereignty they feel would decrease if state borders were abolished. Inside the nation-states there is a strong demand for assimilation, which limits the freedom of migrants to express their culture and identities: those who want to be included by their host society need to adapt themselves to the dominating culture and the mainstream behaviour, values and goals of their host nation (Young, 1990).

Social tensions between ethnic groups in this scenario provide a favourable breeding ground in which centre-right parties create a climate of anxiety by spreading threatening scenarios of globally mobile terrorists, criminals, and fundamentalists and of uncontrollable migration flows, increasing unemployment due to cheap migrant labour, a segmentation of labour markets, and a breakdown of social security systems. Thus they suggest the closing of borders to further migrants to prevent cultural alienation and social problems.

The European project has not been abolished in Scenario 1: rather, the suspicions between old and new and rich and poor Member States have increased during the course of enlargement. EU citizens who emigrate to other EU countries are denied access to welfare benefits and are treated as second-class citizens in many cases. The most notable obstacles to the free movement of labour in this context are the Western welfare states, with their comparatively high benefits. Collective welfare chauvinism legitimates a restrictive citizenship policy and strict migration laws and regulations, such as prolonged transition periods. As a consequence, mobility within Europe remains low, with the exception of the European elite. Middle- and working-class migrants from the new EU countries, on the other hand, face practical difficulties in finding jobs equivalent to their studies and in gaining access to social security systems. In the old Member States, there is a lack of confidence concerning the ability of the new Member States to control external borders and to deal with smuggling. This may cause an anti-EU ambiance in the new Member States and further complicate their integration. Because of the internal problems related to migration, the EU tightens its immigration and asylum policy. Within the European Union, labour markets are rather selective. While specialists and academics from other Member States and selected countries gain unrestricted access to the labour market, migrants from outside

Europe are associated with low-paid, insecure and/or part-time jobs, disregarding their prior education. Ironically, the latter group, which is often said to be a threat to the welfare state, plays an important role in maintaining it – by paying taxes and contributions, not to mention their employment in the social and healthcare sector itself.

Scenario 2 (no internal but rigid external borders)

In Scenario 2, Europe moves from a state-centric to a community-centric policy. As a consequence, progress is made towards equality and regional development. Improving conditions in the poorer regions of Central and Eastern Europe mean that no major migration flows materialize. Richer countries forego the transition periods to avoid labour shortages, to attract important human capital, and to boost their economies. The creation of common markets, the growing cultural exchange, and the gradual harmonization of social security systems lower human mobility barriers among the EU Member States. This also leads to a deepening of European integration.

However, the inner harmony of the EU is obtained only by showing indifference towards global migration challenges. The abolition of internal borders leads to a strengthening of the EU's external frontiers and to an increase of internal monitoring of those perceived to symbolize disrespect to Europe's outer borders, which is to say non-EU migrants.

With regard to asylum and migration issues, the governments transfer their authority to the EU level in order to coordinate their approach. Eclectic controlling practices are abandoned to achieve efficient cooperation between national police forces and monitoring systems and to make it impossible for incomers to circumvent laws by changing their country of residence. The French philosopher Gilles Deleuze (1990) described this situation as a transition from Foucault's disciplinary society (control is compartmentalized) to a society of control (control is continuous and omnipresent). Migration policy is replaced by a control policy of advanced information systems and targeted biotechnical identification mechanisms. In this sense, current restrictive migration policies are better captured by the metaphor of 'Panopticon Europe' than by the popular 'Fortress Europe' notion, because they emphasize the development of advanced identification and internal control systems to better safeguard access to public provisions and the labour market (Engbersen, 2001, p. 223).

Immigration to the European Union from outside is discouraged by cutting off social benefits, complicating family reunification, and making immigrants ineligible for public health services and education. Paradoxically, these discouraging measures and stricter border controls do not prevent people from migrating, but rather promote irregular immigration – as the profitability of human smuggling increases with the difficulty of entering a country. Control defeats itself in a vicious circle: the presence of undocumented migrants supports populist anti-immigration opinions; discourses of stigmatization are used by the media and policy-makers to consolidate the link between criminality and migration; this leads to popular resentment, which again leads politicians to implement even stricter immigration control, and so on.

In order to stem migration and facilitate the deportation of unwanted migrants, cooperation with the biggest departure countries is extended. For the same reason, Europe tries to improve its relations with its direct neighbours to the south and the east. These measures attempt to shift the migration problem from Europe to poorer parts of the world, instead of removing the reasons for forced migration.

Scenario 3 (no internal and permeable external borders)

Scenario 3 pictures a multicultural Europe with vivid cultural exchange among its Member States and with third countries. Social tensions between local and immigrant communities are decreasing, due to the mobilization and empowerment of alternative political groups, grass-root movements, and formerly marginalized non-EU migrants. This in turn leads to more efficient lobbying on behalf of migrants and to a demand for more open EU migration policies and a re-examination of existing identification and control systems.

The reasoning behind the politics of open borders is diverse. The above-mentioned groups refer to moral arguments, such as human rights and global justice, whereas European enterprises and well-organized economic interest groups favour open borders in the name of competitive advantage and the long-term interests of an ageing Europe. This kind of rationale for open borders, however, is problematic, as it is dependent on certain conditions: if economic development changes for the worse, pro-immigration arguments for open borders can easily lead to an anti-immigration spirit, welfare chauvinism and the erection of new borders. Therefore moral arguments appear to be more sustainable in this context.

The call to deregulate labour markets in Europe and the importance placed on liberal values and universal human rights lead to a situation in which the EU runs out of ideas to justify its boundaries and finally adopts a policy of (fairly) open borders on a global scale (see Bader, 1995). Human mobility is steered with the help of the self-regulatory capacity of the labour market. In case of problems, blame is no longer placed on migration and open borders, but on the socioeconomic system and its institutions that are unable to respond adequately to the challenge of human mobility. A Europe of open borders is more or less compelled to engage in projects that remove the reasons behind forced migration, with the help of an international redistribution of resources. These resources are not only distributed to the main departure countries, but focus also on the poorest areas of the world. Within Europe, human mobility is high among all social groups instead of only the academic and professional elite. As a consequence, the EU becomes ever more multicultural: postmodern nomads with overlapping identities are no longer an exception but, rather, the norm. Europe has changed from a 'factory of exclusion' to a cosmopolitan entity of diverse transnational identities. This means in practice that the EU implements multicultural integration policies, in which multiculturalism refers to the right to be different and to foster one's own culture whereas integration refers to an interactive, two-way process in which both parties are actively involved and something new is created (Kumar, 2003; Modood, 1997).

The problem of irregular immigration is solved by giving all EU residents a legal status. This enables us to obtain exact figures of how many people actually reside in Europe. Post-national EU citizenship is a radical step towards greater inclusiveness, as it decouples territory, ethnicity, culture, and nationhood from citizenship. For migrant communities, post-national citizenship means emancipation from the assimilative policies of nation-states and gives them freedom to cherish their particular identities. European citizenship is a transitional stage, one of many steps towards a world citizenship, as Habermas envisioned: 'even if we still have a long way to go before fully achieving it, the cosmopolitan condition is no longer merely a mirage' (1996, p. 515). Cosmopolitan Europe would, nevertheless, require large-scale changes, such as the reformation of taxation systems and the privatization of welfare. The latter is likely to prove the biggest obstacle for a cosmopolitan condition as it is strongly resisted in contemporary Europe.

Conclusion

This chapter set out to discuss whether the metaphor 'Europe without borders' is simply rhetoric, actual reality, or merely a utopian idea. Its examination of the mobility patterns within the European Union, however, alongside migration obstacles and various policy approaches, indicates that talks of a borderless Europe are often not more than rhetoric, at least if the term 'border' is understood in a broader sense, which goes beyond national frontiers and includes administrative, cultural, linguistic, and other obstacles. We could say that a borderless Europe is a reality to some Europeans, such as the professional and academic elite, is mere rhetoric to most EU citizens, and is as yet only a dream to those non-EU migrants whose freedom to move has been restricted by regulations and laws. The borders in Europe thus appear differently to different groups and individuals, whose perceptions of invisible borders are always subjective.

As the European Union is currently working on policies to overcome mobility thresholds, a 'Europe without borders' could become reality one day. However, even in this case, the metaphor would only apply to the visible and invisible boundaries inside the European Union, and not to the EU's external borders. Given the current political situation on the European and the Member State level, along with the widespread public fears concerning uncontrolled migration 'flows', the removal of external borders in Europe is a utopian idea.

With regard to the three scenarios developed above to describe possible future developments of migration and migration policies in the European Union, Scenario 1 (rigid internal and external borders) represents a step backwards compared to the status quo in Europe. Possible preconditions for this scenario are the perception of increasing threats as a result of open borders (e.g., terrorism) and/or a failure of the European enlargement and integration process. Scenario 2 (no internal borders and rigid external borders) goes beyond the status quo if internal borders are understood in a wider sense. External borders will only disappear in very specific cases where economic or image benefits are involved (e.g., a lack of skilled labour or the acceptance of political refugees); otherwise, Europe remains a 'fortress'. It would appear that the EU is currently heading in this direction. Scenario 3 (no internal borders and no impermeable external borders) is a utopian idea.

One reason why Scenario 3 will not prevail in the near future is the widespread stigmatization of (non-EU) migrants in Europe. Public fears of uncontrolled migration flows are once again being used to maintain the boundaries (in the meaning of external frontiers and access to institutions, systems, and key positions) of the European Fortress so as to guard the welfare of the rich, industrialized EU countries. It appears unlikely that Europe will overcome the fears connected with migration in the near future. In addition, the social security systems would need to undergo fundamental changes in order to realize Scenario 3. The current systems are not able to provide healthcare, unemployment benefits and/or income support for everybody who decides to move to Europe or to reside in another Member State. Hence a reduction in benefit levels and an individualization of social security (insurance principle) seem to be preconditions for 'migration without borders'. As the comparably high standard of welfare and social security in Europe is considered a key characteristic of the EU, it is unlikely that Europeans will be willing to give it up for the sake of open external borders.

However, Scenario 3 should not be dismissed without further reflection. The fact that it is a utopian idea does not mean that the EU cannot implement certain aspects of it in its future policies, such as more global responsibility concerning equality, justice, and sustainable development. Discussions about a Europe without external borders are important, as they call the necessity and legitimacy of immigration controls into question. Europe may not be ready for the concept of open borders and the unrestricted movement of people, but one should keep in mind that today's Utopia could become tomorrow's reality.

Note

1. Unless stated otherwise, the term 'Europe' refers to the European Union and its Member States.

Bibliography

Amnesty International U.K. 2003. European Union: asylum – Amnesty International backs UNHCR criticism of EU asylum proposals. www.amnesty.org.uk/deliver/document/15018.html (accessed 23 August 2004).

Angst vor Polen. 2001. *Spiegel Online*. www.spiegel.de/spiegel/0,1518,150587,00.html (accessed 21 December 2006).

Bader, V. 1995. Citizenship and exclusion – radical democracy, community, and justice: or, what is wrong with communitarianism? *Political Theory*, Vol. 23, No. 2, pp. 211–46.

Berg, E, and van Houtum, H. 2003. A border is not a border. E. Berg and H. van Houtum (eds), *Borders between Territories: Discourses and Practices*. Ashgate, Aldershot, pp.1–2.

Best, U. 2003. The EU and the Utopia and anti-Utopia of migration: a response to Harald Bauder. *ACME: An International E-Journal for Critical 0*. www.acme-journal.org/vol2/Best.pdf (accessed 29 April 2004).

Bigo, D. 2000. Migration and security. V. Guiraudon and C. Joppke (eds), *Controlling a New Migration World*. London and New York, Routledge, pp. 121–44.

The Coming Hordes. 2004. http://economist.com/world/europe/displayStory.cfm?story_id=2352862. 15 January (accessed 18 May 2004).

Consolidated Version of the Treaty Establishing the European Community. 2002. 4http://europa.eu.int/eur-lex/en/treaties/dat/EC_consol.pdf (accessed 28 April 2004).

Council of the European Union. 1999. Tampere European Council – presidency conclusions. http://ue.eu.int/en/Info/eurocouncil/index.htm (accessed 29 April 2004).

Deleuze, G. 1992. Postscript on the societies of control. www.modcult.brown.edu/students/segall/deleuze.html (accessed 5 July 2004).

DIW. 2000. EU-Osterweiterung: Keine massive Zuwanderung zu erwarten. *DIW-Wochenbericht* 21, Deutsches Institut für Wirtschaftsforschung. www.diw-berlinde/deutsch/publikationen/wochenberichte/docs/00-21-1.html (accessed 25 August 2001).

Engbersen, G. 2001. The unanticipated consequences of Panopticon Europe. V. Guiraudon, and C. Joppke (eds), *Controlling a New Migration World*. London and New York, Routledge, pp. 222–46.

Entrikin, J. N. 2003. Political community, identity and cosmopolitan place. M. Berezin and M. A. Schain (eds), *Europe without Borders: Remapping Territory, Citizenship, and Identity in a Transnational Age*, Baltimore, Md., Johns Hopkins University Press, pp. 51–63.

EU einigt sich auf Asylrecht. 2004. *Spiegel*. www.spiegel.de/politik/ausland/0,1518,297671,00.html (accessed 29 April 2004).

European Commission. 2001*a*. *Employment in Europe 2001 – Recent Trends and Prospects.* Luxembourg, Office for Official Publications of the European Communities.

———. 2001*b*. The free movement of workers in the context of enlargement. http://europa.eu.int/comm/enlargement/docs/pdf/migration_enl.pdf (accessed 30 August 2001).

———. 2002. Barcelona: Commission sets 2005 target to deliver EU worker mobility. http://europa.eu.int/comm/employment_social/news/2002/feb/034_en.html (accessed 8 May 2004).

———. 2004. Free movement. Information on the transitional rules governing the free movement of workers from, to and between the new Member States. http://europa.eu.int/eures/main.jsp?acro=free&step=0&lang=en (accessed 28 June 2004).

———. 2006*a*. The European Union Policy towards a Common European Asylum System. http://ec.europa.eu/justice_home/fsj/immigration/fsj_immigration_intro_en.htm (accessed 30 November 2006).

———. 2006*b*. Free movement within the EU – a fundamental right. http://ec.europa.eu/justice_home/fsj/freetravel/fsj_freetravel_intro_en.htm (accessed 2 December 2006).

———. 2006*c*. Migration and Asylum in numbers. http://ec.europa.eu/justice_home/doc_centre/immigration/statistics/doc_immigration_statistics_en.htm (accessed 2 December 2006).

———. 2006*d*. Report on the Functioning of the Transitional Arrangements set out in the 2003 Accession Treaty (period 1 May 2004–30 April 2006). http://ec.europa.eu/employment_social/news/2006/feb/com_2006_0048_en.pdf (accessed 2 December 2006).

European Union. 2004*a*. Schengen (Agreement and Convention). http://www.europa.eu.int/scadplus/leg/en/cig/g4000s.htm#s4 (accessed 29 April 2004).

———. 2004*b*. Coordination of the Community Immigration Policy. http://www.europa.eu.int/scadplus/leg/en/lvb/l33155.htm (accessed 29 April 2004).

———. 2004*c*. Eurodac system. http://europa.eu.int/scadplus/leg/en/lvb/l33081.htm (accessed on 12 August 2004).

European Foundation for the Improvement of Living and Working Conditions. 2004. Migration trends in an enlarged Europe: summary. www.fr.eurofound.eu.int/publications/files/EF0432EN.pdf (accessed 18 May 2004).

European Parliament. 2004. Progress towards an area of freedom, security and justice (2003). www2.europarl.ep.ec (accessed 15 July 2004).

European Union. 2004*a*. Glossary: Schengen (Agreement and Convention). http://europa.eu/scadplus/glossary/schengen_agreement_en.htm (accessed 22 April 2004).

———. 2004*b*. Coordination of the Community immigration policy. www.europa.eu.int/scadplus/leg/en/lvb/l33155.htm (accessed 29 April 2004).

———. 2004*c*. 'Eurodac' system. http://europa.eu.int/scadplus/leg/en/lvb/l33081.htm (accessed 12 August 2004).

Eurostat. 2002. *The Social Situation in the European Union 2002.* Luxembourg, Office for Official Publications of the European Communities.

———. 2003. *The Social Situation in the European Union 2003.* Luxembourg, Office for Official Publications of the European Communities.

Foucault, M. 1994. *Dits et écrits 1954–1988.* Paris, Gallimard.

Graham, T. 1992. The single European market and labour mobility. *Industrial Relations Journal*, No. 1, pp. 14–25.

Habermas, J. 1996. *Between Facts and Norms: Contributions to a Discourse Theory of Law and Democracy*. Cambridge, U.K., Polity Press.

Helsingin Sanomat, International Edition. 2000. SAK survey: 400,000 Estonians would like to work in Finland. www2.helsinginsanomat.fi/english/archive/news.asp?id=20000905xx17 (accessed 26 May 2004).

Horsti, K. 2003. Turvapaikan muuttuvat ulottuvuudet Euroopassa. S. Villa and S. Pehkonen (eds), *Kosmopolis: Rauhan, konfliktin ja maailmanpolitiikan tutkimuksen aikakausilehti*, No. 4, pp. 7–23.

Huysmans, J. 1995. Migrants as a security problem: dangers of securitizing societal issues. R. Miles and D. Thränhardt (eds), *Migration and European Integration: The Dynamics of Inclusion and Exclusion*. London, Pinter, pp. 53–72.

Kamppinen, M., Malaska, P. and Kuusi, O. 2003. Tulevaisuudentutkimuksen peruskäsitteet. M. Kamppinen, P. Malaska and O. Kuusi (eds), *Tulevaisuudentutkimus: perusteet ja sovellukset*. Tampere, Finland, Tammer-Paino Oy, pp. 19–53.

Kumar, K. 2003. The idea of Europe: cultural legacies, transnational imaginings, and the nation-state. M. Berezin and M. A. Schain (eds), *Europe without Borders: Remapping Territory, Citizenship, and Identity in a Transnational Age*. Baltimore, Md., Johns Hopkins University Press, pp. 33–50.

Kunz, J. 2002. Labour mobility and EU enlargement: a review of current trends and debates. Brussels, European Trade Union Institute. (Discussion and working paper.)

Langewiesche, R. 2001. EU enlargement: general developments and the free movement of labour – on the way to compromise? E. Gabaglio and R. Hoffmann (eds), *Trade Union Yearbook 2000*, Brussels, European Trade Union Institute, pp. 317–36.

McDowell, M. 2004. Justice Council reach political agreement on Asylum Procedures Directive. www.eu2004.ie/templates/news.asp?sNavlocator=66&list_id=629 (accessed 18 May 2004).

Ministers reach breakthrough on EU asylum policy. 2004. *Deutsche Welle*. www.dw-world.de/dw/article/0,2144,1156465,00.html (accessed 18 March 2004).

MKW GmbH. 2001. Exploitation and development of the job potential in the cultural sector in the age of digitalisation: obstacles to mobility for workers in the digital culture in the European Union. Munich, MKW GmbH. (Study commissioned by the European Commission, DG Employment and Social Affairs, Brussels.)

Modood, T. 1997. Introduction: the politics of multiculturalism in the new Europe. T. Modood and P. Werbner (eds), *The Politics of Multiculturalism in the New Europe: Racism, Identity and Community*. London, Zed Books, pp. 1–24.

PSE Group. 2004. Free movement of workers and transitional agreements. Brussels, PSE Group (The Socialist Group in the European Parliament). (Working paper for the Committee on Social and Employment Affairs.)

Rasmussen, H. K. 1997. *No Entry: Immigration Policy in Europe*. Copenhagen, Copenhagen Business School Press.

Rodrigues, S. 2004. Why are internal security and immigration issues so important for the new Member States. www.ui.se/stephaner.pdf (accessed 28 April 2004).

Samorodov, A. 1992. Labour mobility in Europe as a result of changes in Central and Eastern Europe. *Labour*, Vol. 6, No. 3, Winter, pp. 3–21.

Scagliotti, L. 2003. Raum der Freiheit, der Sicherheit und des Rechts: Einwanderung und Asyl – eine kurze Aktualisierung. Paper presented at PSE-conference, Area of Freedom,

Security and Justice: Four Years after Tampere – Our Proposals for the Future. Tampere, Finland, 13 and 14 October.

Tassinopoulos, A. and Heinz, W. 1998. Mobility and migration of labour in the European Union. A. Tassinopoulos, H. Werner and S. Kristensen (eds), *Mobility and Migration of Labour in the European Union and Their Specific Implications for Young People.* Luxembourg, Office for Official Publications of the European Communities, pp. 5–98.

Vandamme, F. 2000. Labour mobility within the European Union: findings, stakes and prospects. *International Labour Review*, No. 4, pp. 437–55.

Walzer, M. 1994. *Thick and Thin: Moral Argument at Home and Abroad.* Notre Dame, Ind., University of Notre Dame Press.

Wie viele nach EU-Osterweiterung in den goldenen Westen wollen. 2001. *Neue Kronen Zeitung.* 7 June.

Wiegand, I. 2002. Freizügigkeit in der erweiterten EU: Überprotektion oder gelungener Kompromiß? Report of experts' meeting held at Stiftung Wissenschaft und Politik (SWP), Berlin, 11 March. Berlin, SWP and the European Commission.

Young, I. M. 1990. *Justice and the Politics of Difference.* Princeton, N.J., Princeton University Press.

Chapter 8

Creating a borderless West Africa: constraints and prospects for intra-regional migration

Aderanti Adepoju

This chapter chronicles the efforts made by West African states to foster free movement within the region and to establish a borderless West Africa. It reviews some of the regional policy initiatives of the last decades in the field of migration and shows that the migration without borders (MWB) scenario is a policy option in the region: the governments of the Member States of the Economic Community of West African States (ECOWAS) have regularly committed themselves to foster free intra-regional migration, which has resulted in major progresses in facilitating migration. Despite these efforts, however, there remain constraints to, as well as prospects for, the creation of a borderless West Africa. This raises the question of the feasibility and sustainability of the MWB scenario in the region.

West African migration circuit

Migration is historically a way of life in West Africa. For generations, people have migrated in response to demographic, economic, political and related factors: population pressure, environmental disasters, poor economic conditions, conflicts, and the effects of macro-economic adjustment programmes. Migrants have included temporary cross-border workers, seasonal migrants, clandestine workers, professionals and refugees. Cross-border migrants (especially farm labourers, unskilled workers, nomads, and women engaged in trade) paid little attention to arbitrary national borders, and population movements in search of greater security prevailed over wide areas (Economic Commission for Africa, 1983). Today, intra- and inter-country movements continue to be a central feature of many people's lives. Much of this movement has taken place across great distances, from the northern zones to the coastal regions, and has been short-term and male-dominated.

Movements now regarded as international migration historically occurred across frontiers to restore ecological balance. Migrants were in search of new land, safe for settlement and fertile for farming, as well as trade-related opportunities (Economic Commission for Africa, 1983). Indeed, migrants have always considered West Africa as a single socioeconomic unit within which people and trade in goods and services flowed freely. The distinction between internal and international migration is therefore obscured: migration between neighbouring countries with similar social and ethno-cultural features took place on a routine basis; these factors also facilitated the migrants' relocation at the destination (Adepoju, 1998a).

The colonial period provoked large-scale labour migration, required to establish plantations, mines and public administration. A series of economic measures – including compulsory recruitment, contract and forced labour legislation, and agreements to secure cheap labour – sparked clandestine internal and cross-border migration of unskilled men, required for infrastructural work, especially for transport networks in the north and plantation agriculture in the coastal countries (Amin, 1974). Forced recruitment later gave way to the free migration of individuals and families in search of better living conditions, working on cocoa farms, plantations and in forestry in Ghana and Côte d'Ivoire, and in groundnut fields in Senegal and Gambia. Circular savannah–coastal short-term and male-dominated migration – now classified as international migration – spanned wide areas, especially from the north to coastal and prosperous agricultural regions (Zachariah and Conde, 1981).

But the colonialists paid little regard to the socio-cultural realities of these countries, with the result that many ethnic groups split by pencil sketches into adjacent countries (as are the Yoruba in Nigeria and Benin; Ewes in Togo and Ghana; Vais and Kroos in Liberia and Sierra Leone; Hausa-Fulani in Niger and Nigeria, and so on) regarded movements across artificial borders simply as an extension of internal migration, in line with long-standing ethnic solidarity. Free movement across frontiers was facilitated by cultural affinity, especially where immigrants spoke the same language and shared the same customs as the indigenous population of the host country (Adepoju, 1998a). A great deal of migration was undocumented and facilitated by long, unpoliced borders lacking physical landmarks. At the Ghana/Togo and Nigeria/Benin borders, for example, frontier workers commuted daily between their homes and place of employment (Adepoju, 1998a). Nomadic pastoralists also moved clandestinely in search of grazing land for their herds across international frontiers in Sahelian West Africa.

The consolidation of borders at independence initially reduced cross-border migrations only slightly. Border regulations could be circumvented, and extensive borders made effective policing against clandestine migration extremely difficult, even when national governments enacted rules and regulations to control immigration into their newly independent countries, primarily with the intention of safeguarding the scarce jobs available for their own citizens in fulfilment of election promises. Prominent among these regulations are the Immigration Act (1963), the Immigration (Amendment) Act (1973) and the Immigration Manuals and Regulations (1972) in Nigeria, and the Immigration Quota System and issue of work permits in Sierra Leone. The latter was designed to discourage the inflow of unskilled or unqualified people into the country for the purpose of taking up employment. This development introduced a distinction between internal and international migration, both of which once involved free movement across a wide space of the subregion, and between regular and irregular immigration – through the requirement that immigrants must possess valid travel and entry documentation (Adepoju, 1995). In reality, most West African countries are agglomerations of peoples rather than states, and many citizens lack access to national passports. Hence, so-called irregular migrants were not only undocumented at their destination; they had often left their countries irregularly – without appropriate exit documents (passport, visa, health certificate) – and had failed to use designated official departure posts.

Post-independence nationalism was also manifested in other ways, including through changes in immigration laws that prescribed specific procedures for the entry and employment of non-indigenous workers, and later through xenophobia against immigrants. In the case of undocumented migrants already resident in a country, policies often took the form of exclusion and deportation. These were endemic: Senegal expelled Guineans in 1967; Côte d'Ivoire expelled approximately 16,000 Beninese in 1964; Sierra-Leone, and later Guinea and Côte d'Ivoire, expelled Ghanaian fishermen in 1968. Earlier on, Côte d'Ivoire had expelled over 1,000 Benin and Togo nationals in 1958; Chad expelled thousands of Benin nationals who were 'illegal migrants' and not 'law abiding'. In early 1979, Togolese farmers were expelled from Ghana and Côte d'Ivoire. Ghana expelled all 'illegal aliens without valid residence permit' as from 2 December 1969, an exercise that involved an estimated half a million people, mostly from Nigeria, the former Republic of Upper Volta (now Burkina Faso) and Niger (Adepoju, 1991, 1998b).

Many West African countries are now simultaneously immigration, emigration and transit countries. The main countries of immigration in the subregion are Côte d'Ivoire, Ghana, Senegal and Nigeria. The major labour-exporting countries include Burkina Faso, Guinea, Mali, and Togo. Overall, within the West African circuit, a lot of cross-border movements have essentially been intra-regional. The interdependent economies of countries have facilitated, and poverty has propelled, a wide variety of migration configurations, including autonomous migration of women. Rural–urban migration also intensified as farm labourers, deprived of the means to improve their living conditions, abandoned work and life in rural areas in search of waged labour in the cities. In recent years, traditional labour-importing countries have experienced political and economic crises, which have also spurred out-migration of their nationals (Adepoju, 2005b). Macro-economic adjustment measures and huge increases in the number of entrants into the labour market annually have fuelled the job crisis, creating sustained pressure for emigration. Most countries have been ruled by military dictators that mismanaged national economies and spurred exiles of intelligentsia, trade union officials and student union leaders in droves. Conflicts and environmental degradation have further aggravated the pressure for migration from poorer to relatively prosperous regions, within and outside the subregion. In the Sahel, in particular, desertification and cyclical famines have triggered waves of environmentally displaced persons across national frontiers within the subregion.

Re-creating free movement of persons in West Africa

The leaders of West Africa recognized in the early 1970s that regional integration could be an important step towards the subregion's collective integration into the global economy. The treaty creating the Economic Community of West African States (ECOWAS) was signed in Lagos on 28 May 1975 by the following countries: Benin, Burkina Faso, Cape Verde, Côte d'Ivoire, Gambia, Ghana, Guinea, Guinea-Bissau, Liberia, Mali, Niger, Nigeria, Senegal, Sierra Leone, and Togo. Article 27 of the treaty affirms a long-term objective to establish a Community citizenship that could be acquired automatically by nationals of all Member States. A key objective of the Preamble to the treaty is to remove obstacles to the free movement of goods, capital *and* people in the subregion (ECOWAS, 1999).

Phase one of the Protocol on Free Movement of Persons and the Right of Residence and Establishment of May 1979, guaranteeing free entry of Community citizens without a visa for ninety days, was ratified by Member States in 1980 and put into effect immediately. This once again ushered in an era of free movement of ECOWAS citizens within Member States (Adepoju, 2003). But with the ratification of the protocol on the Free Movement of Persons, the smaller countries expressed fear of economic domination by Nigeria, the Community's demographic and economic giant. At the same time, Nigerians were concerned about the possible influx of ECOWAS citizens into their country, and demanded that the effects of the protocol be closely watched, monitored and contained within their national interest (Onwuka, 1982).

The rights of entry, residence and establishment were to be progressively established within fifteen years after the protocol came in force. During the first five years, requirements for visas and entry permits were to be abolished. Community citizens in possession of valid travel documents and an international health certificate could enter Member States without a visa for up to ninety days. Member States could nevertheless refuse admission into their territory to immigrants deemed inadmissible under their national laws (Adepoju, 2002). In the case of expulsion, normally at the expense of the immigrants, states undertook to guarantee the security of the citizen concerned, his/her family and his/her property. The delayed second phase (Right of Residence) of the protocol came into force in July 1986, when all Member States ratified it, but the Right of Establishment has not been implemented until now. In 1992, the revised Treaty of ECOWAS, among others, affirmed the right of citizens of the Community to entry, residence and settlement, and enjoined Member States to recognize these rights in their respective territories. It also called on Member States to take all necessary steps at the national level to ensure that the provisions were duly implemented (ECOWAS, 2000*a*).

Facing the challenge: constraints and achievements

ECOWAS Member States belong to multiple unions with different aims and objectives, different levels and patterns of development, and different political systems and ideologies (Asante, 1990). Countries with small populations are juxtaposed with those with large populations and land masses; some are resource-poor, while others are endowed with human and natural resources. The smaller and economically less-prosperous countries are often suspicious of the demographic and economic giants – Nigeria and Côte d'Ivoire – in the Community.

Wavering political support, political instability, inter-state border disputes (or even wars), and what Lelart (1999) called 'veiled external interference' (especially in the francs zone), have retarded progress in ratifying and implementing ECOWAS's free-movement protocols. The persistent economic downturn has crippled the ability of states to pursue consistent macro-economic policies and has resulted in poor funding of economic unions. The non-convertibility of currencies (about eight currencies are in use in the subregion, excluding the CFA franc that binds former French colonies) hinders financial settlements and the harmonization of macro-economic policies and procedures. The ubiquitous roadblocks across frontiers, the lengthy and costly formalities at border posts and the corruption of officials have further hindered the free flow of persons and trade.

It also seems that the smaller and more homogenous the community is, the easier it is to function cohesively, as is the case of the Union Economique et Monétaire Ouest Africaine (UEMOA), for example, where Member States share a common currency, colonial history and the French language and therefore find it easier to implement joint programmes faster than the larger ECOWAS, which re-groups former colonial francophone, anglophone and lusophone countries (Adepoju, 2005a). The communality of language in the francophone zone tends to facilitate networks and communication across boundaries, especially because a large part of trade across borders consists of informal and clandestine transactions.

The coming into force of the protocol on free movement of persons coincided with a period of economic recession in most of West Africa, especially in countries bordering Nigeria, whose economy was fuelled by huge earnings in the oil sector. Oil-led employment opportunities attracted migrants of all skills, but especially unskilled workers, in their droves from Ghana, Togo, Chad, Mali and Cameroon to work in the oil, construction and services sectors (Adepoju, 1988). But the short-lived oil boom resulted in a rapid deterioration in living and working conditions, including devaluation of the national currency, a wage freeze and high inflation. In early 1983 and in mid-1985, the Nigerian government revoked Articles 4 and 27 of the Protocol so as to expel over a million undocumented migrants, mostly Ghanaians. The ratification of the second phase of the ECOWAS Protocol on Right of Residence, which came into force in July 1986, coincided with the introduction of Nigeria's structural adjustment programme. As the economic crisis deepened, approximately 0.2 million irregular migrants were again expelled in June 1985, a development that created a crisis of confidence in the Community (Adepoju, 2000). Foreigners became scapegoats as governments were confronted with seething economic and political problems; migrants were targets of hostility from the native population and blamed for whatever economic, social and political problems arose in the country.

Most countries of the subregion have enacted, or retained, a series of laws that in effect restrict 'foreigners' (including nationals of ECOWAS) from participating in certain kinds of economic activities; the expulsion of migrants also negated the raison d'être for establishing the Community. As long as the economies of recipient countries accommodated clandestine labour migrants, there was little sign of stress. As economic conditions worsened and unemployment among nationals deepened, however, immigrants quickly become targets for reprisals through expulsion (Ojo, 1999). As noted above, irregular immigrants have been expelled from virtually all West African countries before and even after the formation of ECOWAS.

Some political leaders are using ethnicity and religion to reclassify long-standing residents as non-nationals (as in Côte d'Ivoire); they are also wary of the presence of large numbers of immigrants on their shores during tightly contested elections, fearing that they may swing the vote in favour of the opposition along ethnic or religious alliances (Adepoju, 1998b). The situation in Côte d'Ivoire is the clearest illustration of this process. The country is one of the major immigration-receiving states in the subregion, as it has vast natural resources but a small domestic labour force: foreigners have for many years constituted about a quarter of its waged labour force. The country's first post-independent president, Félix Houphouët-Boigny, ignoring the arbitrary borders drawn by colonial powers, encouraged immigration from its poor neighbours. Immigrants from Burkina Faso, Nigeria, Liberia, Senegal and Ghana flooded the plantations clandestinely and did menial jobs that the local population despised. They brought their families and were allowed to marry cross-culturally, settle and vote. But in recent years, the shift in the country's liberal immigration policy and the growing anti-immigrant sentiments have taken a violent turn. The introduction of the concept of *ivoirité*, and the stripping of some of the rights that immigrants had hitherto enjoyed has sparked discontent and mistrust among immigrants (Adepoju, 2002). The chaos and the war between elements of the predominantly Muslim north and the Christian south threatens the very survival of a once-stable country. Thousands of nationals of Mali, Burkina Faso, Guinea and Nigeria returned home as anti-foreigner sentiments peaked. Dislodged Liberian refugees sought solace in Mali and Guinea.

The policy to register and issue special identity cards to foreigners is also widely viewed as aimed at identifying and deporting irregular immigrants (Adepoju, 2003). The long-delayed National Identity Card scheme launched in Nigeria in mid-February 2003 was designed in part to 'effectively control' undocumented immigrants and their nefarious activities. At about the same time, Liberia introduced a compulsory exit visa for all residents in the country – a move criticized as violating the fundamental right of its citizens to free movement in and out of the country. In March 1999, Ghana requested all aliens in the country to register and be issued with identity cards (Adepoju, 1999). Immigrants are suspicious of this move, recalling the antecedents of the 1969 Alien Compliance Order that culminated in the expulsion of non-Ghanaians.

The refugee regime, for a long time localized in the Horn of Africa and the Great Lakes region, moved swiftly to the subregion as Liberia's contagious civil war spread to Sierra Leone, soon engulfing Guinea and Guinea Bissau and then Côte d'Ivoire in its trail, while uprooting thousands of people internally and across national borders – who became displaced persons and refugees. Nearly 70 per cent of Liberia's population was displaced, and thousands who fled the war to seek refuge in Sierra Leone were soon dislodged as conflict broke out there in March 1991. Refugees were dispersed to Guinea and Côte d'Ivoire, only to be embroiled in another flight for safely, to Mali, Ghana and Burkina Faso. About 750,000 people were displaced in Côte d'Ivoire and another 500,000 'foreign' residents, mostly Burkinabes, were rendered homeless and in desperation fled to their countries of origin (Adepoju, 2005a). Moreover, as soon as one refugee-generating crisis is resolved, a new or renewed crisis emerges sequentially: sporadic border disputes between Senegal and Mauritania, Ghana and Togo, Liberia and Guinea have also led to refugee flows and the expulsion of Community citizens from these territories.

Evidence shows that most Member States have expelled Community citizens, in spite of the protocol on free movement of persons. Sentiments against non-nationals have risen in recent years as a result of the economic downturn, which has increased youth unemployment and political instability. Largely as a result of this, the Protocol on Establishment and Residence has not been implemented, despite the close links between free movement rights, trade integration, tariff regimes and the promotion of labour mobility in the subregion.

It is nevertheless worth noting that, despite the numerous constraints enumerated above, progress has been recorded on many fronts. The free movement of persons, without visas, within the subregion is a major achievement of ECOWAS. Associated with this development is the progress made in the areas of monetary policy, communication, trade and related matters. These include the introduction of ECOWAS travellers' cheques – the West African Unit of Account – to harmonize the subregion's monetary policy; the proposed adoption of a common currency by 2004 (now postponed to 2007) to facilitate cross-border trade transactions, and the introduction of the Brown Card travel certificates, to be used as ECOWAS passports (ECOWAS, 2000c).

The abolition of mandatory residency permit and the granting of the maximum ninety-day period of stay to ECOWAS citizens by immigration officials at entry points took effect from April 2000. Border posts and checkpoints on international highways, which hitherto menaced the free movement of persons and goods, were scrapped, and the Nigerian government dismantled all checkpoints between Nigeria and Benin. Border patrols were set up by Niger, Nigeria, Benin, Togo, Ghana, Burkina Faso and Mali to monitor and police national frontiers, in addition to closer collaboration and information-sharing between the police and internal security agents

(ECOWAS, 2003). The elimination of rigid border formalities and the modernization of border procedures through the use of passport-scanning machines were both designed to facilitate free and easier movement of persons across borders, the ultimate goal being the creation of a borderless West Africa (Adepoju, 2002).

The creation of a *borderless subregion* was the major item on the agenda of the meeting of heads of state and government held in Abuja, Nigeria, early in 2000. During the summit, the ECOWAS passport was adopted as a symbol of unity to progressively replace national passports in circulation over a transitional period of ten years. The subregional private airline (ECOAIR) was launched in Abuja to coincide with the twenty-fifth anniversary of the organization and to facilitate intra-regional travel (ECOWAS, 2000*b*).

Transport and telecommunication links between Member States have been boosted by the trans-coastal, trans-Sahelian and trans-coastal/Sahelian road networks. Regional infrastructure has been rehabilitated and expanded to foster economic integration, with the proposed establishment of two rail links: a coastal route from Lagos to Cotonou, Lomé and Accra, and a Sahelian route linking Lagos to Niamey and Ouagadougou. Border posts and all checkpoints on international airways are to be policed only by customs and immigration officials. In 2000, a zone for the circulation of goods, free of custom duties, was set up to facilitate the free movement of goods and persons across the borders of ECOWAS Member States. Earlier on, in December 1999, the Lomé Protocol on the mechanism for the prevention, management and control of conflicts, and the maintenance of peace and security, was signed.

Conflicts in the subregion are endemic, contagious, very violent and often senseless, as the experience of Liberia, Sierra Leone and Côte d'Ivoire shows. In this context, the Lomé Protocol (1999), and other ECOWAS efforts at conflict prevention and resolution should be reinforced. This mechanism is well ahead of other regional organizations in Africa. What is needed is an overwhelming emphasis on early warning and prevention, backed with the financial and human resources needed to forge ahead in addressing the root causes of conflicts, and to create an environment in which to build peaceful and stable conditions for sustainable development. It is also in this context that the limited achievements of the ECOWAS Ceasefire Monitoring Group (ECOMOG) in the areas of peacekeeping and monitoring engagements, and in curtailing the Liberian leader's regional destabilization plans, must be placed.

The way forward

Migration is an essential tool in integration that should be used effectively to break language and colonial barriers and to correct the historical mistakes made in the subregion that served to categorize its people as francophone, anglophone and lusophone. This colonial heritage promoted national sentiments among West Africans along these divides and above that of the Community (Adepoju, 2005a). Study and exchange programmes in West African countries should be encouraged to redress this colonial heritage. A viable starting point for the formation of attitudes favourable to migration is the formal educational system, using the 'catch them young strategy' to inform young school students of the positive roles and benefits of migration and the duties and obligations of migrants. Youth should be involved in cross-cultural activities, all the more so because they are our leaders-in-waiting, and are expected to assume the mantle of Community leadership in the future. Hence Member States should abolish existing discriminatory fees against non-nationals in their tertiary educational institutions.

Efforts at promoting a borderless scenario must also address the right of residence and establishment of migrants and the obligations of host countries. In that context, Member States should amend national laws and employment and investment codes that conflict with ECOWAS treaties and protocols and in effect restrict 'foreigners', including nationals of Community states, from participating in certain kinds of economic activities. Experience shows that effective free movement of persons cannot be divorced from access to employment at the destination (and, better still, possibly settlement) and ease of remitting earned income through formal banking channels. Currency convertibility and common currency arrangements become imperative and can greatly facilitate transactions, especially for the illiterate merchants, mostly women, who dominate the Nigeria-Benin-Togo-Côte d'Ivoire-Senegal-Gambia trade network.

The ECOWAS secretariat should undertake, or commission, a study to take stock of national laws and treaties that relate to migration; review and update laws, employment and investment codes that are at variance with ECOWAS Protocol on free movement of persons, establishment and settlement; and retrain and inform officials on the revised national laws and treaties, as well as ECOWAS Protocols, to ensure that they (at their level) foster rather than frustrate the objectives, modalities and procedures for free mobility of Community citizens.

Capacity-building of immigration officials is critical. The institutional capacity required to manage migratory flows and for effective policy-formulation and implementation must be strengthened through training and retraining key customs, immigration and security officials and police. Presently functioning as border control and security officials, their role has to be transformed into that of migration management, helping to facilitate rather than restrict migrations in regular situations and in the context of the subregion's MWB agenda. Training of officials to deal with the free movement of persons and goods and to understand the rights and obligation of migrants should be institutionalized to replace on-going ad-hoc arrangements.

To date, the issue of migration has been low on the development and political agenda of the subregion. There is no formal forum for dialogue and consultations among various stakeholders to discuss common approaches to migration concerns and to share ideas and enhance understanding and cooperation in migration management in the subregion. A West African Dialogue on Migration Management for all stakeholders, in particular the media and the public, should be established as a continuous process to combat the misrepresentations, ignorance and xenophobia that currently surround the issue of migration. Discourses on migration, especially from the receiving end, are full of anxiety, misconceptions, myths and prejudices; and are also fed on xenophobia. It is therefore imperative for each Member State to establish an Advisory Board on Migration. Membership of the board should be drawn from all stakeholders (civil society; researchers; officials from a range of relevant ministries and agencies; political, religious and traditional leaders and so on). The primary role of the board would be to serve as a forum to discuss country-specific concerns and options on migration and migration-management issues, and to monitor the status of implementation of national laws and ECOWAS decisions relating to migration.

Public enlightenment, concerted advocacy and public education campaigns should be mounted, possibly simultaneously in all countries of the subregion, to halt unwholesome hostility against migrants and refugees among traditionally hospitable peoples who in the past have been ready to share their meagre resources with strangers. In doing so, accurate information on the positive contribution of immigrants to national development, on the causes and consequences of migration at both their places of origin and destination, and on the fluidity of migration dynamics, which can turn countries of immigration into sending and transit countries, should be emphasized, elaborating the positive aspects of migrants as agents of development in source and destination countries.

An integrated transportation network is required, and must be maintained, to facilitate the smooth movement of persons and the distribution of goods and services. The infrastructural deficits in many states must be addressed and road networks upgraded and maintained. ECOWAS needs to harmonize and implement the intertwined policies of trade, investment, transport and movement of persons integrally.

A sustained sensitization action plan is required to create awareness in the private sector and among the general population of the Single Monetary Zone concept, currently being spearheaded by Nigeria and Ghana, and the Trade Liberalisation Scheme, which are leading to the creation of a Custom Union and a single regional market and to the adoption of a single ECO currency.

These are facilitative factors that, if fully implemented, could considerably enhance intra-Community trade, and especially the movement of persons, goods and services.

Conclusion

The specificity of the MWB scenario in West Africa is that free movement used to exist and, to some extent, still exists informally. In this respect, ECOWAS initiatives to promote a borderless region make a lot of sense and should be interpreted as the re-creation of free movement rather than as the elaboration of a new regional organization. These efforts have been partly successful, as they have made the movements of people much easier than before. It remains that, despite these initiatives and the repeated commitment of ECOWAS states to promote free movement, major constraints remain. This raises critical questions: Is a fully borderless West Africa possible? Could it be sustained?

The first phase of free movement has been achieved. The second and third phases, relating to establishment and residence, respectively, have still not been implemented. The piecemeal implementation of the protocols highlights the need for Member State governments to harmonize national laws that conflict with regional and subregional treaties, and to address the issue of the right of residence and establishment of migrants and the obligations of the host countries by amending national laws and investment codes that restrict 'foreigners', including nationals of Community states, from participating in some economic activities. They should also identify areas of agreement that they can progressively implement, notably the free movement of persons, the need for travel cards and traveller's cheques, a tariff regime, and harmonized customs and immigration formalities to enhance intra-regional labour mobility and cross-border trade. They should then implement other agreements using the variable speed approach, whereby sets of common objectives are agreed upon but component countries move at different speeds towards implementation – some rapidly and others slowly. It is not until Community citizens can move freely within, and work and reside in, Member States that the concept of a borderless West Africa will become fully operational.

ECOWAS's Protocol on Free Movement of Persons, Settlement and Establishment is a trendsetter among regional economic communities (RECs) in Africa. An orderly, well-managed migration can be a veritable instrument for economic, social and political integration in the subregion. Such an orderly movement can blossom only in situations of peace and stability, hence the need for sustainable development, employment creation, conflict prevention, and management and resolution mechanisms to promote stability. This also calls for closer cooperation and coordination among countries to harmonize their employment and investment policies. Above all, national labour migration laws have to be harmonized with ECOWAS Protocol on Free Movement of Persons, Settlement and Establishment. Regular consultations and dialogue among ECOWAS Member States, between them and other RECs in Africa, and, at the national level, among various stakeholders, would help resolve areas of friction and also place migration matters at the top of political agendas.

Nationals, especially potential migrants, should be provided with adequate information on the full provisions of the Protocol on Free Movement of Persons and on the rules and regulations guiding entry, residence and employment in Member States, especially the need for valid travel documents. Efforts should be made to enhance the population's access to national passports – and, in due course, to ECOWAS passports – by decentralizing the issuing authorities to district and local levels. Another major issue regards xenophobia, which is at its height in Côte d'Ivoire and is fanned by the media and politicians. Concerted advocacy and public education is needed to halt unwholesome hostility towards migrants and refugees.

A system of continuous policy dialogue should be instituted to engage all stakeholders – policy-makers, politicians, civil society, the media, migrant associations, etc. – in matters of migration management. Above all, a framework for monitoring the integration scheme and the implementation of decisions at national and subregional levels should be established. This is especially crucial in view of the need for Member States to cede authority to regional bodies. The prospect of a borderless West Africa is a challenging one, but plays a crucial role in fostering tolerance and social cohesion in the region.

Bibliography

Adepoju, A. 1983. Patterns of migration by sex. C. Oppong (ed.), *Females and Males in West Africa*. London, George Allen and Unwin.

———. 1988. Labour migration and employment of ECOWAS nationals in Nigeria. T. Fashoyin (ed.), *Labour and Development in Nigeria*. Lagos, Nigeria, Landmark.

———. 1991. Binational communities and labour circulation in sub-Saharan Africa. D. G. Papademetriou and P. L. Martin (eds), *The Unsettled Relationship: Labour Migration and Economic Development*. New York, Greenwood Press, pp. 45–64.

———. 1995. Emigration dynamics in sub-Saharan Africa. *International Migration*, Vol. 33, Nos 3–4, pp. 315–91.

———. 1998a. Links between internal and international migration: the African situation. R. T. Appleyard and C. Stahl (eds), *International Migration Today*, Vol. 2. Paris, UNESCO and University of Western Australia (Nedlands).

———. 1998b. The role of diverse regional economic communities in the politics of migration in African countries. *Migration at the Threshold of the Third Millennium: IV World Congress on the Pastoral Care of Migrants and Refugees*, Vatican City, Pontifical Council for the Pastoral Care of Migrants and Itinerant People.

————. 1999. Overview of irregular/undocumented migration and regional co-operation in Africa. *Asian Migrant*, Vol. 12, No. 3, pp. 75–83.

————. 2000. Regional integration, continuity and changing patterns of intra-regional migration in sub-Saharan Africa. M. Siddique (ed.), *International Migration into the 21st Century: Essays in Honour of Reginald Appleyard*. Aldershot, U.K., Edward Elgar.

————. 2002. Fostering free movements of persons in West Africa: achievements, constraints, and prospects for international migration. *International Migration*, Vol. 40, No. 2, pp. 3–28.

————. 2003. Migration in West Africa. *Development*, Vol. 46, No. 3, pp. 37–41.

Amin, S. 1974. Introduction to S. Amin (ed.), *Modern Migration in Western Africa*. Oxford, Oxford University Press.

Asante, S. K. B. 1990. Regional economic cooperation and integration: the experience of ECOWAS. P. Anyang'Nyongo (ed.), *Regional Integration in Africa: Unfinished Agenda*. Nairobi, Kenya, Academy Science Publishers.

Economic Commission for Africa (ECA). 1983. *International Migration, Population Trends and Their Implications for Africa*. Addis Ababa, ECA. (African Population Studies Series No. 4.)

ECOWAS. 1999. *An ECOWAS Compendium on Movement, Right of Residence and Establishment*. Abuja, Nigeria, ECOWAS Secretariat.

————. 2000a. *Executive Secretary's Report, 2000*. Abuja, Nigeria, ECOWAS Secretariat.

————. 2000b. *Final Communique: Mini Summit of Heads of State and Government on the creation of a borderless ECOWAS*. Abuja, Nigeria, ECOWAS Secretariat.

————. 2000c. Internal Affairs Ministers' Record Progress on ECOWAS Passport. Abuja, ECOWAS Secretariat.

————. 2003. Achievements and Prospects. Abuja, Nigeria, ECOWAS Secretariat. www.sec.ecowas.int/sitecedeao/english/achievements.htm (Accessed 21 December 2006.).

Lelart, M. 1999. The franc zone and European monetary integration. D. C. Bach (ed.), *Regionalisation in Africa: Integration and Disintegration*. Cambridge, U.K., James Currey.

Ojo, O. B. J. 1999. Integration in ECOWAS: successes and difficulties. D. C. Bach (ed.), *Regionalisation in Africa: Integration and Disintegration*. Cambridge, U.K., James Currey, pp. 119–27.

Onwuka, R. I. 1982. The ECOWAS protocol on the free movement of persons: a threat to Nigerian security? *African Affairs*, Vol. 81, No. 323, pp. 193–206.

Zachariah, K. C. and Conde, J. 1981. *Migration in West Africa: Demographic Aspects: A Joint World Bank-OECD Study*. London, Oxford University Press.

Chapter 9

Histories, realities and negotiating free movement in southern Africa

Sally Peberdy and Jonathan Crush

Throughout the world, more than 190 million people live outside the country of their birth: over half of these cross-border migrants live in developing countries (United Nations, 2006). There are already an estimated 16.3 million migrants on the African continent, and the International Labour Organization (ILO) estimates that by 2025, 10 per cent of Africans will be living outside their country of origin (United Nations Development Programme [UNDP], 2002). Some 20 per cent of all labour migrants in the world live and work in Africa. Africa's history of migration and intra- and inter-continental trade stretches back many centuries. As in the rest of the world, countries on the continent are grappling with how best to manage the movement of people across national borders. This is particularly important given the significance of labour migration to many of Africa's economies, and as the continent endeavours to advance its position in relation to the rest of the world.

Southern Africa perhaps epitomizes the shape of African migration. It is a region with a rich history of migration that dates back long before the arrival of Europeans on the continent. This history stretches into the present, as people continue to move in significant numbers across the region's national borders and from, and into, the rest of the continent and the rest of the world. Although the colonial and apartheid past of the region has shaped contemporary patterns of labour migration, the post-apartheid era has seen changes in patterns of regional migration, particularly to and from South Africa. Despite the long history of intra-regional migration within southern Africa, the movement of migrants and refugees in the region is controlled by nationally based legislation (Klaaren and Rutinwa, 2003). Notwithstanding this long history of intra-regional migration, nationals of the region often show hostile attitudes to regional migration and migrants (Crush and Pendleton, 2004; Mattes et al., 1999; Southern African Migration Project [SAMP] and South African Human Rights Commission [SAHRC], 2001).

Today's Africa, emerging from many of the continents' liberation movements, has had a long, if interrupted, tradition of pan-Africanism. Since 1990 most African countries have renewed their commitment to rejuvenating and reinventing notions of African unity and to finding continental and regional solutions to African development. Key to these initiatives is the promotion of continental and regional economic cooperation and integration. These efforts can be seen in the reinvention of the Organization of African Unity as the African Union (AU) and the formation of the New Partnership for African Development (NEPAD). A number of sub-continental regional bodies also promote regional economic integration, cooperation and development.

The dominant regional organization in southern Africa is the Southern African Development Community (SADC). Since its reconstitution in 1992 there has been renewed commitment from member countries to regional economic cooperation and integration as a strategy for regional development. As part of these efforts, SADC states have ratified a Free Trade Protocol that aims to create a free trade area within the SADC by 2008. However, attempts to facilitate the movement of people within the SADC have not met with the same success. Draft protocols relating to the movement of people have, instead, been highly contentious, and progress on the Draft Protocol on the Facilitation of Movement of People has been slow. First appearing as the Draft Protocol on the Free Movement of People in 1995, re-drafted as the Draft Protocol on the Facilitation of Movement of Persons in 1997–1998, a final Draft Protocol was signed by six states in August 2005, starting the process of ratification. Until ratification, and, as drafted, even after ratification, intra-regional migration in southern Africa will continue to be regulated by national immigration and refugee policies and legislation.

This chapter examines the contradictions between the longstanding history of regional migration, regional commitments to economic integration and cooperation, and the slow progress made by the SADC in facilitating the movement of people through the region. The chapter begins with a brief examination of the long history of migration to the region, identifying some of the significant changes that have taken place over the past decade. It then explores the development of regional organizations and integration initiatives in southern Africa, focusing on attempts to facilitate the movement of people throughout the region.

Changing patterns of migration

Patterns of twenty-first century migration have their origins in the mid-nineteenth century. Indeed, migration was probably the single most important factor tying together all of the various colonies and countries of the sub-continent into a single regional labour market during the twentieth century. Longstanding patterns, forms and dynamics of migration have undergone major restructuring in the last two decades. These changes have had a considerable impact on the livelihood strategies of the poor, and have major implications on national migration policies and policies to reduce poverty and inequality. Southern Africa is now, quite literally, a region on the move (McDonald, 2000).

Several causes are behind this dynamic state of affairs. First, the end of apartheid produced new opportunities for internal and cross-border mobility and new incentives for moving. Second, the integration of South Africa with the SADC region brought an increase in legal and undocumented cross-border flows and new forms of intra-regional mobility. Third, South Africa's reconnection with the global economy opened the country and region up to forms of migration commonly associated with globalization (Crush and McDonald, 2002). Fourth, rural and urban poverty and unemployment have pushed more people out of households in search of a livelihood: one result of this has been the feminization of poverty in rural southern Africa and a significant gender reconfiguration of migration streams (Dodson, 1998). Fifth, HIV/AIDS has had a demonstrable impact on migration: not only is the rapid diffusion of the epidemic itself inexplicable without reference to the mobility of people, but new forms of migration are emerging in response (Williams et al., 2002; Ansell and van Blerk, 2004; International Organization for Migration [IOM], 2003).

Finally, the countries of the SADC are not new to forced migration; the social and economic impact of the Mozambican and Angolan civil wars continue to reverberate, as do continued civil war in the Democratic Republic of the Congo and economic destabilization in Zimbabwe. Recurrent civil strife in other parts of Africa has generated refugee movements and new kinds of asylum seekers to and within the region. At the same time, access to Europe, North America and Australia has become more difficult for asylum seekers from Africa. Furthermore, the cessation of hostilities in some of these countries has confronted countries of asylum with issues of repatriation and integration.

Other significant changes in the last twenty years have been the virtual cessation of immigration from Europe and a dramatic increase in the numbers of skilled migrants leaving southern Africa. Migrant streams have also become far more diverse, and southern Africa has begun to receive migrants from developing countries further afield, including the rest of Africa and Asia.

Visitors and tourists

The number of people legally crossing borders throughout the southern African region has exploded in the last decade. In South Africa, for example, the annual number of border crossings by visitors increased from around 1 million to over 6.5 million between 1990 and 2002.[1] Africans comprised the overwhelming majority of these visitors: border crossings by African visitors increased from 550,000 in 1990 to over 4.5 million in 2002. The majority of African border crossings were visitors from other SADC countries; the number of visits by other SADC nationals increased from 500,000 to over 4 million per year over the same period (Department of Home Affairs [DHA], 2004).

SAMP found that visiting or tourism were the major reasons cited by people who had crossed regional borders: Namibia and Swaziland (58 per cent), Lesotho (36 per cent), Mozambique (17 per cent), and Zimbabwe (16 per cent) (McDonald, 2000, p. 232). Relatively minor reasons included study and medical treatment. Available data from other SADC countries shows a marked increase in inward and outward legal border crossing in most other states (Oucho et al., 2000; Frayne and Pendleton, 2002; Tevera and Zinyama, 2002; Sechaba Consultants, 2002; Simelane and Crush, 2004). Studies also show similar variety in stated reasons for entry. Again, the primary stated reason is not to work but for visiting, trade and business purposes (many of these business travellers are found in the official count of visitors).

Visitors, whether in South Africa as tourists, on short business visits or travelling for trade purposes, spend considerable amounts of money in the country. In 2002, African visitors to South Africa contributed R22 billion (or 45 per cent) of the R48.8 billion total directly spent in South Africa by foreign visitors (Rogerson, 2004). When individual countries are considered, six SADC countries (Zimbabwe, Lesotho, Botswana, Mozambique, Swaziland and Zambia) made the top ten most important contributing countries. The average spend of visitors arriving by air from Angola and Zambia exceeded that of the average spend of European and North American visitors (R14,000–16,700 per visit) (ibid.). Average individual spend by SADC visitors travelling by land varied from R2,200 (Swaziland) to more than R9,000 (Malawi).

As a result of this increase in traffic, border posts throughout the region have experienced increases in the volume of human traffic. The pressure on already limited border-control resources has been enormous, with long delays and inefficiency becoming the norm at many border posts. The region has concurrently experienced a growth in migration of people from other parts of the continent as well as significant growth in tourism arrivals from overseas.

Labour migration

South African stated-purpose-of-entry data is available by country from Statistics South Africa on a monthly basis. Although limited to designated categories (holiday, business, study, work, immigration), the numbers do not suggest that the majority of people enter for work or to seek work. This is confirmed by SAMP research, which reveals a multiplicity of motives for cross-border movement: cumulatively, in a study of six SADC countries, fewer than 25 per cent of immigrant respondents had moved to work or to look for work. However, respondents showed considerable inter-country variation in the percentage who said they had migrated for work: Mozambique (67 per cent), Zimbabwe (29 per cent), Lesotho (25 per cent), Namibia (13 per cent) and Swaziland (9 per cent) (McDonald, 2000, p. 232).

Male contract labour migration to the mines (South Africa, Zambia, Zimbabwe) and commercial farms and plantations (South Africa, Zimbabwe, Swaziland) is the most enduring form of legal cross-border labour migration within the region, beginning in the late nineteenth century and continuing to the present (Crush et al., 1992; Crush and James, 1995; Jeeves and Crush, 1997). Mine migration was most highly regulated through systems of recruitment under a single agency, the Employment Bureau of Africa (TEBA).

By the 1990s, only the South African gold and platinum mines continued to employ large numbers of domestic and foreign migrants; other mining sectors in South Africa (such as coal mining) and elsewhere in the region (Zambia, Zimbabwe) had moved to local and/or stabilized workforces before the 1990s (Crush and James, 1995). During the 1990s, however, the South African mines experienced major downsizing and retrenchments, creating considerable social disruption and increased poverty in supplier areas. Interestingly, the South African mines laid off local workers at a much faster rate than foreign workers. As a result, the proportion of foreign workers rose from 40 per cent in the late 1980s to close to 60 per cent today (Crush and Peberdy, 2004, p. 8). Mozambicans now make up 25 per cent of the mine workforce, up from 10 per cent a decade ago (Crush and Peberdy, 2004). Retrenchments in the mines have led to a fall in remittances, presenting major challenges for households formally reliant on them. Other family members have begun to migrate in response.

An area of great concern to governments in the region is the growth in skilled migration from the region. Despite the poor quality of the data, there can be little doubt that the 'brain-drain' from the SADC region has accelerated since 1990, particularly from South Africa, Malawi and Zimbabwe. Domestically, economic and political circumstances have conspired to create a large pool of potential emigrants. New global job opportunities in many sectors have encouraged skilled workers to act. However, there is uncertainty over the numbers involved. In the case of South Africa, there is evidence that official statistics undercount the numbers by as much as two-thirds (Brown et al., 2000). Studies of other countries in the region show statistics that are either non-existent or very badly outdated. In the vacuum, highly inflated guesstimates are extremely common in the media.

Of particular interest is the sizable intra-regional brain drain ('brain circulation') and emigration from the region (McDonald and Crush, 2002). Some countries, like Zimbabwe, are disadvantaged by both. Some may gain what others lose (South Africa, Botswana). For the region as a whole, within-SADC brain drain means no net loss, but it may cause tensions between countries. As a matter of fact, countries that are able to attract skilled migrants from other parts of the region, for instance South Africa, may be reluctant to admit them, not wanting to cause problems for, and with, their neighbours (Mdladlose, 2004). The impact of the brain drain is affected by regional migration policies. This has led most countries in the region to eschew brain gain strategies, in the form of proactive immigration policies, and to search for replacement skills (Crush, 2002).

Migration for business and trade

Available data suggests that the southern African region is being increasingly integrated into transnational continental and regional trade networks, both formal and informal. The re-entry of South Africa into the SADC has led to a significant increase in travel for business purposes (DHA, 2004). South African data shows that in 2002 there were over 450,000 visits for business purposes to South Africa. The majority of these arrivals (some 300,000 or 65 per cent) came from the rest of the continent (DHA, 2004).

Similarly, informal or small-scale cross-border trade, which has been long established in the region, seems to be growing in volume. A SAMP study shows that trade and shopping (usually for business) comprise a significant reason for movement in the region (McDonald, 2000). An average of 7 per cent of respondents in the SAMP survey said the purpose of their last visit was to buy and sell goods (Lesotho, 3 per cent; Mozambique, 2 per cent; Namibia, 2 per cent; Zimbabwe, 21 per cent). A further 11 per cent said they had travelled to shop (Lesotho, 19 per cent; Mozambique, 4 per cent; Namibia, 1 per cent and Zimbabwe, 21 per cent) (McDonald, 2000, p. 232). Across certain borders, informal trade is likely to exceed formal-sector cross-border movement of goods. Informal merchants or small-scale cross-border traders are among the most enterprising and energetic of contemporary migrants. They face major bureaucratic and other obstacles, even within a region heading for free trade by 2008, and often fail to benefit from the freer regional cross-border trade environment (Peberdy, 2004; Minde and Nakhumwa, 1997; Peberdy and

Crush, 2000; Peberdy and Crush, 1998; Peberdy and Rogerson, 2000; Peberdy, 2000*a*, 2000*b*). Because of onerous visa requirements for business permits, most of these traders travel on visitor permits.

Notwithstanding the importance of cross-border trading as a livelihood strategy for many households and its role in providing employment, it still needs to be better understood and, where possible, facilitated by policy changes in migration and customs and excise regimes. No country in the region yet has a visa or permit to accommodate cross-border traders, although some border posts offer semi-formal arrangements that allow traders to cross borders on certain days. South Africa's recent (2005) immigration regulations may also facilitate access for small-scale cross-border traders from neighbouring countries (Botswana, Lesotho, Mozambique, Namibia, Swaziland and Zimbabwe),[2] as may the new SADC Draft Protocol on the Facilitation of Movement of People, if ratified.

Irregular migrants

The migrant stream that attracts most public and official attention is 'undocumented', 'illegal' or 'unauthorized' migration (Waller, 2006). The first point to emphasize is that clandestine border crossing in southern Africa is nothing new (Peberdy, 1998). And, while the volume has undoubtedly increased in the last two decades, it hardly warrants the often inflammatory language used to describe these flows. Third, undocumented migration tends to be driven by economic circumstances and migration regimes that do not accommodate semi-skilled and unskilled workers. Sectors that are significant employers of undocumented migrants include commercial agriculture, construction and secondary industry (Rogerson, 1999; Crush et al., 2000).

Finally, enforcement in all countries tends to focus on identifying and deporting violators with the minimum of due process. In terms of sheer volume, South Africa is easily the regional leader in this, having deported over a million people since 1990 (many are repeat deportees). Deportations and the treatment of undocumented workers has led to simmering tensions over this issue among countries in the region (for instance, Botswana and Zimbabwe, and South Africa and Zimbabwe and Mozambique). Bilateral commissions have done little either to stop the flow of migrants or to change the mentality of exclusion and control.

Forced migration and refugees

In terms of forced migration, both Mozambique and latterly Angola and the Democratic Republic of the Congo (DRC) have experienced major outflows of refugees to neighbouring countries and significant internal displacement (McGregor, 1998). In the 1990s, the majority of Mozambican refugees to Malawi, Swaziland and Zimbabwe returned home, but not without considerable uncertainty and hardship. However, many of the estimated 350,000 refugees who fled from southern Mozambique to South Africa remained. Angolan refugees are now being repatriated from Namibia, South Africa and Zambia. Refugees fleeing the genocide in Rwanda ended up in the United Republic of Tanzania and the DRC. Now, refugees from the DRC can be found across the region, particularly in Zambia.

In the 1990s, there was a new and steady southward flow of forced migrants, undocumented migrants and students. South Africa now boasts sizeable francophone African and Nigerian urban communities (Morris, 1999; Morris and Bouillon, 2001). Between 1994 and 2004, approximately 186,000 applications for asylum were made in South Africa; 28,000 applications were granted (DHA, 2005). In 2002, foremost among these were applicants from Africa – Zaire/DRC (7,700), Angola (6,900), Somalia (5,900), Nigeria (5,300), Senegal (4,500), Ethiopia (3,200) and Burundi (2,000) – and from Asia – India (6,400), Pakistan (5,300) and Bangladesh (1,300) (UNHCR, 2004; DHA, 2004). However, Zambia is the largest host of forced migrants, and is home to over 250,000 refugees.

SADC does not have a coordinated regional response to the challenge of internal and external refugee movements. Individual countries are left to shoulder the burden as best they can with support from international agencies. All but Botswana are signatories to the major refugee conventions, but few have advanced or adequate systems of refugee determination in place. Nor is there any mechanism to deal with disputes that may arise if SADC countries accept refugees from other SADC countries.

Regional attitudes to migration and migrants

Xenophobia and hostility to migrants are common in the region, and in some countries, for instance South Africa, have involved physical attacks on non-nationals. A SAMP study suggests that nationals of Botswana, Namibia, and South Africa are particularly intolerant of non-nationals, and especially of African non-nationals (Crush and Pendleton, 2004; SAMP and SAHRC, 2001; Mattes et al., 1999). These attitudes are reflected in the media and are often found in government policies and the rhetoric of politicians (Danso and McDonald, 2000).

The 2001–2002 SAMP study of the attitudes of urban-based nationals of six countries in the region (Botswana, Mozambique, Namibia, South Africa, Swaziland and Zimbabwe) revealed that citizens of these countries have a strong national identity and respect for national borders (Crush and Pendleton, 2004). Disturbingly, in the context of this discussion, nationals of these countries did not have a strong regional consciousness and did not distinguish between migrants from the region, the rest of Africa, and those from Europe and North America (Crush and Pendleton, 2004). (However, it should be said that Mozambicans showed a stronger sense of regional identity than other respondents.) The survey found that nationals of all countries consistently overestimated the number of foreigners in their country and saw non-national migrants as a problem rather than an opportunity (Crush and Pendleton, 2004). South Africans and Namibians held the strongest opinions in this regard, followed by Botswanans.

High levels of xenophobia are of concern, not just because they make individual migrants' lives uncomfortable. Xenophobia allows the exclusion of non-nationals from vital services that they may be entitled to (health and education services, for instance) and further marginalizes and excludes vulnerable communities, thereby increasing inequalities – even for non-nationals who are in the country legally (Community Agency for Social Enquiry [CASE], 2003; Peberdy and Majodina, 2000). Furthermore, while the regulatory regime looks relatively protective of migrants, immigrants, refugees and asylum seekers, most governments (including wealthier countries like South Africa) lack the resources to effectively enforce legislation. Finally, relatively high levels of hostility to migrants along with relatively strong support for exclusionary migration policies do little to create a climate for the introduction of legislative changes that recognize the region's long history of migration and as a regional labour market.

Regional organizations, regional integration and strategies for free movement

Migration policy is formulated at various interlocking scales, from the continental (AU/NEPAD) to local government, via regional and national levels. But how are we to get these different levels of governance to interface with one another to develop an integrated approach to policy development and migration management? At the continental level, the attitudes of NEPAD and the African Union (AU) towards migration perhaps epitomize the issue. Both cite freer movement of people across the continent as a key long-term objective. Yet little analysis is presented of the reasons for this position or its likely impacts, and there is no systematic discussion of the institutional mechanisms by which this might be achieved.

Article 4 of the Abuja Treaty of 1991, which established the African Economic Community of the Organisation of African Unity (OAU, now the AU), set as an objective the progressive removal 'of obstacles to the free movement of persons, goods, services and capital and the right of residence and establishment'(cited in Oucho and Crush, 2001, p. 142). Article 43 of the treaty also committed Member States to pursue this aim 'at bi-lateral or regional levels' (ibid.). These sentiments were reiterated by a decision of the OAU Council of Ministers in Lusaka in 2001, which said that Member States should 'work towards free movement of people and to strengthen intra-regional and inter-regional cooperation in matters concerning migration.'[3]

Some movement towards this sizeable objective was made with the reconstitution of the OAU as the AU. In 2004, the Executive Council of the AU was presented with a Draft Strategic Framework on Migration (African Union, 2004). This Draft Framework is more cautious than were earlier AU treaties, but it does explore the significance of migration and its developmental opportunities. The document identifies the importance of migration and its 'untapped potential' for the continent, arguing that attempts to manage and exploit this potential will require 'enhanced dialogue on subregional, regional and pan-African levels' (p. 2). It states that the Framework's objective is to 'encourage Member States to implement and integrate migration issues into their national and regional agenda by developing national migration policies as stated in the Lusaka Decision' (p. 7). In essence, the document again asks Member States to work towards the free movement of people on the continent, but although it makes recommendations for action on specific issues, it provides no directions about how this larger objective might be achieved.

Countries of sub-Saharan Africa have established various subregional bodies with the aim of enhancing economic integration and cooperation and promoting harmonization of policy and legislation. The East African countries of Kenya, Uganda and United Republic of Tanzania formed the earliest economic pact; however this fell apart in 1977 and was only restored in 1996. Some west and central African countries formed the West African Economic Community (CEAO) in 1973. West African countries came together as the Economic Community of West African States (ECOWAS) in 1975 (Asante, 1986). The Treaty of Lagos, which established ECOWAS, gave as a long-term goal the removal of barriers to trade, employment and population movement (Oucho and Crush, 2001, p. 141; see also Chapter 8 in this volume). In 1993, ECOWAS reaffirmed its commitment to establishing the free movement of 'people, services and capital' (cited in Hough, 2000, p. 7).

Southern African states may be members of one or more of three regional organizations, the Southern African Customs Union (SACU), the Southern African Development Community (SADC) and the Common Market for Eastern and Southern Africa (COMESA).

The smallest and the longest-standing southern African organization is the Southern African Customs Union (SACU). SACU encompasses Botswana, Lesotho, Namibia, South Africa and Swaziland. The remit of SACU refers only to trade between these countries and the setting of common tariffs imposed on imports from outside the Union. However, reflecting the historical SACU relationships, free movement of people was allowed between South Africa and Botswana, Lesotho and Swaziland until 1963 (with apartheid racial restrictions on movement once people had entered South Africa) (Peberdy, 1999, 1998). There was also relatively free movement between South Africa and South West Africa (now Namibia) until independence in 1990, while it remained a territory administered by South Africa.

The largest contemporary regional organization including southern African countries is the Common Market of Eastern and Southern Africa (COMESA). COMESA emerged in 1993 from the Preferential Trade Area for Eastern and Southern African States, which was formed in 1981. All countries in the SADC, with the exception of South Africa, are members of COMESA. COMESA has the stated aims of pursuing free trade and free movement of people through its Member States (Oucho and Crush, 2001, p. 141). In 1999, COMESA launched a free trade area, in order to guarantee the free movement of goods and services produced in the community and to promote the removal of tariff and non-tariff barriers to trade (Crush and Oucho, 2001, p. 141). However, this has yet to become operational. The organization also aims to free the movement of capital and investments within the community and to establish a customs union (with a single tariff rate for imports from non-COMESA countries), along with a currency union and common currency.

COMESA is relatively positive about the concept of the free movement of persons between Member States, which it advocates in its founding treaty. In 2000, the organization stated that it intends to enable 'the adoption of a common visa arrangement, including the right of establishment leading eventually to the free movement of *bona fide* persons' (COMESA, 2000). How such an aim will become operational is not clear, nor is it clear what progress, if any, the organization is making on this issue, although it has set a deadline of achieving free movement of people and monetary union by 2025.

The only organization that encompasses all countries of southern Africa is the Southern African Development Community (SADC).[4] In 1979, various southern African countries, excluding South Africa, came together to form the Southern African Development Coordination Conference (SADCC). The purpose of the SADCC was to reduce the dependence of southern African states on the apartheid South African economy and transport network. In 1992, the SADCC was transformed into the Southern African Development Community (SADC) to accommodate South Africa. The Democratic Republic of the Congo also subsequently joined. Article 23 of the SADC Declaration of

Treaty and Protocol of 1992 (signed in Windhoek) states that 'the SADC shall seek to involve fully the peoples of the region and non-governmental organizations (NGOs) in the process of regional integration ... [and] shall cooperate with and support the initiative of the peoples of the region and NGOs contributing to the objectives of this Treaty in areas of cooperation in order to foster closer relations among the communities, associations and peoples of the region' (Mwaniki, 2003, p. 3).

From the continental level of the African Union to the regional level of the SADC, organizations bringing together African countries appear to have committed themselves to at least some of the principles of pan-Africanism. They seem to unanimously agree that the route to continental and regional development, cooperation and integration lies in freeing the movement of people, goods and capital. Most organizations have, as part of their founding documents, and certainly since the 1990s, a commitment to pursuing these aims, including the freer movement of people. Some movement has been made on relaxing constraints on the movement of goods. Yet when it comes to the movement of people, little progress appears to have been made, even though the development of the African Union Draft Strategic Framework on Migration does indicate that migration has moved onto the agenda of the organization. However, the lack of progress in creating zones of free movement of people may reflect the politicized problems of implementation (Oucho and Crush, 2001; Mistry, 2000). This chapter will now turn to look in more detail at the attempts of the SADC to pursue the freer movement of goods and people.

The SADC and freeing the movement of people and goods

When the SADCC was reconstituted as the SADC in 1992, it produced a range of regional protocols to be ratified and implemented by Member States. The intention behind these protocols was to pursue the aims of the SADC to promote development through regional integration and cooperation. The Member States meet at ministerial level on a regular basis to push forward these aims and to promote discussion and dialogue.

Progress has been made on a number of fronts, although some protocols have engendered some controversy and dissention among Member States. The Protocol on Education and Training has been ratified without notable dissent (Ramphele, 1999). Some progress has also been made with the development of a 'Univisa', intended to promote tourism to the region. Directed at nationals of non-SADC states, the visa would allow holders access to more than one country in the region. The development of the Univisa follows the ongoing creation of trans-frontier national parks, whereby countries agree that a park can cut across national boundaries.

Although the process was contentious, the SADC has successfully ratified the SADC Free Trade Protocol (Jenkins et al., 2000). The Protocol introduces a gradual scaling down of tariffs with the aim of creating a free trade area by 2008. Alongside the scaling down of tariffs, some countries have also introduced bilateral arrangements with tariff reductions to promote trade. The focus of the discussions around the Free Trade Protocol was large-scale, formal-sector trade. Yet, as mentioned above, a significant proportion of trade in the region is carried out by small-scale entrepreneurs, often called informal sector traders (Peberdy, 2004). The activities of these traders, who travel with their goods (and therefore encounter migration as well as trade regimes), were not considered in the Free Trade Protocol – nor have they been considered thus far in the scaling-down process.

Attempts by the SADC to promote the freer movement of nationals within the region have been far more fraught and have only made progress in 2005. The first protocol generated by the SADC, the Draft Protocol on the Free Movement of People, was completed in 1995. It emerged from a workshop held in 1993 and a meeting of the SADC Council of Ministers in 1994. The Draft Free Movement Protocol 'was based on a clear vision of a region with a shared history (including free movement before colonial conquest)' and a future 'where capital, goods and people could move freely across national borders' (Oucho and Crush, 2001, p. 144). The protocol aimed for the gradual abolition of barriers to movement across national borders of member countries. Oucho and Crush (2001, pp. 144–5) lay out the three-phase process proposed by the Free Movement Protocol:

1. Phase One (within twelve months): visa-free entry from one state to another would be effected for visits of up to six months, provided that the individual has valid travel documents and enters through an official border post.
2. Phase Two (within three years): any citizen would have the right to reside in another state in order to take up employment, and to enter freely for the purpose of seeking employment.
3. Phase Three (within five years): states would abolish 'all restrictions on the freedom of establishment (permanent residence) of citizens of other Member States in its territory'.

The South African government was sufficiently alarmed by the Free Movement Protocol that it commissioned an analysis from the South African Human Sciences Research Council (HSRC, 1995). The HSRC report was highly critical and urged that the Protocol be rejected. The objections of the HSRC report can largely be grouped into seven areas (HSRC, 1995; Oucho and Crush, 2001):

1. The report argued, incorrectly, that there had never been any kind of free movement in the region.
2. The report argued that the Protocol would add to South Africa's already sizeable unemployment problem.
3. The report falsely suggested that the use of foreign labour in mines would be phased out, creating a demand for jobs from retrenched non-South African mineworkers.
4. The report suggested that it would legitimize (an over-inflated number of) irregular migrants already resident in South Africa.
5. The report suggested that freer movement of southern Africans would lead to an increase in xenophobia and attacks on non-South Africans.
6. The report suggested that the porosity of the borders of the region would lead to an increase in irregular migration from outside the region, particularly into South Africa.
7. Finally, the report concluded that South Africa should only encourage the free movement of goods and capital.

The objections of the report were problematic. First, the report ignores the fact that the borders of the region have always been porous and never effective in keeping out those who really wanted to cross them and, therefore, that irregular migrants have always been able to move through the region if they wanted. The report's concerns regarding labour migration ignore the long-standing role of labour from the region in South Africa's economy, while also ignoring evidence that suggests migrants and immigrants may create work, rather than take it. Its assertions regarding xenophobia are equally problematic, suggesting that the only way to counter anti-foreigner sentiments is to accede to it and restrict the entry of non-nationals. Although its assertions regarding the movement of goods and capital are potentially positive, it does not recognize that the effective movement of goods and capital may involve people crossing borders.

The South African Minister of Home Affairs supported the analysis, arguing that:

> For South Africa to compromise its immigration policy and control and allow free movement will place the citizens in an even more precarious situation than they are in already, with disastrous consequences for the Reconstruction and Development Programme (RDP) and for the realization of our commitment to a right for a better life for all. (Buthelezi, cited in Oucho and Crush, 2001, p. 148)

The SADC Ministers of Home Affairs met in 1996 to discuss the protocol. South Africa, Botswana and Namibia all opposed the Free Movement Protocol, along the lines of the objections outlined by the HSRC. Using the HSRC authors as consultants, the South African Department of Home Affairs decided to draft an alternative protocol: the South African Draft Protocol on the

Facilitation of Movement of People, which was much more restrictive in approach. Essentially it was only willing to go as far as the first stage of the original protocol: visa-free entry for short-term visitors. The SADC Secretariat declined to accept the South African draft and instead revised the Free Movement Protocol as its own SADC Draft Protocol on the Facilitation of Movement of People, which was completed in 1998, although it began to be circulated in 1997. The South African draft fell away.

The SADC Protocol on the Facilitation of Movement of People (or the Facilitation of Movement Protocol) was an attempt to deal with the concerns of Member States without losing sight of the original objectives and principles of the Free Movement Protocol. The language of the Facilitation of Movement Protocol, unlike its predecessor, largely eschews any reference to rights and moves from the terminology of 'promotion' to 'facilitation' (Oucho and Crush, 2001, p. 152). It sought to 'facilitate entry, residence and establishment' for regional migrants. It eliminated the commitment to introduce an SADC passport and reduced the visa-free entry period from six to three months. The Free Movement Protocol, in the third phase, would have given the right of permanent residence to any SADC national in another SADC state at any time. The Facilitation of Movement Protocol only committed countries to give permanent residence to non-nationals already resident in the country. And while the original protocol committed the region eventually to free movement, the new protocol only committed Member States to a progressive reduction in migration controls between Member States.

Overall, although this version of the SADC Draft Protocol on the Facilitation of Movement of People was a far more progressive document than that produced by South Africa, it remained a more restrictive model of regional migration than that provided for in the original SADC Protocol on the Free Movement of People. It did, in some respects, pay attention to the region's shared history of migration, but at the same time, it tried to address the fears of objecting countries.

The SADC Secretariat presented the redrafted Protocol to the SADC Council of Ministers in Maputo in January 1998. The Council deferred discussion to allow Member States time to review the new Protocol. It was then discussed when the Council of Ministers met again in September 1998. Again, South Africa, Botswana and Namibia expressed their concerns, which lay along similar lines to their earlier objections to the Free Movement Protocol. They were worried that the Protocol would commit them to a process, with a timetable and goals, which they opposed. Member States were also concerned that ongoing conflict in Angola and the Democratic Republic of the Congo would result in mass movements of people (Solomon, 2000).

Member States were asked to consult internally and report to the Chairman of the Council. Five years later, in late 2003, there was some impetus within the

SADC Secretariat to revive discussions on the protocol. The SADC body dealing with matters of safety, security and defence tabled the protocol for members' consideration in late 2004.

Discussions on safety, security and defence led to a further rewriting of the drafted Facilitation of Movement Protocol (see Williams and Carr, 2006). This final draft was presented to the twenty-fifth Council of Ministers of the SADC in Botswana in August 2005. Six countries signed the Draft Protocol. The signatures of a further three countries are required before the protocol can be ratified. Member countries will also need to pass the protocol through their national procedures. South Africa, with a new African National Congress Minister for Home Affairs (replacing the old minister from the Inkatha Freedom Party following the elections of 2004), was one of the signatories: it appears to be pursuing a more open policy that fits better with its commitments to the SADC, the AU and NEPAD.

Although the preamble to the document appears progressive ('Recognizing that full popular participation in the process of building the Region into a Community is only possible where the citizens of the Community enjoy freedom of movement of persons, namely: visa-free entry, residence and establishment in the territories of Member States'), the protocol does, as it states, 'adopt a flexible approach' (SADC, 2005). But it seems less flexible than earlier drafts although it does retain a phased approach, with an as-yet undefined time frame. Throughout, it maintains that the measures contained in the protocol will remain subject to national legislation, and seems to be closer to the earlier South African Draft Protocol of the late 1990s.

The new Draft Protocol, if ratified, still aims to facilitate and speed up the movement of SADC nationals wanting to visit another Member State:

1. It advocates that relevant national laws and regulations should be harmonized and should promote the objectives of the protocol.
2. It allows for visa-free entry for visitors for a maximum period of ninety days per year, but with the right to apply for an extension. Visitors will require travel documents and sufficient means of support, and must enter through an official border post.
3. It calls for the introduction of standardized immigration forms and separate desks at ports of entry for SADC nationals, with at least one shared border post open twenty-four hours a day (SADC, 2005, Articles 14–15).

However, its provisions with regard to residence (permanent residence) and establishment (entering for work or to establish a business) are less progressive. The protocol states that residence and establishment will continue to be subject to national legislation, but that there should be no undue delay in processing applications (Articles 16–20). The protocol does contain provisions regarding the expulsion of SADC nationals (Articles 22–25), stating that there should be no 'group indiscriminate expulsion' (Article 24), and does lay out principles that national legislation should include when deportation is to take place (which can be suspended where 'national security, public order or public health' issues are in play). These include provisions that are, for instance, not currently occurring in South Africa, such that people being deported should have the right of recourse to the legal system, right to appeal, and time to wind up their personal business affairs (Article 25).

It seems that the new draft protocol, if ratified, will allow visitors easier movement and speed up the processing of SADC nationals at border posts and of applications for permanent or temporary residence. It should also lead to harmonization of legislation and migration systems, which could in turn lead to better migration management. The new draft protocol reflects its origins, as responsibility for implementation will lie with the committee of ministers responsible for public security 'and any other committee established by the Ministerial Committee of the Organ' (SADC, 2005, Article 29). It also asks Member States to ensure machine-readable travel documents are made available to their nationals, and to maintain a population register of nationals and non-nationals (Articles 9 and 12).

The protocol does appear to encourage Member States to enter bilateral agreements with each other to facilitate the movement of people. Some countries have already embarked on this route. For instance, in 2005, Mozambique and South Africa agreed to visa-free travel for their nationals, and Mozambique is pursuing similar agreements with Malawi, the United Republic of Tanzania and Zimbabwe. The South African regulations for the Immigration Act of 2002, as amended by the Immigration Amendment Act of 2004, also indicate this more positive approach to the region and the rest of the continent. A new six-month 'cross-border permit' will allow multiple entry for short visits to South Africa for visitors, visiting business-people and small-scale traders who come from Botswana, Lesotho, Mozambique, Namibia, Zimbabwe and Swaziland. Furthermore, some of the financial costs of study permits have been relaxed for African applicants.

However, the Draft Protocol on the Facilitation of Movement remains a draft. It is, as yet, not clear how long it will take to secure the necessary three signatures for the protocol to come into force. Nor, once they have been secured, what the time-frame will be for implementation. Furthermore, a recent review of the immigration, refugee and citizenship legislation of SADC Member States suggests they retain an ongoing commitment to nationally based legislation, which does not acknowledge the longstanding history of crossing borders in the region or the commitments of Member States to the SADC aims of cooperation and integration for development (Klaaren and Rutinwa, 2003).

Conclusion

The AU, like its predecessor, the OAU, is committed to preserving the territorial boundaries inherited from the colonial carving-up of Africa in the late nineteenth century. To do anything else would inevitably lead to a rapid increase in territorial disputes and inter-state conflicts. Territorial disputes in post-colonial Africa have rarely escalated above the level of minor squabbles, and most nation-states have accepted these boundaries and have sought to pursue nation-building projects within them, although their success has varied considerably from country to country and region to region. Civil war has been a far more common feature of post-colonial Africa than inter-state conflict. Mozambique, Angola and the DRC aside, studies of national identity in southern Africa show that the vast majority of citizens identify very strongly with their nation-states and are extremely proud to call themselves citizens of those states.

The very success of post-independence nation-building projects poses a significant obstacle to the building of a strong regional consciousness. Despite over two decades of formal cooperation and integration, citizens of southern African countries do not see themselves as members of a larger regional entity in any significant manner. This would, perhaps, not be problematic if all southern Africans remained at home. But they do not. They are extremely mobile and they cross borders for a complex variety of purposes, legally or not, virtually at will. But rather than being welcomed as fellow members of SADC, they are ostracized and marginalized and are subject to abuse and name-calling. They are 'foreigners', 'aliens', 'makwerekwere', stealers of jobs, consumers of resources, spreaders of disease and perpetrators of crime. Many migrants to South Africa now say that the situation is far worse than it was before 1994, at least in terms of the way they are treated by ordinary South Africans. The same situation pertains in Botswana, where Zimbabweans are regularly denounced, deported or caned for being in the country.

Free movement in Africa across the old colonial boundaries is a founding ideal of many continental and regional blocs. Originally rooted in pan-African ideology, contemporary arguments for freedom of movement tend rather to stress the economic benefits for sending and receiving states. When the SADC Secretariat considered the issue in the mid-1990s, it recognized that freer movement of goods, capital and people was a basic building-block of regional integration and development. It has made significant progress on freeing the movement of goods and capital, but it also sought, in a very real way, to recognize and legitimize the decades-old movement of people across boundaries within the region. Unfortunately, the Secretariat ran a little ahead of itself, presenting a Schengen-style agreement that posed, in the eyes of its critics, a fundamental threat to national sovereignty. Surprisingly, perhaps, only three states opposed it – but they were all migrant-receiving states. South

Africa's critique of the Protocol was very problematical, but that was hardly the point. It provided a self-interested rationale for rejection, which was all that was needed. Having failed to move the other SADC states to its own position, it then turned on the considerably less-threatening SADC Facilitation Protocol and ensured that this made no headway either.

People will continue to cross boundaries in ever-greater numbers within the SADC, that much is certain. The question confronting the SADC and its Member States (and now, it seems, the AU) is how to operationalize this reality, bring it above board and manage it in the best interests of regional cooperation, integration and development. The best hope for those who feel that free movement is the future is that the decade-long political logjam within South Africa on this issue is now over. The end of the Buthelezi era and the simultaneous embracing of Africa by the second-term Mbeki presidency must inevitably change the public climate with regard to the principle of greater cross-border movement of people in all directions. The signing of the Draft Protocol on the Facilitation of Movement of Persons by six Member States, including South Africa, is a positive move after a decade of seeming inactivity, and despite the limited provisions of the protocol. Whether it will be able to overcome the many obstacles to the realization of the SADC Secretariat's vision (and that of many of the Member States) remains to be seen. Furthermore, it is unclear whether the still limited provisions of the draft protocol, however welcome, will meet the vision of the preamble of the protocol community, whereby citizens enjoy full freedom of movement. Certainly it seems that for some time to come, goods will be able to move more freely through the region than nationals of the region.

Notes

1. Note that these figures refer to the number of times the border is crossed, not the number of individuals who cross the border.
2. Regulations for Immigration Act (Act no. 13 of 2002) as amended by Immigration Amendment Act (Act no. 8 of 2004).
3. African Union Council of Ministers, 74th Ordinary Session, Lusaka, Zambia, *Decision CM/Dec 613(LXX1V)*, cited in African Union, 2004, p. 5.
4. Countries of the SADC are: Angola, Botswana, Democratic Republic of the Congo, Lesotho, Malawi, Mauritius, Mozambique, Namibia, South Africa, Swaziland, United Republic of Tanzania, Zambia, Zimbabwe. Seychelles is in the process of withdrawing from the SADC.

Bibliography

African Union. 2004. Draft strategic framework for a policy on migration in Africa. Paper presented at the Fourth Ordinary Session of the Executive Council of the African Union, Addis Ababa.

Ansell, N. and van Blerk, L. 2004. *HIV/AIDS and Children's Migration in Southern Africa*. Cape Town and Kingston, Southern African Migration Project (SAMP). (Migration Policy Series No. 33.)

Asante, S. 1986. *The Political Economy of Regionalism in Africa: A Decade of the Economic Community of West African States (ECOWAS)*. New York, Praeger.

Brown, M., Kaplan, D. and Meyer, J.-B. 2002. The brain drain: an outline of skilled emigration from South Africa. McDonald and Crush, op. cit., pp. 99–112.

Common Market of Eastern and Southern Africa (COMESA). 2000. Background information: objectives of COMESA, www.comesa.int/background/backobjv.htm. (Also available at www.comesa.int/comesa/about/vision/vision_chapter_5/en/view)

Community Agency for Social Enquiry (CASE). 2003. *National Refugee Baseline Survey: Final Report*. Johannesburg, JICA and UNHCR.

Crush, J. 2002. The global raiders: nationalism, globalization and the South African brain drain. *Journal of International Affairs*, No. 56, pp. 147–72.

Crush, J. and James, W. (eds). 1995. *Crossing Boundaries: Mine Migrancy in a Democratic South Africa*. Cape Town, Idasa.

Crush, J., Jeeves, A. and Yudelman, D. 1992. *South Africa's Labor Empire: A History of Black Migrancy to the Gold Mines*. Cape Town/David Philip and Boulder, Col./Westview Press.

Crush, J., Mather, C., Mathebula, F. and Lincoln, D. 2000. *Borderline Farming: Foreign Migrants in South African Commercial Agriculture*. Cape Town and Kingston, Southern African Migration Project (SAMP). (Migration Policy Series No. 16.)

Crush, J. and McDonald, D. (eds). 2002. *Transnationalism and New African Immigration to South Africa*. Kingston/Southern African Migration Project and Ontario/Canadian Association of African Studies.

Crush, J. and Peberdy, S. 2004. Towards a fairer deal for South African labour. South Africa, Department of Labour.

Crush, J. and Pendleton, W. 2004. *Regionalizing Xenophobia? Citizen Attitudes to Immigration and Refugee Policy in Southern Africa*. Cape Town and Kingston, Southern African Migration Project (SAMP). (Migration Policy Series No. 30.)

Danso, R. and McDonald, D. 2000. *Writing Xenophobia: Immigration and the Press in Post-Apartheid South Africa*. Cape Town and Kingston, Southern African Migration Project (SAMP). (Migration Policy Series No. 17.)

Department of Home Affairs South Africa. 2002. *Immigration Act, 2002*. www.dha.gov.za (Accessed 21 December 2006.)

———. 2004. Unpublished statistics.

———. 2005a. *Immigration Regulations*. www.dha.gov.za.

———. 2005b. Unpublished statistics.

Dodson, B. 1998. *Women on the Move: Gender and Cross-Border Migration to South Africa*. Cape Town and Kingston, Southern African Migration Project (SAMP). (Migration Policy Series No. 9.)

Frayne, B. and Pendleton, W. 2002. *Mobile Namibia: Migration Trends and Attitudes*. Cape Town and Kingston, Southern African Migration Project (SAMP). (Migration Policy Series No. 27.)

Hough, M. 2000. Free movement of people within the SADC region: where is it going? *Institute of Strategic Studies Bulletin*, No. 1. University of Pretoria, South Africa.

Human Sciences Research Council (HSRC). 1995. *A Research Review of the Policies Surrounding the Issue of the Free Movement of People across International Borders with Specific Reference to Southern Africa and the Particular Effect Thereof on South Africa*. Pretoria, HSRC.

International Organization for Migration (IOM). 2000. *IOM Migration Policy Framework for Sub-Saharan Africa*. Geneva, IOM.

———. 2003. *Mobile Populations and HIV/AIDS in the Southern African Region*. Pretoria, IOM and UNAIDS.

Jeeves, A. and Crush, J. (eds). 1997. *White Farms, Black Labour: The State and Agrarian Change in Southern Africa*. New York/Heinemann, London/James Currey and Pietermartizburg/University of Natal Press.

Jenkins, C., Leape, J. and Thomas, L. 2000. *Gaining from Trade: Complementary Policies to Underpin the SADC Free Trade Area*. New York, St Martin's Press.

Klaaren, J. and Rutinwa, B. (eds). 2003. *Towards the Harmonization of Immigration and Refugee Policy in the SADC*. Cape Town/Idasa and Kingston, Canada/Queen's University. (Migration Dialogue for Southern Africa [MIDSA] Report No 1.)

Mattes, R., Taylor, D., McDonald, D., Poore, A. and Richmond, D. 1999. *Still Waiting for the Barbarians: South African Attitudes to Immigrants and Immigration*. Cape Town and Kingston, Southern African Migration Project (SAMP). (Migration Policy Series No. 14.)

McDonald, D. (ed.). 2000. *On Borders: Perspectives on International Migration in Southern Africa*. Cape Town/SAMP and New York/St Martin's Press.

McDonald, D. and Crush, J. (eds). 2002. *Destinations Unknown. Perspectives on the Brain Drain in Southern Africa*. Pretoria, Africa Institute of South Africa.

McGregor, J. 1998. Violence and social change in a border economy: war in the Maputo hinterland, 1984–1992. *Journal of Southern African Studies*, Vol. 24, No. 1, pp. 37–60.

Mdladlose, R. 2004. Migration and health in South Africa. The Migration Dialogue for Southern Africa, Cape Town, November.

Mercy, B., Kaplan, D. and Meyer, J. 2000. An outline of skilled emigration from South Africa. *Africa Insight*, No. 2.

Minde, I. J. and Nakhumwa, T. O. 1997. *Informal Cross-Border Trade between Malawi and Her Neighbouring Countries*. Nairobi, USAID, Regional Economic Development Support Office for Eastern and Southern Africa.

Mistry, P. 2000. Africa's record of regional cooperation. *African Affairs*, No. 99, pp. 553–73.

Morris, A. 1999. *Bleakness and Light: Inner-City Transition in Hillbrow, Johannesburg*. Johannesburg, South Africa, Wits University Press.

Morris, A. and Bouillon, A. (eds). 2001. *African Immigration to South Africa: Francophone Migration of the 1990s*. Pretoria, Protea and IFAS.

Mwaniki, J. 2003. The impact of informal cross-border trade on regional integration in SAD and its implications on wealth creation. Geneva, Development innovations and networks (IRED), East and Southern Africa.

Niessen, J. 2002. International mobility in a globalising world. Paper presented at ACP-EU Joint Parliamentary Assembly Workshop on Migration and Development, Cape Town, 20 March.

Oucho, J., Campbell, E. and Mukamaambo, E. 2000. *Botswana: Migration Perspectives and Prospects*. Cape Town and Kingston, Southern African Migration Project (SAMP). (Migration Policy Series No. 19.)

Oucho, J. and Crush, J. 2001. Contra free movement: South Africa and the SADC migration protocols. *Africa Today*, Vol. 48, No. 3, pp. 139–58.

Peberdy, S. 1998. Obscuring history? Contemporary patterns of regional migration to South Africa. D. Simon (ed.), *South Africa in Southern Africa: Reconfiguring the Region*. Oxford/James Currey, Athens, Ohio/Ohio University Press, and Cape Town/David Philip, pp. 206–21.

———. 1999. Selecting immigrants: nationalism and national identity in South Africa's immigration policies, 1910–1998. Ph.D. Thesis, Queen's University, Canada.

———. 2000*a*. Border crossings: small entrepreneurs and informal sector cross-border trade between South Africa and Mozambique. *Tjidschrift voor Economische en Sociale Geographie*, Vol. 91, No. 4, pp. 361–78.

———. 2000*b*. Mobile entrepreneurship: informal cross-border trade and street trade in South Africa. *Development Southern Africa*, Vol. 17, No. 2, pp. 201–19.

———. 2004. Overview of informal sector cross-border trade. London, Department for International Development (DFID).

Peberdy, S. and Crush, J. 1998. Trading places: cross-border traders and the South African informal sector. Cape Town and Kingston, Southern African Migration Project (SAMP). (Migration Policy Series No. 6.)

———. 2000. Invisible trade, invisible travellers: the Maputo Corridor Spatial Development Initiative and informal cross-border trading. *South African Geographical Journal*, Vol. 83, No. 2, pp. 115–23.

Peberdy, S. and Majodina, Z. 2000, Finding a new home? A report on the lives of Somali refugees in Johannesburg. South Africa, Forced Migration Studies Programme and the Somali Association of South Africa.

Peberdy, S. and Rogerson, C. 2000. Transnationalism and non-South African entrepreneurs in South Africa's small, medium and micro-enterprise (SMME) economy. *Canadian Journal of African Studies*, No. 34, pp. 20–40.

Ramphele, M. 1999. *Immigration and Education: International Students at South African Universities and Technikons*. Cape Town and Kingston, Southern African Migration Project (SAMP). (Migration Policy Series No. 12.)

Rogerson, C. 1999. *Building Skills: Cross-Border Migrants and the South African Construction Industry*. Cape Town and Kingston, Southern African Migration Project (SAMP). (Migration Policy Series No. 11.)

———. 2004. *Regional Tourism in South Africa: A Case of Mass Tourism of the South*. Southern African Migration Project (SAMP). www.queensu.ca/samp/ (Accessed 21 December 2006.) (Migration Policy Brief No. 14.)

Sechaba Consultants. 2002. *Poverty and Livelihoods in Lesotho, 2000: More than a Mapping Exercise*. Maseru, Sechaba Consultants.

Simelane, H. and Crush, J. 2004. *Mobile Swazis: Patterns and Perceptions of Migration in Swaziland*. Cape Town and Kingston, Southern African Migration Project (SAMP). (Migration Policy Series No. 32.)

Solomon, H. 2000. Strategic responses to illegal population flows within the southern African context. Paper presented at the Regional Seminar on Labour Migration in SADC. Lusaka, Zambia.

Southern African Development Community. 2005. *Draft Protocol on the Facilitation of Movement of Persons, 2005.* www.sadc.int

Southern African Migration Project (SAMP) and South African Human Rights Commission (SAHRC). 2001. *Immigration, Xenophobia and Human Rights in South Africa.* Cape Town and Kingston, Southern African Migration Project (SAMP). (Migration Policy Series No. 22.)

Tevera, D. and Zinyama, L. 2002. *Zimbabweans Who Move: Perspectives on International Migration in Zimbabwe.* Cape Town and Kingston, Southern African Migration Project (SAMP). (Migration Policy Series No. 25.)

United Nations High Commission for Refugees. 2004. Unpublished statistics.

United Nations Population Division (UNDP). 2002. *International Migration Report 2002.* New York, United Nations.

———. 2006. *International Migration 2006.* New York, United Nations.

Waller, L. 2006. *Irregular Migration to South Africa during the First Ten Years of Democracy.* Southern African Migration Project (SAMP). www.queensu.ca/samp/ (Accessed 21 December 2006.) (Migration Policy Brief No. 24.)

Williams, B., Lurie, M., Gouws, E. and Crush, J. 2002. *Spaces of Vulnerability: Migration and HIV/AIDS in South Africa.* Cape Town and Kingston, Southern African Migration Project (SAMP). (Migration Policy Series No. 24.)

Williams, V. and Carr, L. 2006. *The Draft Protocol on the Facilitation of Movement of Persons in SADC: Implications for State Parties.* Cape Town and Kingston, Southern African Migration Project (SAMP). www.queensu.ca/samp/ (Accessed 21 December 2006.) (Migration Policy Brief No. 19.)

Chapter 10

Migration without borders: a long way to go in the Asian region

Graziano Battistella

Borders matter. Borders define territories, and the notion of territoriality has been very relevant for the formation of nation-states. But we are currently living in a globalized world, where 'a new generalized perception of a massive weakening of territoriality' (Lapid, 2001, p. 9) is ever more common. Consequently, 'the function of borders as barriers is losing in importance compared to their function as bridges' (Albert and Brock, 2001, p. 36). Migrants are considered among the forces contributing to the understanding of the world as shaped by something else than just territorialized spaces.

In the past, migrants who settled tended to form minority communities – an indicator of their 'otherness' from mainstream society – today, however, there is the possibility of forming transnational communities. This trend is facilitated by safer, faster and cheaper transportation; by the availability of economic and cultural goods, such as ethnic food and ethnic media; and most of all, by instantaneous and affordable communication. Like globalization, transnationalism can easily become an overused term, both in its application to any migrant community and in the excessive implications attributed to it. Nevertheless, it points towards the weakening of the border as a state device with which to achieve control and forge a 'national' identity.

While migration is eroding the functions of borders, it continues to be regulated by borders. In a time of heightened concern for national security, controlling borders is considered indispensable in stopping the danger coming from outside. Stopping the entry of migrants has thus become essential in curbing infiltration. A recent and impressive symbol of such security concerns is the U.S.'s decision to erect a 700-mile wall along its southern border with Mexico, detailed in the Secure Fence Act signed into law by President George Bush in October 2006. In addition to national security, economic reasons militate against the free movement of people. Migration costs are considered (mostly by destination countries) to be too high to allow free circulation. By contrast, the voices of a number of liberal philosophers and economists are among those in favour of the migration without borders scenario, such as political scientist Mancur Olson, who writes that 'The gains from migration from poor to rich countries are so colossal that this migration cannot be prevented by any measures that are acceptable to the sensibilities of modern democracies' (1998, p. 371).

From a review of policy analyses, Massey (1999) concludes that policies in destination countries are affected by macro-economic health, the volume of international flows, and broad ideological currents. Consequently, developed countries will tend to restrict immigration from developing countries, and precisely at a time in which those countries are finding it more in their interest to promote emigration. What will prevail? Although resources dedicated to border controls have increased, it is quite clear that immigration persists despite the limits imposed by countries of destination. Furthermore, although receiving countries have official policies to counter unauthorized migration, there is nonetheless a certain tacit acceptance of a 'reasonable' level of unauthorized migration.

In the presence of such powerful global forces, what should the right policy attempt to achieve? Increase border controls in an attempt to stop irregular immigration? Acknowledge the impracticality of border controls and agree on the free movement of people? Or reaffirm the current direction of migration management, including accepting some level of unauthorized migration? This chapter examines migration in Asia as a case study. The first part describes the origin and development of migration in Asia over the last thirty years and its current grouping into five subsystems. Then, irregular migration flows in these subsystems are presented as an indication of the limited impact of migration policies that aim to curtail the right to migrate. The next section recaps the basis for such a right and its specificities. This leads to a consideration of incorporation and citizenship as dismantling external borders to elevate internal ones, which would result in a largely cosmetic effort. The chapter concludes that the Asian region might not be one in which migration without borders will be implemented soon. At the same time, the inadequacy of national policies in facing the issue is recognized, at least indirectly, through regional dialogues on migration management. In the long road to free circulation of labour through open borders, an intermediate step might consist of regional agreements for closer integration of labour markets.

The development of migration in Asia

Current labour migration in Asia appears as a multitude of migration flows moving in various directions. However, these did not develop simultaneously. Rather, they came about in response to economic opportunities and policy regulations. Perhaps three specific phases can be identified, marking the progressive diffusion of migration in the region.

The beginnings: labour migration to the Middle East (1970s)

The Middle East began attracting labour migration from the Asian region in the early 1970s. The origin and growth of this movement are well known (Amjad, 1989; Appleyard, 1999). It began with major infrastructure projects in the Gulf countries, following their increased revenues from the sale of oil, the prices of which had skyrocketed in the 1970s. Economic recession and the closing of labour migration to northern Europe shifted the attention of firms and technical expertise towards the Middle East, which had until then drawn its migrant labour from neighbouring Arab countries. It turned to Asia as a source of labour, at first to India and Pakistan, and then reaching farther east to the Republic of Korea, Thailand and the Philippines.

This first phase, marked by migration from a few South Asian and South-East Asian countries in one direction, peaked in the early 1980s and established a system that then spread to other areas. The system has three major characteristics: the involvement of the private sector in handling the recruitment and placement of migrants; the hiring of migrants for a limited time only (mostly two years); and the avoidance of long-term migration by requiring migrant workers to return to their country of origin before renewing their contracts and not allowing family reunification. Contrary to the experience of labour migration in Europe, where government-to-government agreements had been used to manage labour flows, the system in Asia was handed over to the private sector, and soon became a lucrative business. Myriads of recruitment agencies mushroomed in the various countries of origin, while in countries of destination workers were handled by sponsors, allegedly according to real job opportunities available.

The expansion of labour migration: the opening of new destinations in East and South-East Asia (1980s)

The bonanza of labour opportunities in the Middle East came to an end in the middle of the 1980s, when most infrastructure projects were completed and the price of oil fell back to less than U.S.$10 per barrel. However, the demand for labour soon shifted, with construction and engineering workers being substituted by maintenance and service workers. As a system was already in place, all parties involved had an interest in keeping it running. Other countries too came into the picture as sources of migrant workers for the Middle East, particularly Bangladesh and Sri Lanka in South Asia, and Indonesia in South-East Asia. Migration from the Republic of Korea and Thailand, however, dried up: but for two different reasons. In the case of the Republic of Korea, better development opportunities appeared in the country of origin, while for Thailand, a political incident put an end to labour flows to Saudi Arabia.

The decline of migration to the Middle East and the opening of opportunities in other countries channelled migration flows to different directions, particularly towards countries in East and South-East Asia. The level and type of migration flows were partially shaped by the type of border control exercised by the countries of destination. In East Asia, the major destination should have been Japan, which, in the 1980s, was becoming the second largest economy in the world. However, Japan resisted the importation of unskilled labour, opting instead to expand the employment of women, to increase the technological content of its production processes, and to begin locating industries in countries where the cost of labour was low. Japan did not escape labour migration altogether, as some migration did take place, mostly in the form of tourists overstaying their visas and remaining as irregular workers. Japan also crafted a number of schemes to address its labour shortage. As a labour market, Japan is distinctive in its demand for entertainers (who come mostly from the Philippines). Entertainers are considered as professionals in Japan and therefore can obtain working visas.

In South-East Asia, Singapore and Malaysia soon developed into major countries of destination. These two migration flows differed significantly because of their different migration policies. Singapore had made use of migration from its beginnings as an independent nation; first from Malaysia, then from nearby countries such as Bangladesh, Thailand and the Philippines. The management of foreign labour was designed to spur economic growth, but with a view to avoiding dependence on unskilled migrants. The two instruments for managing migration were a quota system (each sector was allowed a certain percentage of migrant workers in its workforce) and the imposition of a levy on employers who hired less-skilled foreign workers. The intention was to prevent the replacement of 'cheap' migrant workers for local workers and to encourage technological improvements (Wong, 1997). In 1986, when Singapore went into a recession, employers were encouraged to retrench foreign workers. In 1997, in the wake of the crisis in the region, Singapore did not automatically retrench foreign workers, pursuing instead a policy aimed at maintaining its competitiveness.

Malaysia became a country of immigration without having any clear policy programme, through the hiring of migrants (who mostly came from Indonesia, but also from the Philippines, Thailand and Bangladesh) mainly to provide workers for the plantation, construction and service sectors. From the very beginning, the flow of migration from Indonesia was heavily characterized by unauthorized entries and stays in Malaysia. Various agreements with countries of origin provided Malaysia with the legal instruments to increase or decrease its foreign workforce, but not the ability to control its borders.

Consolidation: labour migration throughout Asia (1990s)

The 1990s were marked by the consolidation of labour migration through its spread to new countries, the development of new 'labour migration' schemes, and continuing migration even during a time of economic crisis. Three new countries opened up, willingly or not, to migration in the early 1990s. First was Taiwan, which formally set up a labour-migration policy intended to bring in additional workers for major infrastructural projects. Some migration had already begun in an irregular form a few years earlier. To avoid temporary labour migration turning into de facto settlement (as had happened in Europe), Taiwan decided to limit the duration of contracts (first to one year, then two, then later extended to three and more recently to a maximum of six years) without giving contract-holders any possibility to renew them. It initially decided to allow migration only from four countries (Indonesia, Malaysia, the Philippines and Thailand – Viet Nam was added in 1998 and Mongolia in 2004); it limited employment of migrants to certain specific industries and decided to assign labour recruiting only to a handful of recruitment agencies, whose activities it could monitor to avoid irregularities. However, the difficulties of managing migration quickly emerged: recruiting agencies began to subcontract their licenses; employers from other sectors succeeded in obtaining the importation of foreign workers; and migrants, dissatisfied with only one working term, returned under a different name. An industry of employment agencies quickly emerged, which increased the costs of migration borne by migrants (Tsay, 1995).

Whereas Taiwan formally adopted an immigration policy, the Republic of Korea tried to circumvent it by establishing a trainee scheme, similar to the scheme implemented by Japan. Under this scheme, the country was to train foreign workers who then would be employed in joint ventures involving Korean firms abroad. However, the joint ventures did not materialize, and trainees, initially from South-East Asian countries and later also from countries in South Asia, soon turned into irregular migrants and found employment in small and medium industries that did not have the resources to relocate abroad (Park, 1995).

Thailand also was stormed, almost by surprise, by a wave of unauthorized immigration. In this case, it mostly originated from Myanmar, with which

Thailand shares a long and porous border, with the involvement of officials at the border facilitating entry and placement of migrants in construction, in fishing industries and in rice mills. In addition to Burmese (who comprise more than 80 per cent of all foreign workers), immigrants also came from neighbouring Cambodia and Laos, following routes established when Thailand had functioned as the first asylum country for refugees during the Indochinese crisis.

Examples of the schemes used by countries of destination are those developed by Japan, which still resists the admission of low-skilled migrants. Although the 1990s was a period of economic crisis for Japan, this did not stop migrants from trying to find a crack in the Japanese labour market. To respond to the demand for foreign labour, Japan first adopted a trainee system, bringing in 'trainees' from developing countries who underwent a period of training for a year, followed by a period of employment (initially a year; more recently this was expanded to two years). But this system did not bring in high numbers of people (less than 50,000 entrances annually). More significant was the number of foreign workers who were admitted because of their Japanese descent, mostly from Brazil, with a small number from Peru – these arrivals were also able to bring in their families, and were permitted to work for three years (Tsuzuki, 2000). The *Nikkeijin* scheme is a telling example of how non-economic factors play an important role in migration policies; it is also an example of a country opening to labour migration without admitting it.

The 1990s were marked by two major crises. The first was the Gulf War in 1991, which caused the abrupt repatriation of some 1.5 million migrants. However, when the crisis was over, the number of migrants in the Gulf countries actually increased, reaching new heights in 1995. The war had a more lasting impact on Yemenis and Palestinians, who were expelled by Saudi Arabia because their governments took the side of Iraq. The second crisis was a financial and then economic crisis that swept across Asia, beginning with Thailand and then the Republic of Korea and Malaysia, and eventually the whole region. Mass repatriations of migrants were carried out by Malaysia and Thailand, while the Republic of Korea encouraged voluntary departure. However, little voluntary departure took place from the countries affected by the crisis as conditions in the countries of origin were no more favourable, and local workers were not eager to take the migrants' jobs. This also set the conditions for the return of repatriated foreign workers and a rethinking of repatriation policies (Battistella and Asis, 1999). The lesson of the 1990s is that migration flows, once set in motion, are hard to reverse. Rather, migration tends to acquire a structural role, so that the control of borders has to adjust to it.

Migration in Asia in the new century

The development of migration in Asia has led to an understanding that migration is here to stay. This not only refers to the dependence on migrant workers in destination countries – particularly in countries with a high proportion of migrants in the labour force, such as Singapore (28 per cent) and Malaysia (16 per cent), or in sectors with a high concentration of migrants (such as construction, fishing industries, or domestic work) – but also on the dependence of countries of origin on labour migration as a safety valve (or as part of their development strategies). At this point, after a three-decade history of labour migration, migration dynamics and routes have been fairly well established.

The current situation can best be summarized by grouping migration flows into five migration subsystems.

1. **The Gulf Cooperation Council (GCC) subsystem.** This is the oldest subsystem. It has a great need for foreign labour, as these oil-dependent economies do not have enough trained workers to meet the needs of the private sector. The foreign population of the GCC countries grew from 8.6 million in 1990 to 12.8 million in 2005, representing an increase of 48.5 per cent (UN, 2006a). The core nation in this system remains Saudi Arabia. It hosted 6.4 million migrants in 2005, equivalent to 25.9 per cent of the total population. Such proportion reaches 62.1 per cent for Kuwait and 71.4 per cent for the United Arab Emirates. GCC countries are committed to increase the employment of their local labour force and decrease the presence of foreign labour (UN, 2006b). However, such efforts, together with repeated efforts to diminish irregular migration, have not proven very effective. GCC countries, particularly Saudi Arabia, are the primary (almost the exclusive) destination of migrants coming from countries in South Asia. Approximately 3 million Indians are living and working in the Middle East (Srivastava and Sasikumar, 2003).

2. **The Indian Subcontinent system.** Although traditionally considered to be a sending region – some 1.5 million Sri Lankans are employed abroad, and in 2003 Bangladesh changed its rules to allow for women who are over 35 years of age to work abroad as domestic workers (*Migration News*, October 2005) – it also constitutes a destination for migrants from within the region. India, in particular, hosts migrants from Nepal, but estimates on the number vary from as low as 250,000 to as many as 3 million (Prasad, 2000). Many migrants from Bangladesh also go to India, mostly to the state of Assam (Srivastava and Sasikumar, 2003). India is also opening its hospitals to foreigners who seek treatment. Healthcare costs in India are up to 80 per cent lower than in the U.S., and 150,000 foreign patients were treated in Indian hospitals in 2005 (*Migration News*, October 2006). Pakistan hosts

3.5 million foreign-born residents (UN, 2006*b*), particularly from Bangladesh and Myanmar, as well as refugees from Afghanistan, whose number reached 1.08 million people in June 2006 (UNHCR, 2006).

3. **The Indo-Chinese system**. This has three distinct foci. The first is Singapore, with 1.8 million foreigners and at least 600,000 migrant workers, of whom 160,000 are domestic workers, mostly from Indonesia and the Philippines (*Migration News*, October 2006). The second focus for migration, Malaysia, has a mixture of regular and irregular migrants both on the peninsula and in Sabah. According to government sources, as of July 2006 there were some 1,823,431 foreign workers from 22 countries employed in Malaysia, particularly in manufacturing and construction services and on plantations. The top five source countries were: Indonesia, accounting for 1,172,990 workers; Nepal, 199,962; India, 130,768; Viet Nam, 96,892; and Bangladesh, 64,156 (*Asian Migration News*, 15 September 2006). The third focus for migration is Thailand, which has approximately 2 million foreign workers, mostly from Myanmar, Cambodia and Laos (*Migration News*, April 2006). Major countries of origin in this system are Indonesia, which has 3.5 million workers abroad, with remittances expected to reach U.S.$3.3 billion by the end of 2006 (*Asian Migration News*, 15 July 2006), and the Philippines, which in 2005 deployed some 733,970 workers by land (mostly to the Middle East and Asia) and 247,707 by sea, and earned U.S.$10.6 billion in remittances (POEA, 2006). A recent addition is Viet Nam, which sent 70,600 migrants abroad in 2005, including 25,000 to Malaysia, 23,000 to Taiwan and 12,000 to the Republic of Korea (*Migration News*, April 2006).

4. **The Hong Kong–Taiwan system**. There are two different destinations in this system. Hong Kong is the prime destination for domestic workers (over 250,000): three-quarters of them come from the Philippines. Taiwan, however, has a labour immigration policy that concerns a number of different sectors, with migrants coming primarily from Thailand (98,322), Indonesia (49,094), the Philippines (95,703) and Viet Nam (84,185), with also a few from Malaysia and Mongolia, for a total of 327,396 at the end of 2005 (CLA, 2006). Small companies that rely on less-expensive foreign labour have in recent years been moving their production processes to mainland China.

5. **The north-east Asia system**. The main destinations are Japan and the Republic of Korea. Japan hosted 1.97 million foreign nationals at the end of 2004, of whom the largest group were Koreans (607,000), followed by Chinese (488,000), Brazilians (287,000) and Filipinos (199,000) (Kashiwazaki and Akaha, 2006). The overall policy orientation remains to not allow the immigration of unskilled workers. Japan has a visa for professional entertainers (issuing 134,879 such visas in 2004), under which

many women from the Philippines, China and Thailand enter for work, particularly in the nightclub industry. However, the tightening of entry requirements in 2005, following Japan being named by the U.S. State Department as a country not doing enough against the trafficking of migrants, has sharply lowered the number of yearly entries. The Republic of Korea, after many years of unsuccessful attempts, has approved a formal programme of labour migration that took effect in September 2004. This move was expected to reduce hitherto high levels of unauthorized migration. The trainee system (which was the source of most of the country's irregular immigration) remained operative until the end of 2006. In June 2006, the estimated 346,000 foreigners included 189,000 unauthorized migrants (*Migration News*, October 2006). The People's Republic of China, where massive internal migration has been a major policy issue (in recent years perhaps 120 million have moved from the rural to the coastal areas) must be considered separately. Since the reform period, authorities have progressively adopted measures that have moved from prohibiting migration (1979–1983), to allowing migration (1984–1988), to restricting migration (1989–1998), to regulating migration (1999–2000) and, finally, to encouraging migration (Ping and Pieke, 2003). China is also progressively participating in the international labour market.

Considered from the perspective of the main countries of origin in the region, the development of migration has been constantly increasing, and practically doubled in the 1990s. Saudi Arabia and the Middle East in general are the main destinations for migrants from South Asia. In addition, Malaysia is a major destination for Bangladeshis; Singapore for Indians; and Lebanon for Sri Lankans. Among countries in South-East Asia, Saudi Arabia is also the top destination for Indonesians and Filipinos. The other main destinations for Indonesians are outside the Middle East: particularly in Malaysia. Among the destinations of Filipino migrants, Hong Kong (domestic workers) and Japan (entertainers) figure prominently. Taiwan is by far the most common destination for Thai migrants, while Malaysia and Taiwan are the main destinations for Vietnamese migrants (International Organization for Migration [IOM], 2003).

Irregular migration in Asia

In its origin and expansion, migration in Asia has developed through unauthorized channels. At times, unauthorized channels have been the only ones available, especially in countries with no formal migration policies. Later, these channels persisted, while new ones were provided by the various parties involved. As in other parts of the world, irregular migration in Asia is first of all a response to inadequacies in the management of migration (Battistella and Asis, 2003). But it is also a symptom of deeper incongruities in the world order, ultimately questioning the restriction of freedom of movement across borders.

A brief overview of the dynamics of irregular migration in the various subsystems indicates that, while there are specificities in how the phenomenon develops and operates in each subsystem, there are also significant similarities. It also reveals why irregular migration should be understood not in isolation, but in conjunction with regular migration. As such, comprehensive policies are necessary to reach a common understanding of labour movements across borders.

Systematic and periodic irregularity

Irregular migrants in the Gulf countries constitute an issue that local authorities must address periodically. Regardless of various registration programmes, irregular migrants keep showing up, thanks to two mechanisms. One is ingrained in the *khafeel* or sponsorship system, which enables some nationals to control the importation of labour through the issuance of bloc visas. *Khafeels* are designed to only bring into the country migrants who have work waiting for them. However, sponsors recruit more workers than there are jobs to increase their earnings from fees, often placing them, also for a fee, with other labour brokers. Without even knowing it, migrants in this way find themselves in an irregular situation. The other mechanism is the annual pilgrimage to Mecca, after which several thousand people remain in Saudi Arabia as irregular migrants. Preventive measures against these irregularities have not been successful and registration programmes – forfeiting penalties in exchange for showing up and being repatriated – are only temporary remedies.

Irregularity created by colonial legacies

Irregular migrants in Pakistan are mostly the result of flows that emerged in the 1970s and 1980s, after the creation of Bangladesh. Unlike the emigration flows of the 1950s and 1960s, which had been supported by the government, the later migrants were poor workers who settled in major cities. Reliable figures for the number of irregular immigrants in Pakistan are not available, although estimates vary from 1 million to 3 million; most are Bengalis, but there are also some Burmese (Gazdar, 2003). Irregular migrants in India, particularly in the state of Assam, also often originate from Bangladesh. The issue has caused some controversy, to the point that a fence has been erected between the two states. Irregular migration flows also include trafficking, particularly of women, for sex work in Indian brothels.

Irregularity as extension of border crossings

South-East Asia is a region with various migration foci. Irregular migration takes different forms in the different subsystems. However, the most prevalent mode of entry is through border crossing. Thailand and Malaysia are the two countries with a large number of irregular migrants. Both also happen to share long borders with their neighbours – Thailand with Myanmar, Malaysia with Indonesia. In addition, the ethnic, cultural and religious similarities between Indonesia and Malaysia make the insertion and permanence of irregular migrants relatively manageable. A similar tradition of border crossing, which continues to this day, exists also between Filipinos in the archipelago of Sulu and Malaysian Sabah (Battistella and Asis, 2003). To stop irregular migration from Thailand, the Malaysian government has erected a wall across a section of the border. The passage is also used by irregular migrants from Bangladesh, some of whom find themselves stranded in Thailand.

Irregularity prior to integration

In the case of Hong Kong and Taiwan, irregular migration is mostly from mainland China. In spite of a firm policy allowing limited admission of Chinese, quite a number of mainlanders succeed in entering, finding work and settling. Migrants cross borders that will eventually be eliminated when Hong Kong becomes part of one China. In the case of Taiwan, it is difficult to predict how the situation with China will evolve. It is possible that irregular migration will subside, as, with the development of mainland China, even the entry of regular migrants is decreasing. In both Hong Kong and Taiwan, other forms of irregular migration consist mostly of migrants from countries of origin in the region who overstay their visa or who enter with forged documents.

Tolerated irregularity

In East Asia, irregular migration consists largely of migrants who initially entered regularly but overstayed their permits and engaged in remunerated activity without proper authorization. While the Republic of Korea hopes this issue will be resolved with the end of its trainee system in 2007, Japan is still resisting adopting a labour immigration policy. An increasing number of irregular migrants are apprehended every year in Japan. The Ministry of Justice estimated that there were 240,000 irregular migrants in the country at the beginning of 2005, comprised mostly of those who had overstayed their visas

(207,000), along with some 30,000 who were smuggled in by boat. Although the Japanese authorities have detailed information about irregular immigrants, they have not responded by introducing forceful crackdowns or repatriation campaigns. This suggests that Japan is addressing the issue with pragmatism and tacitly allowing a certain number of irregular immigrants to remain in the country. Some consideration should be given to the flow of Chinese towards the Russian Far East. Although initial high estimates have been reduced to approximately 200,000 immigrants, who have sought opportunities created by the declining population in the region (Akaha, 2004), it still remains a relevant presence of foreign population that is little discussed.

A cursory overview of irregular migration in the various subsystems in Asia, which differs in the specific modes of entry and the means used to stay in the receiving country, reveals deep similarities in its causes and dynamics. Among them are the following:

1. Legal and irregular migration channels prosper side by side. Often, migrants involved in regular or irregular migration are not distinctly different from each other. This illustrates the fact that irregularity is shaped not by the character of migrants, but through policy or procedural factors that determine possibilities and limitations for legal migration.
2. The form in which irregularity takes place is very much dependent on external circumstances. Irregular migration is more likely to occur when two countries share a land border crossing.
3. In addition to geography, history also plays an important role in irregular migration. When administrative measures do not take sufficient consideration of historical traditions, they are bound to fail.
4. Whether originating in undocumented entry or in breaching visa terms, irregular migration always implies engaging in working activities without authorization. The ultimate magnet and the most convincing reason for engaging in irregular migration is the availability of jobs and of employers willing to hire migrants without the required permits. The issue, then, is ultimately the lack of congruence between economic and migration policies.
5. To access regular or irregular channels, potential migrants need information. Research has indicated that migrants rely more on unofficial channels (social networks) rather than official channels (Battistella and Asis, 2003).
6. Recruiting agencies are key players in irregular migration. The dilemma for policy-makers is how to control irregularities committed by agents, when the system as a whole has come to rely so much on them.
7. Regardless of the main responsibilities of the different actors (recruiters, social networks, relatives, other intermediaries, and migrants themselves) it appears evident that irregularity requires the connivance of more than one actor, and often includes government officials. It is also difficult to police

those in charge of enforcement, because of intricate webs of interests, connivance and blackmailing.

8. Regularity correlates with the openness and ease of the migration process.

Policies against irregular migration normally target all actors involved. However, they differ substantially in destination and origin countries. In destination countries, the first target of enforcement is always the migrants themselves. Control measures also involve the punishment of people smugglers, employers and even citizens who provide lodging to irregular migrants. Undoubtedly, such measures have a deterrent effect. However, they are not sufficient to stop irregular migration, because the causes behind such movements are more powerful than control measures. Policies against irregular migration in the countries of origin, on the other hand, do not target migrants. Rather, they are directed at recruiters and intermediaries, although their efficacy is rather limited. Borders do not have the same meaning when examined from one side as from the other, and the significance of irregular crossings changes with the change of perspective.

The poor rate of effectiveness of migration policies, as indicated by widespread irregular migration and the ultimate inefficacy of control measures against it, points to conflicting philosophies. At times, the zeal with which these measures are pursued has tragic consequences for migrants. Migration is pursued because of its advantages for those involved: employers, countries of destination, countries of origin, recruiters, migrants. Ideally, it could be a win/win situation. However, migration is not without costs, and the interests of those involved do not always coincide. Policies are generated to maximize the interests of regulators, in general countries of destination and their constituents (employers and citizens). When those policies conflict with the interests of recruiters, migrants or even employers, irregularity results.

Irregularity could be considered to represent a behaviour that deviates from a just regulations; or a behaviour that is too costly (either in economic or civic terms) to control, and calls for a change of the regulations; or simply a practical, and often costly, affirmation of the right to migrate. Mainstream views support the first idea, and nations continue to devise new ways to stop irregular migration, but without much success, and regardless of certain economists' arguments regarding the ineffectiveness of borders closed to the free movement of labour (Iregui, 2005). The following section examines the discussion on the right to migrate.

Open borders, the right to migrate

International law does not recognize a right to migrate. The right that is affirmed in the Universal Declaration of Human Rights (Article 13-2) and in other covenants and conventions is the right to leave one's country and to return to it.[1] This is not an absolute right. In the Covenant on Civil and Political Rights, for example, the typical restrictions apply (protecting national security, public order, public health or morals, or the rights and freedom of others). Nevertheless, there is solid support for this right in liberal democracies (restrictions to it have been and are still exercised in totalitarian regimes). It is considered part of the right to self-determination, in parallel with the right to self-determination of peoples (Hannum, 1987, p. 4). It touches on the essence of government based on consensus, because if freedom to leave is not granted, the relation between government and citizen is based on coercion. Lauterpacht said that 'a state which denies to its citizens the right to emigrate reduces itself to the level of a prison' (Dowty, 1987, p. 16). The right to migrate is closely linked with non-discrimination, because if people are discriminated against on their right to leave they are also constrained from exercising other rights. And someone whose rights are violated will often try to leave, as is the case of refugees.

The right to leave as codified in international law cannot be translated as a right to migrate. In fact, this term has been carefully avoided. The concept of 'migration' also includes entering another country, and such a right is not granted by any international instrument. Therefore, the right to leave does not imply a duty on the part of another country to admit, except in the case of specific treaties or for specific persons, such as diplomats, representatives of international organizations, members of armies of another state, or victims of *force majeure*, such as shipwreck survivors (Goodwin-Gill, 1978). It can be argued that immigrants with permanent residence in a country of destination also enjoy the right to be admitted (Plender, 1988). Asylum seekers, on the other hand, do not exactly enjoy the right of admission but, as long as they succeed in entering the territory of a state, are granted the right of not being repatriated (non-refoulement) until their case is fully adjudicated.

The incoherence of having a right to leave without a corresponding right to enter has not escaped the attention of many commentators. There are various nuances in philosophical positions in this regard, but they can be organized into two camps: those who are in favour of freedom of movement across international borders and those who are against it. Liberal egalitarians are the most vocal in supporting freedom of movement, which they consider 'an important liberty in itself and a prerequisite for other freedoms' (Carens, 1992, p. 25). To not grant freedom of movement is to reduce people to serfdom. The same arguments that support freedom of movement within a country are also valid for transnational movement. In Cole's words (2000, p. 202), it is necessary to overcome 'incoherence between the liberal polity's internal and external principles: those within its boundaries are subjected to liberal principles and practices, while those at the border are subjected to illiberal principles and practices.' At the heart of the liberal egalitarian approach is a commitment to the moral equality of humanity.

By contrast, the starting principle for the camp of political realists is that it is 'morally acceptable that we should prefer the interests of our own collective to those of mankind in general' (Hendrickson, 1992). A state has a right to self-determination which prevails over the right to personal self-determination of people from other states. The right of the state to impose conditions on admission of foreigners to its territory is inherent to its sovereignty. To control entry of foreigners is essential 'for without it a society has no control over its basic character' (Dowty, 1987, p. 14).

Actually, even liberal egalitarians have taken a less radical position, and admit that there are situations in which border control is necessary, such as cases in which immigration could result in invasion or if it threatens to change the basic character of the receiving society, or there is a need to protect disadvantaged people within the destination country (Isbister, 1996). Nevertheless, they maintain that pragmatic limitations to freedom of movement do not invalidate it in principle, and that the onus of proof does not rest on the reasons for an immigrant to be admitted, but on the claims of the state to have a right to exclude would-be immigrants (Dummett, 2001).

This discussion raises the question of whether the right to migrate does not exist because it is not really a right, or because it is a right not recognized in international law. Although this might appear moot to those who have a positivist view of human rights (rights that are given by the international community and are not inherent to the human person), and although I have no intention to engage in a discussion on the bases for human rights, this is a valid question. Human rights can indeed be considered inherent to the person and necessary to safeguard human dignity; therefore, they are not established, but simply recognized by the international community. Thus the full meaning of the right to migrate should be recognized, and should not be limited to the right to leave and to return.

The immediate and full recognition of the right to migrate, and therefore of freedom of movement, in a world deeply divided by social, economic, political and cultural differences might appear utopian. A progressive course could be set, however, which might consist of intermediate steps (freedom of movement within specific regions) along the way to its full realization. In the meantime the standard limitations can apply, as communities, both in the country of origin and in the country of destination, also have rights. Finding the balance between the common good and individual guarantees would then be the object of migration policies.

In this intermediate stage, what changes would such a position bring to the management of migration policies? Essentially three: it would overcome the now-exclusive national approach to migration policies and insert a dialogical frame; it would require establishing international principles for the management of migration; and it would require the establishment of an international agency to supervise respect for (and adherence to) such principles.

Overcoming internal borders

Concentrating on the issue of freedom of movement through open borders might be a radical but incomplete effort. Actual possibilities of movement through social stratification within societies must also be examined. In fact, the whole problem of limitations to the transnational circulation of labour can be considered as a problem of distributive justice on the international scenario (Schwartz, 1995; Jordan and Düvell, 2002). Such a problem would not be solved if distributive justice were denied within national boundaries. There are at least two sides to this problem: one has to do with equal treatment in regard to a variety of economic and social aspects (access to employment, training, unemployment insurance, housing, health, education); and the other, closely related to this, has to do with incorporation, including the ultimate incorporation: citizenship.

The migration-policy model prevalent in the Asian continent is that of temporary labour migration. Migrants are admitted with a work contract for a strictly limited period of time, normally no more than two years, and are then required to return to their home country before renewing their contract. The system is designed to avoid the establishment and formation of minorities. Contract workers are not allowed to be joined by family members, and, in some cases (such as Singapore and Malaysia), their integration with the local community is so discouraged as not to allow or favour marriages with local citizens. Obviously, possibilities to naturalize are not even considered.

The situation is rather different for highly skilled and professional migrants, whose earnings enable them to have access to long-term or permanent settlement, to bring their families with them and to be considered for naturalization. In addition, even admission and circulation are much easier for them, which strengthens the argument that free movement is an issue of distributive justice. In fact, circulation for business people has been made easier with the issuance of the Asia-Pacific Economic Cooperation (APEC) Business Travel Card, which allows business people from the sixteen participating Asia-Pacific countries to enter any other of these countries without a visa and to stay up to sixty days.

Once again, however, reality precedes imagination. Although largely precluded from settling and naturalizing, migrant communities have developed in some Asian countries, and unconventional forms of participation in the running of local communities have consequently been forged. Participation is the key indicator that internal borders have fallen, and citizenship is the most fundamental entitlement to participation. In a world that is progressively characterized by transnational membership, even the notion of citizenship is going through transformation. Four unorthodox modes of citizenship that migrants have achieved in Asia have been identified (Battistella and Asis, 2004).

The first is the 'unauthorized citizenship' of Filipinos in Sabah and Indonesian migrants in Malaysia in general. They have established communities which have achieved de facto permanent settlement. Of course, their unauthorized status makes them a target for expulsion, which occurs occasionally because of internal politics. But this does not deter them from remaining with practical acceptance by the local community.

'Permanently temporary citizenship' refers not to the status of individuals but of communities in places such as Hong Kong, Singapore and Taiwan. The individuals are bound to return at the end of their working contract, but the communities remain as a permanent component of local societies. Their permanent status is recognized by governments, who provide them certain recognition, such as Migrants Day in Singapore.

The incorporation of the Korean community in Japan, comprising people who remained after the Second World War and newcomers, can be described as 'shunned citizenship'. Although access to naturalization is available to them, most have opted not to naturalize not only to preserve their identity but also as an alternative form of political participation in local society. As non-citizens, they have been able to influence citizenship reforms and the advancement of multicultural issues.

Some local governments in Japan with a sizeable foreign population have taken the initiative ahead of the central government to include migrants in their local administration through consultation processes. This is a limited implementation of what is elsewhere called 'residence citizenship': the recognition that residence, which implies participating in the local labour force, in educational and cultural activities, and paying taxes, should be accompanied by civic participation.

Obviously, these unorthodox forms of citizenship only reveal the practical engagement of migrants in the life of the local community and do not provide any of the guarantees that come from citizenship. In many cases, even the benefits of social citizenship are denied to them. But they also reveal the willingness on both sides to break down internal boundaries, and indicate that internal boundaries must fall first, before external borders can be dismantled.

Conclusion

A discussion on open borders may not be promising in Asia at this time. The Westphalian principles of nation-state formation – border control, freedom from external intervention, de-legitimizing subnational identities and loyalties (Heisler, 2001) – must be maintained in the post-colonial period in which various countries in Asia still find themselves, even though they are challenged by migratory flows. As discussed, migration in Asia is strongly organized as temporary contract labour, with minimal entitlements. In such a context, discussions on the freedom of movement for workers across open borders are rare, if they exist at all.

But the situation in Asia is not static. Although migration policies still subscribe to the national framework, regional gatherings to consider these questions have become more frequent. Two initiatives have taken place since 1996: the Manila Process, which has served as a platform for informal discussions for more than a dozen countries in East Asia and Oceania; and the Asia-Pacific Consultations (APC), organized in cooperation with UNHCR, with a broader participation of countries. A special moment of regional cooperation was the international symposium on 'Migration: Towards Regional Cooperation on Irregular/Undocumented Migration', held in Bangkok in April 1999, which concluded with the Bangkok declaration on irregular/undocumented migration. A similar initiative focusing on smuggling and trafficking of migrants was organized in Bali in 2004. These regional meetings are mostly talks or dialogues, and they involve minimal commitment. The road to open borders will not be short nor easy. The experience of the European Union may be instructive here; freedom of movement for workers for member countries was established in the Treaty of Rome in 1957, but was only achieved forty years later. Furthermore, when it became a reality, workers from EU countries were no longer migrants, but EU citizens, reaffirming the notion that freedom of movement is a citizen's, not a migrant's, prerogative.

For the moment, Asian countries are coming to grips with the notion that they cannot properly manage migration unilaterally. As regional discussions progress, more favourable conditions for citizens of member countries will be considered, and freedom of movement across borders will become less unthinkable (as examples from Africa and Latin America illustrate). The established path on this road is that economic disparities among nations must first be narrowed, and freedom of movement will follow. Economists would contend that the opposite should be done: freedom of movement should be granted as a way of achieving greater equality among nations. Unfortunately, theoretical work on the impact of free circulation of labour has not obtained the same acceptance as theories on the free circulation of goods. That is partially the reason why we have a World Trade Organization but no World Migration Organization.

In the everyday life of millions of people, however, migration is the opportunity to escape inequality. Such opportunity is not granted equally, as those who least need it can more easily obtain it. Thus, many people affirm their right to migrate through unauthorized behaviour, often with exploitative outcomes for migrants. Unauthorized migration should not be encouraged, but it cannot be dismissed as deviant behaviour. To understand it requires us to examine the underpinnings on which our society is organized, keeping in mind that the horizon extends beyond the borders of our nation – and our time.

Note

1. UN instruments include the International Covenant on Civil and Political Rights (Article 12); the International Convention on the Elimination of All Forms of Racial Discrimination (Article 5); the Convention on the Rights of the Child (Article 10–?); and the International Convention on the Protection of the Rights of All Migrant Workers and Members of Their Families (Article 8).

Bibliography

Akaha, T. 2004. Cross-border human flows in northeast Asia. *Migration Information Source*, 1 October.

Albert, M. and Brock, L. 2001. What keeps Westphalia together? Normative differentiation in the modern system of states. M. Albert, D. Jacobson and Y. Lapid (eds), *Identity, Borders, Orders: Rethinking International Relations Theory*. Minneapolis, Minn., University of Minnesota Press, pp. 29–49.

Amjad, R. (ed.). 1989. *To the Gulf and Back: Studies on the Economic Impact of Asian Labour Migration*. New Delhi and Geneva, ILO.

Appleyard, R. (ed.). 1999. *Emigration Dynamics in Developing Countries. Volume IV: The Arab Region*. Aldershot, U.K., Ashgate.

Battistella, G. and Asis, M. B. 1999. *The Crisis and Migration in Asia*. Quezon City, Philippines, Scalabrini Migration Center.

———. 2003. *Unauthorised Migration in Southeast Asia*. Quezon City, Philippines, Scalabrini Migration Center.

———. 2004. Citizenship and Migration in Asia. Human Movements and Immigration (HMI) World Congress, Barcelona 2–5 September.

Carens, J. H. 1992. Migration and morality: a liberal egalitarian perspective. B. Barry and R. E. Goodin (eds), *Free Movement: Ethical Issues in the Transnational Migration of People and of Money*. New York, Harvester Wheatsheaf, pp. 25–47.

Central Intelligence Agency. 2003. *The World Factbook 2003*. www.cia.gov/cia/publications/ factbook/

Cole, P. 2000. *Philosophies of Exclusion: Liberal Political Theory and Immigration*. Edinburgh, U.K., Edinburgh University Press.

Council of Labor Affairs, Taiwan. 2006. *Yearbook of Labor Statistics*, Taipei.

Dowty, A. 1987. *Closed Borders: The Contemporary Assault on Freedom of Movement*. London and New Haven, Conn., Yale University Press.

Dummett, Sir M. 2001. *On Immigration and Refugees*. London, Routledge.

Gazdar, H. 2003. A review of migration issues in Pakistan. *Migration, Development and Pro-Poor Policy Choices in Asia* series. Department for International Development, U.K. www.livelihoods.org/hot_topics/docs/Dhaka_CP_4.pdf (Accessed 21 December 2006.)

Goodwin-Gill, G. 1978. *International Law and the Movement of Persons between States*. Oxford, Clarendon Press.

Hannum, H. 1987. *The Right to Leave and to Return in International Law and Practice*. Dordrecht, Netherlands, Martinus Nijhoff.

Heisler, M. O. 2001. Now and then, here and there: migration and the transformation of identities, borders, and orders. M. Albert, D. Jacobson and Y. Lapid (eds), *Identity, Borders, Orders: Rethinking International Relations Theory*. Minneapolis, Minn., University of Minnesota Press, pp. 225–47.

Hendrickson, D. C. 1992. Migration in law and ethics: a realist perspective. B. Barry and R. E. Goodin (eds), *Free Movement: Ethical Issues in the Transnational Migration of People and of Money*. New York, Harvester Wheatsheaf, pp. 213–31.

International Organization for Migration (IOM). 2003. *Labour Migration in Asia: Trends, Challenges and Policy Responses in Countries of Origin*. Geneva, IOM.

Iregui, A. M. 2005. Efficiency gains from the elimination of global restrictions on labour mobility: an analysis using a multiregional CGE model. G. J. Borjas and J. Crisp (eds), *Poverty, International Migration and Asylum*. Basingstoke, Palgrave Macmillan, pp. 211–39.

Isbister, J. 1996. Are immigration controls ethical? *Social Justice*, Vol. 23, No. 3, pp. 54–67.

Jordan, B. and Düvell, F. 2002. *Irregular Migration: The Dilemmas of Transnational Mobility*. Northampton, Mass., Edward Elgar.

Kashiwazaki, C. and Akaha, T. 2006. Japanese immigration policy: responding to conflicting pressures. *Migration Information Source*, November.

Lapid, Y. 2001. Identity, borders, orders: nudging international relations theory in a new direction. M. Albert, D. Jacobson and Y. Lapid (eds), *Identity, Borders, Orders: Rethinking International Relations Theory*. Minneapolis, Minn., University of Minnesota Press, pp. 1–20.

Massey, D. S. 1999. International migration at the dawn of the twenty-first century: the role of the state. *Population and Development Review*, Vol. 25, No. 2, pp. 303–22.

Olson, M. 1998. Mancur Olson on the key to economic development. *Population and Development Review*, Vol. 24, No. 2, pp. 369–79. (Reprint of M. Olson, 1989, The key to economic development, IUSSP *International Population Conference, New Delhi, September 20–27, 1989*, Vol. 3, Liege, Belgium, International Union for the Scientific Study of Population [IUSSP].)

Park, Y. 1995. Korea. *ASEAN Economic Bulletin*, Vol. 12, No. 2, pp. 163–74.

Philippine Overseas Employment Administration (POEA). *Overseas Employment Statistics*. www.poea.gov.ph (accessed 29 November 2006.)

Ping, H. and Pieke, F. N. 2003. China migration country study. *Migration, Development and Pro-Poor Policy Choices in Asia* series. Department for International Development, U.K.. www.livelihoods.org/hot_topics/docs/Dhaka_CP_3.pdf (Accessed 21 December 2006.)

Plender, R. 1988. *International Migration Law*. Dordrecht, Netherlands, Martinus Nijhoff.

Prasad, B. 2000. Nepal. *ILO Asia Pacific Regional Trade Union Symposium on Migrant Workers, 6–8 December 1999*. Proceedings. Geneva, Bureau for Workers Activities (ACTRAV) and International Labour Office (ILO).

Schwartz, W. F. (ed.). 1995. *Justice in Immigration*. New York, Cambridge University Press. (Cambridge Studies in Philosophy and Law.)

Srivastava, R. and Sasikumar, S. K. 2003. An overview of migration in India, its impacts and key issues. *Migration, Development and Pro-Poor Policy Choices in Asia* series. Department for International Development, U.K. www.livelihoods.org/hot_topics/docs/Dhaka_CP_2.pdf (Accessed 21 December 2006.)

Tsay, C. 1995. Taiwan. *ASEAN Economic Bulletin*, Vol. 12, No. 2, pp. 175–90.

Tsuzuki, K. 2000. *Nikkei* Brazilians and local residents: a study of the H housing complex in Toyota City. *Asian and Pacific Migration Journal*, Vol. 9, No. 3, pp. 327–42.

United Nations. 2006a. *International Migration 2006*. New York, UN Department of Economic and Social Affairs, Population Division.

———. 2006b. *International Migration in the Arab Region*. Proceedings of UN Expert Group Meeting on International Migration and Development in the Arab Region: Challenges and Opportunities, Beirut, 15–17 May, 2006. New York, UN.

United Nations High Commissioner for Refugees. 2006. www.unhcr.org/statistics (Accessed 29 November 2006).

Wong, D. 1997. Transience and settlement: Singapore's foreign labor policy. *Asian and Pacific Migration Journal*, Vol. 6, No. 2, pp. 135–68.

Chapter 11

A world without borders?
Mexican immigration, new boundaries
and transnationalism in the United
States

Alejandro I. Canales and Israel Montiel Armas

Introduction

A walk through certain areas in any large Western city, such as the Raval in
Barcelona, Brixton in London, or East Los Angeles, is bound to give the unwary
visitor an odd feeling: most of the people he or she comes across will belong to
ethnicities from elsewhere in the world, speak unintelligible tongues, and in
some cases even wear picturesque costumes without a trace of self-
consciousness, because after all this is 'their' neighbourhood and it is the visitor
who looks out of place. This feeling is not just produced by the manners and
aspect of the residents: the whole morphology of the place, from the appearance
of the shops and the products they sell to the very smells and colours, does not
correspond to what is normally considered indigenous to the country. The most
striking feature of all this is that these areas are not curiosities for tourists
craving exotic images for their holiday photographs (although there is some of
that) or a kind of theme park showing in the flesh what everyday life is like in
other parts of the planet. Although visitors may have the feeling that they have
been inadvertently transported to another continent, what they are actually
looking at is a typical neighbourhood in the globalized West, as authentic as any
other but of a kind unknown outside the First World.

Actually, this experience is not peculiar to today's world. The numerous 'Chinatowns' and 'Little Italies' scattered all over the planet, many of which are among the longest established and most traditional neighbourhoods of the cities concerned, show that international migration is not a phenomenon of recent date. Although people often tend to forget it, its history is as old as human existence on earth. To be more precise, it dates back to the appearance of the first international borders.[1] In fact, with the sole exception of the so-called countries of settlement (chiefly the United States, Canada, Argentina, Australia and New Zealand), all Western countries plus Japan experienced large population outflows until well into the twentieth century, accounting until that time for the bulk of international emigration. Even what are now highly developed countries such as Italy, Spain and Ireland were sources of large-scale emigration until as recently as thirty years ago. If there is one thing that distinguishes the current situation from what happened in earlier periods, it is that international migration has not only intensified, but *extensified*, so that while Western countries have reduced their contribution to emigration flows in the last few decades, the starting points, destinations and characteristics of these flows have diversified as a result of the combination of processes we term globalization.[2]

In turn, migratory dynamics are reinforcing and rendering irreversible the interdependence between countries that characterizes globalization, so that each of the migratory routes forming a regular link between a country of origin and a country of destination is progressively consolidated. By virtue of what Massey (1990) calls the mechanism of *cumulative causality*,[3] each migratory movement establishes the conditions for new migrations by people to whom the migrant is related. This is why, once a route is established, the growth of migration ceases to be linear and becomes exponential, thus creating ever closer ties between the two countries in a process that is continually feeding back upon itself. A brief review of migration figures from 1973 to date confirms the existence of population flows of this kind between the Caribbean Basin (Mexico, Central America and the West Indies) and the United States, between the Maghreb and some Mediterranean countries in Europe (France, Italy and Spain), between South Asia and the United Kingdom, between South-East Asia and Australia, and between Guangdong Province and the rest of China (although this is not really an international flow), to cite just a few of the best-known examples showing the extent to which this phenomenon has spread around the globe.[4]

Experience shows that, in all these cases, the first population movements are the trigger for an expansion in contacts of all kinds between the two countries: immigrants return to their countries of origin for vacations and are visited by friends and relatives, they send home goods purchased in the host country but also consume goods produced in their country of origin which have to be imported, they transfer remittances to their country and send news of employment opportunities for new migrants, receiving in exchange information about events affecting their families and taking decisions about them; and so we could go on citing examples of a web of contacts of ever increasing density. To cope with this increase in contacts, meanwhile, an entire communication and transport infrastructure is developed (establishment and extension of scheduled flights, improvements to telecommunications systems, creation of money-transfer mechanisms), and this in turn facilitates new migratory movements, leading to the appearance of what we might call *migration circuits* between the two countries. Consequently, one of the characteristics of migration today is that it is no longer confined to the flow of people, but increasingly drives a no-less copious flow of material and symbolic goods, information, capital and cultural values between the territories linked by these migratory circuits. An important consequence of this is that the links may become so deep and extensive that the origin and destination countries come to form twin poles of what in practice is an integrated system. Despite being a factor of external origin, immigration acquires a growing influence on the development of key elements in the structure of host countries, such as their demographic pyramid or the characteristics of their labour supply.

The case of the pairing formed by Mexico and the United States may be considered the supreme example of this phenomenon in its advanced phase: in terms of the percentage of each country's total population represented by the migrants concerned, Mexican emigration to the United States has acquired a critical mass such that the interdependence between the two extends into the sensitive core of their socioeconomic structures, to the extent that the administrative boundaries separating the two countries have in a sense been blurred by a reality that inexorably overflows them.[5] On a smaller scale, the conurbation formed by Ciudad Juárez (Chihuahua, Mexico) and El Paso (Texas, United States), separated from each other only by the Rio Bravo, but cut off by desert from the rest of their respective countries, constitutes a kind of laboratory experiment in extending this integration to all aspects of economic and social life. This is a truly binational city in which each half fulfils a function indispensable to the survival of the whole. In fact, the existence of an international border does not necessarily mean a sharp separation, but rather, by creating differences between the two sides, lays the basis for increased integration thanks to the complementarity that these differences make possible.

Although in most instances the degree of integration is less than that now developing between Mexico and the United States, it is possible to describe some of the characteristics of this phenomenon in a general way, while bearing in mind that its progress and outcome will be different in each country depending on its existing models of social, economic, political and cultural cohesion and, of course, on the political decisions taken in response to the issues raised by international immigration. One example of the influence of each country's peculiarities on the integration of immigrants is the importance of the informal sector to the economy: depending on its size, a larger or smaller proportion of immigrants will be undocumented, and the way they integrate into the host society will accordingly be different as well, i.e., involving more or less friction. It might be worth noting that in many Western countries there is also a demand for informal labour that often has to be met by undocumented immigrants, and this is one of the main causes of this type of migration.

In this chapter, we examine the experience of Mexican emigration to the United States to reveal the implications that international migration has for the survival of borders between countries in an era of globalization. We show that this process has a dual nature: although frontiers are becoming blurred in practice, at the same time border and immigration controls are stiffening, and the living conditions of immigrants are worsening as a result. We then analyse how this situation, combined with the labour market segmentation that has been driven by the restructuring of the production model and by social differentiation processes (what we call 'internal boundaries'), has been turning immigrants into a population group characterized by social vulnerability and overexploitation in the workplace. Nonetheless, we regard this not as a process of social exclusion but as the way inclusion is taking place for immigrants in the current context. Lastly, we analyse the appearance of transnational communities and the role of transnationalism as a mechanism that is shaping the profile of migrants as social actors situated in this context of structural differentiation.

International migration and the erosion of traditional frontiers

If the experience of Mexican migration to the United States is any example, the emergence of pairings between countries of emigration (newly industrializing countries and Third World countries) and countries of immigration (the West) is having two principal effects on the status of frontiers between these two types of country: increasing diversity in the host countries, showing that their borders do not isolate them from other parts of the world, and increasing integration between origin and destination countries.

Cultural diversity

The most striking effect of this process is that it increases the ethnic, cultural and linguistic diversity of the host countries, which eventually absorb some of the characteristics of the emigrants' home countries. The eastern part of Los Angeles to which we referred earlier has the highest concentration of inhabitants of Mexican origin in the United States. In fact, its population is almost exclusively Mexican, and Spanish is practically the only language spoken. But this part of the city is not just a piece of Mexico grafted onto the United States; it is also a type of neighbourhood that can be found, with the same composition and characteristics, in many other cities in the country. In other words, East Los Angeles is not just a Mexican neighbourhood, but is now a typical United States neighbourhood. In the era of globalization, areas of this type, defined by their migratory origin, are not just ethnic enclaves but an intrinsic characteristic of global cities.

It could be argued that what is occurring in these cases is a phenomenon of juxtaposition without any great consequences, i.e., that immigrant communities are creating autonomous subcultures in epidermic contact with the rest of society, a situation that will gradually disappear as the group fully assimilates or that will harden and lead to the appearance of ghettos isolated from the rest of society. Indeed, the immigrant tradition of the United States, with its constant assimilation of successive waves of immigrants after two or three generations, would appear to support this diagnosis (see Portes and Rumbaut, 1997, for a discussion of the immigration history of the United States). Nonetheless, one example will serve to illustrate the importance that a critical mass of immigrants of like origin can have as a factor for change in the host society.

After several decades of increasing immigration from Latin America, the United States has become one of the major Spanish-speaking countries in the world. The 2000 U.S. census found that a little over 28 million people over five years of age spoke Spanish at home, a number that is rising at such a rate that the U.S. will soon have more Spanish speakers than any other country except Mexico. While it is true that most United States citizens do not know the language, in the near future bilingualism is likely to be an almost indispensable requirement for any elected office in many states; it should indeed be remembered that, in the U.S., elections are held for many local posts that in other Western countries are filled by unelected officials, such as state judges, local police chiefs and others. It is not too rash to predict, then, that before long this tacit obligation will progressively spread to many positions of an executive or technical character, so that Spanish comes to join English as one of the United States' own languages, even if this status is not made official. This would imply an alteration in the traditional logic of assimilation, with immigrants integrating into the host society, yet at the same time profoundly transforming its social and cultural structure.

Indeed, the adverse reaction in large sections of U.S. society to the growing presence and influence of Hispanics, which was given intellectual expression in Samuel Huntington's essay *Who Are We? The Challenges to America's National Identity* (2004), demonstrates the plausibility of this scenario and the perception of it as an imminent threat. Although the subtitle of Huntington's work is rather unfortunate (after all, Hispanics are American as well), it shows that what is at stake and what its defenders seek to preserve is a particular conception of national identity, defined by certain shared values embodied in a nation occupying a territory that is its exclusive possession. But regardless of whether this type of community ever really existed, this conception is becoming increasingly debatable as the diversity of Western societies increases. In any case, this reaction should not be regarded as simply populist in nature, since it is also the outlook of the elite that Huntington represents, with many supporters among decision-makers. These adverse reactions should be regarded as another of the effects of international migration and as a factor influencing the way it develops.

Social dynamics

Another consequence of this phenomenon is that through migration the social dynamics of the countries of origin become major factors in the development of the social dynamics of the destination countries – so that, in practice, they become endogenous factors. This means that the socioeconomic and sociodemographic structures of migrant-receiving countries become more open to the outside, not just because the migratory flow contributes to their evolution but also because, through emigration, the social dynamics of the countries of origin have a direct impact on the internal dynamic of the recipient countries. This refers not only to emergency situations, like the devastation produced by Hurricane Mitch in Central America in 1998, the civil wars of the 1980s in that same region, or the collapse of the Mexican economy in 1982 and 1994 (all of which produced large rises in emigration to the United States at the time), but also and mainly to processes that are structural in nature.

One of the processes that reveal this structural interdependence is the historical population dynamics of destination countries. Analyses of demographic developments show that immigration is not just a supplement to organic growth but, for many of these countries, an intrinsic part of the population reproduction system. This contribution is not confined to the population increase that immigration generates directly; there is also the subsequent contribution of immigrants and their descendants to the natural growth of the population. This is evident in the so-called countries of settlement, but it is also true of countries, such as France, which have historically been characterized by low birth rates. In these cases, population growth is largely due to the continuing arrival of immigrants and the twofold contribution they make: when they immigrate, and when they and their descendants reproduce.[6] We thus encounter a demographic complementarity between countries of emigration and destination that is structural in nature, even if the actors have changed over time. Developing countries are now in the position formerly occupied by certain Mediterranean and Slavic countries in Europe, among others. Another feature of the present situation is that population ageing in Western countries is certainly going to accentuate this complementarity yet further.

Regarding the other half of this pairing, emigration also plays a vital role as a population-regulation mechanism because it mitigates the effects that situations of stagnation and social change alike have on countries with a peripheral position in the world economic system. It is obvious that a situation of stagnation and backwardness can lead to emigration, but changes can have this effect as well.[7] An example is provided by developing countries whose productive apparatus is modernized and integrated into the international economy. It used to be thought that, by promoting development and welfare in countries of actual or potential emigration, processes of this kind would act as a check on population outflows. Consequently, development assistance, foreign direct investment and free trade were proposed as possible instruments to halt these flows. One indication of how widely accepted this idea has become is the fact that, in line with this approach, the 1986 Immigration Reform and Control Act not only created stricter controls on immigration into the United States but supplemented these by providing for the creation of a Commission for the Study of International Migration and Cooperative Economic Development in Congress, with a mandate to recommend economic cooperation and development assistance measures to offset the adverse effects that increased border controls would have on the countries from which immigrants came, and thus to reduce these flows. But this approach is too simplistic. Bringing these countries into the international economy has led to the breakdown of traditional local communities and reduced the means of subsistence of large sections of the population, thus often triggering an increase in migration flows to other countries; capital mobility thus generates international migration (Sassen, 1988). The industrialization of the European countries and Japan likewise led to massive emigration from countryside to city, and also overseas.

Transnational communities

A third effect of international migration on borders that we wish to highlight, namely the appearance of transnational communities, is more local in its manifestations, although it is having a very substantial impact as it spreads. For this reason, we analyse the phenomenon more fully in the last section. In any event, the two processes that we have just described mark an irreversible trend towards growing integration between countries. Although integration is making it impossible for the borders between states to separate the different countries effectively, traditional frontiers have not disappeared. Rather, as we shall now see, interregional integration is coinciding with the strengthening of traditional borders between states and the imposition of greater obstacles to immigration.

Frontiers old and new

International migration is thus part of a long-term trend, and its effects are likely to intensify in the future. This would suggest that the progressive disappearance of borders as constraints on social processes and peoples' movements is irreversible or, at least, that frontiers are gradually to become so porous that they will ultimately amount to no more than lines drawn on the map, with little impact on reality. Yet this process is occurring alongside a progressive stiffening of immigration laws and growing restrictions on new immigration, a trend that is fostered by the so-called 'war against terrorism', but which started, let it be remembered, well before the attacks of 11 September 2001. This leads to a paradoxical situation: while stricter controls on border crossings and raising obstacles to migration may moderate flows towards Western countries and probably bring more friction into the process, they will certainly not halt it.

The border between Mexico and the United States at Tijuana-San Diego is a clear example of this contradictory situation. On the one hand, this is the world's busiest border post, reflecting the growing interconnection between California and Mexico. Indeed, San Diego and Tijuana constitute to some extent a transnational metropolis, with many Mexicans crossing the border daily to work or shop in the San Diego area, just as Tijuana is a habitual place of recreation for residents of San Diego. The proximity of San Diego and its well-developed business services infrastructure is also an important comparative advantage for Tijuana when it comes to attracting international investment in its *maquila* industry (Alegría, 1992; Herzog 1990). On the other hand, the border is an imposing wall that runs out to sea and into the desert, and those who try to cross it clandestinely are pursued implacably by the border patrol. The two facts co-exist and represent a dual reality: the frontier does not exist in practice for some, but for others it does. In other words, the border has never been so permeable, but at the same time it has never been so closely watched.

Immigrants have responded by adopting new methods to overcome these obstacles, even if this means greater risk and effort. When it becomes impossible for undocumented migrants to cross at frontier towns, they make the attempt through the desert or over mountains, and when surveillance is stepped up along sections of coast where immigrants have traditionally landed, they try to reach other, more distant parts of the coast that are not yet watched. But even when they succeed in crossing the border in a less dramatic way (and this is usually the case), many immigrants are condemned to a legal limbo of indefinite duration that limits their life prospects and exposes them to the worst forms of exploitation. Traditional international borders and the restrictions created by migration laws remain, for many, if not an insurmountable barrier, then at least an obstacle to be overcome. The perception that borders are disappearing is a Eurocentric one, since they are still there, and are a greater challenge than ever, for most of humanity.

Furthermore, these traditional borders are just the first barrier that migrants encounter in their new lives; in practice, international migration causes the border to be displaced into the interior of the recipient country: migrants carry it with them like an aura, so that the border becomes diffuse and multiple, while always shadowing and restricting their movements. In this creation of internal borders we can identify two closely related key factors that account for their existence. Firstly, employment has become increasingly segmented and polarized in the new deregulated labour market that has resulted from economic restructuring in the Western countries. Secondly, there is the ethnic and cultural segregation of Mexican migrants in the United States, which has prevented this community from following the traditional assimilation pattern of previous waves of migrants.

Migration and employment in post-industrial society

In considering the relationship between immigration and the employment structure, attention needs to be paid to the changes that globalization has wrought in the organization of work and to the leading role played by immigrant labour in these changes. Without denying the importance of cultural factors when interpreting the integration of immigrants into the host society, we believe that because work is at the core of the social structure, the function it discharges in this process will determine how immigrants fit into the new society. We shall not go into the details of the new organization of work, however, but will concentrate only on those aspects that are most relevant to our theme.[8]

One of the characteristics of the new occupational structure is its growing polarization, owing to the deregulation of labour relations. On the one hand, there has been an expansion of executive, professional and technical posts whose common characteristic is that they are based on information processing, and these are becoming the core and apex of the new occupational structure. At the same time, though, there has been an increase in lower-level and less-skilled service occupations, essentially in the field of what are called 'personal services'. This increase in the number of low-level occupations whose function is to improve other people's quality of life is the necessary counterpart of the growth in occupations at the apex of the occupational structure, since this expansion of the number of people with a high level of purchasing power has created a greater demand for personal services work, both skilled (interior designers, psychoanalysts, pet veterinarians, etc.) and unskilled (cleaning and maintenance services, jobs in eating and drinking outlets, care of dependent persons, etc.).

Besides this growing demand for unskilled labour in service industries, immigrants are also the main victims of another phenomenon, namely the new conditions of employment that have arisen as a result of contractual and labour deregulation, not only in many branches of industry and in construction, but in almost all leading-edge sectors as well. Because so many companies are outsourcing services and production processes, unskilled, repetitive jobs that offer no prospect of training are providing increasingly little in the way of stability or benefits either. In the case of industries in which Fordist methods of work organization still apply, we are also seeing an expansion of more temporary and informal (if not downright illegal) forms of hiring.[9] This is a strategy used by businesses to respond to the challenges of global competition without having to confront the costs of technological innovation or delocalization. The downgrading of working conditions ('casualization' – Sassen and Smith, 1992) drives local labour out of these jobs, which are then filled by immigrant labour hired on worse terms. By contrast with personal services, what we are seeing here is not net new job creation, since industrial employment is diminishing in relative terms (and often in absolute terms as well) in Western countries, but a growing demand for immigrants to fill these jobs, owing to the downgrading of contractual conditions.

Earlier waves of immigrants were similarly subjected to poor working conditions and exploitation,[10] but what characterizes the current situation is that the employment flexibility and adaptability seen among immigrants are not just a survival strategy for families impoverished by economic restructuring but also, and primarily, the result of patterns of change in the production apparatus of the United States economy. In the past, low-level occupations of this kind provided earlier immigrants with modest employment, but because they were stable and society deemed them honest, they enabled complete assimilation to take place over the course of a generation or two. The situation has now changed radically, for while there is upward mobility in the employment structure over time (the share of occupations requiring greater training and higher education is still growing more quickly than the share of lower-level occupations), what is happening is that workers are automatically allocated to particular occupations and production sectors in accordance with their sociodemographic characteristics, particularly their gender, ethnicity and migration status. In other words, although it is obvious that the occupational structure has always produced some kind of inequality, there are factors of a cultural nature that are limiting the mobility of certain workers and confining them to particular places within that structure. This is why there has been a large increase in immigrants working in jobs such as maintenance and cleaning, gardening, dish-washing, restaurant work, house-cleaning, domestic service and other low-skilled occupations of a similar kind. Furthermore, the automatic allocation of immigrants to jobs of this type for cultural reasons leads to a demand monopoly that makes their working conditions even less satisfactory.

The result is an asymmetrical labour market. The extreme vulnerability of immigrant workers puts them at the mercy of their employers, so that they have to accept the wages and conditions offered by these without any opportunity for negotiation. Let us recall that this vulnerability is the result not of economic factors but of extra-economic ones, such as migration status. This reveals the inadequacy of traditional approaches to migration that have interpreted it with reference to local imbalances in the employment market that are resolved by a transfer of factors, in this case labour. While this is part of the explanation, it must be stressed that the operation of this employment market for immigrants is governed by asymmetrical power relationships (more asymmetrical, that is, than those applying in the case of local workers) that have their origin in extra-economic factors. Drawing on Max Weber's formulation, Jorge Bustamante (1997, pp. 238–56) analyses the characteristics of this *imperfect market* for labour, in which the vulnerability forced upon migrants deprives them of the negotiating power that should by rights derive from the indispensable role they play in the normal functioning of the United States' economy.

This segmentation in the labour market provides the basis for a wider segmentation of the population into differentiated economic, social and cultural categories. Although the stratification of the different occupational groups follows the economic logic of the labour deregulation process, the composition of each of them is not determined by a strictly economic logic but by extra-economic social differentiation processes, the main factors of differentiation being culture, ethnicity, demography, gender and migration status. These social differentiation factors are the basis for the new internal borders that have arisen with globalization and that are contributing to the segmentation of the social structure in the information society.

As a result of these social differentiation factors and differing roles in the labour market, vulnerability levels also differ between population groups, a situation that has been worsened by a context where the political and social negotiating mechanisms that arose in industrial society and were enshrined in the welfare state have ceased to operate for the most vulnerable groups. This is the mechanism that creates social and cultural minorities like immigrants (but also female household heads, for instance), whose socially constructed vulnerability is transferred to the labour market in the form of a devaluation of their work, and thus of their conditions of existence and reproduction as well. As we can see, the poverty and insecurity of these workers are not the result of exclusion from the labour market but, on the contrary, of the way they participate in it. The fact is that, in the current context of economic and labour deregulation, modernization generates and reproduces its own forms of poverty, since the social vulnerability of individuals (due to their membership of a social, demographic or cultural minority) ceases to be a factor that exposes them to possible economic exclusion and becomes instead the necessary condition for their inclusion. Consequently, it is doubtful whether the current modernization process will overcome poverty and social inequality, since these, far from being hangovers from pre-modern societies, are an intrinsic part of globalization itself.

Migration, transnationalism and internal borders

In this context, the transnational communities developed by immigrants take on a particular importance. Transnational communities are indeed another result of international migration that has its origin in factors of a micro-social nature and is manifested on a local scale. Although the deepest causes of population movements are structural, they are of course the outcome of an aggregation of individual migrations by people who make decisions based on what is happening in their immediate environment. Most of these individual migrations are determined in practice by the existence of family and community networks, which shape a specific itinerary and geographical (and often occupational) destination for emigration. Although it has always been found that members of a given community tend to emigrate to and settle in the same place, thus tending to constitute a micro-society in the destination country that reproduces their community of origin, this phenomenon now evinces a greater complexity.

Traditional approaches distinguished between temporary and permanent migration. In the latter case, it was considered that, although immigrants might maintain close contacts with their countries of origin, their intention was to establish themselves and integrate in their *adoptive* country, so that these contacts would weaken over time until the group was fully assimilated (or 'Americanized'). This assimilation need not mean that the link with the country of origin disappears or that immigrants give up all their customs, and immigration consequently has effects on the characteristics of the host society. It should be recalled that while the United States was originally a refuge for various Protestant sects that were persecuted in Britain, which has shaped the country's collective image of itself, it now has a large Catholic population as a result of immigration from Ireland, Italy, Poland and other Catholic majority countries. Another example is the U.S.'s policy towards the conflict in Ulster, visibly influenced by its large population of Irish origin. Nonetheless, maintenance of these links does not call integration or the 'American dream' into question. Rather, they often go to swell the cultural heritage of the United States (Saint Patrick's Day parades, pizza, artists of Jewish origin, etc.).

By contrast, Mexican migration was traditionally seen as a typical example of temporary migration. Although many Mexican migrants settled in the United States during the twentieth century, most of them did not intend to integrate. Indeed, it might be said that migrants lived in the migratory circuits to which we referred earlier, rather than in a specific location, while still maintaining their Mexican national identity. Since the 1980s, though, a significant change has taken place: many of these migratory circuits have turned into transnational communities because the *density* of movements and social ties has extended the community of origin to all the places where its migrants are to be found.

The result is that the reproduction of communities of origin in Mexico is directly and inseparably linked to its migrants' different settlements in urban and rural areas of the United States. In other words, it is a single community dispersed around different locations. This new social and spatial form of the communities created by migration makes it necessary to reformulate traditional ideas about migration and migrants. To start with, in such cases, migration no longer entails a radical change in socioeconomic context; rather, migrants go and live in a different section of their own community, but with the same forms of social reproduction. Irrespective of the fact that the two settlements may be separated by thousands of miles and an international border, they continue to form a single community and this enables their residents to maintain not only their original national identity, but their local one as well. Thus, it often happens that an immigrant neighbourhood maintains a closer relationship with its community of origin than with those around it.[11]

The consequences for the communities of origin are quite substantial, although there is debate as to whether the effects are positive or negative. Up until the 1980s the negative aspects were emphasized, the argument being that emigration reduced the amount of labour available, heightened social inequalities and caused dependency or a 'migration syndrome', as Reichert (1981) famously termed it, restricting the potential for endogenous local development. Since then, however, there has been a tendency to stress the positive impacts, particularly the potential offered by remittances sent home by migrants, when used for productive investment. This point of view is shared by international development organizations, which are trying to encourage the development of emigration countries by this route.[12]

In any event, what we wish to emphasize is that, in the context of the new productive and occupational structure of the Western countries described earlier, transnational communities are taking on a special significance. The social networks of reciprocity, trust and solidarity on which they are based also act as a mechanism for coping with the social vulnerability that derives from their members' position as immigrants. Immigrant workers, marginalized in a context of inequality and insecurity produced by globalization, develop forms of response (although not of 'exit') to this process by turning back to their own communities. Thus, the links they maintain through transnational communities provide them with defence mechanisms for coping with situations of vulnerability such as relocation risks, settlement costs, job-seeking, participation in destination communities or the day-to-day reproduction of the family in the communities of origin. All these needs can be met thanks to the resources provided by the system of social networks and relationships that make up transnational communities.

Transnationalization, then, results from the behaviours migrant workers employ to cope with their subordinate role in the labour globalization process – a process marked by a strengthening of the traditional borders between states and, above all, by the existence of internal borders that limit their work and life prospects. Although the function of this mechanism is to cope with internal borders, it also has the effect of blurring the borders between states. Where the social identity of migrants is concerned, transnational communities are based on a feeling of 'belonging' that is very different from citizenship. It is about configuring an identity that precedes but also transcends citizenship, a transnationalization of the sense of community that is not confined by national borders. In this way, Mexican migrants living in the United States maintain and increase their links with their communities of origin even once they have taken up legal, stable and permanent residence. For them, possible integration into the destination country does not mean renouncing their communities of origin, since their attachment to these is deeper and more vital than politically constructed attachments. In many cases, indeed, people integrate only the better to defend and maintain these community ties.

To sum up, transnational communities and social networks, which constitute the *social capital* of migrants, have two sides. On the debit side, as strategies of response but not of 'exit', they serve to reproduce the conditions of social subordination generated by globalization. In other words, they make possible the social reproduction of immigrants in a hostile environment, but by failing to challenge the system of social stratification that is at the root of migrants' vulnerability, they allow this system to perpetuate itself. Furthermore, in ensuring social reproduction, this mechanism also serves the interests of a system that is based on the overexploitation of migrants.

As regards the credit side, by providing an alternative field of belonging and action, transnational communities may also act as a social base from which migrants (who usually occupy a subordinate position in both the origin and the destination country) can escape from the narrow frameworks of negotiation imposed by globalization and by the persistence of borders. One example of this are the so-called 'home town associations', popularly known as 'migrants' clubs'.

These associations originally arose as a way for the natives of a particular country to hold festivities and maintain some traditions from their communities of origin, and as mutual aid and solidarity mechanisms. However, they soon extended their activities to their communities of origin, chiefly by channelling financial and material resources to these and improving the living conditions of their compatriots. These activities have elevated such immigrants to the status of political actors influential enough to negotiate with the Mexican authorities, especially at the state and local levels. Some of these associations have adopted a political profile in the destination country as well, actively standing up for the economic, occupational, human and political rights of their compatriots in the United States. This is often done by creating coalitions with community organizations, unions, non-governmental organizations and other civil associations that defend the rights of the U.S. population in general, and it is also an active way of participating in the destination country.

These are, broadly speaking, the characteristics of transnational communities and the framework in which they function. However, the relations that are established between these communities and the host society are not predetermined. They will depend on the decisions taken by the different actors and on the integration models that develop in each particular case. Accordingly, we can imagine different integration scenarios, all with their quota of strain and conflict.

For example, transnational communities might dissolve like ice in a bucket of water, so that the amount of water increases but there is no change in its composition. Or they could rather behave somewhat like sugar – ultimately dissolving in the host society, but contributing a new 'flavour' to its culture and identity ('sweetening' U.S. society in this case). In other words, an integration model could foresee the host society absorbing not just the immigrants but also their culture, and itself changing in the process. Another possibility, though, is that transnational communities might instead behave like a rock in that same bucket of water, with a strict, long-term separation continuing between the two. While the effects of erosion would see pieces of the transnational community gradually becoming detached, they would never be absorbed or assimilated by the host society. A much more improbable scenario, in our view, is the one apparently envisaged by Huntington, where integration resembles a sponge and the transnational community ends up absorbing and supplanting the community that was there originally.

Conclusions

For all our efforts to systematize it, reality will always be a step ahead. In the case of international migration, the growing integration between countries caused by globalization has rendered obsolete many of the theories and concepts used to approach the phenomenon, since migrations have been taking on new forms that do not fit well into the traditional moulds. By contrast with previous episodes, they are not the result of temporary or cyclical imbalances in the labour market of the Western countries or of a need to colonize, nor are immigrants assimilating by adopting the national identity of the destination society. The new conditions of production in Western societies now mean that the demand for migrant labour to take up low-skilled, unstable employment is permanent in character. The development of migration circuits means that this need for labour can be met uninterruptedly – but, inevitably, the increase in flows and the vulnerability of the migrants have given rise to transnational communities, and this in turn is changing the way migrants integrate.

In this context, transnationalism is not just an emerging social phenomenon, but is proving to be a paradigm that enables us to interpret the peculiarities of international migration in the globalization era. For this reason, one of the first tasks of the social sciences is to develop this new paradigm if they wish to address the phenomenon of international migration. With the knowledge we have now, however, we can draw some conclusions of a political nature that could help ensure that the intensification of international migration and the appearance of transnational communities, as irreversible historical phenomena, develop with as little trauma as possible.

1. As we have noted, two parallel phenomena are occurring in the contemporary world: the virtual disappearance of borders as obstacles to mobility for some and their entrenchment for others. While the former development is a necessary adaptation to globalization, the latter is no more than a futile attempt to halt an irreversible process. We need to be aware of the irreversible nature of integration and of the advantages it can generate. It would be advisable, therefore, to analyse the benefits deriving from increased labour mobility more thoroughly as an educational exercise for the benefit of public opinion in Western countries, to lay the political and social groundwork for a less traumatic integration of immigrants. The ageing of Western countries (especially Japan and Europe), for example, shows that increased labour mobility is not just inevitable but necessary.

2. Despite attempts to check immigration, it has emerged as one of the main drivers of globalization. The globalization process certainly has its good and bad sides, but proper management of it could ensure a better quality of life for all at the lowest possible cost. Consequently, it is wholly unfair that immigrants should bear such a disproportionate share of the cost of globalization, in the form of obstacles to movement and overexploitation in the workplace. In many countries of emigration, for example, the remittances sent by international migrants to their households of origin

exceed the volume of foreign direct investment (to say nothing of development aid). Consequently, it is migrants who are making the greatest contribution to the development and welfare of their countries of origin. Facilitating the sending of remittances and reducing the commission on these operations should be considered not just an act of decency, but also an effective way of fostering development.

3. The configuration of the production system, and in particular the automatic allocation of migrants to particular sectors and occupations, has the effect of creating internal borders. These borders are not a necessity of the production system but the outcome of certain ideological prejudices that also yield an abusive advantage from the overexploitation of migrant labour. For this reason power relations in the labour market, which tend to be weighted in favour of employers at the best of times, are particularly skewed against migrant workers. This is especially true of undocumented migrants, who cannot take advantage of the protections enjoyed by other workers. Considering that the need for migrant labour is an intrinsic characteristic of labour markets in Western countries, the continuation of this state of affairs suggests a desire to keep immigrants in a position that makes it easier to overexploit their labour. While this problem is a complex one to resolve, measures to bring the underground economy to the surface would substantially improve the living conditions of many migrant workers.

4. In particular, we consider that the current character of migration as a process which generates transnational fields of belonging and action renders useless the efforts of states to restrict people's mobility. This is so, firstly, because the ways actors participate in and experience migration are becoming more and more extensive and diverse, making strict control of immigration impossible, particularly when the aim is to reduce it. And secondly, because these transnational fields are not confined to the mobility of persons but, crucially, include a system of networks through which material and symbolic goods are moved and exchanged. Given this situation on the ground and the need to defuse the possible strains and conflicts of the process, integration policies should concentrate on two things: a revised conception of citizenship that reflects the new multicultural reality of Western countries, and vigorous efforts to combat the forms of exclusion suffered by immigrants, although to be really effective these would undoubtedly require profound changes in the production model. Accordingly, and in view of the leading role that the new forms of public policy implementation give to civil society, it would be desirable to recognize the institutions and actors forming part of transnational communities as social interlocutors in the decision-making process.

Notes

1. To challenge the received wisdom about the supposed explosive increase in migrations over recent years, Tapinos and Delaunay (2000) highlight the continuities in international emigration over time, arguing that the current situation does not differ substantially from that of earlier periods. Durand and Massey (2003) similarly analyse the continuities of Mexican emigration to the United States over the last hundred years.

2. Without entering into the controversy about how globalization should be interpreted, a controversy that extends even to the term itself, we have adopted the appellation that is most widely used and accepted in academic circles to refer to a set of processes that are intensifying social relations and interdependence on a planetary scale. Overviews of the relationship between globalization and international migration can be found in Castles and Miller (2003) and in Sassen (1998), particularly Section I.

3. A term adapted from the work of Gunnar Myrdal (1958), who referred to *cumulative circular causation* to explain the set of processes that perpetuate underdevelopment.

4. While attempts to date the moment when one stage of a historical process ends and the next begins are somewhat arbitrary, experts agree that the current stage of migration is a historical phenomenon that began with the 1973 energy crisis and the consequent restructuring of the production model, which has turned Western countries into post-industrial societies. This historical phenomenon is characterized by: increasing diversity and informality; the predominance of newly industrializing and Third World countries as sources of migration; and the tendency of migrants to find work in the activities and occupations most affected by economic deregulation, along with certain unskilled personal and community services that have experienced enormous growth in recent years (care of dependent persons, services in eating and drinking establishments, maintenance work). The fact that most people migrating to other countries do so for work reasons fully justifies this association between the different stages in the development of the world capitalist system and the historical phases of international migration. This subject will be returned to later.

5. Although the strategic importance of emigration to the United States for the socioeconomic stability of the country is widely recognized in Mexico, initiatives like California's short-lived Clause 187, which restricted undocumented migrants' access to social, health and education services and obliged employees of these services to report them to the migration authorities, show that public opinion on the other side of the border does not regard the benefits of migration as reciprocal. The academic debate in the United States about the impact of Mexican immigration on the country's economy is moving towards a consensus that its net effects are positive, but this view has not yet penetrated the political debate and public opinion, where the contrary belief has so far prevailed. Without looking further afield, an initiative similar to the Californian one was approved by referendum in the state of Arizona in November 2004, although the news was overshadowed by the presidential election held at the same time.

6. Demographer Anna Cabré (1999) has developed this thesis for the case of Catalonia, which received immigrants from the rest of Spain for a century and now receives them from other parts of the world. Cabré shows that, of women born between 1856 and 1960, only those born between 1936 and 1950 achieved a net reproduction rate in excess of one. She calculates that, without immigration, the population of Catalonia would now be only 2.4 million instead of the actual figure of just over 6 million. Estrella Valenzuela et al. (1999) put forward a similar argument for Mexico's northern frontier.

7. Paul Singer (1975) developed this thesis in depth, although he was dealing with migration from the countryside to cities within a given country.

8. The theoretical background to our discussion can be found in Castells (2000), Sassen (1991, 1998), Piore (1979) and Beck (2000).

9. Examples in the United States in which local workers have been replaced by immigrants employed on worse terms are documented in Colón-Warren (1994), Zlolniski (1994), Fernández Kelly et al. (1987) and Sassen and Smith (1992).

10. De Tocqueville, writing as long ago as the early nineteenth century, made a telling observation about the employment prospects of European immigrants in the United States: 'An erroneous notion is generally entertained that the deserts of America are peopled by European emigrants, who annually disembark upon the coasts of the New World, whilst the American population increases and multiplies upon the soil which its forefathers tilled. The European settler, however, usually arrives in the United States without friends, and sometimes without resources; in order to subsist he is obliged to work for hire, and he rarely proceeds beyond that great belt of industry which adjoins the ocean. The desert cannot be explored without capital or credit; and the body must be accustomed to the rigours of a new climate before it can be exposed to the chances of forest life. It is the Americans themselves who daily quit the spots which gave them birth to acquire extensive domains in a remote country. Thus the European leaves his cottage for the trans-Atlantic shores; and the American, who is born on that very coast, plunges in his turn into the wilds of central America. This double emigration is incessant; it begins in the remotest parts of Europe, it crosses the Atlantic Ocean, and it advances over the solitudes of the New World. Millions of men are marching at once towards the same horizon; their language, their religion, their manners differ, their object is the same. The gifts of fortune are promised in the West, and to the West they bend their course.' (*De la Démocratie en Amérique* 1835: see De Tocqueville and Reeve (trans.), 1951).

11. For an overview of transnational communities see the collective works of Glick-Schiller et al. (1992), Mummert (1999) and Smith and Guarnizo (1997). Two works on transnational communities from an anthropological perspective are Kearney and Nagengast (1989) and Smith (1995). A summary of these studies can be found in Canales and Zlolniski (2001).

12. Excellent critical reviews of the literature on this subject are provided by Durand and Massey (1992), who offer a positive overview of the role of emigration in the development of communities of origin, and by Binford (2002), who takes a somewhat more sceptical approach. See Canales and Montiel (2004) for a discussion of the economic role of remittances in the case of Mexico.

Bibliography

Alegría, T. 1992. *Desarrollo urbano en la frontera México-Estados Unidos: una interpretación y algunos resultados*. Mexico City, Consejo Nacional para la Cultura y las Artes.

Beck, U. 2000. *The Brave New World of Work*. Cambridge, U.K., Polity Press.

Binford, L. 2002. Remesas y subdesarrollo en México. *Relaciones: Estudios de Historia y Sociedad*, Vol. 90, No. 23, pp. 115–58.

Bustamante, J. A. 1997. *Cruzar la línea: La migración de México a Estados Unidos*. Mexico City, Fondo de Cultura Económica.

Cabré, A. 1999. *El sistema català de reproducció*. Barcelona, Spain, Proa.

Canales, A. I. and Montiel, I. 2004. Remesas e inversión productiva en comunidades de alta migración. El caso de Teocaltiche, Jalisco. *Migraciones Internacionales*, Vol. 2, No. 3, pp. 142–72.

Canales, A. I. and Zlolniski, C. 2001. Comunidades transnacionales y migración en la era de la globalización. *La Migración internacional y el desarrollo en las Américas*. Santiago, Chile, ECLAC, IDB, IOM and UNFPA.

Castells, M. 1996. *The Rise of the Network Society*. Vol. 1 of *The Information Age: Economy, Society and Culture*. Malden, Mass., Blackwell.

Castles, S. and Miller, M. J. 1993. *The Age of Migration: International Population Movements in the Modern World*. Basingstoke, U.K., Macmillan.

Colón-Warren, A. 1994. Puerto Rican women in the Middle Atlantic region: employment, loss of jobs and the feminization of poverty. C. A. Torre, H. R. Vecchini and W. Burgos (eds), *The Commuter Nation: Perspectives on Puerto Rican Migration*. Puerto Rico, Editorial de la Universidad de Puerto Rico, pp. 253–88.

de Tocqueville, A. and Reeve, H. (trans.). 1951. Principal causes maintaining the democratic republic. P. Bradley (ed.) and H. Reeve (trans.) *Democracy in America*, Vol 1, Chap.17. New York, Knopf. (1835 title, *De la Démocratie en Amérique* [in French].)

Durand, J. and Massey, D. 1992. Mexican migration to the United States: a critical review. *Latin American Research Review*, Vol. 27, pp. 3–43.

———. 2003. *Clandestinos: Migración México-Estados Unidos en los albores del siglo XXI*. Mexico City, Porrúa-Universidad Autónoma de Zacatecas.

Estrella Valenzuela, G., Canales Cerón, A. and Zavala de Cosío, M. E. 1999. *Ciudades de la frontera norte: Migración y fecundidad*. Mexicali, Mexico, Universidad Autónoma de Baja California.

Fernández-Kelly, M. P. and García, A. M. 1988. Economic restructuring in the United States: the case of Hispanic women in the garment and electronics industries in Southern California. B. A. Gutek, A. H. Stromberg and L. Larwood (eds), *Women and Work: An Annual Review*. Beverly Hills, California, Sage, pp. 49–65.

Glick Schiller, N., Basch, L. and Blanc-Szanton, C. (eds). 1992. *Towards a Transnational Perspective on Migration: Race, Class, Ethnicity, and Nationalism Reconsidered*. New York, New York Academy of Sciences. (Annals of the New York Academy of Sciences Vol. 645.)

Herzog, L. A. 1990. *Where North Meets South: Cities, Space and Politics on the U.S.-Mexico Border*. Austin, Texas, University of Texas Press.

Huntington, S. P. 2004. *Who Are We? The Challenges to America's National Identity*. New York, Simon & Schuster.

Kearney, M. and Nagengast, C. 1989. *Anthropological Perspectives on Transnational Communities in Rural California*. Davis, California, California Institute for Rural Studies.

Massey, D. 1990. Social Structure, Household Strategies, and the Cumulative Causation of Migration. *Population Index*, Vol. 56, No. 1, pp. 3–26.

Mummert, G. (ed.). 1999. *Fronteras fragmentadas*. Zamora, Michoacán, Mexico, El Colegio de Michoacán/CIDEM.

Myrdal, G. 1958. *Economic Theory and Under-Developed Regions*. London, G. Duckworth.

Piore, M. 1979. *Birds of Passage: Migrant Labor and Industrial Societies*. New York, Cambridge University Press.

Portes, A. and Rumbaut, R. G. 1997. *Immigrant America: A Portrait*. Berkeley, California, University of California Press.

Reichert, J. 1981. The migrant syndrome: seasonal U.S. wage labor and rural development in central Mexico. *Human Organization*, Vol. 40, No. 1, pp. 56–66.

Sassen, S. 1988. *The Mobility of Labour and Capital: A Study in International Investment and Labor Flow*. Cambridge, U.K., Cambridge University Press.

———. 1991. *The Global City: New York, London, Tokyo*. Princeton, N.J., Princeton University Press.

———. 1998. *Globalization and Its Discontents: Essays on the New Mobility of People and Money*. New York, The New Press.

Sassen, S. and Smith, R. 1992. Post-industrial growth and economic reorganization: their impact on immigrant employment. J. A. Bustamante, C. W. Reynolds and R. A. Hinojosa (eds), *U.S.-Mexico Relations: Labor Market Interdependence*. Palo Alto, Calif., Stanford University Press, pp. 372–93.

Schmidley, D. 2001. *Current Population Reports, Series P23–206: Profile of the Foreign-Born Population in the United States: 2000*. Washington DC, U.S. Census Bureau, Government Printing Office.

Singer, P. 1975a. *Economía política de la urbanización*. Mexico City, Siglo XXI.

———. 1975b. Migraciones internas: consideraciones teóricas para su estudio. Singer, 1975a, op. cit., pp. 31 70.

Smith, R. 1995. *Los Ausentes Siempre Presentes: The Imagining, Making, and Politics of a Transnational Community between New York and Ticuani, Puebla*. Unpublished thesis, New York, Columbia University.

Smith, M. P. and Guarnizo, L. E. (eds). 1997. *Transnationalism from Below*. Somerset, N.J., Transaction.

Tapinos, G. and Delaunay, D. 2000. Peut-on parler d'une mondialisation des migrations internationales? *Mondialisation, Migrations et Développement*. Paris, OECD, pp. 37–53.

Zlolniski, C. 1994. The informal economy in an advanced industrialized society: Mexican immigrant labor in Silicon Valley. *The Yale Law Journal*, Vol. 103, No. 8, pp. 2305–35.

Chapter 12

The free circulation of skilled migrants in North America

Rafael Alarcón[1]

Introduction

It is perhaps illusory to imagine a scenario of migration without borders when one is in the city of Tijuana, on the border between Mexico and the United States. The municipality of Tijuana and San Diego County are separated by a dark metal wall. It is reinforced with additional fencing in some sections and closely guarded by hundreds of U.S. Border Patrol agents who, with electronic equipment of military origin, try to stop people crossing clandestinely from the Mexican side. In October 2006, United States President George Bush signed into law the Secure Fence Act, which directs the Department of Homeland Security to construct 700 miles of additional fencing along the border between Mexico and the United States.

These developments can be traced back more than a decade: in late 1993, the United States government decided to reinforce surveillance of its border with Mexico to halt the migration of undocumented persons by applying two important measures: a substantial increase in the budget of what is now called the Department of Homeland Security and a concentration of resources to install walls and electronic surveillance equipment on border routes that have been traditionally used by undocumented migrants (Cornelius, 2001; Reyes et al., 2002).

This has brought into being a fortified border, which in turn has forced those now crossing the border without proper documentation to go deep into wilder and more dangerous areas where many of them drown in rivers and canals or die of heat in the desert or of cold in the mountains. Over 3,000 people are recorded as having died attempting to cross the border since 1994 (Alonso Meneses, 2003).

The nearest approximation to migration without borders in the context of North America is the case of skilled migrants from Mexico who can cross the borders of the United States and Canada more freely. For this chapter, I define 'skilled migrants' as those of twenty-five years of age and over who have completed at least four years of study at university level or have been awarded a master's degree or doctorate.[2] Immigration policies, the power of corporations, and their own class resources enable such migrants to cross borders and participate in labour markets within the global economy more easily than unskilled migrants (Alarcón, 2000).

Robert Reich (1992) argues that the expansion of the global economy is creating conditions for the advent of 'symbolic analysts' who identify, negotiate and solve problems through the manipulation of symbols. Some of these professionals with a global labour market are scientific researchers, engineers, lawyers, real estate developers, marketing strategists, art directors, writers, musicians and university professors. Manuel Castells (1996) further shows that there is a global labour market for a small but growing segment of professionals and scientists who carry out innovative research and development, cutting-edge engineering, financial management, and advanced business services and entertainment. In his opinion, national borders do not readily constrain these professionals in view of the existence of an economy that is both informational and global. Castells nevertheless does not think that there is a genuine global labour market for all because this global economy, too, is segmented.

This chapter examines the effect of the immigration policies of the United States and Canada on (temporary or permanent) skilled migration from Mexico in the context of the development of the North American Free Trade Agreement (NAFTA). The agreement entered into force on 1 January 1994 and was the outcome of a difficult and complex negotiation between the governments of Canada, Mexico and the United States. Of the three countries, Mexico was the source of a large number of unskilled workers employed in the United States without legal authorization. NAFTA permitted the free circulation of goods, services and information, but excluded the free movement of workers in the North American region. From the outset, the issue of the mobility of workers was removed from the agenda of the negotiation by the Mexican delegation so as not to impede the approval of the agreement (Castañeda and Alarcón, 1991). However, the three member countries of NAFTA instituted what are known as 'NAFTA visas' to facilitate the temporary employment of professionals in the North American region as a timid form of promoting the circulation of these workers in the region to enhance NAFTA goals.

This chapter is divided into four parts. The first part offers an overview of emigration from Mexico, with special emphasis on skilled migration. The next two sections explore the immigration policies of the United States and Canada, using as an analysis framework data on Mexican migration to those two countries in the first few years of the twenty-first century. The fourth part concentrates on the distribution of NAFTA visas in the three countries in 2003. The conclusion considers the main arguments put forward in this study.

The migration of skilled workers from Mexico

According to figures of the General Census of Population and Housing, Mexico had 97,361,711 inhabitants in 2000 (Puig, 2000). For its part, the United States Census of Population found that in the same year there were 9,177,487 Mexican immigrants residing in the United States, nearly 10 per cent of Mexico's total population. With this population of emigrants, Mexico at present has the largest diaspora in the world, concentrated almost entirely in the United States. In 2000, Mexicans were the largest group in that country, and they accounted for 30 per cent of all immigrants, trailed far behind by nationals of China, the Philippines, India and Viet Nam (Malone et al., 2003). In addition, Mexican immigration has the highest proportion of people lacking legal authorization. Jeffrey Passel (2004) estimates that in March 2002 there were around 9.3 million undocumented immigrants in the United States, of whom 5.3 million (57 per cent) were from Mexico.

Mexican migration to Canada, on the other hand, is minimal, and Mexicans constitute only a small portion of Canada's total intake of immigrants. The only substantial migratory process between the two countries is through a recruitment programme under which every year a few thousand Mexican farmworkers go to Canada for seasonal work.

Mexican migration to the United States mainly consists of workers with very low levels of schooling, which more or less channels them to unskilled jobs and low pay. A study by Dianne Schmidley (2001) reveals that, as compared with immigrants from Europe, Asia, Africa, the Caribbean, Central America, South America and Canada, Mexicans are, among other things, the youngest, those with the highest proportion of men over women, and those with the lowest educational attainment.

Only a third of Mexican immigrants in the United States of twenty-five years of age and over (33.8 per cent) have an education equivalent to or higher than high school or secondary level. By contrast, 81.3 per cent of Europeans, 83.8 per cent of Asians and 94.9 per cent of Africans of twenty-five years of age and over have that level of schooling. Only immigrants from Central America come close to the Mexicans, with 37.3 per cent, but immigrants from South America and the Caribbean are more educated than Mexicans, with, respectively, 79.7 per cent and 68.1 per cent.

Mexican immigrants have likewise lived fewer years in the United States and have the lowest proportion of naturalized citizens. They are part of a labour market that works for low wages, and their participation in managerial and professional specialities and in technical, sales, and administrative support occupations is very low. Where they are heavily concentrated is in jobs as operators, fabricators and labourers, or in farming, forestry and fishing (Schmidley, 2001, p. 41).

Is there any reluctance on the part of Mexican professionals to migrate to the United States? Little can be said about this since there is scant information on the migration of skilled workers from Mexico. In a previous study (Alarcón, 2000), I used a qualitative method to examine how engineers and scientists born in Mexico have become integrated into the high-technology industry of Silicon Valley, the world's most successful region, located in Northern California. Most of these professionals belong to the Association of Mexican Professionals of Silicon Valley and reached the region via different routes. The majority originally went to the United States for postgraduate studies at a U.S. university and, on completing their studies, were recruited by high-tech companies that helped them arrange temporary or permanent residence. The second group consists of those who started working in subsidiaries of high-tech enterprises in Mexico and were then transferred to the central plant in Silicon Valley. A few reached the United States as members of families of migrants and went through its education system. Finally there are the 'high-tech *braceros*' who, like the Mexican seasonal labourers of the past, work temporarily in the United States. Most of these migrants have the H-1B visa allowing them to stay for a maximum of six years but making them then eligible for permanent residence.

In a recent study on brain drain in Mexico, Castaños-Lomnitz et al. (2004) found that professionals in engineering stood the best chance of being hired abroad. The United States, Canada and the United Kingdom are the main destinations for those seeking to engage in academic activity outside Mexico.

This chapter examines how skilled migrants from Mexico enter the United States or Canada permanently or temporarily. The Mexican population census data offer an approximate estimate of the number of professionals who may be eligible to work in these countries. Table 12.1 shows the distribution of the population aged twenty-five years and above by sex who declared they had completed at least four years of study at university level or had a master's degree or doctorate.

Table 12.1 shows that of the total population of Mexico, almost 4 million people (3,981,753) of twenty-five years of age or more had a higher education

Table 12.1: Distribution by sex of the Mexican population aged 25 years and above with a professional or postgraduate education, 2000

	Number			Percentages by sex		
	Academic Level			Academic Level		
	Professional	Master's or Doctorate	Total	Professional	Master's or Doctorate	Total
Men	2,095,468	226,900	2,322,368	57.8	63.5	58.3
Women	1,528,840	130,545	1,659,385	42.2	36.5	41.7
Total	3,624,308	357,445	3,981,753	100.0	100.0	100.0

Source: Based on sample of Mexico's 12th General Census of Population and Housing, 2000.

(a professional qualification, a master's degree or a doctorate) in 2000. This is the estimate of the pool of skilled workers who might be eligible for temporary or immigrant visas from Canada and the United States. In 2000, more than half of the professionals (51.3 per cent) were distributed among the following eleven disciplines, by order of importance: accounting, law, administration, basic education, medicine, civil engineering, computer engineering, architecture, industrial engineering, agricultural engineering and mechanical engineering.

U.S. immigration policy and Mexican migration

The immigration policy of the United States is based on four fundamental principles: family reunification; the admission of immigrants with occupational skills in demand; the protection of refugees; and the diversity of immigrants by country of origin (Wasem, 2004, p. 1). While the numerical significance of family reunification has been very clear since the implementation of the 1952 Immigration and Nationality Act, only in 1990 did the United States Congress take more direct account of the human capital of immigrants by emphasizing the education and occupational skills of new immigrants. The 1990 Immigration Act significantly expanded the proportion of visas for employment reasons, raising their annual ceiling from 54,000 to 140,000.

Under the 1990 Immigration Act, 40,000 immigrant visas are granted each year for priority workers: immigrants with 'extraordinary' ability in the sciences, arts, education, business or athletics. This category includes outstanding professors and researchers and certain executives and managers of multinational corporations. The second category provides 40,000 visas annually for immigrants with advanced university degrees or with 'exceptional' abilities in the sciences, arts or business. The third category, with a further 40,000 visas, is for other skilled and unskilled workers, although only 10,000 visas are available for the latter. The category of special immigrants is designed for certain religious ministers and workers, and for employees of the United States government working abroad, who have access to 10,000 visas a year. Finally, the fifth category provides 10,000 visas a year for entrepreneurs who set up a new commercial enterprise and invest between U.S.$500,000 and U.S.$3 million in the United States. Such investment must create at least 10 full-time jobs for workers in the United States (Calavita, 1994; Papademetriou, 1996; Yale-Loehr, 1991).

As shown in Table 12.2, the United States admitted a total of 705,827 immigrants in 2003. The largest segment to be admitted – 332,657 people (47.1 per cent) – consisted of immediate relatives of U.S. citizens (spouses, parents and children), on whom there is no numerical restriction. In addition, 158,894 (22.5 per cent) were admitted under the family reunification preference system governed by a four-category quota system; 82,137 (11.6 per cent) under the

Table 12.2: Immigrants admitted to the United States by type and class of admission, 2003

Preference Immigrants		
Family-sponsored immigrants		**158,894**
Unmarried sons/daughters of U.S. citizens	21,503	
Spouses of alien residents	53,229	
Married sons/daughters of U.S. citizens	27,303	
Siblings of U.S. citizens	56,859	
Employment-based immigrants		**82,137** *
Priority workers/aliens with exceptional ability	14,544	
Professionals with advanced degrees	15,459	
Skilled workers, professionals, other workers	46,613	
Special immigrants	5,452	
Employment creation	65	
Immediate relatives of U.S. citizens		**332,657**
Refugees and asylees		**44,927**
Diversity immigrants		**46,347**
IRCA legalization		**39**
Other immigrants		**40,826**
Total (all immigrants)		**705,827**

Source: U.S. Department of Homeland Security, 2004 (Table 5).

* The total of the original table 5 of the U.S. Department of Homeland Security (2004) on employment visas is given as 82,137 which is wrong since the correct figure is 82,133.

employment preference system, in accordance with the limits in the five different categories; and 46,347 (6.5 per cent) became permanent residents through the Diversity Visa program. The remaining 85,792 (12.2 per cent) comprise refugees and other types of immigrants admitted under other categories.

It is important to note, with respect to employment-based visas, that of the 140,000 visas available annually a mere 82,137 persons were granted admission in 2003. Meyers and Yau (2004) report a 53 per cent reduction as against the number of visas of this type granted in 2002.

Table 12.3 shows the seven countries accounting for the largest number of immigrants admitted to the United States as permanent residents on employment-based preferences in 2003. Foremost is Mexico, which obtained the highest number of immigrant visas (115,864) but only 3,261 of them (2.8 per cent) were employment-based. With the exception of Viet Nam, the Asian countries provide markedly higher proportions of employment-based immigrants than do the Latin American countries. For example, while 40.8 per cent of immigrants from India were admitted on employment-based preferences, the corresponding figure for Mexicans was 2.8 per cent.

What mechanism is at work to explain such a low proportion of employment-based Mexican migrants? Clearly, the bulk of Mexican migration to the United States is for reasons of family reunification. This is attributable to geographical proximity, the existence of large Mexican communities in several regions, and access to strong social networks. But why do these factors not come into play for skilled migration?

With regard to the temporary H-1B employment visas, which were designed for temporary workers employed in 'special occupations' requiring highly specialized knowledge and at least one bachelor's degree or equivalent,

Table 12.3: Immigrants admitted to the United States on employment-based preferences, 2003

	Total immigration	Employment-based preferences	Percentage of total immigration
Mexico	115,864	3,261	2.8
India	50,372	20,560	40.8
Philippines	45,397	9,756	21.5
China	40,659	7,511	18.5
El Salvador	28,296	752	2.6
Dominican Republic	26,205	159	0.6
Viet Nam	22,133	119	0.5
All countries	705,827	82,137	11.6

Source: U.S. Department of Homeland Security 2004 (Table 8).

the data of the Department of Homeland Security (2004) again show that migrants from India are in the fore with a fifth of the visas offered in 2003. There is already ample evidence that a great many software engineers from India use these visas to work in the high-tech industry of the United States (Lakha, 1992; Alarcón, 2001).

According to the Department of Homeland Security (2004, Table 25), 360,498 persons were admitted with H-1B visas in 2003. Of them, migrants from India obtained 75,964 (21.1 per cent of the visas), followed by migrants from the United Kingdom with 31,343 (8.7 per cent), Canada with 20,947 (5.8 per cent), Mexico with 16,290 (4.5 per cent) and France with 15,705 (4.3 per cent).

The participation of Mexico as the fourth recipient of this type of visa, with more than France, Germany, Japan, China, Colombia and Brazil, suggests a greater inclination on the part of Mexican skilled migrants to enter the United States labour markets temporarily by means of the H-1B visa, which is initially granted for three years and may be renewed for a further three. It may also open the door to permanent residence.

Canadian immigration policy and Mexican migration

Canada's immigration policy comes down firmly on the side of skilled immigrants. The system puts immigrants into five categories: skilled workers (also called 'economic immigrants'); spouses and dependents of skilled workers; entrepreneurs, investors and the self-employed admitted under what is known as the 'business class'; those admitted for family reunification purposes; and refugees. Since 1995, the categories of skilled workers and their spouses and dependents have become the most numerous. This process has been accompanied by a marked reduction in the family reunification category, which includes distant family members who are sponsored by residents of Canada (Minister of Public Works and Government Services, 2003a).

Up to the 1960s, the bulk of immigration to Canada was of people with practically no formal education. In 1967, however, a points system was introduced for the selection of skilled immigrants (Reitz, 2004, pp. 100–6). Under the 2002 Immigration and Refugee Protection Act, the selection criteria for skilled workers emphasize human capital qualities and flexible skills more than the specific occupations laid claim to by the immigrants, as in the past. This new points system highlights education, language ability, work experience, age, the employment offered and adaptability (Tolley, 2003). The Department of Citizenship and Immigration Canada has a website (http://www.cic.gc.ca/english/skilled/qual-5.html) detailing this points system that would-be immigrants to Canada can use to assess their potential in accordance with the human capital and flexible skills they possess. Table 12.4

Table 12.4: Distribution of skilled immigrant workers admitted to Canada by top ten countries of last permanent residence, 1996–2000

Country	Number	Percentage
China	38,486	17.8
India	17,448	8.1
Hong Kong	15,301	7.1
Pakistan	13,930	6.4
Taiwan	9,636	4.4
France	9,492	4.4
Philippines	7,887	3.6
Iran (Islamic Republic of)	6,518	3.0
United Kingdom and Colonies	6,330	2.9
Romania	5,984	2.8
Top ten countries	131,012	60.5
Other countries	85,696	39.5
Total	216,708	100.0

Source: Citizenship and Immigration Canada 2004 (Table 6).

shows the top ten countries of last permanent residence of the skilled immigrants admitted to Canada between 1996 and 2000. China, India, Hong Kong and Pakistan feature prominently. Mexico is not on the list of top 10 countries providing Canada with skilled migrants.

Jeffrey Reitz (2004, p. 101) points out that, during the 1990s, Canada admitted between 200,000 and 250,000 immigrants a year, a per capita immigration rate representing three times that of the United States. Table 12.5 shows that between 1961 and 2000, while immigration from the United Kingdom and the United States decreased markedly, immigration from Asia rose rapidly, particularly that originating in Hong Kong. In this context, immigration from Mexico has been insignificant, not even topping 1 per cent, up from 2,100 persons in the 1960s to 12,700 in the 1990s.[3]

Mexico is very prominent, however, when it comes to providing Canada with temporary workers. In 2002 Canada admitted 87,910 persons on temporary work visas, of which the United States accounted for 20,302 (23 per cent) and Mexico 11,393 (13 per cent). Of the remaining countries, the United Kingdom, Australia, Jamaica and Japan supplied at least 5,000 workers (Minister of Public Works and Government Services, Canada, 2003b).

A fundamental component of the Mexican temporary migrants going to work in Canada is made up of those doing so under the Mexican Seasonal Agricultural Workers Programme, an agreement signed by the governments of

Table 12.5: Distribution of immigrants to Canada by country of origin, 1961–2000: selected countries

Country of Origin	1961–1970		1971–1980		1981–1990		1991–2000	
	Number	%	Number	%	Number	%	Number	%
Hong Kong	36,500	2.6	83,900	5.8	129,300	9.7	240,500	10.9
China	1,400	0.1	600	0.7	36,200	2.7	181,200	8.2
Philippines	–	–	54,100	3.8	65,400	4.9	131,100	5.9
Taiwan	–	–	9,000	0.6	14,300	1.1	79,600	3.6
United States	161,600	11.4	178,600	12.4	75,700	5.7	60,600	2.7
United Kingdom	341,900	24.2	216,500	15.0	92,300	6.9	57,200	2.6
South Korea	–	–	16,000	1.1	16,500	1.2	43,200	2.0
Mexico	2,100	0.1	6,100	0.4	6,900	0.5	12,700	0.6
Australia	26,400	1.9	14,700	1.0	5,100	0.4	8,600	0.4

Source: Reitz, 2004, p. 104, Table 3.1

both countries in 1974. According to Gustavo Verduzco (1999, p. 177–78), the Canadian government originally designed the programme as a means of assisting the least developed countries, starting in 1966 with Jamaica and a year later with Trinidad and Tobago and with Barbados. In 1974, 203 Mexican workers began to seek work in Canada, and in 1996 the figure reached 5,211. Verduzco considers the programme to have been a success both for Canada and for Mexico since, although it has been operating for many years, it has not produced a migratory flow of Mexicans to Canada. Furthermore, there have been few cases of desertion by workers.

Trade NAFTA (TN) visas and Mexican professionals

NAFTA visas were an outcome of the North American Free Trade Agreement and of the special trading relationship that has existed since 1994 between Canada, the United States and Mexico. Granted by all three countries, they are intended to enable professionals from any one of these countries to work temporarily in either of the other two for the sake of effective trading relations. From the point of view of the United States, a 'trade NAFTA' non-immigrant alien is a citizen of Canada or Mexico who is admitted to the United States to engage in business activities at a professional level as agreed to under NAFTA (Office of the Federal Register, 2004). Article 1601 of NAFTA addresses the need to facilitate the temporary migration of these workers in keeping with the principle of reciprocity, and the importance of establishing transparent criteria and procedures for this purpose.[4]

There are four categories of NAFTA visas: business visitors, merchants and investors, intra-company transferees and professionals. The requirements for obtaining the NAFTA visa to work in the United States differ for Canadians and Mexicans. The requirements for Mexican citizens are the following. The employer has to present a letter of employment stating that the position in question requires the professional capacities stipulated in Chapter 16, Annex 1603, Appendix 1603 of NAFTA. The applicant for his or her part must submit to the United States Consul a letter of offer of professional employment describing the activity to be performed, the purpose of entry and the duration of the stay, together with evidence of the worker's professional status.[5]

In contrast to the Mexicans, Canadian citizens do not need a visa to enter the United States but they can obtain this status from the Citizenship and Immigration Services (CIS) at the port of entry. The NAFTA visa is valid for one year, which may be extended indefinitely if the employer so requests. However, unlike the H-1B visa, the NAFTA visa does not pave the way to permanent resident status in the United States. Table 12.6 shows the number of NAFTA visas granted by the three North American governments in 2003.

What comes as a surprise in the first place is that, while Mexico receives the largest number of NAFTA workers of the three North American countries, it sends the lowest number of them. Part of the explanation for this considerable imbalance is that, to work in the United States or Canada, one needs to speak English or French. In addition, we can take it that there are more professionally qualified persons in Canada and the United States than in Mexico. There is also more Canadian and U.S. investment in Mexico than Mexican investment in

Table 12.6: Number of TN Trade NAFTA visa holders admitted to Canada, Mexico and the United States by country of citizenship, 2003

Country of citizenship	Country of destination		
	Canada	Mexico	U.S.
Canada	–	21,676	58,177
Mexico	110	–	1,269
United States	5,657	282,533	–
Total	5,767	304,209	59,446

Source: Citizenship and Immigration Canada (2005), Instituto Nacional de Migración de Mexico (2004, FMTV table) and the U.S. Department of Homeland Security (2004, Table 25).

Canada and the United States, so that what the number of workers with NAFTA visas reflects is rather that the economies of Canada and the United States are stronger than the Mexican economy.

The latter assumption seems to be borne out by the data provided by Mexico's National Institute of Migration back in 2003, when business visitors accounted for the bulk of those using the NAFTA visa. The Institute found that in 2003 a total of 304,209 Canadian and U.S. citizens travelled to Mexico on NAFTA visas, 75 per cent of whom were business visitors, 20 per cent professionals, 3.5 per cent investors and merchants, and only 1.5 per cent intra-company transferees.[6] This suggests that skilled workers travel in North America more as part of corporate strategies than by their own decision.

Conclusions

One of the first conclusions of this paper is that 'migration without borders' is still a complicated process for Mexican skilled migrants. Although the immigration policies of the United States and Canada explicitly encourage their migration, very few of them manage to avail themselves of the opportunity. This suggests that it is not enough to 'open borders'; what is needed is information, access to social networks and language skills, among other things.

Given that in 2000 there were some 4 million Mexicans with at least 4 years of study at university level or with a master's degree or a doctorate, the number of those admitted to the United States in 2003 as permanent residents under the employment-based preferences system seems very low (3,261). This number dwindles further when one considers that it includes both the principal immigrants and their families. By comparison, in the same year 112,603 people were admitted because they were close relatives of United States citizens or entered under the family reunification preference quotas. In Canada, the permanent migration of skilled Mexicans remains very low.

The temporary migration of skilled Mexican migrants prompts different reflections. In the first place, the figure of 16,290 Mexicans obtaining H-1B visas to work in the United States is relatively high. On the other hand, the number of Mexicans receiving a NAFTA visa in 2003 was very low, at a mere 110 to enter Canada and 1,269 to enter the United States, respectively. The H-1B visa's ability to lead to permanent residence in the United States is most probably one of the factors explaining this difference, since the NAFTA visa lacks this feature.

This points to the social and cultural mechanisms behind the relative reluctance of Mexican professionals to migrate temporarily or permanently to countries like Canada and the United States. One central aspect may be the lack of information, particularly regarding the NAFTA visas. There are, nevertheless, other obstacles such as a required language proficiency. It is also probable that Mexican professionals perceive their socioeconomic status as acceptable in the context of a country where a very high proportion of the population is officially categorized as poor. Mexico's urban middle classes might see international migration as a sign of failure, and Mexican professionals may have no wish to be identified with their less-educated compatriots who swell the ranks of those migrating to the United States.

It is paradoxical that, unlike professionals, unskilled Mexican migrants encounter severe restrictions on their international mobility. There are only a few limited temporary work programmes, such as Canada's scheme for agricultural workers and the H-2A programme for agricultural workers in the United States. Unskilled workers would like to migrate 'without borders' to the United States, but their employers, despite depending on them, do not step in to encourage their government to promote their decent and secure migration, as do the employers of skilled migrants in the United States. As long as immigration policies are made more restrictive, the only course open to these workers is access to their social networks, which, for all the obstacles, including the risk of death, enable them to cross international borders.

Notes

1. I am grateful for the comments and suggestions of Antoine Pécoud and María Eugenia Anguiano, and for the valuable technical assistance of Maricarmen Ochoa, Télesforo Ramírez and Manuel Tapia.
2. I follow the definition of 'professionals' used by the Instituto Nacional de Estadística, Geografía e Informática of Mexico (INEGI) 1995.
3. According to Mueller (2005), a possible explanation for the recent increase of the Mexican-born population in Canada is the return of Mennonites who emigrated to Mexico in the 1920s.
4. North American Free Trade Agreement, between Canada, the United States and Mexico. http://tratados.sre.gob.mx/tratados/MEX-AMERICAN.PDF
5. See U.S Department of State website: http://travel.state.gov/visa/tempvisitors_types_temp_nafta.html
6. See Instituto Nacional de Migración website: www.inami.gob.mx/paginas/estadisticas/ene04/registro.mht

Bibliography

Alarcón R. 2000. Skilled immigrants and Cerebreros: foreign-born engineers and scientists in the high-technology industry of Silicon Valley. N. Foner, R. Rumbaut and S. Gold (eds). *Immigration and Immigration Research for a New Century*. New York, Russell Sage Foundation, pp. 301–21.

————. 2001. Immigrant niches in the U.S. high-technology industry. W. A. Cornelius, T. J. Espenshade and I. Salehyan (eds), *The International Migration of the Highly Skilled: Demand, Supply, and Development Consequences in Sending and Receiving Countries*. La Jolla, Calif., University of California, San Diego, Center for Comparative Immigration Studies.

Alonso Meneses, G. 2003. Human rights and undocumented migration along the Mexican-U.S. border. *UCLA Law Review*, Vol. 51, pp. 267–81.

Calavita, K. 1994. U.S. immigration and policy responses: the limits of legislation. W. A. Cornelius, P. L. Martin and J. F. Hollifield (eds). *Controlling Immigration: A Global Perspective*. Palo Alto, Calif., Stanford University Press, pp. 52–82.

Castañeda J. G. and Alarcón, R. 1991. Workers are a commodity, too. *Los Angeles Times*. 22 April 1991.

Castaños-Lomnitz, H., Rodríguez-Sala, M. L. and Herrera Márquez, A. 2004. Fuga de talentos en México: 1970–1990, un estudio de caso. H. Castaños-Lomnitz (ed.), *La migración de talentos en México*. Porrúa, Mexico City, IIEC-UNAM.

Castells, M. 1996. *The Rise of the Network Society*. Vol. 1 of *The Information Age: Economy, Society and Culture*. Malden, Mass., Blackwell.

Citizenship and Immigration Canada. 2005. *Facts and Figures 2005*. www.cic.gc.ca/english/pub/index-2.html (Accessed 20 December 2006).

————. 2004. *Immigrant Occupations: Recent Trends and Issues*. www.cic.gc.ca/english/research/papers/occupations/occupations-c.html (Accessed 20 December 2006).

Cornelius, W. 2001. Death at the border: efficacy and unintended consequences of U.S. immigration control policy. *Population and Development Review*, Vol. 27, No. 4, pp. 661–85.

Instituto Nacional de Estadística, Geografía e Informática de Mexico (INEGI). 1995. *Atlas de los Profesionistas en Mexico*. Mexico, Instituto Nacional de Estadística, Geografía e Informática de Mexico.

Iredale, R. 2000. Migration policies for the highly skilled in the Asia-Pacific region. *International Migration Review*, Vol. 34, No. 3, pp. 882–906.

Lakha, S. 1992. The internationalization of Indian computer professionals. *South Asia*, Vol. 15, No. 2, pp. 93–113.

Malone, N., Baluja, K., Constanzo, J. N. and Davis, C. J. 2003. *The Foreign-Born Population, 2000*. Census 2000 Brief. Washington DC, U.S. Census Bureau.

Meyers, D. and Yau, J. 2004. *U.S. Immigration Statistics in 2003*. Migration Policy Institute, November. www.migrationinformation.org/Feature/print.cfm?ID=263 (Accessed 21 December 2006.)

Minister of Public Works and Government Services, Canada. 2003*a*. Immigrant occupations: recent trends and issues. www.cic.gc.ca/english/research/papers/occupations/occupations-toc.html (Accessed 21 December 2006.)

————. 2003*b*. Facts and figures 2002: statistical overview of the temporary resident and refugee claimant population. www.cic.gc.ca/english/pdf/pub/facts-temp2002.pdf (Accessed 21 December 2006.)

Mueller, R. E. 2005. The rise of Mexican immigrants and temporary residents in Canada: current knowledge and future research. *Migraciones Internacionales 8*, Vol. 3, No. 1, pp. 32–56.

Office of the Federal Register, National Archives and Records Administration (NARA). 2004. *Federal Register*. Vol. 69, No. 140. July 22.

Papademetriou, D. 1996. U.S. immigration policy after the Cold War. Pittsburgh, Penn., University of Pittsburgh Press.

Passel, J. S. 2004. Mexican immigration to the U.S.: the latest estimates. Migration Policy Institute, *Migration Information Source*, November, www.migrationinformation.org/Feature/display.cfm?ID=208 (Accessed 21 December 2006.)

Puig Escudero, A. 2000. *La población en el año 2000*. DEMOS 13. Mexico City, IIS and the Universidad Nacional Autónoma de México.

Reich, R. 1992. *The Work of Nations: Preparing Ourselves for 21st-Century Capitalism*. New York, Vintage Books.

Reitz, J. G. 2004. Canada: immigration and nation-building in the transition to a knowledge economy. W. Cornelius, T. Tsuda, P. L. Martin and J. F. Hollifield (eds), *Controlling Immigration: A Global Perspective*. 2nd edition. Palo Alto, Calif., Stanford University Press, pp. 79–113.

Reyes, B., Johnson, H. and Van Swearingen, R. 2002. *Holding the Line? The Effect of Recent Border Build-Up on Unauthorized Immigration*. Public Policy Institute of California.

Schmidley, D. 2001. *Current Population Reports, Series P23–206: Profile of the Foreign-Born Population in the United States: 2000*. Washington DC, U.S. Census Bureau, Government Printing Office.

Tolley, E. 2003. The skilled worker class: selection criteria in the Immigration and Refugee Protection Act. *Metropolis Policy Brief*, No. 1, January.

U.S. Department of Homeland Security. 2004. *Yearbook of Immigration Statistics 2003*. Washington DC, Government Printing Office.

Verduzco Igartúa, G. 1999. El programa de trabajadores agrícolas mexicanos con Canadá: Un contraste frente a la experiencia con Estados Unidos. *Estudios Demograficos y Urbanos 40*, Vol. 14, No. 1, pp. 165–91.

Wasem, R. E. 2004. U.S. immigration policy on permanent admissions. CRS Report for Congress, Congressional Research Services. Washington DC, the Library of Congress, February.

Yale-Loehr, S. 1991. *Understanding the Immigration Act of 1990*. Washington DC, Federal Publications.

Internet sources consulted

Citizenship and Immigration Canada:
http://www.cic.gc.ca/english/

Instituto Nacional de Migración de México:
http://www.inami.gob.mx/paginas/estadisticas/ene04/registro.mht

Secretaría de Relaciones Exteriores de Mexico:
http://tratados.sre.gob.mx/tratados/MEX-AMERICAN.PDF

United States Department of State:
http://travel.state.gov/visa/tempvisitors_types_temp_nafta.html

Chapter 13

Migration policies and socioeconomic boundaries in the South American Cone

Alicia Maguid

Introduction

Migration to, from and within the Southern Cone of Latin America is taking place in an international setting marked by economic, political and social change. The universalization of market economics and the ever-increasing interdependence of the world economy are leading to the globalization of socioeconomic activities at the international level and in Latin America, encompassing not only the exchange of goods, technology and services, but also the movement of people. Alongside this is a process of regional economic integration: in Latin America, three subregions have emerged (the Andean, Central American and Southern Cone subregions), among which the last one – the MERCOSUR – shows a high dynamics with the recent incorporation of several countries.[1]

Human mobility is an integral part of this regional integration and has intensified in recent decades. As in other parts of the world, states have reacted through largely restrictive and national migration policies, and discussions of migration issues within MERCOSUR have long been limited to border control issues. However, in the early years of this century there has been a qualitative change in terms of how migration is perceived politically in the region, which has inspired the establishment of an agreement meant to facilitate the movement and residence of nationals of MERCOSUR states parties.

This new regional context therefore provides a paradigmatic example that sheds light on the possible impact of the migration without borders (MWB) scenario on the countries involved, especially as these are characterized by marked differences in their levels of development, in the dynamics and structure of their labour markets, and in the living conditions of their inhabitants generally. The MERCOSUR example may also illustrate the consequences of the MWB scenario for the size of migratory flows, as well as for migrants' human rights and conditions of entry into labour markets.

This chapter analyses the changes that have occurred in recent migratory trends and identifies their determinants by exploring the role played by socioeconomic factors and migration policies. It shows that, in addition to territorial boundaries, there are socioeconomic boundaries in receiving societies that force immigrants to accept precarious employment, low wages and long working hours in occupations within increasingly narrow segments of the labour market. Overcoming such employment discrimination is difficult to envisage against a general background of deteriorating working and living conditions for both migrants and the population as a whole. In this respect, the chapter emphasizes the internal boundaries that, as much as state borders, have a very strong impact on the situation of migrants in destination states.

Migratory patterns in the Southern Cone[2]

International migration is a complex social process that is historically linked to the development of the Latin American countries, and to those of the Southern Cone in particular, and which has reflected and continues to reflect the economic, social and political imbalances between countries and regions. It is useful to identify three migration stages connected with different phases in the region's development.

Between 1870 and 1929, this region saw large-scale immigration from overseas, predominantly from Europe, fostered by policies clearly formulated to attract immigrants in response to a perceived need to populate these vast territories and consolidate the new national states. In this period, immigration played a major role in the development of the receiving societies. (There was subsequently a second and final wave during the post-Second World War era, albeit smaller than the previous one.) It is possible to distinguish a second stage of migration between 1930 and 1960, which, unlike the earlier agro-export model, adopted a development strategy based on import substitution, promoting the development of national industries. Along with these changes, there was rapid urbanization in a context marked by internal migration to the large cities accompanied by intra-regional movements, which took place essentially between border areas.

Lattes and Recchini de Lattes (1992) estimate that around 10.9 million people arrived in the Southern Cone between the late nineteenth century and

1970. Three-quarters of these people are concentrated in Argentina and Brazil, with 38 per cent and 35 per cent respectively.

The third stage began in the late 1960s, with the emergence of two major migration patterns that have become more intense in recent decades, one involving interchanges within the Southern Cone region and the other extra-regional – for the most part to the United States of America, and subsequently to other destinations including Canada, European countries and Japan.[3] Although movements between the region's countries date back a long way, in this stage they became more pronounced and assumed increased visibility as a result of the disappearance of migratory flows from overseas. This third migration stage took place in a setting marked by the economic crisis that began in the late 1970s and intensified in the 'lost decade' of the 1980s, with a sustained fall in these nations' gross domestic product (GDP). The profound changes in the economic model of the 1990s resulted in increased economic growth in the first half of the decade, but did not bring about real improvements for the people: by the end of the decade, poverty and inequality in income distribution had increased, while conditions in national labour markets had worsened. Economic vulnerability in the face of crises in other regions – Mexico in 1994 and Asia in 1997 – and the region's high dependence on external financing also became apparent.[4]

International migration in the Southern Cone: recent trends[5]

The population of the Southern Cone region reached 244 million in 2000, which represents 48 per cent of the total population of Latin America. This figure is more than three times greater than that for 1950: the most significant increases occurred up to 1970, with high growth rates of around 3 per cent on average per annum for the region as a whole. The six countries making up the Southern Cone began their demographic transition at different times and vary considerably with regard both to the size and rate of growth and the factors involved in their population dynamics (ECLAC/CELADE, 2004b).

From 2000 to 2005, Brazil, with almost 175 million inhabitants, accounted for 72 per cent of the region's population, followed a long way behind by Argentina, with a population one-fifth its size. At the other extreme, Uruguay, with only 3.3 million, suffered most from the impact of emigration, which, in conjunction with its low birth rate, means it saw very limited population growth. Argentina, Chile and Uruguay began to experience a fall in fertility rates and mortality rates very early; Brazil did so later, but reached similar levels by around 1990. By contrast, Bolivia and Paraguay were, at the start of the twenty-first century, still maintaining high birth rates, with close to four children born per woman, and consequently had higher growth potential. They also had the highest mortality levels: the life expectancy of Bolivians and

Paraguayans is fourteen and seven years less, respectively, than that of Chileans (who have the greatest life expectancy in the region).

Projections by ECLAC/CELADE (2004b) predict a low net migration rate in the near future, which does not mean that migratory movements will disappear. The limited impact of the migratory balance is the result of a combination of several factors. First, the decline and non-renewal of migration from overseas and the gradual reduction in the numbers of immigrants through mortality are contributing to a reduction in the total numbers of persons born abroad. The decline in total immigrants to the region is thus partly due to the reduction in those 'born in the rest of the world' – survivors of migration from overseas. This figure fell to one-half in Argentina and Brazil, the main recipients of these migrants, and also declined markedly in Uruguay. In addition, increasing emigration serves to partly offset the entry of new and predominantly intra-regional flows (Table 13.1 shows the number of international immigrants recorded in the 1980, 1990 and 2000 census rounds).

Within the context of Latin America, the Southern Cone remains a region with high migration dynamism. In the early 1990s, it accounted for 52 per cent of all international migrants who changed their country of residence in Latin America.

The number of intra-regional immigrants increased between 1980 and 2000 for the region as a whole by 24 per cent, rising from 1 million to close to 1.4 million. The growth during the 1990s, precisely when MERCOSUR was developing, was similar to the growth of the previous decade. Nevertheless, it did not reach the level experienced in the 1970s, when the economic crisis had still not become acute and levels of unemployment in the main receiving country, Argentina, were very low.

Over the last twenty years, the greatest relative increase has occurred in Chile, where the number of migrants born in the region has risen 2.5 times, Bolivia occupying second place with a 1.6 times increase. However, both countries account for only a small percentage – 5 per cent and 4 per cent respectively – of the region's total movements.

Argentina stands out as the largest contributor, accounting for 68 per cent of movements recorded at the start of the present decade. It is historically and currently the main destination of intra-regional migration, forming the core of the small migratory subsystem of the Southern Cone.

While migration has been and still is predominantly intra-regional, the most notable increases have occurred in the number of immigrants from the rest of the American continent, in particular from Peru, although this volume is still insignificant.

At the start of the present decade, this region had 281,000 immigrants who had been born in other countries of the Americas, a figure three times higher than that of the early 1980s. Argentina and Chile account for the largest rise,

Table 13.1: Southern Cone countries: total population and impact of international migration in the 1980, 1990 and 2000 census rounds

Country	Census	Total population	Born abroad		Born in countries of the region		Born in the rest of the Americas[1]		Born in the rest of the world	
			Total	% of population	Total	% of foreign nationals	Total	% of foreign nationals	Total	% of foreign nationals
Region[2]	1980	168,857,592	3,426,365	2.0	1,091,610	31.9	96,968	2.8	2,237,787	65.3
	1990	205,864,159	2,837,407	1.4	1,229,845	43.3	128,018	4.5	1,479,544	52.1
	2000[3]	237,796,903	2,758,372	1.2	1,355,096	49.1	281,226	10.2	1,122,050	40.7
Argentina	1980	27,926,693	1,993,159	6.8	753,428	39.6	29,353	1.5	1,120,378	58.9
	1991	31,953,140	1,615,473	5.1	841,597	52.1	37,960	2.3	735,816	45.5
	2001[3]	36,260,130	1,517,904	4.2	916,264	60.4	115,302	7.6	486,338	32.0
Bolivia	1976	4,613,486	58,070	1.3	31,834	54.8	15,963	27.5	10,273	17.7
	1992	6,420,792	59,807	0.9	31,606	52.8	18,932	31.7	9,269	15.5
	2001	8,274,325	95,764	1.2	51,917	54.2	29,890	31.2	13,957	14.6
Brazil	1980	119,002,606	1,110,910	0.9	96,241	8.7	29,240	2.6	985,429	88.7
	1991	146,825,475	767,780	0.5	102,758	13.4	27,261	3.6	637,761	83.1
	2000	169,799,170	683,830	0.4	118,512	17.3	41,120	6.0	524,098	76.6
Chile	1982	11,329,736	84,345	0.7	29,380	34.8	14,378	17.0	40,587	48.1
	1992	13,348,401	114,597	0.9	49,036	42.8	24,769	21.6	40,792	35.6
	2002	15,116,435	195,320	1.3	73,474	37.6	76,292	39.1	45,554	23.3

Table 13.1: *continued*

Country	Census	Total population	Born abroad		Born in countries of the region		Born in the rest of the Americas[1]		Born in the rest of the world	
			Total	% of population	Total	% of foreign nationals	Total	% of foreign nationals	Total	% of foreign nationals
Paraguay	1982	3,029,830	166,879	5.5	145,653	87.3	5,482	3.3	15,744	9.4
	1992	4,152,588	187,372	4.5	161,357	86.1	7,781	4.2	18,234	9.7
	2002	5,183,080	173,176	3.3	151,438	87.4	7,307	2.0	14,431	8.3
Uruguay	1985	2,955,241	103,002	3.5	35,074	34.1	2,552	2.5	65,376	63.5
	1995[4]	3,163,763	92,378	2.9	43,391	47.0	11,315	12.2	37,672	40.8

Source: ECLAC/CELADE, 2004a; INDEC, 2001; DGEEC, 2002.

Notes:

1 Includes persons born in other countries of Latin America and the Caribbean and persons born in the United States and Canada.

2 For the whole region, the 1976 figure for Bolivia was included in 1980 and the 1995 census figure for Uruguay was replicated in 2000.

3 The foreign nationals total includes persons born abroad in cases where the country of birth is unknown.

4 This is the latest census.

which occurred during the last decade. These changes are reflected in migrant composition. Because of the decline in European migration, there was an increase in the share of intra-regional migrants among foreign nationals, who make up almost one-half of the regional total, and that of people from other Latin American countries, who represent 10 per cent.

With the exception of Chile, which has similar proportions of intra-regional migrants and migrants from the rest of the Americas, the predominance of movements between countries of the region is clearly visible. The range of variation is wide: from 87 per cent in Paraguay – which receives migrants almost exclusively from neighbouring countries – to just 17 per cent in Brazil. The percentage of such migrants in the receiving population is highest in Argentina and Paraguay, where they constitute over 2.5 per cent of the population.

Intra-regional migration: significant changes of the 1990s

During the 1990s, the increase in migrants moving within the Southern Cone brought about changes in the size of migratory flows from several countries, but did not alter migratory patterns. Table 13.2 shows migration between these countries in around 1990 and 2000.

Argentina was still the main recipient. In this period, for all countries other than Brazil, Argentina remained the destination of around 90 per cent of intra-regional migrants. Other countries that also continued to be recipients, albeit receiving a much small number of immigrants, were Paraguay (with people arriving mainly from Brazil and Argentina) and, in third place, Brazil (where the majority came from Paraguay, Argentina and Uruguay). A further common feature that was maintained was that all nationalities of the region were represented in Argentina and Brazil, while Argentineans predominated in the other countries.

In Argentina, the number of Chilean and Uruguayan immigrants decreased, a fact that marks a break in the historical trend in evidence since the middle of the twentieth century. This suggests either that there has been no renewal of those flows, or that the few people who have arrived have not made up for those who returned to their countries of origin. Conversely, Bolivian immigrants virtually doubled and Paraguayan immigrants also increased in number, while the number of immigrants born in Brazil remained constant. As a result, the relative proportion of immigrants changed. In 2001, Paraguayans still predominated (35 per cent), but second place was occupied by Bolivians (25 per cent), followed by Chileans (23 per cent); the percentage of Uruguayans fell (13 per cent) and the very small share represented by Brazilians was maintained (4 per cent).

Specific mention should be made of the case of Chile, in view of the significant changes that occurred there. The country experienced a considerable

Table 13.2: Southern Cone countries: intra-regional immigrants by country of birth: 1990 and 2000 census rounds

Country of residence	Intra-regional immigrants	Country of birth					
		Argentina	Bolivia	Brazil	Chile	Paraguay	Uruguay
Total 1990	1,229,845	151,814	168,134	167,645	272,746	272,618	160,549
Argentina	841,697	–	143,659	33,476	244,410	250,450	133,453
Bolivia	31,606	17,829	–	8,586	3,909	955	327
Brazil	102,758	25,468	15,694	–	20,437	19,018	22,141
Chile	49,036	34,415	7,729	4,610	–	683	1,599
Paraguay	161,357	47,846	766	107,452	2,264	–	3,029
Uruguay	43,391	26,256	376	13,521	1,726	1,512	–
Total 2000[1]	1,355,096	196,003	265,320	151,525	236,755	357,914	147,579
Argentina	916,264	–	231,789	33,748	211,093	322,962	116,672
Bolivia	51,917	28,615	–	15,075	4,469	3,297	461
Brazil	118,612	27,531	20,388	–	17,131	28,822	24,740
Chile	73,474	50,448	11,649	7,589	–	1,321	2,467
Paraguay	151,438	63,153	1,118	81,592	2,336	–	3,239

Source: ECLAC/CELADE, 2004a. INDEC, 2001. DGEEC, 2002.

1 The regional total was calculated with the inclusion of the data from the 1995 census of Uruguay.

increase in the number of immigrants, which, while still less than the total of Chilean emigrants, reflects the improvement in its economic situation.

A final important aspect is the gradual feminization of migratory flows: most intra-regional migrants at both dates were women, and the trend shows that this trait has been intensifying. Between 1990 and 2000, the index fell from ninety-two to eighty-four males for every hundred females.

The new subregional integration setting: migration policies and socioeconomic asymmetries

During the 1990s, throughout the course of the regional integration process, migratory movements took place against a changing socioeconomic background, with advances, standstills and setbacks, which failed to overcome the disparity between countries and widened the social gaps within them.

This brought about a migration 'governability crisis', which highlighted the ineffectiveness of the earlier unilateral policies of states (Mármora, 2003). In response, new joint areas emerged for the multilateral treatment of international migration, i.e., apart from MERCOSUR itself, bilateral and multilateral agreements between countries (which preceded and continued to exist alongside the Treaty of Asunción) and the establishment of regional consultative bodies such as the South American Forum on International Migration.[6] What is novel about this strategy is that the countries of origin and destination enter into agreements together.

While highly positive, this shift towards alternative strategies did not initially alter the predominance of restrictive approaches aiming to limit immigrants' entry and lawful stay in the countries of destination. Only in late 2002 was the region's integration process tackled from a different perspective, with the creation of MERCOSUR citizen status as a guarantee of legal residence in any of the member countries. This new political commitment is aimed at increasing the transparency of the migration situation and preventing illegality and discrimination with regard to immigrants, but does not go so far as to entail establishing a genuine MWB scenario, even if the persistence of migratory movements appears to be linked to socioeconomic factors (such as relative differences between labour markets, wages and the exchange value of national currencies) rather than to the effect of migration policies and agreements, which until the early part of the twenty-first century pursued a restrictive approach.

With regard to extra-regional emigrants, some policies have been strengthened to protect their integration abroad, to respect their human rights and the maintenance of links with their countries of origin by facilitating the transfer of remittances; to improve their political participation in national elections; and to augment the exchange of knowledge in scientific and technological fields.

Examination of migration within MERCOSUR

From the outset, the objectives of the Treaty of Asunción and the mechanisms to achieve them have been essentially economic, commercial and customs-related – being directed at bringing about a process of integration that would in the future lead to the construction of a common market. As set out in Chapter 1 of the treaty, entitled 'Purposes, principles and instruments', the intention is to build a broad market based on 'free movement of goods, services and factors of production between countries'. This statement could be assumed to include free movement of labour as one of the factors of production.

By contrast, the very way in which the Common Market Group (GMC) – the executive body of MERCOSUR – is organized shows the lack of importance attached to the migration variable: of the ten working subgroups which it originally comprised, and of the fourteen currently in existence, not one deals specifically with the issue of migration and its many linkages with the integration process.

Migration was, however, addressed throughout the decade in certain subgroups – particularly with regard to border controls – and also tangentially, given its links with labour and social security issues.

Three stages in the treatment of the migration variable since the establishment of MERCOSUR can be identified.

First stage

This stage, regarded as a transition phase in the formation of the common market, came to an end in late 1994. The issue of migration was dealt with in two working subgroups, which approached it from different angles. In the Subgroup on Customs Issues (No. 2), comprising migration management specialists, steps were taken to implement mechanisms to regulate and expedite controls at frontier crossings, such as the gradual establishment of unified border crossing points and the use of a common registration form for entries and departures. Also, cross-border movement of people who live in frontier areas was facilitated. In the Subgroup on Labour Relations, Employment and Social Security (No. 11), comprising labour ministers and representatives of the business sector and trade unions, migration was dealt with as a social process extending beyond mere border controls.

The idea of the future establishment of free movement of persons formed part of Subgroup No. 11's working guidelines. Mármora and Cassarino (1999) explain this approach by pointing out that it was assumed that the common market would be established by 1 January 1995, meaning free movement of factors of production. They also refer to the difficulties and disputes that arose from the discussion of this topic. As a result, a proposal was formulated for the gradual implementation of free movement, but it was not followed up owing to the subsequent redefinition of MERCOSUR.

Second stage

The initial transition phase was continued – not, as originally planned, with the formation of a common market, but under the terms of its redefinition as an 'imperfect customs union', established under the Ouro Preto Protocol in December 1994. With this decision, the free movement of goods and capital became MERCOSUR's exclusive focus. Mobility was viewed solely in terms of labour migration, which was examined in various areas of the new organizational structure. There were limited achievements, most notably the signing of the Multilateral Agreement on Social Security and the MERCOSUR Socio-Labour Declaration – which recognizes the same rights and obligations for migrant workers as for nationals – and facilitation of mobility and employment of highly skilled personnel in the service sector (promoting the so-called third freedom) and of professionals in other selected categories. At the same time, the issues of border controls and integration continued to be discussed (Perez Vichich, 2003).

Third stage

The first years of the present century have seen several important events, reflecting a change in the political approach to the treatment of the issue of migration. First, progress has been made in the conclusion of agreements guaranteeing freedom of residence for citizens of states parties, which indirectly puts the debate concerning free movement of persons back on the MERCOSUR agenda. Secondly, border controls have been improved and steps towards their computerization are continuing. These two seemingly contradictory developments suggest that there is still no intention to open up the borders, but there is a more realistic recognition of the ineffectiveness of restrictive policies in curbing migratory movements. Given that such movements continue to occur despite the measures adopted to prevent them and that greater restriction causes increased irregularity, attempts are being made to facilitate the regularization of immigrants and thus overcome the negative consequences of this situation.

The initiative to establish a right of residence arose at the meeting of interior ministers with the adoption of the Agreement on Residence for Nationals of States Parties of MERCOSUR. This agreement and a similar one that includes Bolivia and Chile were signed by the presidents of the expanded MERCOSUR on 6 December 2002. The agreement applies both to those wishing to enter and those already residing in one of the states parties, irrespective of the migratory status under which they entered. With the sole criterion of nationality, and subject to presentation of identity documents from their country of origin, immigrants qualify for temporary residence for two years, which can subsequently become permanent. The agreement establishes their right to move freely within the receiving country and their right to equal civil, social, cultural and economic rights in relation to nationals; it also provides for equality of treatment under labour legislation, especially in connection with wages, conditions of employment, and social security. Right of residence is extended to members of immigrants' families irrespective of their original nationality. The agreement also establishes the right to transfer remittances to countries of origin, and the right of immigrants' children to their own identity and their right of access to education, even in cases where their parents are in an irregular situation. It defines measures for preventing undeclared employment, including penalties imposed on employers, rather than on immigrants, and on persons or organizations profiting from trafficking in migrants or from employment in abusive conditions. The agreement has been ratified by all countries with the exception of Paraguay. However, not all have advanced at the same pace, because of the political and bureaucratic difficulties in amending or adapting their migration legislation. Given its multilateral nature, the agreement will not enter into force until it is ratified by all countries; which is why Argentina has signed bilateral agreements with Brazil, Bolivia, Chile, Uruguay and Peru while Paraguay's ratifying of the agreement is currently being negotiated.

Another noteworthy development in this new stage was the inclusion in 2003 and 2004 of Peru, Colombia, Ecuador and Venezuela in MERCOSUR as associate states, which poses new challenges for the integration process and extends the mobility facilities and rights of their citizens.

National migration policies

While regional negotiations were going on, restrictive approaches still prevailed at the national level, at least until the late twentieth century, in the Southern Cone countries and in most countries of the American continent. That approach can be traced back to the 1930s, when the felt need was to protect labour markets in crisis, although the arguments in support of it naturally varied over time.

According to Mármora (1995, 2003), there is a clear connection between the arguments adopted in each period and the changing political and economic circumstances in the region's countries. For example, during the 1970s and early 1980s, when military dictatorships predominated in the Southern Cone countries, the national security approach was the framework for strict migration control policies. In the 'lost decade' of the 1980s, when democratic regimes were restored in several countries, the focus was again placed on protecting the native labour force. During the 1990s, foreigners were increasingly perceived as a threat, not only as regards the displacement of labour and greater levels of poverty, unemployment and crime but also in relation to the use of education and health services – even though several studies carried out in Argentina showed that immigrants had no effect on the worsening of those problems (Maguid, 1995; Mármora and Gorini, 1995). The issue of security, which is linked to the rise in drug trafficking and terrorism, became closely associated with international migration following the attacks of 11 September 2001 in the United States.

It is striking to see that, even though most countries are mostly on the sending side of the migration process, the central features of the region's migration policies remain the negative perception of the consequences of immigration and the persistence of security and control strategies. Bolivia is the only country to have promulgated a decree supporting immigration, in the 1990s, to encourage demographic growth and development while putting forward proposals to prevent emigration of nationals. Both aspects reflect the requirements of a country of emigration attempting to retain and increase its population.

The case of Argentina warrants special treatment, as it is the only country that recently made substantial amendments to its migration legislation, taking steps towards implementing the MERCOSUR Agreement on Residence. Historically, policies of promotion and tolerance with regard to European immigration have been accompanied by other highly selective policies for bordering countries. However, the build-up of undocumented migrants, in particular during the military dictatorships, gave rise to various amnesties aimed at alleviating the situation of irregularity, the majority being implemented under democratic governments in 1958, 1965, 1974, 1984 and 1992.

In 1981, during the last military dictatorship, the General Migration Act was adopted with a political strategy based on a national security doctrine that denied undeclared migrants the right to engage in remunerated occupations and access to healthcare and education, and laid down a series of requirements that hampered their regularization. That law remained in force for more than twenty years, albeit accompanied by bilateral agreements and measures that from time to time lessened its discriminatory aspect. It was not until December 2003 that a new migration act was promulgated. It adopted the same residence criterion based on nationality and is fully consistent with the principles and rights established for migrants in the MERCOSUR Agreement on Residence. Also, the Migration Department is no longer permitted to detain and expel irregular migrants, such action now requiring the intervention of the judiciary.

It is also laid down that the treatment of foreigners is to be governed by the most favourable terms set out in the Act or in specific agreements.

Thus the country experiencing the greatest impact from regional migration is precisely the one that appears to have been promoting changes to facilitate the entry of immigrants and the regularization of those already established. These changes have occurred following the severe economic crisis of 2001, which brought about the end of currency convertibility, and Argentina can therefore be assumed not to expect any rise in immigration as a result of greater liberalization. It is unquestionably seeking to increase the transparency of the situation of those who are already there. In order to implement the new law and the MERCOSUR Residence Agreement, Argentina launched in 2006 a large-scale regularization process: the National Program of Regularization of Migratory Documents 'Patria Grande', aimed at the insertion and integration of the immigrant population coming from Bolivia, Brazil, Chile, Colombia, Ecuador, Paraguay, Peru, Uruguay and Venezuela (which are the Member and Associated States of the subregional integration treaty), thus facilitating their access to residence.

Changes in recent migratory patterns and socioeconomic asymmetries

The limited impact of migration policies in terms of regulating migratory flows confirms that structural factors should be given the greatest importance in explaining the causes and consequences of international migration. In an exhaustive review of theories of international migration, Massey (1993) puts forward the world systems theory, which links peoples' movements to the expansion and globalization of the market economy. Accordingly, in peripheral societies, a population group with a propensity to emigrate is generated and supplies the demand in central societies for unskilled, casual and low-paid jobs. At the same time, material and cultural links are strengthened, which increases transnational communities as well as social and institutional networks – in a process that is further made possible by facilitated means of communication and transport. In the case of the Southern Cone, push factors can thus be found in countries of emigration with surplus labour supply (particularly in Bolivia and Paraguay), while pull factors linked to better employment opportunities and higher wages have historically characterized Argentina (Marshall, 1983).

In addition, the processes of adjustment, deregulation and liberalization of the economy, along with the changes in the role of the state, have brought about transformations that have profoundly altered productive systems and, as a result, the economic dynamics and regulation of labour markets. This is the setting in which recent migratory movements have been occurring, and which shows marked economic and social asymmetries over the last decade, as indicated by the data in Table 13.3. The relative differences favouring

Table 13.3: Southern Cone countries and Peru: economic and social indicators, 1990–2002

Country	Per capita GDP (1995 U.S.$)	Declared unemploy-ment rate[1]	Percentage of population below the poverty line	Infant mortality rate o/oo	Illiteracy rate[2]
Argentina					
1990	5,545	6.3	21.2	24.3	3.7
1999	7,435	13.8	19.7	21.8	3.2
2002	6,055	17.8	41.5		
Bolivia					
1990[3]	804	9.4	53.1	75.1	17.9
1999	941	7.1	48.7	66.7	14.6
2002	938	6.4	52.0		
Brazil					
1990	3,859	4.5	41.2	47.2	15.3
1999	4,217	11.4	32.9	42.2	13.1
2002	4,340	10.7	34.1[4]		
Chile					
1990	3,779	8.7	38.4	14.0	5.1
1999	5,631	10.1	20.7	12.8	4.2
2002	5,952	10.6	20.1[4]		
Paraguay					
1990	1,697	6.3	49.9	43.3	8.1
1999	1,603	10.1	49.0	39.2	6.7
2002	1,477	11.5	50.1[4]	20.1	2.9
Peru					
1990	1,879	–	–	55.5	12.2
1999	2,310	7.3	36.1	42.1	10.1
2002	2,376	7.2	42.0[5]		
Uruguay					
1990	4,707	8.9	17.8	17.5	2.4
1999	5,984	11.2	9.4		
2002	4,946	16.9	15.4		

Notes:

1 In urban areas.

2 Based on the population group aged fifteen years and over for 1990–1995 and 1995–1999.

3 Corresponds to 1989 as regards GDP and poverty.

4 Corresponds to 2001.

5 This figure slightly overestimates poverty owing to methodological changes.

Source: ECLAC, 2004b; INDEC, 2001.

Argentina, Chile and Uruguay were for example significant in the period from 1990 to 1999 with regard both to per capita GDP and to social indicators (infant mortality, illiteracy and poverty levels).

By contrast, unemployment rates did not follow the other indicators. In particular, unemployment rates alone cannot explain Argentina's attractiveness throughout the decade. In that country, the unemployment rate held at low levels – between 4 per cent and 6 per cent – over a long period (1974 to 1993). It then began to rise, reaching a maximum of 17 per cent in 1996, falling to 13.8 per cent in 1999. Despite these fluctuations, unemployment affected natives and migrants in a fairly similar way. Greater flexibility enabled them to survive by accepting poorer employment conditions in marginal occupations, essentially in the informal sector.

In addition to *territorial* boundaries there are *socioeconomic* boundaries, which have traditionally given rise to migrants' marginal integration into labour markets and limited their access to education and health services. In Argentina, a segmented pattern of labour-market participation has persisted, allowing migrants' entry solely into specific sectors such as construction, small-scale industry, and domestic service in the case of women (Marshall, 1983; Maguid, 1995, 1997).

Until the early 1990s, against a background of low unemployment rates, the role of immigrants was supplementary, in that they performed jobs not filled by the native population. Subsequently, with a decline in the labour market, they would appear to have gained a certain competitiveness in those segments and succeeded in displacing internal migrants by accepting more precarious employment conditions, working longer hours and earning lower wages (Cortés and Groisman, 2004). A further attraction factor was added to this situation: currency convertibility, which gave a dollar-equivalent value to currencies and enabled migrants to make up for the precariousness of their employment through the possibility of achieving savings and transferring remittances to their countries of origin.

The economic crisis in 2001 led to a sharp contraction of employment and to an increase in poverty that involved wide population sectors. This unfavourable scenario in terms of boundary migration was reinforced by the end of currency convertibility, which reduced the possibility of migrants sending remittances to their countries of origin. Recent studies reveal that the crisis discouraged new arrivals but did not provoke massive returns. The bordering country migrants remain in the Argentinean labour market at the cost of precarious, unstable and poorly paid jobs (Maguid and Arruñada, 2005).

Uruguay constitutes a special case since, despite similar social conditions and lower poverty levels than Argentina and Chile, it is a country that has had high emigration for thirty years. Pellegrino (1995) attempts to explain this atypical characteristic by pointing out that the personal aspirations of advancement in such a small country, with limited national projects, and other cultural factors created a veritable 'emigration culture', particularly among young people.

In short, socioeconomic factors, strengthened by the persistence of migration networks, have played an important role in defining migratory patterns in the Southern Cone. The indicators relating to 2002 clearly show the consequences of the process of decline at the start of the present century. Chile and Brazil are the exception, as they are achieving slight increases in per-capita GDP and are maintaining unemployment and poverty levels. At the other extreme, as a result of the severe economic and financial crisis that began in late 2001, Argentina is showing marked increases in unemployment, which has reached 18 per cent, and, particularly, in poverty, which affects almost 42 per cent of its population, a percentage that brings it close to the region's more disadvantaged countries. This slump in the main receiving country is a key element in any examination of the potential future impact of a possible MWB scenario.

Some ideas on the impact of migration without borders

Progress towards opening up borders and regularizing the situation of undocumented migrants, as set out in the MERCOSUR Agreement on Residence and in national migration policies (in particular those of Argentina), is taking place against the background of a severe economic crisis that is affecting the employment market's ability to absorb the labour supply in the face of high unemployment rates and a huge growth in poverty. Moreover, the end of convertibility, which meant that its currency's exchange value fell three times in relation to the dollar, is making Argentina a less attractive country for its neighbours in the region. In the meantime, the application of the new migration policies (whose implementation began in Argentina in 2006) and the future ratification of the Agreement on Residence in all countries of the region should enable some progress to be made, provided that countries surmount the traditional bureaucratic and administrative obstacles to successful migration policies.

The situation in the Southern Cone at the beginning of the twenty-first century therefore provides a paradigmatic example for considering the potential impact that free movement of persons would have. The preliminary ideas set out below should be understood as questions aimed at contributing to the debate on the impact of open borders in the future, both on the size of migratory flows and on the prospects for improving the living conditions of migrants.

Migratory flows

With respect to the size of migratory flows, the MWB scenario could be expected to have the following consequences:

1. A rise in alternative, circular forms of mobility between the countries of the region (such as temporary migration or commuting) that do not entail any change of permanent residence.
2. An increase in migration to Chile from both Southern Cone countries and other Latin American countries, in particular from Peru, Ecuador and Colombia, with an intensification of the trends that emerged in the previous decade.
3. In the case of Argentina, the future of migration will be very closely linked to developments in its economy and to its capacity to generate employment, improve income distribution and overcome the social exclusion of broad sectors of the population that have undergone a rapid descent into poverty.

If the situation remains as it is today, an increase in immigration is not to be expected even in the case of open borders (or as a result of the new regional migration policies aimed at facilitating entry and residence) and of the progressive reduction in the unemployment rate, which fell around 10 per cent during 2005 and 2006. The most recent data from the Permanent Household Survey show for example that, between 1998 and 2005 (i.e., following the economic crisis), the number of border migrants hardly varied, suggesting that there was no renewal of migratory flows or that offsetting occurred, albeit of slight significance, between the few people who returned and new immigrants.[7]

Migrants and human rights

With respect to migrants and human rights, the MWB scenario could generate the following consequences:

1. By eliminating situations of irregularity, it would have a positive impact in guaranteeing the social, economic, cultural and political rights of migrants.
2. It would overcome discrimination suffered by immigrants with regard to community participation and access to healthcare, social security, and education for children and young people.
3. It would help to weaken xenophobic arguments that, based on myths that exaggerate the number of undocumented migrants, attribute rising unemployment and declining social services to immigrants.

Xenophobia in Argentina reached a peak when unemployment began to rise, but it diminished with the crisis of 2001, which reduced the living and working standards of migrants along with that of the working and middle classes.

With regard to Chile, Martinez Pizarro (2003) notes that the increase in immigration over the past decade, which has reached hitherto unknown levels, has aroused alarmist perceptions exacerbated by the media to the point of referring to a 'wave of migration' and presenting stigmatized images of immigrants, especially those from Bolivia and Peru. However, the number of immigrants recorded in the 2002 population census is far smaller than the number of Chileans living abroad, and its relative size is minimal, barely exceeding 1 per cent of the total population (Table 13.2).

Employment

With respect to conditions of employment, the transparency and legality of migration would have different consequences depending on the general economic and sectoral situation, developments in the labour market and compliance with labour legislation in the countries:

1. In conditions of dynamic labour markets and economic growth, employment standards of migrants and also of the most disadvantaged native workers would be likely to improve. This would occur through eliminating the particular disadvantages faced by the undeclared migrant labour force, which is necessarily more flexible and more willing to accept employment conditions that contribute to depressed wage levels and precarious labour.
2. Restrictive policies generate irregularity and thus condition employer practices that seek to reduce costs by hiring migrants for longer hours at lower wages. With the opening up of borders, the seeming paradox of maintaining measures of control directed at migrants, while not penalizing employers who recruit undeclared migrant workers, would come to an end.
3. By contrast, if conditions of high unemployment, underemployment and casual labour persist in the medium term, the free movement or regularization of migrants would not have these effects.

In Argentina, the rise in unemployment contributed to the stagnation or lowering of real wages of workers performing standardized unskilled jobs in industry and the services. In addition to immigrants, the lower-income population sectors, young persons, and older adults have also been obliged, through fear of being unemployed, to accept more precarious working conditions. Therefore, until the labour supply situation as a whole improves, the current situation will not change – even if borders are opened up and migration is regularized.

Conclusions

Free mobility of persons in a context of full integration would contribute to a better organization of production and productivity levels and to the successful and harmonious regulation of labour markets, both at the regional and national levels. Above all, it would enable an improvement in the living and working standards of migrants and of the population as a whole by widening the scope of opportunities for labour-market participation and making more efficient use of the region's human resources. These principles underlie the 'formal' declarations set out in the MERCOSUR platform. However, we are still far from achieving MWB, which will rely on the recognition of its advantages by receiving societies.

Logically, for the benefits of free movement and expanded markets to be effective, it is necessary to overcome the profound disparities that exist between countries, a process that will require a long period of time that is difficult to estimate. Intra-regional and extra-regional mobility have increased and become more widespread throughout the region in recent decades, despite restrictive policies and measures of control, suggesting once again that migration is conditioned by structural factors that lead to marked differences in employment opportunities and living conditions between countries. Both within the expanded MERCOSUR and in the main receiving country's migration policy there have been significant advances in the regularization of the entry of migrants and the conditions of their stays.

The concept of the 'MERCOSUR citizen' is an important step towards an intra-regional version of the MWB scenario, but it should be borne in mind that measures to improve and computerize border controls are at the same time being strengthened, indicating that there is no intention of removing them. While a number of theories have been put forward in this chapter, it is difficult to forecast the impact that these new measures would actually have, because that depends on the development of socioeconomic factors and on the political resolve of states to amend bureaucratic obstacles erected over the course of many years.

Notes

1. In March 1991, the presidents of Argentina, Brazil, Paraguay and Uruguay signed the Treaty of Asunción, thereby setting in motion a regional integration process whose aim was the formation of a common market, known as MERCOSUR – Mercado Común del Sur/Mercado Comum do Sul (Southern Common Market). Bolivia and Chile were subsequently included as associated states, with increasing involvement. The term 'expanded MERCOSUR' is used in reference to this group of countries, which together make up Latin America's Southern Cone region. In

2003 and 2004, Colombia, Ecuador, Peru and Venezuela also joined the MERCOSUR. Thus, the group of countries that are part of (or associated with) the MERCOSUR are those that make up Latin America's Southern Cone, with the exception of Guyana and Surinam.

2. The Southern Cone of Latin America comprises Argentina, Bolivia, Brazil, Chile, Paraguay and Uruguay. These countries make up the expanded Southern Common Market (MERCOSUR).

3. The number of people born in Southern Cone countries residing in the United States rose from 101,000 in 1970 to 449,000 in 2000, according to data from the United States Census Bureau.

4. See ECLAC, 2001, 2002 and 2004b.

5. To analyse the trends we used data from population censuses. While presenting some limitations, these constitute one of the most reliable sources for studying migration.

6. The declarations of the four South American conferences can be consulted at www.mininterior.gov.ar

7. Based on data from the INDEC Permanent Household Survey for October 1999, 2000, 2001, 2002 and 2005. The survey covers the main urban centres, which make up approximately 70 per cent of the urban population and 63 per cent of the total population.

Bibliography

Cortés, R. and Groisman, F. 2004. Migrations, the labour market and poverty in Greater Buenos Aires. *CEPAL Review*, No. 82, pp. 173–92.

DGEEC. 2002. *Censo 2002 Vivienda y Población* [National Population and Housing Census, 2002]. Paraguay, Dirección Nacional de Estadística, Encuestas y Censos (DGEEC).

ECLAC. 2001. *Una Década de Luces y Sombras. América Latina y El Caribe en los años noventa*. Santiago, Chile, ECLAC/Alfaomega.

———. 2002. *Social Panorama of Latin America 2000–2001*. Santiago, Chile.

———. 2004a. *Social Panorama of Latin America 2002–2003*. Santiago, Chile.

———. 2004b. *Una década de desarrollo social en América Latina. 1990–1999*. Santiago, Chile.

ECLAC/CELADE. 2004a. *Demographic Bulletin*, 73. Santiago, Chile.

———. 2004b. *Investigación sobre la Migración Internacional en Latinoamérica y el Caribe (IMILA)*. www.eclac.org/default.asp?idioma=IN.

INDEC. 2001. *Censo Nacional de Población Higares y Vivienda* [National Population, Household and Housing Census]. Buenos Aires, Argentina, Instituto Nacional de Estadística y Censos (INDEC).

Lattes, A. E. and Recchini de Lattes, Z. 1994. International migration in Latin America: patterns, determinants and policies. M. Macura and D. Coleman (eds), *International Migration: Regional Processes and Responses*. Geneva/United Nations Economic Commission for Europe and New York/United Nations Population Fund, pp. 1–45. (Economic Studies, No. 7.)

Maguid, A. 1995. L'immigration des pays limitrophes dans l'Argentine des années 90, mythes et réalités. *Revue Européenne des Migrations Internationales*, Vol. 11, No. 2, pp. 167–88.

————. 1997. Migrantes limítrofes en el mercado de trabajo del Area Metropolitana de Buenos Aires, 1980–1996. *Estudios Migratorios Latinoamericanos*, No. 35, pp. 31–62.

Maguid, A. and Arruñada, V. 2005. El impacto de la crisis en la inmigración limítrofe y del Perú hacia el Área Metropolitana de Buenos Aires. *Revista de Estudios del Trabajo*, No. 30, pp. 95–122.

Mármora, L. 1995. Logiques politiques et intégration régionale. *Revue Européenne des Migrations Internationales*, Vol. 11, No. 2, pp. 13–33.

————. 2003. Políticas migratorias consensuadas en América Latina. *Revista Estudios Migratorios Latinoamericanos*, No. 50, pp. 111–42.

Mármora, L. and Cassarino, M. 1999. La variable migratoria en el MERCOSUR. *Revista de la OIM sobre Migraciones en América Latina*, Vol. 17, No. 1. Santiago de Chile, OIM.

Mármora, L. and Gorini, J. 1995. Impacto de la inmigración en la estructura de la seguridad de la República Argentina. Buenos Aires, Ministry of the Interior.

Marshall, A. 1983. Inmigración de países limítrofes y demanda de mano de obra en la Argentina, 1940–1980. *Revista Desarrollo Económico*, Vol. 23, No. 89, pp. 35–58.

Massey, D. S., Arango, J., Hugo, G., Kouaouci, A., Pellegrino, A. and Taylor, E. 1993. Theories of international migration: a review and appraisal. *Population and Development Review*, Vol. 19, No. 3, pp. 431–66.

Martinez Pizarro, J. 2003. El encanto de los datos. Sociodemografía de la inmigración en Chile según el censo de 2002. *Serie Población y Desarrollo*. Santiago, Chile, ECLAC/CELADE.

Pellegrino, A. 1995. La propension des jeunes à émigrer: le cas de l'Uruguay. *Revue Européenne des Migrations Internationales*, Vol. 11, No. 2, pp. 131–43.

Perez Vichich, N. 2003. La movilidad de los trabajadores en la agenda del MERCOSUR. *Studi Emigrazione*, No. 149, pp. 45–61.

Notes on contributors

Aderanti Adepoju is Chief Executive at the Human Resources Development Centre in Lagos and serves on the Editorial Advisory Board of *International Migration* and *International Migration Review*. Both an economist and a demographer, he has researched issues of internal and international migration at the Universities of Ife and Lagos in Nigeria and with the ILO and the UN. From 1992 to 1996 he led the IOM\UNFPA Research Team on Emigration Dynamics in Sub-Saharan Africa. His numerous publications on international migration and regional integration in Africa include 'Review of research and data on human trafficking in sub-Saharan Africa' (*International Migration*, 2005); 'Trends in international migration in and from Africa' (in Douglas Massey and J. Edward Taylor [eds], *International Migration Prospects and Policies in a Global Market*, Oxford University Press, 2004); 'Continuity and changing configurations of migration to and from the Republic of South Africa' (*International Migration*, 2004) and *International Migration in and from Africa: Dimensions, Challenges and Prospects* (with T. Hammar [eds]; PHRDA /CEIFO, 1996).

Rafael Alarcón is Professor in the Department of Social Studies at El Colegio de la Frontera Norte in Mexico. A specialist on international migration, he holds a Ph.D. in City and Regional Planning from the University of California, Berkeley. He was the founding editor of *Migraciones Internacionales*, which he edited from 2001 to 2005. His publications include *Return to Aztlan: The Social Process of International Migration from Western Mexico* (with Douglas Massey, Jorge Durand and Humberto Gonzalez; University of California Press, 1987) and 'The role of states and markets in creating global professionals' (in Han Entzinger, Marco Martiniello and Catherine Wihtol de Wenden [eds], *Migration between States and Markets*, Ashgate, 2004).

Graziano Battistella is Director of the Scalabrini International Migration Institute (SIMI) in Rome. He worked for nine years in the 1980s at the Center for Migration Studies in New York, where he was on the Editorial Board of *International Migration Review*, before becoming Director of the Scalabrini

Migration Center in Quezon City, Philippines, for twelve years, where he founded and edited the *Asian and Pacific Migration Journal*. In addition to articles published in specialized magazines, he has edited or co-edited: *Unauthorized Migration in Southeast Asia* (Scalabrini Migration Center, 2003; with Maruja Asis); *Asian Women in Migration* (Scalabrini Migration Center, 1996; with Anthony Paganoni); *The Human Rights of Migrant Workers: Agenda for NGOs* (Scalabrini Migration Center, 1993); and *Philippine Labor Migration: Impact and Policy* (Scalabrini Migration Center, 1992; with Anthony Paganoni).

Alejandro I. Canales was born in Santiago (Chile) and holds a Ph.D. in Social Sciences from El Colegio de México. He is President of the Asociación Latinoamericana de Población (Latin-American Population Association) and has been a Research Professor and Director of the Centre for Population Studies at the University of Guadalajara, Mexico, since 1998. He has directed several research projects on international migration at the University of Guadalajara and gives graduate courses on population, development and international migration in Mexico and Latin America. He has published widely in European and Latin American journals. His most recent books are *El Norte de Todos: Migración y trabajo en tiempos de globalización* (with Jesús Arroyo Alejandre and Patricia Noemí Vargas; University of Guadalajara/University of California Los Angeles, 2002); *Desafíos teóricos y metodológicos en los estudios de población en el inicio del milenio* (with Susana Lerner [eds]; University of Guadalajara/El Colegio de México, 2003), and *Gente Grande: Situación actual y perspectiva del envejecimiento en Jalisco* (with Israel Montiel and Tarsicio Torres; University of Guadalajara, 2004).

Jonathan Crush is Director of the Southern African Research Centre at Queen's University, Canada, and Honorary Professor in the Department of Geographical and Environmental Sciences at the University of Cape Town. He is Director of the Southern African Migration Project (SAMP) and has written and published extensively on migration and development issues in southern Africa. His most recent publications include *Destinations Unknown: Perspectives on the Brain Drain in Southern Africa* (with David A. McDonald [eds]; Africa Institute, 2002) and *Transnationalism and New African Immigration to South Africa* (with David A. McDonald [eds]; SAMP/Canadian Association of African Studies, 2002).

Han Entzinger is Professor of Migration and Integration Studies at Erasmus University Rotterdam. From 1986–2001 he held a similar chair at Utrecht University, where he co-founded the European Research Centre on Migration and Ethnic Relations (Ercomer). He is Past President of the Research Committee on Migration of the International Sociological Association and has been actively involved in research on migration, multiculturalism, public policy and the welfare state for over thirty years, in which time he has been a consultant to various governments, the European Union, the Council of Europe, the ILO and other international organizations. His latest book is *Migration between States and Markets* (with Marco Martiniello and Catherine Wihtol de Wenden; Ashgate, 2004).

Bimal Ghosh is Emeritus Professor at Colombia's Graduate School of Public Administration and an international consultant on migration, development and human rights issues. A former Senior Director in the United Nations system, he has led numerous United Nations/World Bank programmes in Asia, Africa and Latin America and pioneered the UN/UNHCR programme on refugee integration through area development. He was Scientific Coordinator of the 2000 West African Ministerial Conference on Migration and Development (Dakar), and Senior Consultant to the 1991 European Ministerial Conference on East–West Migration (Vienna). In 1997 he launched a UN-supported global project on migration management, New International Regime for Orderly Movements of People (NIROMP), and in 1998–1999 was a member of the UNCHR Working Group of Intergovernmental Experts on the Human Rights of Migrants. He has been associated with universities in the U.S., Europe and Asia and is a recipient of various honours and academic awards for his contribution to development and international cooperation. He has written a great number of books, reports and articles on international economic, political and human rights issues, with a focus on migration, trade, development aid and globalization. His recent publications on migration include *Elusive Protection, Uncertain Lands: Migrants' Access to Human Rights* (IOM, 2003); *Managing Migration: Time for a New International Regime?* (Oxford University Press, 2000); *Return Migration: Journey of Hope or Despair?* (IOM, 2000); *Huddled Masses and Uncertain Shores: Insights into Irregular Migration* (Martinus Nijhoff, 1998); and *Gains from Global Linkages: Trade in Services and Movements of Persons* (Macmillan, 1997).

Paul de Guchteneire is head of the Programme on International Migration and Multicultural Policies at UNESCO and Director of the *International Journal on Multicultural Societies*. He has worked as an epidemiologist at the Netherlands Cancer Research Foundation and is a past Director of the Steinmetz Institute of the Royal Netherlands Academy of Arts and Sciences and a former President of the International Federation of Data Organizations (IFDO). His current research focuses on the human rights dimension of international migration and the development of policies for migration management at the international level. His publications include *Best Practices on Indigenous Knowledge* (with Ingeborg Krukkert and Guus von Liebenstein

[eds]; UNESCO-MOST/CIRAN, 1999) and *Democracy and Human Rights in Multicultural Societies* (with Matthias Koenig [eds]; UNESCO/Ashgate, 2007), as well as several works on data collection and analysis in the social sciences.

Nigel Harris is Emeritus Professor of the Economics of the City at University College London, Senior Policy Adviser on Migration at the European Policy Centre, Brussels, and Chairman of the Royal Society of Arts Migration Commission. The author of a great number of articles and books on migration, economic development, urbanization, and cities in developing countries, his latest works include *Thinking the Unthinkable: The Immigration Myth Exposed* (Tauris, 2003) and *The Return of Cosmopolitan Capital: Globalization, the State and War* (Tauris, 2004).

Jan Kunz is national team leader of the EU-funded ELOST-Project at Tampere University and a Scientific Assistant to a Member of the European Parliament in Brussels. He has a Diploma in Social Sciences and a Master of Arts in Political Science at the Justus-Liebig-University in Giessen, Germany (1997). His dissertation on unemployment and employment policy at the local level was published in 2004 at the University of Tampere, Finland. His research interests include urban sustainable development, unemployment and labour market issues, and labour mobility and migration, as well as population ageing and social exclusion.

Mari Leinonen was born in 1977 in Kuopio, Finland. She has a Master's degree in Economics and Administration from the University of Tampere, Finland, where her main fields of study were regional science, administrative science and environmental policy. Her Master's thesis was entitled 'The EU-Financed Suburb Development Project of Hervanta' (2003). In 2004 she began research towards a Ph.D. at the European Ph.D. in Socio-Economic and Statistical Studies graduate school at the University of Tampere. Her current research is focused on urban planning and development in Finnish and European contexts.

Alicia Maguid is a Senior Researcher at the National Council of Scientific and Technological Research (CONICET), Argentina. A sociologist and demographer, she is Director of Social Statistics at the National Institute of Statistics and Censuses (INDEC) and Professor of Social Demography at the National University of Lujan, Buenos Aires. In 2002/2003, she coordinated the Statistical Information System on International Migration in Central America and Mexico (SIEMCA), developed by the International Organization for Migration (IOM) and the Latin American and Caribbean Demographic Centre of the Economic Commission for Latin America and the Caribbean (ECLAC/CELADE). She has worked as a consultant for ECLAC, CELADE, IOM, UNHCR and ILO and has published widely on international migration patterns, international labour markets, and poverty in Latin American countries.

Israel Montiel Armas was born in Tenerife, Spain, in 1975. He holds a degree in Political Sciences and Administration and is a doctoral student in Human Geography at the University of Barcelona. He is currently working as a Research Assistant at the Centre for Population Studies at the University of Guadalajara (Mexico), on a project regarding Mexican immigration to the United States. His recent publications include 'Remesas e inversión productiva en comunidades de alta migración a Estados Unidos. El caso de Teocaltiche, Jalisco' [Remittances and productive investment in communities of high migration to the United States: the case of Teocaltiche, Jalisco] (with Alejandro I. Canales; *Migraciones Internacionales* 2004) and 'Vivir del dólar: hogares, remesas y migración' [Living on the dollar: homes, remittances and migration] (with Alejandro I. Canales; in G. López Castro (ed.), *Diáspora michoacana*, El Colegio de Michoacán y Gobierno del Estado de Michoacán, 2003).

Sally Peberdy is Project Manager with the Southern African Migration Project (SAMP) in Johannesburg. Her work has centred on migration issues in southern Africa since moving to South Africa in 1994 to research and write her Ph.D. thesis 'Selecting Immigrants: Nationalism and National Identity in South Africa's Immigration Policies, 1910–1998' for Queen's University, Canada. She has worked with SAMP on a range of research projects on regional migration; her particular areas of interest include migration and small-scale cross-border trade; migration and HIV/AIDS; and regional migration in the context of the SADC, the AU and NEPAD.

Antoine Pécoud has been with UNESCO's Section on International Migration and Multicultural Policies since 2003 and is a Research Associate at the Unité de recherche Migrations et Société (URMIS), University of Paris VII and at Migrations internationales, espaces et sociétés (MIGRINTER), University of Poitiers. He holds a B.A. from the University of Lausanne and a Ph.D. in social and cultural anthropology from the University of Oxford. His research has focused on migration policies, immigrant entrepreneurship in Germany and the human rights implications of international migration. His work has notably been published in the *International Journal of Urban and Regional Research*, the *Journal of Ethnic and Migration Studies* and the *Revue Européenne des Migrations Internationales*.

Mehmet Ugur is Jean Monnet Reader in European Political Economy at the University of Greenwich, U.K. His research draws on the economics of information and institutional design to study regional integration, EU migration policy, EU-Turkey relations, corporate governance, and institutions and economic performance. His current projects focus on the migration implications of Turkey's EU membership and institutional determinants of economic performance in Turkey. Mehmet Ugur's latest book is *Turkey and European Integration* (with Nergis Canefe [eds]; Routledge, 2004).

Catherine Wihtol de Wenden is Director of Research at France's Centre national de la recherche scientifique, Centre d'études et de recherches internationales (CNRS-CERI) and also teaches at the Institut d'Etudes Politiques in Paris. Both a political scientist and a lawyer, she specializes in issues of international migration and has been an external expert for the OECD, the International Organization for Migration (IOM), the European Commission, the Council of Europe and the UNHCR. Among her recent publications are *L'Immigration en Europe* (La Documentation Française, 1999); *L'Europe des Migrations* (La Documentation Française, 2001); *La Beurgeoisie: Les trois âges de la discrimination* (with Rémy Leveau; CNRS, 2001); and *Police et discrimination: le tabou français* (with Sophie Body-Gendrot; Atelier, 2003).

Index